The Right to Learn

Linda Darling-Hammond

The Right to Learn

A Blueprint for Creating Schools That Work

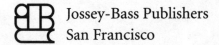

Jossey-Bass Publishers
San Francisco

Chapter One epigraph from *W.E.B. Du Bois Speaks,* vol. 2. Copyright © 1970 by Philip S. Foner and Shirley Graham Du Bois. Reprinted by permission from Pathfinder Press.

Chapter Two epigraph reprinted by permission of David Kearns.

Chapter Four epigraph from *The Unschooled Mind* by Howard Gardner. Copyright © 1991 by Howard Gardner. Reprinted by permission of BasicBooks, a division of HarperCollins Publishers, Inc.

Chapter Eight epigraph from *Savage Inequalities* by Jonathan Kozol. Copyright © 1991 by Crown Publishers Inc.

Chapter Nine epigraph from *To Know as We Are Known* by Parker J. Palmer. Copyright © 1983, 1993 by Parker J. Palmer. Reprinted by permission of HarperCollins Publishers, Inc.

"To You" in Chapter Ten from *Collected Poems* by Langston Hughes. Copyright © 1994 by the Estate of Langston Hughes. Reprinted by permission of Alfred A. Knopf Inc.

For sales outside the United States, please contact your local Simon & Schuster International Office.

Jossey-Bass Web address: http://www.josseybass.com

 Manufactured in the United States of America on Lyons Falls Turin Book. This paper is acid-free and 100 percent totally chlorine-free.

Library of Congress Cataloging-in-Publication Data

Darling-Hammond, Linda, date.
    The right to learn : a blueprint for creating schools that work /
Linda Darling-Hammond. — 1st ed.
       p.   cm. — (The Jossey-Bass education series)
    Includes bibliographical references and index.
    ISBN 0–7879–0261–6 (cloth : acid-free paper)
      1. School management and organization—United States.
2. Educational change—United States. 3. Education and state—
United States. 4. Learning. 5. Teaching—United States.
I. Title. II. Series.
LB2805.D16 1997
371.2'00973—dc21   97–4736

FIRST EDITION
HB Printing   10 9 8 7 6 5 4

The Jossey-Bass Education Series

Contents

This book is dedicated to my parents, who understood the importance of learning, and who sparked and stoked my quest to understand.

~ Preface

This book describes how we can radically improve not only individual schools but our overall system of education. In the view of most educators, parents, employers, and students our current education system is failing. Rigid and bureaucratic, it was never designed to teach *all* children effectively, to teach learners in all their varieties, to attend to each child's particular mix of aptitudes and barriers to learning. Educating all children effectively is the mission of schools today, yet great numbers of children still have no reasonable opportunity to acquire the knowledge and abilities that will help them thrive in and contribute to today's society. In *The Right to Learn* I examine the lessons of history and our expanding knowledge of what works in schools and classrooms to describe how school reforms might transform our education presumptions and policies so that our education system supports learning for all.

In some sense, I have been writing this book for at least forty years. I have always felt that the most exciting thing any person could do is to learn and the most challenging and satisfying thing anyone could do is to teach. That teaching and learning secure the foundations of civilization—of both civility and civitas—did not occur to me until much later. However, the idea that anyone should be denied the opportunity to learn or should experience education that is boring or demeaning has always distressed me. Learning, I have always felt, is as essential as breathing.

During the 1950s and 1960s, in the days when school systems were rapidly growing and reforming, my parents moved and sacrificed many times to ensure that my siblings and I got the best public education my parents could obtain. They managed to find schools where we profited from programs stimulated by that era's education reformers and funded by a government eager to catch up with the Russians. I was the beneficiary of curricula informed by Jerome Bruner, Joseph Schwab, and Jean Piaget as well as the efforts of scholars like

Kenneth Clark. I was one of the fortunate young people of that era who had access to powerful education. I studied and loved the *new math, hands-on science,* and new approaches to foreign language instruction. (I also remember my parents and some teachers complaining about this math stuff that they didn't understand and were eager to get rid of.) I was enchanted by open education experiments that gave students choices and opportunities to tackle rich, interesting projects. I loved the provocative discussions and intellectually challenging assignments used by teachers who adopted inquiry-based approaches to the teaching of humanities. I profited from opportunities to learn music and to connect it to other parts of my life.

I benefited from some extraordinary teachers whose path into teaching had been paved by federal grants that underwrote their preparation and made it possible for them to learn new methods. I had some great teachers who were the beneficiaries of Teacher Corps programs and National Science Foundation investments. Through another federal program, I had a chance to serve as a teacher's aide, an opportunity that triggered my zeal for teaching and, as it turned out later, sealed my fate. I was enabled to attend an Ivy League college thanks to equal access financial aid policies, and I entered teaching myself on a National Defense Student Loan.

I knew enough to be grateful for these opportunities because I had seen something of the alternative in schools I had passed through: a teacher who, on her good days, used erasers rather than books to hit children on the head; teachers who counted reading directly from the teacher's manual as teaching and who assigned workbook pages by the hundreds; and an occasional encounter with the behaviorist curriculum innovations that evolved from the Skinnerian studies of rats and pigeons popular just before and after World War II. I recall being dumbfounded by programmed instructional texts intended to teach English grammar through endless series of one-sentence skill bites, with minitests after each one. And I could not imagine why anyone would make students stop reading books to march their way through color-coded SRA reading kits. (I remember having to put Dostoyevsky aside to demonstrate that I could make my way from green to purple cards featuring short decontextualized passages followed by multiple-choice questions.)

It was the periodic experience of exhilarating education—floating above a flat sea of routine skill and text coverage—that first encouraged me to learn and later persuaded me to teach. At the same time I saw how my brother, who had a number of disabilities, had a much less supportive experience because, although we went to the same schools, we were placed in different tracks. But I did not see the full extent of U.S. inequality in education—or the backward curriculum policy created for the segregated poor—until I began student teaching in Camden, New Jersey. In this grossly underfunded district, which has been a subject of school finance lawsuits for more than twenty-five years, I found a crumbling warehouse high school managed by dehumanizing and sometimes cruel procedures and staffed by underprepared and often downright unqualified teachers. It had a nearly empty book room and a curriculum so rigid and narrow that teachers could barely stay awake to teach it.

Although all of my 12th-grade students had failed English the year before and many had barely learned to read or write (hence their assignment to a novice teacher), the curriculum instructed me to spend a large chunk of time teaching them to memorize the Dewey Decimal system. When I instead engaged them in reading and writing about material they cared about, I was warned about the penalties for failing to "follow the curriculum." I began to understand what it was my parents were escaping as they moved in search of good schools. Not incidentally, I found some brilliant students in that Camden classroom and many others who were thoughtful, serious, and willing to work hard. When given a chance to do so, virtually all of them learned to read and write. Having been regularly denied the right to learn did not render them incapable of learning.

I have since seen the same confluence of underfunding, underqualified teachers, and rigid, thoughtless curriculum mandates in my teaching and research in many other cities. Today as then, the education offered the children of the poor is one equally uninformed by education research and democratic principles.

There are many reasons for the failure of our education system to provide high-quality education for all children. These reasons are complex and not to be oversimplified. But they are not, I believe, insurmountable. In the more than twenty years since I started teaching I have wrestled with the issues of how to provide engaging successful education for all students—education that helps them locate who they are and how they can make a contribution to the world—that stretches them to achieve very high standards yet affirms their basic humanity and right to pursue what matters most to them.

As I have worked with children and youth at the preschool, elementary, junior high, and high school levels, as well as with older students in college and graduate school, I have tried to understand how people learn—when it is difficult for them as well as when it is easy. When I cofounded a school and later when I studied many more schools and worked with dozens of them on school reform initiatives, I tried to understand what allows schools to support powerful learning for all of their members—students and teachers alike—and what stands in the way. As I have worked with policymakers and studied policy effects, I have tried to understand how the contexts within which schools work affect educators' ability to achieve their goals and how the understandings of policymakers affect their ability to fashion policies that can achieve their goals.

As a policy analyst and adviser I have helped to shape initiatives, knowing they would often stand in contradiction to policies that came before or after. In 1992, however, I had the privilege of working with New York State's then education commissioner, Thomas Sobol, to put together a coherent plan for learner-centered education policy. As chair of the New York State Council on Curriculum and Assessment, I worked with a vociferous and committed cross-section of the state's stakeholders to develop plans for curriculum, assessment, professional development, school support, and accountability that could bring alive the *New Compact for Learning* envisioned by Sobol and the State Regents. The council painted a forward-looking vision of twenty-first-century schools and of the policy strategies needed to develop them:

> The schools we envision are exciting places: thoughtful, reflective, engaging, and engaged. They are places where meaning is made. They are places that resemble workshops, studios, galleries, theaters, studies, laboratories, field research sites, and newsrooms. Their spirit is one of shared inquiry. The students in these schools feel supported in taking risks and thinking independently. They are engaged in initiating and assessing their ideas and products, developing a disciplined respect for their own work and the work of others. Their teachers function more like coaches, mentors, wise advisors, and guides than as information transmitters or gatekeepers. They offer high standards with high levels of support, creating a bridge between challenging curriculum goals and students' unique needs, talents, and learning styles. They are continually learning because they teach in schools where everyone would be glad to be a student, or a teacher—where everyone would want to be—and could be—both.

More important, we struggled through the policy dilemmas inherent in developing top-down supports for bottom-up reform—strategies for change that could help schools get well beyond rhetorical flourishes or regulatory mandates. New student and teacher assessments, teacher education policies, supports for school learning, and new approaches to funding and organizing schools are all part of the policy work that has typically been ignored because states have relied more on controlling schools than on building schools' capacity for knowledge about teaching and learning. This policymaking process continues today among many inside and outside of government. Sometimes we struggle in common cause, and sometimes we argue with one another. Our work not only progresses but also continually unravels and tangles, demanding readjustment and reinvention to account for changing political and practical conditions. The work is never easy and it is never done. It is part of the commitment democracies must make to developing schools that serve *all* of their children and their societies well.

The Right to Learn describes the systemwide changes in policy and practice needed to make all our schools both learner centered and learning centered. Although it has been possible in every major era of education reform to create extraordinary schools that accomplish extraordinary levels of learning with all kinds of students, such schools have never become widely available in most communities. The failure of highly effective schools to spread occurs in large part because such schools exist in a policy environment that does little to nourish them and much to uproot them.

In particular, prior reform efforts have not been buttressed by the ongoing professional development needed to prepare teachers to teach in the complex ways that learner-centered practice demands. Reforms have not been accompanied by policies that reinforce the pursuit of challenging forms of learning through associated changes in curriculum resources, funding, testing policies, and school organization.

Finally, most reforms have not been supported by a public understanding of educational ideas and possibilities. The task of developing such understanding has been neglected throughout the twentieth century, as the bureaucratization of schools has separated families and communities from engagement with the "technical" aspects of school operations. New models of school reform must seek to develop communities of learning grounded in communities of democratic discourse.

Only in this way can communities come to want for all of their children what they want for their most advantaged—an education for empowerment and an education for freedom.

Clearly, issues of power and privilege contribute to the continuation of poor schooling for many children, and the effects of racism and classism cannot be ignored. Yet, in the course of my work, I have also come to believe that much of the reason for the current sorry state of many schools is a genuine lack of understanding on the part of policymakers and practitioners about what is needed to produce schools that can teach for understanding in the context of a complex pluralistic society. My goal in this book is to deepen our collective conversation about how we can create policies and practices that enable schools to teach all students well.

New York City   LINDA DARLING-HAMMOND
February 1997

⟶ Acknowledgments

I am indebted to a great many people who have helped to nurture my own thinking and understanding over many years. My own first mentor, Bernard Charles Watson, kindled the spirit of inquiry and the appreciation of educational possibilities that kept me digging into tough questions year after year. Arthur Wise was a close partner in much research on teaching and policy, including some reported here, and he helped me develop a policy sense that has led to a theory of democratic professionalism. Many colleagues have sharpened and enriched my thinking. They include, especially, Deborah Ball, Bill Clune, David Cohen, James Comer, Richard Elmore, Howard Gardner, John Goodlad, Maxine Greene, Jim Kelly, Gloria Ladson-Billings, Magdalena Lampert, Ann Lieberman, Milbrey McLaughlin, Richard Murnane, Hugh Price, Seymour Sarason, Lee Shulman, Theodore Sizer, and Gary Sykes.

Deborah Meier has been an inspiring partner and a beacon of unswerving dedication and forceful perseverance and intelligence in the cause of better schooling for all children. Among others who daily invent the schools of the future, I am indebted to Edwina Branch, Ann Cook, Alan Dichter, Faye Freeman, Mary Futrell, Evelyn Jenkins Gunn, Haven Henderson, David Hirschy, Sherry King, Olivia Lynch, Lucy Matos, Floretta McKenzie, Nancy Mohr, Tom Mooney, Eric Nadelstern, Pat O'Rourke, Sharon Robinson, Paul Schwarz, Adam Urbanski, and many more wonderful teachers too numerous to name.

Thanks are also due to my colleagues past and present at the National Center for Restructuring Education, Schools, and Teaching (NCREST), who have informed this work in many ways: Jacqueline Ancess, Marcella Bullmaster, Lori Chajet, Velma Cobb, Beverly Falk, Kathe Jervis, Elaine Joseph, Maritza Macdonald, Kemly McGregor, Peter Robertson, Jon Snyder, Rob Southworth, and David Zuckerman. Ellalinda Rustique, Margaret Garigan, and Janet Brown-Watts deserve special thanks for their research assistance on the final drafts of the manuscript. Some of the work in this book originated years ago at the Rand Corporation, where lively conversations with Paul Hill, Tom Glennon, Jeannie Oakes, and Arthur Wise shaped ideas, and where research assistants Lynde Paul and Tamar Gendler provided support.

Most of all, I thank my husband, Allen, who shares my commitments and supports these dreams in hundreds of ways from the lofty to the mundane, and my children, Kia, Elena, and Sean, who motivate and make possible all of my work on behalf of other children.

L.D.H.

~ The Author

Linda Darling-Hammond is William F. Russell Professor in the Foundations of Education at Teachers College, Columbia University, where she is also codirector of the National Center for Restructuring Education, Schools, and Teaching (NCREST) and executive director of the National Commission on Teaching and America's Future. She is actively engaged in research, teaching, and policy work on issues of school restructuring, teacher education reform, and the enhancement of education equity. She is author or editor of six other books, including *Professional Development Schools: Schools for Developing a Profession* (1994), *A License to Teach: Building a Profession for 21st Century Schools* (with A. E. Wise and S. Klein, 1995), and *Authentic Assessment in Action* (with J. Ancess and B. Falk, 1994). In addition she has authored more than 150 journal articles, book chapters, and monographs on issues of education policy and practice.

Darling-Hammond is past-president of the American Educational Research Association, a member of the National Board for Professional Teaching Standards, and a member of the National Academy of Education. She has served on many national advisory boards, including the National Academy's Panel on the Future of Educational Research, the White House Advisory Panel's Resource Group for the National Education Goals, and on the boards of directors for Recruiting New Teachers, the Spencer Foundation, the Carnegie Foundation for the Advancement of Teaching, and the National Foundation for the Improvement of Education.

As chair of the New York State Council on Curriculum and Assessment, she has helped fashion a comprehensive school reform plan that supports curriculum and assessment for more challenging learning goals linked to professional development and greater equity in opportunities to learn. As chair of the Model Standards Committee of the Interstate New Teacher Assessment and Support Consortium (INTASC), she has helped develop licensing standards for beginning teachers that reflect current knowledge about what teachers need to know to teach diverse learners to these higher standards.

Darling-Hammond began her career as a public school teacher and was cofounder of a preschool and day-care center. Before joining the Teachers College faculty in 1989, she was senior social scientist and director of the Rand Corporation's Education and Human Resources Program. She earlier served as director of the National Urban Coalition's Excellence in Education Program, conducting research on exemplary city school programs and urban school finance issues.

Darling-Hammond received her B.A. degree magna cum laude from Yale University in 1973 and her doctorate in urban education, with highest distinction, from Temple University in 1978. She received the Phi Delta Kappa George E. Walk Award for the most outstanding dissertation in the field of education in 1978, the American Educational Research Association's Research Review Award in 1985, the American Federation of Teachers' Quest Award for Outstanding Scholarship in 1987, the Association of Teacher Educators' Leadership in Teacher Education Award in 1990, and Educational Equity Concepts' Woman of Valor Award in 1995. She has received honorary degrees from Temple University and the Claremont Graduate School.

The Right to Learn

## CHAPTER ONE

The Right to Learn

Of all the civil rights for which the world has struggled and fought for 5,000 years, the right to learn is undoubtedly the most fundamental. . . . The freedom to learn . . . has been bought by bitter sacrifice. And whatever we may think of the curtailment of other civil rights, we should fight to the last ditch to keep open the right to learn, the right to have examined in our schools not only what we believe, but what we do not believe; not only what our leaders say, but what the leaders of other groups and nations, and the leaders of other centuries have said. We must insist upon this to give our children the fairness of a start which will equip them with such an array of facts and such an attitude toward truth that they can have a real chance to judge what the world is and what its greater minds have thought it might be.

—W.E.B. Du Bois, "The Freedom to Learn"
([1949] 1970b, pp. 230–231)

Many books have been written in recent years about what is wrong with America's schools and how they might be fixed. This rush of concern from educators, policymakers, businesspeople, and others is in many respects well founded. As the United States moves from a simpler society dominated by a manufacturing economy to a much more complex world based largely on information

1

technologies and knowledge work, its schools are undergoing a once-in-a-century transformation. Never before has the success, perhaps even the survival, of nations and people been so tightly tied to their ability to learn. Consequently, our future depends now, as never before on our ability to teach.

Although the right to learn is more important than ever before in our history, schools that educate all of their students to high levels of intellectual, practical, and social competence continue to be, in every sense of the word, exceptional. Although many such schools have been invented throughout this nation's history, they have lived at the edge of the system, never becoming sufficiently widespread for most young people to have access to them. Over the last decade reformers have created and redesigned thousands of schools that are now educating rich and poor, black, brown, and white students alike to levels of success traditionally thought impossible to achieve. Yet these schools, too, remain at the margins, rarely embraced or supported by the systems in which they struggle to exist and generally unexamined for what they can teach the education enterprise. This book asks how we can reinvent the system of U.S. public education so that it ensures a right to learn for *all* of its students, who will enter a world in which a failure to learn is fast becoming an insurmountable defeat.

THE RIGHT TO LEARN IN ACTION

At International High School in New York City, teenagers who are recent immigrants to the United States can be seen clustered around lab tables, talking and gesturing intently as they work out a physics problem. Two students who speak mostly Spanish are working through the implications of one of Newton's laws with one student who speaks mostly Polish and another who speaks mostly Chinese. The four students communicate successfully with one another using sketches, mathematical notations, role-playing, and phrases in English and their native languages. Their teacher, working in turn with each classroom group, stops by briefly to ask a few questions that evaluate the students' understanding and to graphically illustrate a point with which they have been struggling. He asks if they can connect a concept they studied yesterday with the problem they are working on now. Smiles of recognition crease one face after another as the students realize how the ideas come together. Amid muted cheers and back-slapping they record their results. When the seventy minute period ends, the students are too engrossed in their work to leave until the teacher shoos them off to their next class.

International High School was launched by a group of teachers determined to reverse their students' failures. In a traditional New York City high school most of these students would drop out before 12th grade, but for ten years International has graduated virtually all its students, enabling them to pass both the New York State competency tests and a set of much more rigorous performance assessments developed within the school, and sending more than 90 percent to college. Equally important, students leave this school with a clear sense of themselves and their talents, an ability to frame and solve problems, and a capacity to work well with a wide range of other people (Darling-Hammond, Ancess, & Falk, 1995). The teachers believe, and research supports their view, that International High School's success is a function of its small size, the knowledge and commitments of its teachers, and the freedom it experiences as an alternative school. Alternative status allows faculty to structure teaching and schooling practices that are much more productive than those possible under state and city mandates.

Although the 450 students from more than fifty countries who attend International arrive speaking little or no English, they are immediately immersed in challenging content through an activity-based curriculum that allows them to practice English as they also learn to examine ideas through social sciences and literature, think mathematically and scientifically, and test their views against reason, evidence, and alternative perspectives. Most of their work is conducted in groups and facilitated by teachers who coach them toward proficient performances. Teachers also work in teams, sharing curriculum ideas and teaching strategies with one another and reviewing one another's practices. Teachers have developed structures that allow them to focus on student success and that give them continual opportunities to get better at what they do. Here is more of the picture.

In another International classroom pairs of students are reading each other's autobiographies and asking questions to guide revisions. Before they are done they will have revised their writing several times to refine their ideas and clarity of expression. A student from Ghana asks one from Puerto Rico if she can explain more about the culture of San Juan in her autobiography. As these two converse they are learning about other societies, expanding their view of the world, building a new relationship, and developing their ability to communicate. The obvious seriousness with which they undertake this exchange is coupled with the enjoyment of sharing ideas with a friend. The classroom hums with the sound of purposeful learning that is, in Paulo Freire's words, both rigorous and joyous (Freire, 1970).

A DIFFERENT STORY: DOING SCHOOL

Only a few miles away from International, students in a mathematics classroom in a traditional suburban high school of more than 2,500 are shoehorned into desks still riveted to the floor in rows as they were when the building was constructed many decades ago. Their teacher stands with her back to them, scrawling the steps for solving a quadratic equation on the blackboard. She calls over her shoulder, "Just write this down. You need to memorize it by Monday." Most students write obediently; a few are whispering to one another; one is sleeping unnoticed. As the teacher recites one of the procedures used in the solution, a young man raises his hand halfway and asks, "Why do you do that?" Standing more than ten feet away with her back turned, the teacher does not hear him. She continues writing, calling out as she goes which terms are to be squared, summed, or subtracted, "teaching" without regard to learning. The young man cups his forehead in his hands and puts his pencil down, defeated by the unrequited effort. Most of the others keep copying, willing to accept the fact that they are not supposed to understand. This mathematics class is one of the academic courses serving a relatively small number of students, mostly white and Asian, in the second highest of the school's six tracks.

Down the hallway a remedial English class, composed largely of African American and Latino students and other recent immigrants, is working its way through a lesson on prepositional phrases. The teacher reads aloud from the text and pauses to ask whether anyone can identify the phrase he has read as an adjective or adverb phrase. Those students whose heads are not on their desks look back at him blankly. One girl asks why they should know this, and the teacher replies that it will be on a test. Another young woman raises her hand to answer. The teacher looks at a seating chart to identify the student's name; she is one of more than 140 he sees every day. When she answers incorrectly, the teacher grimaces, states the correct answer, and instructs the students to complete the questions at the end of the chapter. He retreats to his own desk, unsure of how to make the material meaningful and defeated by the only substantive exchange of the hour.

JOINING THE ISSUE

This real tale of two schools is a common one in U.S. education today. Although the right to learn is prominent in the rhetoric of schooling, teaching in many schools is managed by procedures that hold little chance of producing satisfying learning. It is rare to encounter the kind of democratic education seen at International High School—education that teaches young people to think well and independently, to use what they learn to produce high-quality work, to take initiative, and to work effectively together.

These abilities are central to the changing demands of society and to the goals of current school reforms. Since the release of *A Nation at Risk* (National Commission on Excellence in Education, 1983), hundreds of commission reports have been issued and thousands of pieces of legislation have been passed to try to redesign schools so they can prepare a more diverse group of future citizens to learn at much higher levels, cope with complexity, use new technologies, and work cooperatively to frame and solve problems. In just over a decade we have experienced a "first wave" of reforms that sought to raise achievement though course and testing mandates, a "second wave" that argued for improvements in teaching and teacher education (Holmes Group, 1986; Carnegie Forum on Education and the Economy, 1986; National Governors' Association, 1986), and a "third wave" that is focused on defining more challenging standards for learning while restructuring schools so that they can produce dramatically better outcomes (Smith & O'Day, 1990; Sizer, 1992; Schlechty, 1990).

Increasingly, the redesign task is defined as one of transforming the education system rather than merely getting schools to do better what they have always done. If the challenge of the twentieth century was creating a system of schools that could provide minimal education and basic socialization for masses of previously uneducated citizens, the challenge of the twenty-first century is creating schools that ensure—for all students in all communities—a genuine right to learn. Meeting this new challenge is not an incremental undertaking. It requires a fundamentally different enterprise.

Building a system of schools that can educate people for contemporary society requires two things U.S. schools have never before been called upon to do:

To *teach for understanding*. That is to teach all students, not just a few, to understand ideas deeply and perform proficiently

To *teach for diversity*. That is, to teach in ways that help different kinds of learners find productive paths to knowledge as they also learn to live constructively together.

I suggest that this task will require a new paradigm for education policy—one that shifts policymakers' efforts from *designing controls* to *developing capacity* among schools and teachers to be responsible for student learning and to be responsive to student and community needs and concerns. This means (1) redesigning schools so they focus on learning, foster strong relationships, and support in-depth intellectual work; (2) creating a profession of teaching to ensure all teachers have the knowledge and commitments they need to teach diverse learners well; and (3) funding schools equitably so that they invest in the front lines of teaching and learning rather than in the side offices of system bureaucracies.

The rekindled vision of democratic education that motivates many current reforms is powerful—yet also profoundly problematic. A candid assessment of long-standing barriers and a commitment to fundamental reform will be necessary if we are to build the kinds of education needed to support a twenty-first-century democracy in a multicultural technological world.

In the first part of this book (Chapters One through Three) I describe the genesis of our current system of education and the obstacles we face. The remainder of this chapter reveals how barriers to democratic education were established and why they remain solidly planted in so many schools. Chapter Two shows how the U.S. education system evolved its deeply ingrained bureaucracy and why that bureaucracy has failed to produce the schools we need. Chapter Three treats the central issue of teaching and learning in classrooms, describing what we now know about the realities of teaching diverse learners and examining how specific policies help or hinder student learning.

In Part Two (Chapters Four through Six) I describe how restructured schools have produced new approaches to education and extraordinary results for students. Chapter Four presents specific examples of schools that work, identifying nine features these schools have in common and how each feature could be supported by education policy. Chapter Five looks at how successful schools are structured for success and suggests how their strategies can be adapted in other schools. In Chapter Six, I show how staff and other resources can be allocated to better support teaching and learning, examining practices in some other countries as well as in restructured schools here that contain some object lessons for us.

In Part Three (Chapters Seven through Nine) I describe the policy changes needed to develop a system of democratic education able to support successful schools in all communities. Chapter Seven discusses how standards can be developed and used to support students while avoiding bureaucratic pitfalls. In this chapter, I explain why top-down curriculum reform strategies have never worked and what would be needed to create the conditions for powerful teaching and learning in all schools. Chapter Eight shows how greatly access to knowledge varies within and across schools and discusses how we can begin to ensure that all children have a genuine opportunity to learn. Finally, Chapter Nine describes how we can change teacher preparation and teaching conditions in order to build a profession of teaching that can enact a broader, more inclusive vision of education opportunity.

BARRIERS TO DEMOCRATIC EDUCATION

Providing most Americans with an empowering and equitable education has always been a struggle, and it remains one today. Relatively few schools offer all their students a rich, active curriculum that teaches for understanding. Even fewer manage to educate a diverse set of students for constructive social interaction and shared decision making. From the time many Southern states made it a crime to teach an enslaved person to read and Northern states opted to establish differently funded schools for the rich and the poor, through decades of separate and unequal schooling that continue to the present, the right to learn in ways that develop both competence and community has been a myth rather than a reality for many Americans.

The struggle was articulated in the great debates between W.E.B. Du Bois and Booker T. Washington about whether black children must be trained as laborers or might be educated to think for a living (Du Bois, [1930] 1970a). It appeared in the ideological battles that shaped urban schools for the children of immigrants at the turn of the century (Tyack, 1974). Large impersonal factory-model schools with rigid tracking systems were created to teach rudimentary skills and unwavering compliance to the children of the poor. The more affluent and advantaged were taught in small elite private and public schools or carefully insulated special tracks within comprehensive schools, where they were offered a stimulating curriculum, personalized attention, high-quality teaching, and a wealth of intellectual resources.

At the same time, some genuinely democratic schools were built from the work of reformers like John Dewey, Ella Flagg Young, and

Lucy Sprague Mitchell at the turn of the century, in the 1930s, and in the 1960s. In these eras, many individuals worked to create an "equity pedagogy" (Banks, 1993) that challenged diverse groups of students to think independently; to create, invent, and understand academic subjects through research, writing, and inquiry; to experience ideas firsthand; and to make decisions democratically. Efforts to create what John Dewey called a "new education" featured reforms that reappeared in each of these eras and again recently: interdisciplinary curricula aimed at making connections among ideas; disciplinary learning conducted through student experiences; research studies and other projects emphasizing the use of knowledge and the development of higher-order thinking skills; cooperative learning; shared decision making among teachers, students, and parents; and detracking that makes a challenging curriculum available to more students.

These features of progressive education are sometimes posed as antithetical to the acquisition of rigorous and disciplined understanding in subject matter areas. They are decidedly not, but the source of these claims is instructive. For example, progressive education has been recently caricatured by E. D. Hirsch in *The Schools We Need* (1996). Hirsch rightfully rejects false dichotomies between the building of shared knowledge and attention to children's interests and between clear purposeful instruction and engaging and effective learning. In his claims that progressive education has undermined U.S. schools, however, he is wrong about three things: the goals of progressive practice, the nature of prevailing practice in U.S. schools, and the body of research evidence about effective teaching and learning. He also misunderstands why less effective teaching practices—whether labeled progressive or traditional—are so difficult to change and what is needed to help all students acquire the disciplined understanding of subject matter and the ability to apply that understanding that both he and I, and many others, agree they need.

In this and later chapters I present extensive evidence on these questions. The following summary introduces the central points. First, what Hirsch calls the "anti–subject matter principles of progressivism" (p. 49) do not exist. On the contrary, major thinkers and practitioners of education who might be called progressive—John Dewey, Jean Piaget, Jerome Bruner, Howard Gardner, Theodore Sizer, Deborah Meier, and many more—have sought deeper and more disciplined understanding of academic subjects and have developed curricula and assessment strategies for securing it. Teachers College at Columbia

University—the institution that Hirsch fingers as the purveyor of fuzzy-headed anti–subject matter thinking—has in fact long maintained a most traditional form of subject matter–based organization in its teacher education programs, arguing in the face of various attempts at reorganization that the disciplines are a central foundation of knowledge for teaching. However, enacting schooling that attends both to student needs and subject matter demands is extremely difficult, and Hirsch is right when he perceives that many teacher preparation institutions and many schools are confused about how to do *both* well.

Second, Hirsch contends that the problem with U.S. schools, and the reason they perform more poorly than schools in other countries, is that they have widely adopted such progressive practices as research projects and discovery methods and have abandoned good old-fashioned rote learning and memorization. This claim is far from true. In fact, both national and international studies consistently show that the large majority of U.S. schools emphasize rote learning with heavy doses of lecture, drill-and-practice, memorization, and multiple-choice and short-answer testing. The exceptions are found in more affluent communities and higher tracks. Schools in European countries require more extensive projects and rarely use multiple-choice testing, favoring oral and essay examinations instead. In addition, schools abroad are much more likely than U.S. schools to engage students in research and writing, experimentation, and extended discussion of problems and ideas.

Finally, Hirsch selectively cites "mainstream research," most of it from the 1970s, to argue that direct whole-group instruction emphasizing drill-and-practice is the path to developing disciplined understanding and that progressive education as he has characterized it has failed. He ignores research before, during, and after that time that documents the success of "progressive" methods at engendering higher-order thinking skills and that illustrates repeatedly the failure of his favored prescriptions for enabling students to remember ideas, apply them in new contexts, or perform well on tests of complex skills (for reviews see Good & Brophy, 1986; Resnick, 1987a; Gardner, 1991). He also fails to note that many of the researchers he cites have published other studies reporting that the kinds of teaching found useful for engendering recall and recognition of facts on multiple-choice tests are decidedly different from the teaching that develops student success on tasks that require deep understanding and highly developed performance skills (for a review see Darling-Hammond, Wise, & Pease, 1983). And in a stunning display of ignorance, he alleges that "the research literature offers not one example of success-ful implementation of progressivist methods in a carefully controlled longitudinal study" (p. 216).

Although Hirsch is wrong about this, he is right that progressive reforms have often failed to take hold at the system level even when they have succeeded at improving student achievement in the class-rooms where they have been applied. The reasons for this are impor-tant to understand. The following sections of this chapter explain why ineffective teaching practices are so difficult to change and how strate-gies that help all students learn both subject matter and thinking skills can be undertaken on a wide scale.

The Successes and Failures of Progressive Reforms

In each reform era of the past century, many of the schools launched by progressive educators were extraordinarily successful. In the 1930s, the famous Eight-Year Study, led by Ralph Tyler, painstakingly documented how students from experimental progressive schools were ultimately more academically successful, practically resourceful, and socially re-sponsible than matched samples of 1,475 peers from traditional schools (Aiken, 1942; Smith & Tyler, 1942; Chamberlin, Chamberlin, Drought, & Scott, 1942). Like the highly successful schools of today's reform initiatives, these school communities were small and organized around internally developed common goals. They sought to build a core cur-riculum linked to community concerns as well as to students' interests and developmental needs. The schools that showed the most extraor-dinary successes were those that differed most from mainstream prac-tice: their teaching was the most experiential and inquiry oriented and their governance systems the most democratic.

Although the case for this approach to education was carefully proved, progressive education virtually disappeared during the war years. By 1950, even the schools that had been studied and found suc-cessful had mostly reverted to "fundamentals" (Redefer, 1950, p. 35). Communities skeptical about reform ideas were never persuaded that the changes were important enough to merit their spread. School-level reformers rarely engaged the political system in considering the im-plications of their work for policies ranging from course requirements, facilities standards, and Carnegie Units to teacher certification and accreditation rules. Journalists focused only on test scores, not on the changes in school practices that were creating such productive and competent students. Thus policymakers never understood the systemic changes needed to support and maintain the reforms the successful schools had produced, and parents and teachers in other communities never fully understood what the successful schools had done (Kahne, 1994).

A text-based, transmission-oriented curriculum focused on superficial coverage and rote learning returned in force in U.S. schools during the 1940s and 1950s. It was not until *Sputnik* persuaded politicians that the United States needed to become competitive with the Soviets that a press for more intellectually challenging education was revived. Curriculum reforms launched by the National Science Foundation and the Office of Education during the 1960s aimed to prepare students to think critically and independently as well as to understand ideas well enough to apply them to novel situations. Reforms like "discovery learning," "open education," "team teaching," "differentiated staffing," and "democratic decision making" also began to proliferate once again.

A substantial body of research developed during these years showed that intellectually challenging curricula and inquiry-oriented teaching produced noticeable learning gains for students, especially in terms of their abilities to think critically and solve problems, their abilities to express themselves orally and in writing, their creativity, and their self-sufficiency as learners (for reviews see Dunkin & Biddle, 1974; Glass et al., 1977; Good & Brophy, 1986; Horwitz, 1979; Peterson, 1979).

However, these 1960s reforms also failed to overcome the weight of traditional practice and were overrun by the back-to-basics movement of the 1970s and 1980s. Despite extensive dissemination efforts, neither coercion nor persuasion could get teachers to implement the new curricula faithfully (Huberman & Miles, 1986; Gallagher, 1967). Especially where professional development was absent (which was most places), teachers' practice remained substantially the same: textbooks, lecture-recitation methods, and an emphasis on rote learning predominated (Shaver, Davis, & Helburn, 1979). Although there were some successful adaptations (Berman & McLaughlin, 1978), almost none of the progressive curricula developed in these projects are still in evidence in schools.

Despite their successes in the places where they were well understood and implemented, the reforms of previous eras were unsuccessful when they left the high-intensity hotbeds where they were spawned. Many practitioners urged to implement these ideas were unable to do so effectively. Often the ideas were poorly understood, the practices were complex and took time to develop, and they typically required changes throughout the entire school environment, not just behind classroom doors. Even in schools where the reforms had succeeded, they gradually disappeared as individual superintendents, principals, and teachers who had been involved in the changes left and were replaced by traditionally trained (or untrained) practitioners.

THE DEMANDS OF PROGRESSIVE TEACHING   Perhaps the single biggest obstacle to maintaining progressive reforms is the extensive skill needed to teach both subjects and students well. In all the previous reform eras practitioners asked to implement reforms like "open education" or "the project method" knew they were supposed to make learning relevant and attend to student needs. However, they often did not know how to fashion work that was rigorous as well as relevant, how to employ variable student-based strategies and also teach for high levels of disciplined understanding in content areas. And schools were often unable to support the new pedagogies with new forms of organization, governance, and professional development. Many teachers lost track of either their students or the curriculum goals as they broke with their previous routines, trying to become more child centered by letting go of subject matter standards or more subject centered by ignoring students while the curriculum marched on ahead. In the 1960s, many educators' inability to manage both sets of goals led to the perception that schools had lost academic rigor in their eagerness to be relevant.

Teaching practice that succeeds in developing deep understanding of challenging content for a wide range of learners is highly complex: it maintains a dialectic between students and subjects, allowing neither to overwhelm the other. Such teaching presses for mastery of content in ways that enable students to apply their learning and connect it to other knowledge as they develop proficient performances in the field of study. Because students will necessarily come to any learning experience with different learning strategies and prior experiences— and thus with different starting points for the material to be learned— successful teachers must know how to create experiences that let students access ideas in a variety of ways yet always press for deeper and more disciplined understanding.

This kind of teaching is purposeful and may be highly structured, but it is also inevitably improvisational. Because real understanding is always hard-won and human beings bring different mixes of abilities and insights to the task, there is no prepackaged set of steps or lessons that will secure understanding for every learner in the same way. Teachers have to bring a great deal of knowledge and analytic ability to the task of developing understanding with their students.

Transmission teaching is much simpler. Teachers can "get through" texts and workbooks. Classroom routines are straightforward; controls are easier to enforce. There is a sense of certainty and accomplishment when a lecture has been given, a list of facts covered, or a chapter finished, even if the result is little learning for students. When a teacher has transmitted information, it is easy to say "I taught that"—even when students have not learned it. Active learning situations infuse more uncertainty into the teaching process. When a student is building her own understanding through a research project, for example, the teacher needs to construct a careful scaffolding to guide the learning process and have well-designed strategies for eliciting the student's thinking in order to assess what is being learned. Many teachers' preparation has not taught them how to create situations in which learners can have real breakthroughs in understanding or how to evaluate learning and adapt their teaching. Thus they teach as they remember being taught, creating a flow of lessons and activities aimed at fairly superficial coverage that moves along comfortably oblivious to student learning.

Efforts to develop thoughtful democratic classrooms have repeatedly been killed by underinvestments in teacher knowledge and school capacity. Lawrence Cremin (1965) argued that "progressive education . . . demanded infinitely skilled teachers, and it failed because such teachers could not be recruited in sufficient numbers" (p. 56). In each era of change, progressive reforms gave way to standardizing influences: in the efficiency movement of the 1920s, the teacher-proof curriculum reforms of the 1950s, and the back-to-the-basics movement of the 1970s and 1980s. A backlash is forming against current reforms as well. The reasons for these reactions are always the same: when educators denied access to appropriate preparation and training prove unable to manage complex forms of teaching, policymakers typically revert to simplistic prescriptions for practice, even though these prescriptions cannot achieve the goals they seek. The failure of reforms today would be an even greater problem than in times past because the demands for higher levels of performance from a much greater number of citizens are acute, and the failure of society to meet these demands holds much greater social dangers.

EXPECTATIONS, FEARS, AND THE STATUS QUO   Providing a thinking education for all students is a difficult matter, not only because it requires sophisticated teaching but also because it is, from many perspectives, a subversive activity. Even if all educators were prepared to teach all students to think and perform at high levels, there would still be people who find the rearing of a group of independent-minded young people threatening to the rules that govern social life, and others who fear upsetting the social order from which they benefit. Conservative groups that have sought to defeat reforms in many states have sometimes argued that teaching students such skills as critical thinking might undermine parental authority. And when a Connecticut commission issued its call for school reform in 1995, there was a strong backlash among affluent towns against the notion that "all children can learn" and should be taught for high levels of performance. If that were to happen, many advantaged parents reasoned, "slow" children might be mixed up in the same classrooms as "bright" ones, leading to unhappy consequences: either the slow children might retard those on a fast track, or equally problematic, they might achieve well enough to compete for the slots in selective colleges that lead to top-tier jobs traditionally reserved for the advantaged.

Though these parents held understandable concerns about the potential classroom effects of a less-than-careful approach to detracking, their concerns about preserving selective access to the benefits of good education cut to the heart of schooling's purposes and the changing conditions of society. Democratic rhetoric and the presumptions of meritocracy have long rested on the fiction that all people have access to good education. Practically if not idealistically, poor education for many students was not a social problem when plenty of low-skilled jobs offering good wages were to be had. It is a problem today when most jobs demand much greater competence. Yet middle-class fears of growing competition for high-paying knowledge work jobs trigger a crabs-in-a-barrel syndrome: communities and households clamber to stay on top of a precarious heap rather than make an effort to raise the caliber of education for all. This is not always the result of mean-spiritedness. It is simply easier to try to hang on to what one thinks one has than it is to imagine improving the outcomes of an operation as big, cumbersome, unwieldy, and poorly understood as the U.S. public education system.

For all these reasons, true democratic education is both rare and unequally distributed. Although progressive influences have softened the edges of schooling during periodic eras of reform, they have made little dent in most students' experiences. Recent critiques by scholars and students are remarkably alike. They describe a system that seeks to manage schooling simply and efficiently by setting up impersonal relationships, superficial curricula, and routinized teaching. Together, these practices overwhelm the best intentions of all concerned (Boyer, 1983; Goodlad, 1984; Sizer, 1984). Structural problems of school size, bureaucratization, and fragmentation exacerbate the problems of uninspiring pedagogy. A dropout from a well-regarded New York City comprehensive high school explains how:

> At one time school was important to me. I liked getting good grades and making my parents proud of me. [But in high school] I never felt part of the school. It didn't make a difference if I was there or not. Teachers were unwilling to be flexible in their teaching and to allow students to deviate from set ways of doing things. The teachers just threw me aside, probably because I was Spanish. The school had too many dumb rules that weren't realistic. I felt like I was being ignored, like I wasn't important [Carrajat, 1995].

Another dropout from the same school offered the kind of analysis an organizational theorist might make:

> I had passing grades when I decided to drop out, but nobody tried to stop me. Nobody cared. . . . None of the counselors paid any attention to me. The individual classes were too big for students to learn. Students should have longer exposure to individual teachers. If students could have the same subject teachers throughout their high school careers, this would allow teachers to get to know them better. . . . No high school should have more than four hundred students max, and they should be all on one floor. Who needs seven floors in a school? [Carrajat, 1995].

A California high school student put it more succinctly: "this place hurts my spirit" (Poplin & Weeres, 1992, p. 11). His view was echoed by an administrator in the same school, who voiced the poignant dilemma of caring educators trying to make a dysfunctional organization work for children, "Yes, my spirit is hurt, too, when I have to do things I don't believe in" (Poplin & Weeres, p. 23). Poplin and Weeres's study of California schools found that "teachers perceive themselves to be very caring people who went into teaching to give something to youth. [They] struggled to articulate how their attention had been focused away from students. Teachers felt they were pressured to cover the curriculum, meet bureaucratic demands and asked to do too many activities unrelated to the students in their classrooms. Teachers and others felt the size of their classes and numbers of students they saw each day, particularly in middle and high schools, made it difficult to care" (pp. 21–22).

Over and over again, research and casual observation reveal that in most bureaucratically organized schools, students feel alienated from teachers, who appear to have little time for students unless they are unusually "bright" or "problematic." Teachers feel at odds with administrators, who appear to have little time for them unless their concerns pertain to contractual matters, mandates, or paperwork. And everyone feels victimized by "the system," which demands attention to reports and procedures when teachers, students, and administrators would rather devote their time to each other and to learning.

HOW THE CURRENT SYSTEM FAILS TO EDUCATE FOR DEMOCRACY   Unfortunately, the bureaucratic school created at the turn of the twentieth century was not organized either for intellectual development or for individual responsiveness. As the United States moved from an agrarian to a manufacturing economy, efforts to create a system from thousands of haphazardly managed one-room schoolhouses adopted the then-popular factory-line technology for batch processing the huge numbers of students arriving en masse.

The Effects of the Factory Model   Like manufacturing industries, schools were developed as specialized organizations run by carefully prescribed procedures engineered to yield standard products. Based on faith in rationalistic management, in the power of rules to direct human behavior, and in the ability of administrators to discover and implement common procedures to produce desired outcomes, twentieth-century education policy has assumed that continually improving the design specifications for schoolwork—required courses, textbooks, testing instruments, and management systems—will lead to student learning. Knowledgeable teachers were not part of the equation because the bureaucratic model assumed that important decisions would be made by others in the hierarchy and handed down in the form of rules and curriculum packages. Investments in teacher learning in this country are therefore small compared to those in other countries and in other professions.

Large age-graded departmentalized schools were designed for the efficient batch processing of masses of children in the new age of compulsory education and large-scale immigration. Their mission was not to educate all students well. A few students were selected and educated for thinking work, but most students were trained in the basic workplace socialization they would need to conduct simple tasks neatly, punctually, and obediently. The rote learning that satisfied these early twentieth-century objectives still predominates in today's schools, reinforced by curriculum packages and texts, standardized tests that focus on low-cognitive-level skills, and continuing underinvestment in teacher knowledge.

The school structure created to implement this conception of teaching and learning is explicitly impersonal. Students move along a conveyer belt from one teacher to the next, grade to grade, and class period to class period to be stamped with lessons before they move on. They have little opportunity to become well known over a sustained period of time to any adults who can consider them as whole people or as developing intellects. Secondary school teachers may see 150 or more students a day, unable to come to know any individual student or family well. Between start-ups and wind-downs, elementary teachers have only about seven or eight good months with their students before they have to pass them off to another teacher who will start all over trying to get to know them. Teachers work in isolation from one another with little time to plan together or share their knowledge. Students, too, tend to work alone and passively, listening to lectures, memorizing facts and algorithms, and engaging in independent seatwork at their separate desks.

In urban areas, such factory-model schools are likely to be huge warehouses, housing 3,000 or more students in an organization focused more on the control of behavior than the development of community. With a locker as their only stable point of contact, a schedule that cycles them through seven to ten overloaded teachers, and a counselor struggling to serve the "personal" needs of several hundred students, teenagers struggling to find connections have little to connect to. Heavily stratified within and substantially dehumanized throughout, such schools are adversarial environments where "getting over" becomes important when "getting known" is impossible. Adults find their capacity to be accountable for students' learning constrained by factory-model structures that give staff little control over most of what happens to the students they see only briefly.

Even suburban schools, though often "nice," well-funded places, are typically not hotbeds of intellectual provocation. As Theodore Sizer (1984) noted after visiting dozens of such schools, "save in extracurricular or coaching situations, such as in athletics, drama or shop classes, there is little opportunity for sustained conversation between student and teacher. The mode is a one-sentence or two-sentence exchange. . . . Dialogue is strikingly absent, and as a result the opportunity of teachers to challenge students' ideas in a systematic and logical way is limited. Given the rushed, full quality of the school day, it can seldom happen. One must infer that careful probing of students' thinking is not a high priority" (p. 82).

Education Results at the End of the Line   The result of this system is education that does not prepare students to understand and produce much thoughtful work. According to the National Assessment of Educational Progress (National Center for Education Statistics, 1994c), in 1992, for example:

- Only 43 percent of seventeen-year-old high school students could read and understand material such as that typically presented at the high school level, and only 7 percent could synthesize and learn from specialized reading materials.

- Fewer than half could evaluate the procedures or results of a scientific study, and just 10 percent could draw conclusions using detailed scientific knowledge.

- Just 36 percent could write well enough to communicate their ideas, and only 2 percent could write in an elaborated fashion.

- Only 7 percent could use basic algebra or solve math problems with more than one step.

These indicators show modest improvement over previous years (see, for example, Educational Testing Service, 1989a). However, few students have the skills needed to cope easily with the complexities of today's society. International comparisons of student performance in mathematics and science tell a similar story. U.S. students have tended to score at about the median of other countries at 5th grade, dip below the average by 8th grade, and rank below most other industrialized countries by 12th grade, especially on tasks requiring higher-order thinking and problem solving (McKnight et al., 1987; International Association for the Evaluation of Educational Achievement, 1988). Even when the U.S. launched a separate international study to ensure the results were not biased against a U.S. view of curriculum, American thirteen- and seventeen-year-olds ranked near the bottom in both mathematics and science (Educational Testing Service, 1989b). The Third International Mathematics and Science Study, released in 1996, found U.S. eighth-graders ranking near the median of forty-one countries, below most European and Asian countries, and just above developing nations. The United States ranked a bit higher in science.

These studies have found that in contrast to teaching in many higher-scoring nations, U.S. teaching is dominated by textbooks, lectures, and teachers' chalkboard explanations followed by individual seatwork, with little cooperative work, project or laboratory work, or use of resources such as computers, calculators, or manipulatives. Researchers note that these "strategies geared to rote learning" reflect a view that "learning for most students should be passive—teachers transmit knowledge to students who receive it and remember it mostly in the form in which it was transmitted. . . . In the light of this, it is hardly surprising that the achievement test items on which U.S. students most often showed relatively greater growth were those most suited to performance of rote procedures" (McKnight et al., 1987, p. 81).

In a wide-ranging review of assessment results, Stedman (1996) notes that in addition to these troubling results in mathematics and science, "history and civics classes are dominated by textbooks, tests, quizzes, and short-answer questions. It is unusual to find students working in groups or writing long papers. Writing instruction in the schools is also limited and is focused on mechanics. Only about a fourth of 8th graders report that their teachers spend more than an hour a week on writing. . . . What we're seeing is that, particularly at the high school level, students are often disengaged, teachers' work is often factory-like, and intellectual life is often poor."

The Neglect of Teaching   The U.S. education system's failure to focus on teaching quality has taken a large toll. For most of this century, it was thought that learning could be improved by ever more precise specification of teaching procedures: a more tightly prescribed curriculum, more teacher-proof texts, more extensive testing, and more carefully constrained decision making. The problem with this approach is that although policies must be uniform, students are not standardized in the pace and manner in which they learn. The tendency to prescribe practices thought to be desirable on statistical grounds has deflected attention from what works with particular children, creating a "focus on service delivery rather than on successful learning . . . [on] the provision of instruction rather than the effective educating of students" (Raywid, 1990, p. 162).

Furthermore, the assumption that rules for practice can be enforced through regulatory systems has created an elaborate bureaucracy to design and manage education prescriptions, a bureaucracy that is an expensive exercise in futility. The century-old U.S. decision to invest in large highly specialized school organizations that design and monitor teaching rather than in knowledgeable teachers who could make decisions themselves has led to a system that fails at the most critical tasks of teaching. Moreover, it drains resources out of classrooms to support functions peripheral to teaching.

In short, although the system we have inherited accomplished the goal of many decades ago—the creation of a structure for providing basic schooling on a mass basis—it is not organized to achieve more ambitious intellectual or social goals for learning. Furthermore, international assessments reveal that in the aggregate, not only do U.S. schools offer less thoughtful teaching and produce lower average achievement than schools in many other countries but they are also the most administratively top heavy and the most educationally unequal in the industrialized world in terms of spending, curriculum offerings, and teaching quality (McKnight et al., 1987; Educational Testing Service, 1989b; Organization for Economic Cooperation and Development, 1995).

The idea of hiring low-paid teachers and micromanaging their work has proved to be a Faustian bargain that has created a continual shortage of highly competent individuals, particularly in fields like mathematics and science, and a large superstructure of supervisors, specialists, and other nonteaching staff to direct teaching and to deal with the learning problems created by the lack of investment in teacher knowledge (National Commission on Teaching and America's Future, 1996). By the early 1990s, U.S. school systems spent only 33 percent of their funds on teacher salaries and just over half (53 percent) on instruction (National Center for Education Statistics, 1995a, tables 72, 77, 161) and hired more administrative and nonteaching staff than any other industrialized country (Organization for Economic Cooperation and Development, 1995).

Many European and Asian countries have adopted a more professional model, in which teachers are extensively prepared, well-supported, and responsible for most school decisions. Because more teachers are hired, they have more time for planning and learning together. And because they have more sustained time with their students, they are more effective in teaching to high levels. Furthermore, most of these countries fund schools centrally and equally while the United States continues to spend more than ten times as much on the education of some of its children as it does on the education of others (Educational Testing Service, 1989a; 1991). U.S. communities have some of the best schools in the world, but they also have some of the worst.

For all these reasons, in the United States of America, children who are required by law to attend school are not guaranteed the right to a qualified teacher. More than 25 percent of those hired into teaching each year are not fully prepared and licensed for their jobs (National Commission on Teaching and America's Future, 1996), and these underprepared teachers are assigned primarily to schools and classrooms serving the most educationally vulnerable children (Darling-Hammond, 1988; 1992; Oakes, 1990). These teachers tend to be more autocratic in the ways they manage their classrooms, less skilled at managing complex forms of instruction, less capable of identifying children's learning styles and needs, and less likely to see it as their job to do so, blaming students when their teaching is not successful (Darling-Hammond, 1992). Then, because the competence of the teaching force is so uneven, more legions of supervisors and specialists are hired to develop systems to guide and inspect the work of teachers who are not trusted to make competent decisions. And so the cycle that favors bureaucracy over teaching repeats itself.

This allocation of resources might be justifiable if it produced student learning. Unfortunately it does not. The effort to regulate schools ever more aggressively merely deflects money from the front lines of teaching and learning where it could be used to hire more highly trained teachers and provide them with greater planning time, smaller teaching loads, and more up-to-date materials. The further we push the twentieth-century model of education management, the less well served many students will be. Those denied well-prepared teachers because the funds needed to hire them are absorbed elsewhere and those whose needs do not fit the mold on which prescriptions for practice are based will be "taught," but they will not learn.

Is Reform Really Needed?

It might be said that Americans are always fixing their schools. Each decade another set of fads emerges (often recycled ideas with new names), such as new math, back to basics, project methods, block scheduling, management by objectives, or school-based budgeting. Schools are usually asked to adopt these fads as single ideas laid on top of old structures. Such ideas are poorly assimilated and quickly rejected. Schools chew up and spit out undigested reforms on a regular basis. This creates a sense within schools that whatever the innovation, "this too will pass"—and that it probably should. Despite all the current education hubbub, many people wonder whether U.S. schools aren't really fine and all the reform rhetoric isn't just a lot of hype. Many others fear that change will disrupt familiar patterns. Even change agents find the work of reform extremely difficult and tempting to abandon. Thus, as the difficulty of serious change has become more apparent, the question of whether we should bother at all has become more important.

Not everyone thinks school reform is needed. First, there are fundamentalists who cherish tradition and believe that if schools would just go back to the basics, all would be well. They are joined by those who argue that schools need improving and standards should be raised but that this really means trying harder to do what schools have always done (Hirsch, 1996; Public Agenda, 1994). More discipline, more attention to core subjects, more spit and polish are all that is needed. This view seems motivated by a fear of radical change married to a faith that "tried and true" methods will ultimately work.

The argument for more of the same is not supported by research on school effectiveness, but as shown by public opinion polling, it does tap widespread public sentiment. And it is occasionally stoked by distortions of public views. For example, the Public Agenda (1994) reported that "people reject the notion that schoolwork should be tailored to suit the interests and preferences of young people" (p. 21) based on one peculiar public poll question: whether "schools should use street language to teach inner city kids"—a question more suited for tapping racial prejudices than pedagogical concerns. The same poll's finding that more than 90 percent of parents and the public want schools to make learning more interesting to students was overlooked by the poll report authors and the press. The message of those fearful of reform is that a return to such "time-honored values" as memorizing arithmetic facts and spelling words, enforcing order, and maintaining traditional courses, tracks, and programs as they are will make things right.

Second are those who believe that public schools are in pretty bad shape; however, the answer is not to reform the system but to create voucher systems and charter schools that allow some students to escape. Some advocates of this view believe that competition alone will breed school quality (Chubb & Moe, 1990). However, the part of their argument that assumes that private schools invariably succeed where public schools fail is disproved by the evidence. When student background factors are taken into account, public school students do as well or better than private school students, despite the fact that private schools are able to select for student ability and behavior as well as parent income (Mullis, Jenkins, & Johnson, 1994). In addition private schools that succeed with a wide range of students have organizational features also present in many public schools that succeed—a strong core curriculum, communal organization, and shared values— but neither all private nor all public schools have these features, and the presumption that market pressure will produce them is far from proved (Lee, Bryk, & Smith, 1993). In fact, in the day-care and technical school sectors, where private, for-profit, and proprietary schools flourish, evidence suggests that private-sector quality is dramatically uneven and often far worse than in the public sector (Kagan & Newton, 1989; Shanker, 1990). Privatization alone is not an adequate answer to low quality.

Others propose public school choice. Although choice is certainly better than coercion as a foundation for public education, smart proponents know that choice is not enough. New York City district school superintendent Anthony Alvarado, whose famous public school choice plan in Community District #4 stimulated the creation of many successful schools, notes that other schools in this district remained unsuccessful because their teachers and principals lacked the knowledge and skills needed to change. In his current efforts in Community District #2, Alvarado focuses almost all his investments on professional development, in the belief that building the capacity of teachers and principals is the key to improving schools. The district's steadily climbing achievement suggests his belief is well founded (Elmore, in press). Unless choice plans are accompanied by policies that build the overall supply of excellent teachers and well-designed schools, they will not help the large majority of students who cannot get into the limited slots available in the schools they want to choose, nor will they improve schools that are dysfunctional and desperately need help.

Charter schools are the newest panacea. They are relieved from the usual regulations so they can create new options, exactly as alternative schools were in the 1960s. Although charters may be useful as a small-scale approach to change, they are not likely by themselves to transform the system. Of the thousands of new experimental, alternative, and demonstration schools created with special dispensations in each previous era of reform, most came and went quickly because policymakers did little to change the system as a whole—to increase the supply of knowledgeable teachers, to reallocate funding, and to revise or abolish regulations that shape "regular" schools. Likewise, recent studies of charter experiments in California and Minnesota found these new schools have had little or no effect on their sponsoring districts (Buechler, 1996). If past experience is a guide, strategies that rely on competition or special schools without increasing the capacity of the system to offer good education will produce improved education for only a few and with little lasting effect.

Finally, there are those who argue that American schoolpeople are doing the best they can and better than ever before. In a spirited defense of public education, David Berliner and Bruce Biddle (1995) suggest that the current press for reform is based in part on a "manufactured crisis." They are absolutely correct that the problem is not that U.S. schools are doing worse than they were in the "good old days." In fact schools are doing as well as they ever did for a greater number of students: graduation rates have risen dramatically throughout the century, basic literacy rates have risen, and more students are participating in a greater range of educational opportunities at the secondary and postsecondary levels. Furthermore, public schools are much more inclusive and diverse places than they were in 1950, when nearly half of all seventeen-year-olds had dropped out. Most of the students who are the focus of special programs in today's schools were not in school. Handicapped students were largely excluded from schooling. Large numbers of African American, Latino, and Native American students were relegated to miserably funded segregated systems or denied access entirely. Students who did not speak English coped on their own or dropped out.

Furthermore, U.S. educators work in a less supportive social environment than do their peers in industrialized countries that have much lower rates of child poverty, mortality, and abuse and much greater support for child health, welfare, and preschool education. A growing share of U.S. children (nearly one in four) now live in poverty; many arrive at school hungry, unvaccinated, and frightened by the violence that surrounds their lives. Most live in a single-parent home at some time while they are growing up. Children who encounter a wide variety of stresses in their families and communities are present in virtually every classroom. Defenders of today's schools are right to point out that school bashing does not solve the substantial problems of unequal wealth, inadequate supports for child welfare, social violence, and prejudice that plague our society.

Berliner and Biddle argue that U.S. students achieve as much as students elsewhere once you control for the fact that other countries have less unequal education and social systems and offer more of their students greater opportunities to learn. U.S. students provided with high-level coursework in mathematics and science, for example, do as well as average students in countries where these opportunities are provided for most students (Westbury, 1992). However, U.S. students take such courses later and in smaller numbers. Moreover, the quality of teaching matters. For example, U.S. performance in reading is better than in mathematics when compared to other countries. This is especially true in the early grades (Elley, 1992), a probable result of recent strides in knowledge about literacy development and more extensive preparation of elementary school teachers to teach reading. In contrast, over 30 percent of secondary mathematics teachers lack training in the field they teach. In some states more than 60 percent of mathematics teachers are out of field (National Commission on Teaching and America's Future, 1996).

Teachers' preparation is highly related to what students learn. For example, students in high-achieving states like Iowa, Minnesota, and North Dakota do as well in mathematics as those in high-scoring countries like Korea and Japan while students in low-achieving states like Alabama, Louisiana, and Mississippi do far worse, ranking at the bottom of the distribution with nations like Jordan (see Figure 1.1). Interestingly, the high-scoring states regulate education very little, and none has a statewide testing system, but all three have professional standards boards for teachers that have enacted rigorous requirements for teacher education and licensing and that refuse to allow districts to hire unlicensed teachers. The lowest-scoring states regulate schools

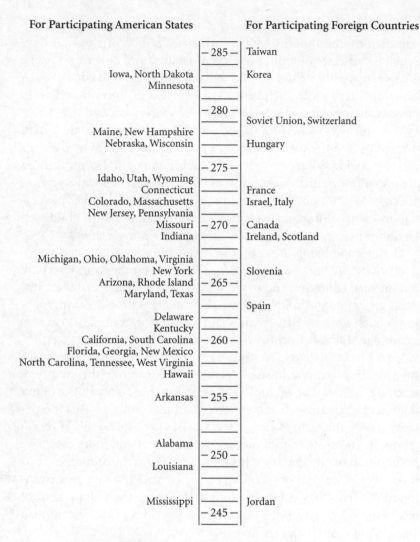

For Participating American States   **For Participating Foreign Countries**

	— 285 —	Taiwan
Iowa, North Dakota	———	Korea
Minnesota	———	
	— 280 —	
	———	Soviet Union, Switzerland
Maine, New Hampshire	———	
Nebraska, Wisconsin	———	Hungary
	— 275 —	
Idaho, Utah, Wyoming	———	
Connecticut	———	France
Colorado, Massachusetts	———	Israel, Italy
New Jersey, Pennsylvania	———	
Missouri	— 270 —	Canada
Indiana	———	Ireland, Scotland
Michigan, Ohio, Oklahoma, Virginia	———	
New York	———	Slovenia
Arizona, Rhode Island	— 265 —	
Maryland, Texas	———	
	———	Spain
Delaware	———	
Kentucky	———	
California, South Carolina	— 260 —	
Florida, Georgia, New Mexico	———	
North Carolina, Tennessee, West Virginia	———	
Hawaii	———	
Arkansas	— 255 —	
Alabama	———	
	— 250 —	
Louisiana	———	
Mississippi	———	Jordan
	— 245 —	

**Figure 1.1.   Average Mathematics
Proficiency Scores for Thirteen-Year-Olds.**

Note: Scores are from 1991 or 1992. The states of Alaska, Illinois, Kansas,
Montana, Nevada, Oregon, South Dakota, Vermont, and Washington did not
participate. The District of Columbia is not displayed. Mathematics proficiency
scores range from 0 to 500. A score of 250 = proficiency in numerical operations
and beginning problem solving. A score of 300 = proficiency in moderately
complex procedures and reasoning.
Source: U.S. Department of Education, 1993, pp. 56–57,
as published in Berliner & Biddle, 1995, p. 61.

heavily and test students frequently, but they have low standards for teacher education and hire large numbers of unqualified teachers each year (National Commission on Teaching and America's Future, 1996).

These disparities are the crux of the issue. If all U.S. schools could function as well as the most advantaged do, there would be no need for systemic change. It is not that U.S. teachers and students cannot succeed when they are well supported, it is that the system fails to support so many of them. This is the real crisis of American education. As Sizer (1984) concludes: "It is astonishing that so few critics challenge the system. In an absolute sense, the learning exhibited by even a 'successful' student after over twelve thousand hours in classrooms is strikingly limited. When one considers the energy, commitment, and quality of so many of the people working in the schools, one must place the blame elsewhere. The people are better than the structure. Therefore the structure must be at fault" (p. 209).

The fundamental problem is that we have pushed the current system as far as it can go, and it cannot go far enough. If we care about all students and about the fate of the society as a whole, we cannot ignore real problems or merely seek to "get around" the present system. We must re-create it so that it, in turn, reshapes the possibilities for the great majority of schools.

THE CHALLENGE FOR SCHOOLS

In the last decade, aggressive efforts to reform schools have been launched not only in the United States but all over the world. With major economic and technological changes that make both daily life and employment much more complex and with burgeoning migration worldwide, virtually all societies are simultaneously seeking to educate more diverse populations and to ensure higher levels of skill for more citizens. In most cases these demands are imposed upon educational institutions designed a century ago for different purposes. Schools must respond to major economic and social challenges that other institutions have barely begun to recognize, much less address.

The Economic Challenge

The question is not whether schoolpeople are working as well as they can under the circumstances—and most surely are—but whether the current system of schooling allows them to educate in ways that support new social, economic, and human goals. Is the learning produced by our schools adequate to today's and tomorrow's demands? Some suggest that the U.S. economy, which has recently shown the most growth in the service sector (traditionally full of low-skill jobs), is more than adequately fed by the current education system (Berliner & Biddle, 1995, p. 100; Mishel & Teixeira, 1991). However, many others note that the restructuring of work today demands higher skills of even service employees (Berliner & Biddle, 1995, p. 238; Murnane & Levy, 1996a).

The terms of the debate are shifting rapidly. Between 1992 and 1995, for example, the proportion of new jobs paying above the national average income and requiring high levels of skill increased from 22 percent to 45 percent (Dobrzynski, 1996). Most are in the service sector, but they are in skilled occupations ranging from accounting to data processing. As one analysis noted: "For all this demand, many Americans . . . simply do not have the education or the skills to qualify for good jobs. Some are chronically impoverished, while others are white-and blue-collar workers who lost high-paying jobs in corporate downsizings even as new positions have been created elsewhere. They have been unable to find employment with pay and benefits comparable to those of their previous jobs" (Dobrzynski, 1996, pp. 3–1).

Peter Drucker (1994) notes that the rise and fall of the blue-collar class between 1950 and the year 2000 is the most rapid of any class in the history of the world. From half of all jobs at midcentury, blue-collar employment will decline to only about 10 percent of total U.S. employment by the end of the century. People once able to earn high wages for routine forms of work are often unable to move into the more intellectually and interpersonally demanding jobs the new economy has to offer, which require more capacity to take initiative, to organize work with others, to deal with novel problems, and to use technologies as well as higher levels of basic literacy and numeracy skills: "The great majority of the new jobs require qualifications the industrial worker does not possess and is poorly equipped to acquire. They require a good deal of formal education and the ability to acquire and to apply theoretical and analytical knowledge. They require a different approach to work and a different mind-set. Above all, they require a habit of continuous learning. Displaced industrial workers thus cannot simply move into knowledge work or services the way displaced farmers and domestic workers moved into industrial work" (Drucker, 1986, p. 62).

Murnane and Levy (1996a) show that the attainment of these skills is rapidly becoming the major predictor of employment and wages, and demand for these skills has created growing disparities in wages between high school and college graduates—with the former declining over time while the latter rise. Longitudinal studies of high school graduates show that even among individuals with the same degrees, those with higher levels of skill increasingly have greater earning capacity. Surveys of employers indicate that even entry-level jobs require workers who have mastered higher levels of basic skills, are technologically literate, and can plan and monitor much of their own work.

Meanwhile, jobs requiring technical skills and knowledge are expected to constitute nearly half the total by the year 2010. And the rapid pace of economic change means that most workers will need to change occupations at least two or three times during their lives (Drucker, 1994; Hudson Institute, 1987). These new conditions mean that the traditional outcomes of our school system—academic success for some and failure for many others—are now more problematic than they have ever been. In contrast to only twenty years ago, today there are few jobs in mills and factories to accommodate most of those for whom schooling has not been a success. High school dropouts, for example, now have less than one chance in three of finding work, and if they do find a job, they typically earn less than half as much as they would have twenty years ago (William T. Grant Foundation, 1988). They increasingly become part of a growing underclass, cut off from productive engagement in society. And working-class youngsters and adults prepared for the disappearing jobs of the past teeter on the brink of downward social mobility. These changes are provoking legitimate fears about this society's future and growing tensions between races and classes.

The Human and Social Challenge

Because the economy can no longer absorb many unskilled workers at decent wages, lack of education is increasingly linked to crime and delinquency. As schools in California have experienced continual cutbacks over the last decade, the state's prison population has increased by more than 600 percent. More than half the adult prison population has literacy skills below those required by the labor market (Barton & Coley, 1996), and nearly 40 percent of adjudicated juvenile delinquents

have treatable learning disabilities that went undiagnosed and un-
treated in the schools (Gemignani, 1994). Nationwide, as prison populations expand and a growing underclass despairs of participating in
the American dream, our failure to invest in schools that can create
adequate life chances for so many has increasingly devastating consequences for individual citizens and for society as a whole.

In addition to a rapidly changing industrial base, the United States
is experiencing major demographic shifts that will demand higher
productivity from a smaller number of workers. In 1950, for example,
there were sixteen workers for every person on Social Security; by
2010, there will be only three (Social Security Administration, 1996).
If not all of these potential workers are productive, our nation's social
compact will crumble.

Meanwhile, the growth in the U.S. population and its potential for
social renewal is largely among immigrants and people of color, who
will make up 40 percent of the public school population and over a
third of the entering workforce by the year 2000 (Hudson Institute,
1987). This nation's ability to embrace and enhance the talents of
those who have long struggled for voice and educational opportunity
will determine much of its future.

Meeting America's twenty-first-century challenge is not just a matter of improved teaching of academic content in schools that are now
failing, although that is surely important. Repairing the torn social
fabric that increasingly arrays one group against another will require
creating an inclusive social dialogue in which individuals can come to
understand diverse experiences and points of view. This suggests not
only education *for* democracy, in the sense that we think of students'
needing to learn trades and good citizenship, but education *as* democracy (Glickman, in press)—education that gives students access to
social understanding developed as they actually participate in a pluralistic community, talking together, making decisions, and coming to
understand multiple views.

Most schools, however, are poor places in which to learn democracy. They often illustrate authoritarian and coercive forms of social
control and social stratification both across schools and across tracks
within schools. Two-thirds of minority students, for example, still attend predominantly minority schools (Orfield, Monfort, & Aaron,
1989), and of the remainder another two-thirds are isolated in low
tracks that provide a separate and unequal educational experience,

qualitatively different in form, function, and content from that offered to high-track students (Oakes, 1985, 1990). This experience too often fails to prepare them to participate fully as democratic citizens or to meet the requirements of contemporary economic life.

If the United States is to maintain a healthy democracy, its education system will need to sustain a shared social life and a more ambitious pursuit of human possibility. Schools will need to develop knowledge, skills, and talents that cannot be fully specified or predicted in advance, creating "the kinds of conditions in which people can be themselves" (Greene, 1984, p. 4) so that they can find and act on who they are; what their passions, gifts, and talents may be; what they care about; and how they want to make a contribution to each other and the world.

Increasing social complexity also demands citizens who can understand and evaluate difficult problems and alternatives and who can manage complicated social systems. As Thomas Jefferson so keenly understood, popular intelligence coupled with democratic decision making provides the best protection against tyranny. In response to Alexander Hamilton's famous assertion "Thy people, sir, are a beast!" Jefferson argued that education would enable the people to make good decisions. Public education's ostensible mission, the development of an intelligent populace and a popular intelligence, requires that all individuals have access to education that prepares them to debate and decide among competing ideas, to weigh the individual and the common good, and to make judgments that sustain democratic institutions and ideals.

Finally, growing up humane and decent people who can appreciate others and take satisfaction in doing things well requires schools that model humanity and decency, that cultivate appreciation, and that support learning about things that matter to the people in them. Education should be a source of nurturance for the spirit as well as a means of reaching understanding, though it can be, and too often is, conducted in a way that deadens and demoralizes. Tedious, coercive schooling creates frustrations that must emerge sooner or later in self-deprecation, despair, or violence against others. However, where a real connection is made between students and teachers in the pursuit of meaningful accomplishments, the possibilities for developing lifelong capacities for learning, doing, and relating to others are greatly expanded.

CREATING A RIGHT TO LEARN

Securing all children's right to learn in the way that new standards suggest and today's society demands requires a change in teaching much more profound than merely covering more facts or getting through more chapters in a textbook. Our very concept of teaching will have to change. Teachers will need to go far beyond dispensing information, giving a test, and giving a grade. They will need to know how to construct ambitious work aimed at more proficient performances while taking advantage of students' different starting points and approaches to learning. Schools will need to reorganize themselves to support this kind of teaching.

To engender serious learning, schools must dramatically increase the intellectual opportunities they offer, becoming more focused on developing understanding and competence (Cohen, McLaughlin, & Talbert, 1993; Gardner, 1991). And as they become more *learning centered,* they must also become more *learner centered,* that is, deliberately organized to attend to the varied developmental and cognitive needs emerging from students' differing experiences, talents, learning styles, language backgrounds, family situations, and beliefs about themselves and what school means for them. This means shifting from a selective mode "characterized by minimal variation in the conditions for learning" and in which "a narrow range of instructional options and a limited number of ways to succeed are available" to an adaptive mode in which "the educational environment can provide for a range of opportunities for success" (Glaser, 1990, pp. 16–17).

To do this, teachers must understand how their students think as well as what they know. They need a deep knowledge of subject matter and a wide repertoire of teaching strategies combined with intimate knowledge of students' growth, experience, and development (Piaget, 1970; Berliner, 1986; Shulman, 1987; Carter & Doyle, 1987). They also need to work in schools that are responsive to students, that foster relationships, and that support teacher learning. Research over the last several decades suggests that schools that develop high levels of both competence and community share nine features that I return to in Chapter Three: active in-depth learning organized around common goals, a focus on authentic performance, attention to student development, appreciation for diversity, collaborative learning, a collective perspective within the school, structures for caring, support for democratic learning, and connections to family and community.

Although yet in a minority, a growing number of schools—fostered by grassroots networks like the Coalition of Essential Schools, the School Development Program, the National Network for Educational Renewal, Accelerated Schools, and many others—have already begun restructuring in many of the ways suggested in this book. The agenda of all these school initiatives is fundamentally democratic: to join empowering forms of education to the quest for educational equity by creating humane, intellectually challenging, and pluralistic learning communities for students who represent all of America.

THE FOUNDATIONS OF A RIGHT TO LEARN: A NEW PARADIGM FOR EDUCATION POLICY

Research has begun to document restructuring schools' accomplishments in supporting much higher levels of challenging learning for a greater range of students than ever before. Striking successes have occurred in central cities, suburbs, and rural areas (Elmore & Associates, 1990; Darling-Hammond, Ancess, & Falk, 1995; Fine, 1994; Lee & Smith, 1994; Lieberman, 1995; Newmann & Wehlage, 1995). It is becoming clear that ordinary schools can succeed in extraordinary ways when they refocus their work on the needs of students rather than the demands of bureaucracies. The work of restructuring is difficult but not impossible. Yet this work is still unsupported by the policy environment. Instead, it is conducted largely by exception, on waivers, and at the margin of the system. Restructuring schools remain in constant tension with the central offices and state agencies that oversee a regulatory system invented for a different time and a different view of schooling.

Moving from several thousand successful schools to nearly one hundred thousand is the much steeper mountain of work ahead. To succeed, we will need an education infrastructure shaped by policies that support appropriate teaching and learning, more effective school organizations, opportunities for powerful professional learning, and resources that enable new practices to take root. School reformers cannot afford to neglect the task of developing new policy while they are growing new schools. Dewey understood this well, noting, in 1902, that "it is easy to fall into the habit of regarding the mechanics of school organization and administration as something comparatively external and indifferent to educational purposes and ideals." It is, however, such matters as "the classifying of pupils, the way decisions are made, the manner in which the machinery of instruction bears upon the child that really control the whole system" (quoted in Tyack, 1974, p. 197).

Progressive education requires more than committed teachers striving for classroom-level reform. It requires a set of systemic conditions—including widespread teacher knowledge and schools structured for strong relationships—that turn-of-the-last-century managers could not understand and did not believe in. School reformers have focused on how to get around the system, but it is the system's deeply ingrained mechanisms for organizing schooling that have thus far prevented the enactment of widespread change. These same structures will kill reforms once again if the system itself is not transformed.

The success of today's efforts will ultimately rest on whether education policies continue to enforce a bureaucratic approach that emphasizes standardization and prescription of practice or whether they support a professional approach that arms teachers with the knowledge they need to teach skillfully and make appropriate decisions. Getting the procedures right will never be enough to improve learning on a wide scale. As Benveniste explains: "Since rules and routines work well when tasks are predictable, unvaried, and well understood, they are used extensively. However, when tasks are varied and unpredictable, when learning is important in the task situation, and when adaptability is required, discretion and trust have to replace routines. This is where the professional in the organization takes on new importance. . . . In an uncertain environment and task situation, the professional has the necessary knowledge and experience to act independently. The professional can search for solutions, determine which alternative to adopt, and implement new approaches" (1987, p. 256). This alternative is only viable, however, where teachers have the knowledge they need to act responsibly and the opportunity to search for solutions to problems of practice that lack straightforward answers.

Teachers in restructuring schools speak eloquently about how the chance to expand their own learning and create adaptive practices has made a difference to their teaching and their students:

> Being a member of the research-into-practice team has been the most rewarding learning experience of my teaching career. . . . No matter what problems arise in teaching, I'll never have to face or solve (them) alone. . . . My team members have been in my classroom, understand

what I am dealing with and are always there to help [a teacher from New Suncook School in western Maine, quoted in Goldsberry et al., 1995, p. 138].

Customizing teaching to each child's level, believe me, is time consuming. But once you try it and see how it works and how much more you enjoy teaching, you just accept it. You start thinking of teaching as a career and not just a job [a teacher from Wheeler School in Jefferson County, Kentucky, quoted in Whitford & Gaus, 1995, p. 34].

Policies that support teachers' professional learning can make a major difference in student success. But figuring out what kinds of policies will support teaching that meets today's new and very different goals for students is not at all simple. The challenges of today's society pose difficult questions for practitioners and policymakers who are the agents of democratic schooling. What would it actually mean to teach all children to the high standards politicians are talking about and educators are trying to fashion? What are the real education implications of the school reform mantra "all children can learn"? What kinds of teaching practices will support learning that enables higher levels of performance and understanding for different kinds of learners? What kinds of knowledge and skills do teachers need to develop such practices? What kinds of school organizations can allow this kind of teaching to occur? How can this restructuring be done in ways that also build cross-cultural understanding and cooperative possibilities across individuals and groups? What do our policy system and our schools of education have to do to make all of this possible?

These are central questions for the contemporary reinvention of democratic education, and they are ones this book tries to address. There are at least three difficult issues posed by a quest to teach in ways that provide a genuine right to learn. First is the issue of how to construct this more complex form of teaching practice in classrooms and schools. This new practice must manage the dialectic between a set of high common expectations for learning and the distinctive pathways by which students construct their understanding. If well tended, this process should also enable students to go beyond the common expectations to develop their unique talents in ways that allow for "individually configured excellence" (Gardner, 1991).

The companion issues pertain to professional development and policy development: How can we create the kind of learning experiences for educators that will allow them to teach in these ways? And how do we create the kind of policy structure that will support them in this work? Building democratic education is extremely knowledge intensive for all actors in the system. It cannot be accomplished by top-down mandates or teacher-proof curricula of the sort most policies have relied upon throughout this century. In order to create the kind of schools I have described, educators must know a great deal about learning and teaching, school organizations, and education change.

In the chapters what follow, I lay the groundwork for the kinds of policy and professional education that could support democratic education for all students.

## CHAPTER TWO

The Limits of the Education Bureaucracy

The task before us is the restructuring of our entire public education system. I don't mean tinkering. I don't mean piecemeal changes or even well-intentioned reforms. I mean the total restructuring of our schools. . . . Successful firms have discarded the archaic, outmoded, and thoroughly discredited practices that are still in place in most of our large school districts. Those districts are organized like a factory of the late 19th century: top-down, command-control management, a system designed to stifle creativity and independent judgment.

—David Kearns, *"An Education Recovery Plan*
for America" (1988)

When reformers of the late nineteenth and early twentieth centuries created the bureaucratic organizations that are the basis for today's schools, they had many laudable goals in mind. To replace a set of badly funded one-room schoolhouses that haphazardly educated children with untrained teachers and ad hoc materials, they hoped to build a system that would provide equal and uniform treatment by standardizing services and decisions based on predetermined rules.

Max Weber ([1946] 1958) described the primary virtue of bureaucracy as its ability "to specialize administrative functions according to purely objective considerations. . . .The 'objective' discharge of business primarily means a discharge of business according to calculable rules and 'without regard for persons'" (p. 215). Unfortunately, it is this very "virtue" that has made teaching and learning so difficult in modern schools.

Today's challenge—to create strategies that can support the individually appropriate teaching needed to produce high levels of success for diverse learners—was not the goal of the last century's reformers. They wanted to use methods that could teach "without regard to persons," and to a remarkable extent they did. Their quest for the "one best system" (Tyack, 1974) drew upon then-popular *scientific management* techniques and modern bureaucratic organizational models to centralize decision making, specialize offices and staff roles, and develop rules governing production. In addition to businesses and factories, they could look to the German and Prussian schools of their time, which offered centralized, highly structured procedures such as age grading and sequenced curriculum compatible with an assembly-line view of the educational process. The image of a moving conveyer belt on which students were placed while teachers performed a predetermined series of operations on them was a powerful metaphor for order and efficiency.

Today, however, many schoolpeople sense that the capacity of assembly-line schools to meet the demands they face is inherently limited. As one teacher put it: "How do we teach these kids in a way that they can learn? I don't believe the present educational structure is able to do that anymore. It's like trying to run a battleship with a tugboat engine" (quoted in Poplin & Weeres, 1992, p. 40). And further efforts to perfect the education bureaucracy have seemed only to make matters worse. In a study that Arthur Wise and I conducted in the early 1980s,[1] teachers in three mid-Atlantic school districts reported that policymakers' efforts to control schools by creating detailed procedures for classroom practice were undermining the teachers' ability to teach well. When asked if there were any policy that might make them leave teaching, the teachers' single most frequent answer did not pertain to low salaries, poor working conditions, student misbehavior, or lack of funding. Instead, they most often cited increased prescription of curriculum and teaching methods as the major threat to their continuation in teaching. These teachers feared that any greater bureaucratization of their work would render them ineffective and eliminate the remaining joys of teaching. As one teacher put it: "The only thing that would make me leave teaching is if they ever computerize all these objectives and I have to sit there and check off forms for thirty-eight kids and 250 different objectives. I think if it got down to that, I would simply resign because I would feel like I was spending more time on forms than on kids."[2]

To understand what needs to change in U.S. schools and what alternatives are possible, we first need to see how the schools evolved to their present stage, what choices were made, and what assumptions supported those choices. As I noted in Chapter One, many other countries have chosen a different course—one that invests more heavily in highly skilled teachers than in prescriptions for practice, in schools that are smaller and less specialized, and in teaching that is conducted *with* regard for persons instead of largely by procedure. Other realities are possible if we can imagine what they are.

This chapter examines how past policies produced bureaucratic schools and assembly-line teaching and how current school failures continue to be linked to the bureaucratization of schools, through the influence of behaviorist learning theories, ongoing curriculum controls, and prescribed testing. I describe the dysfunctional outcomes of these influences and the shape of potential alternatives.

SYSTEMATIZING SCHOOL

The application of scientific management to U.S. schools followed the rush of excitement about the efficiencies of Henry Ford's assembly-line methods. Schools were expected to be the most efficient means to produce a product whose uniformity and quality could be programmed by carefully specified procedures. This led to the gradual adoption of grades and textbook series for sequencing instruction and examinations for evaluating curriculum mastery and placements. Great emphasis was placed on preparing students for their later work in factories. The habits of punctuality, regularity, attention, and silence were viewed by superintendents and college presidents as the most important for eventual success in an industrial society (Harris and Doty, 1874, p. 14).

In most city schools, punishments were meted to those who spoke, moved, or otherwise failed to obey; tardiness was computed down to the second and third decimal point; and children were expected to march in rows. Questioning by children was rarely tolerated; their work required drill and memorization but not thinking or analysis.

Helen Todd (1913) reported that over 80 percent of the children she found working in factories preferred the long hours, filthy conditions, and drudgery of that work to the conditions they had experienced in school.

Although today's schools are less regimented than this, they carry the marks of their industrial origins. The short segmented tasks stressing speed and neatness that predominate in most schools, the emphasis on rules from the important to the trivial, and the obsession with bells, schedules, and time clocks are all dug deep into the ethos of late-nineteenth-century America, when students were being prepared to work in factories on predetermined tasks that would not require them to figure out what to do.

Applying Scientific Management

The advent of the "Taylor system" in the decade after 1910 called for a separation of responsibilities between a new class of managers, who were to do all the thinking, and workers, who were to conduct routine tasks following procedures developed by the managers. As Frederick Taylor (1911) put it, "One type of man is needed to plan ahead and an entirely different type to execute the work" (pp. 37–38).

Taylor's system determined the one best way of doing any job, organized work so that each worker could conduct a narrow repetitive task in exactly the same way, specified the amount and kind of work to be done by each worker each day, and created a supervisory system in which a different foreman oversaw each type of job. This system also created planning departments to design the work, managers and superintendents to coordinate it, and clerks to maintain records of inputs, outputs, and procedures.

Although Taylor was criticized for the number of unproductive people his plan introduced, his tactics spread to schools, where the layers of nonteaching personnel grew. In 1890, the only nonteacher in most districts was the school superintendent. By the 1920s, "there was a whole galaxy of principals, assistant principals, supervisors of special subjects, directors of vocational education and home economics, deans, attendance officers, and clerks, who do no teaching but are concerned in one way or another with keeping the system going" (Lynd & Lynd, 1929, p. 210). Today nonteaching personnel constitute more than half of the U.S. education workforce (Organization for Economic Cooperation and Development, 1995). They are supposed to design, plan, and monitor the work of teachers who are expected merely to "do" that work.

PERFECTING THE FACTORY SCHOOL Efficiency experts' cost calculations led educators to replace small intimate schools with huge ones. Chicago superintendent William McAndrew noted that building a school of 4,000 pupils could save $11.80 per pupil over the construction costs for a school of 2,500 (1926, p. 61). Although studies have since shown that the dysfunctions of large schools negate these savings (Public Education Association, 1992), similarly crude concepts of costs and efficiencies maintain the practice of building large schools even today.

The concept of the "platoon school," originated by William Wirt in 1908, completed school regimentation. Hoping to save on wasted plant space and solve overcrowding, Wirt devised the system in which students circulate through the school from one classroom to another, with different teachers teaching them different subjects for short periods of time. Under this system, teachers began to teach only one subject, over and over again, all day. This "improved school machine" as Wirt called it, lowered both plant costs and teacher costs per pupil.

Although most administrators loved the platoon plan, many teachers and parents did not, seeing all too clearly how the long lines of children marching from room to room looked, as one mother put it, like "nothing so much as the lines of uncompleted Ford cars in the factory, moving always on, with a screw put in or a burr tightened as they pass—standardized, mechanical, pitiful" (Haley, 1924, p. 18). Nonetheless the plan "eliminated waste," and it spread rapidly until it was used in most schools, as it is to this day.

THE BIRTH OF PAPERWORK Of course calculating organizational efficiencies on a regular basis required the creation of planning offices and the hiring of legions of clerks. Soon systems were invented to control purchasing and other functions. These systems, complete with elaborate forms requiring sign-offs in triplicate, "not only converted the simplest act (e.g. ordering a box of chalk) into a major, complicated operation but also indicated a strong distrust of teachers and principals by forcing them to record every action and giving a clerk the right to decide whether supplies should be granted" (Callahan, 1962, p. 173). In 1914, New York City school superintendent William H. Maxwell warned that if teachers did all the paperwork urged by efficiency experts they "would have no time and energy left for teaching." Since then his fears have very nearly come true.

In many large city school systems such procedures continue to operate just as they did when they were invented. By now, however, the forms number in the hundreds, and the required approvals frequently paralyze sensible action altogether, giving rise to unending opportunities for corruption in order to get things done. As Maxwell warned, enormous amounts of staff time are consumed by reports of attendance, tardiness, truancy, testing, expenditures, personnel assignments, uses of time, credit hours accumulated, pass rates, promotion rates, individualized education plans, and on and on and on. Teachers complain bitterly about the teaching time they sacrifice to feed the insatiable administrative appetite for reports. Though they worked in different districts, the teachers Art Wise and I interviewed told similar stories:

> [What is burdensome is] having to spend a lot of my time doing unnecessary paperwork, which does not free me to do other things I would like to do for the students. . . . I walk in in the morning and some child wants to talk to me and I realize that somebody has handed me a form that has to be filled out and it has to be handed back in fifteen minutes . . . I think the tremendous amount of paperwork is really unnecessary.

> Recording of grades, putting grades on computer sheets, keeping attendance records takes time away from the actual process of teaching. Before you're done, you make anywhere from five to seven copies of your attendance. That could be done once and then given to a secretary, and other copies needed could be done from that, instead of taking my time that should be for teaching and planning.

> If we could get the administration to leave us alone and let us teach, we'd be able to. . . . We spend probably a good 30 percent or more of our time doing paperwork. A good percentage of that is completely unnecessary and another percentage is something that could be done by a teacher's aide or secretary. Time that we could and should be using to teach we're doing paperwork.

That the demand for paperwork intended to improve school accountability actually undermines productivity by taking time away from the core functions of the school is a paradox most policymakers and administrators have not yet fully appreciated. In the logic of bureaucratic management, as concerns about school and student performance increase, so do the numbers of reports on every aspect of schooling requested by those far from schools. A vicious cycle is launched: the more paperwork teachers are asked to do, the less time they have for teaching; the less time for teaching, the less learning occurs; the less learning, the more the demand for paperwork intended to ensure that teachers are teaching as the bureaucracy insists they should.

ESTABLISHING HIERARCHICAL CONTROL   The adoption of scientific management also meant excluding community members and teachers from decision making. Tyack (1974) notes that although school superintendents often used the language of social engineers, "they were actually trying to replace village forms in which laymen participated in decentralized decision-making with the new bureaucratic model of a closed 'nonpolitical' system in which directives flowed from the top down, reports emanated from the bottom, and each step of the educational process was carefully prescribed" (p. 40).

The imposition of hierarchical decision making over matters great and small was made easier by the feminization of the teaching force. The egg-crate school structure headed by a male administrator and staffed by female teachers was established by Boston educator John Philbrick, whose model school contained twelve classrooms built for fifty-six students and one teacher per classroom. "Let the Principal or Superintendent have the general supervision and control of the whole," Philbrick advised, "and let him have one male assistant or sub-principal, and ten female assistants, one for each room" (1856, p. 263). This was the start of what Tyack (1974, p. 45) called the "pedagogical harem" and of the subordination of teachers to the directives of those "above" them.

The feminization of teaching simultaneously reduced teachers' wages and the discretion they were allowed to exercise. As women were paid less than men and many were more willing to take orders, school boards set out to hire them. In a book widely used for teacher training between 1907 and 1930, the need for "unquestioned obedience" was stressed as the "first rule of efficient service" for teachers (Bagley, 1910, p. 2). By 1911, when over 70 percent of teachers were women, a study observed that their predominance "has been due in part to the changed character of the management of the public schools, to the specialization of labor within the school, to the narrowing of the intellectual range or versatility required of teachers, and to the willingness of women to work for less than men. . . . [Almost] all of the graded school positions have been preempted by women; men still survive in public school work as 'managing' or executive officers." Teachers with limited training were seen as an advantage: "such teachers will almost invariably be in hearty sympathy with graded-school work"(Coffman, 1911, p. 82). The less educated teachers were, the more they accepted and encouraged greater simplification and routinization of teaching tasks.

Not all women were glad to be exploited by public schools or managed by administrators' reporting schemes. In 1880, former teacher turned journalist Mary Abigail Dodge deplored the "degradation of the teacher":

> All the time writing silly reports and gathering meaningless statistics for administrators, teachers hardly have time to teach. . . . The men who are capable of doing a man's work in the world will have no time to spend in twitching a woman's apron-strings and hindering her from doing hers. . . . The thing which a school ought not to be, the thing which our system of supervision is strenuously trying to make the school into, is a factory, with the superintendents for overseers and the teachers for workmen. [Instead], teachers ought to run the schools exactly as doctors run a hospital [Tyack, pp. 64, 82].

Complaints against the restrictions placed on teachers were registered by Jane Addams, Hull-House founder and a school board member in Chicago, and Ella Flagg Young, who quit as assistant superintendent in Chicago to protest the "petty degradation" created by supervisory processes that drove many women and men from the classroom. English educator Sara Burstall noted of U.S. education that so little initiative was granted to teachers that they must feel "like a cog in a machine" and many must be driven from the profession (Tyack, 1974, p. 259). Humanizing schools and asserting the teachers' role in decision making were, along with wage issues, key rallying cries for early teachers unions.

But to no avail. In the early years of the century, decisions about teaching, curriculum, assessment, and learning passed from the hands of teachers, individually and collectively, to administrators, commercial textbook publishers, and test makers, who were not swayed by such distractions as the needs of individual students. To a substantial extent and in contrast to the tradition in many other countries, decisions about these matters still remain outside the purview of teachers in U.S. schools.

Setting Standards

In the new scientifically managed schools, efficiency experts conducted stopwatch studies to set standards for classroom work: the number of arithmetic problems students should be able to do at each grade and at what speed, the words they should be able to spell, the facts they should be able to recall. Learning tasks were picked not because they led to key abilities but because they were set out in textbooks and easily measurable. Standards were incorporated into extensive tests that would be of great value to the teacher, it was thought. As management expert Franklin Bobbitt put it, "having these definite tasks laid upon her, she can know at all times whether she is accomplishing the things expected of her or not" (1913, p. 23).

Tests were expected to serve both public relations and incentives purposes, making it important that they be developed and scored outside of classrooms by "experts" rather than teachers. Otherwise how could superintendents guarantee the public that the results were scientific, that no cheating had occurred, and that the scores were comparable? Thus it was that U.S. teachers, unlike teachers elsewhere in the world, lost control of curriculum and testing.

Tests were also used to sort students into grade levels and programs so that, it was imagined, teachers could teach all students in a particular group alike. Separate student tracks were created to correspond to the distinct layers of society. In 1909, Harvard University president Charles Eliot counted four of these layers, each requiring a different form of education: a thin layer of managers and leaders, two larger layers of skilled workers and merchants, and a great thick layer of manual laborers. It was widely agreed that in the cause of social efficiency, city schools should "give up the exceedingly democratic idea that all are equal, and that our society is devoid of classes" and prepare students for their future place in the social structure (Cubberley, 1909, pp. 56–57).

The advent of IQ testing provided the necessary machinery. Adapted from the work of Alfred Binet in France and the IQ scales used in the U.S. Army in World War I, group IQ tests for children took the education world by storm in the 1920s. The technology of norm referencing was a major breakthrough for sorting purposes because it selected questions based on their ability to rank order test takers along an artificially constructed normal curve rather than on a straightforward conception of knowledge. These tests were used to sort students into tracks starting in elementary school.

Although some argued that using tests to track students would enhance social justice, the motives for tracking students—like the rationales for using IQ scores to set U.S. immigration quotas—were often motivated by racial and ethnic politics. Just as psychologist Henry Goddard suggested with his testing experiments in 1912 that 83 percent of Jews, 80 percent of Hungarians, 79 percent of Italians, and 87 percent of Russians were feebleminded (Kamin, 1974), so did Lewis Terman, developer of the Stanford-Binet intelligence test, find that "[Indians, Mexicans, and Negroes] should be segregated in special classes. . . . They cannot master abstractions, but they can often be made efficient workers" (quoted in Oakes, 1985, p. 36).

Terman found many inequalities among groups on his IQ test. Most of these differences seemed to confirm the views of the times that various groups were inherently unequal in their mental capacities. However, when girls scored higher than boys on his 1916 version of the Stanford-Binet, he revised the test to correct for this apparent flaw by selecting items to create parity among genders in the scores (Mercer, 1989). Other inequalities—between urban and rural students, rich and poor students, native English speakers and immigrants, whites and blacks—did not occasion such revisions because their validity seemed patently obvious to the test makers of the time.

Analyses of test results were major fodder for the nature-nurture controversy about the origins of intelligence, which had substantial influence on how children were viewed and treated in school. Although some studies found high correlations between measures of school quality and IQ scores by state and found Northern blacks outscoring Southern whites (Bagley, 1925; Bond, 1934; Dearborn, 1928), the idea that education might actually develop intelligence rather than be rationed by it was a view whose day had not yet come. It is an idea still rare in U.S. schools.

Tracking was also encouraged by the deskilling of the teaching force. In theory, tracking allowed for uniform teaching within classes. The effort to manage diversity by categorizing students so that they can then be processed according to standardized methods has been a continuing quest of bureaucratically run schools, and it has resulted in literally dozens of classifications in modern schools—from "gifted and talented," "advanced," and "potentially gifted" on one end to "compensatory," "remedial," "limited English proficient," "learning disabled," "emotionally disturbed," and a battery of special education classifications on the other.

But the bureaucracy's need to employ procedures that will allow it to continue to function "without regard for persons" turns out to be the ultimate source of its failure to manage the job of educating people well.

THE BUREAUCRATIC FOUNDATIONS OF CURRENT SCHOOL FAILURES

From the vantage point of a century later, we may view the scientific managers with a sense of relief that the worst of their follies seem behind us. However, the structures of today's schools are deeply rooted in this tradition. Although schools have changed some in the last one hundred years, most are still organized to impart a largely fact-based, rote-oriented curriculum through structures that do not allow long-term teacher-student relationships or in-depth study. Schools are still viewed as best administered by hierarchical decision making. Policies are still made at the top of the system and handed down to administrators who translate them into rules and procedures. Teachers follow the rules and procedures (class schedules, curricula, textbooks, rules for promotion and assignment of students), and students are processed according to them.

Moreover the roots of the system's current limitations continue to be nourished by the behaviorist learning theories, curriculum prescriptions, and specialized organizational structures planted by scientific managers a century ago.

Behaviorist Learning Theories

Most policies aimed at controlling teaching continue to presume that learning is simple and predictable. This view was reinforced during the first half of the twentieth century by education psychologists who developed theories of learning by manipulating the behavior of rats and pigeons in mazes and cages, making them learn arbitrary behaviors they would never have had reason to pursue in their natural habitats. As American Educational Research Association president Ann Brown explained in a 1994 address, by studying artificially induced animal behaviors and drawing inferences across species and contexts, behavioral psychologists came to believe that children too could learn simple skills only through decontextualized drills under conditions of heavy positive and negative reinforcement. Like the rats and pigeons who were the first subjects of behaviorist learning studies, children were asked to run mazes and stack boxes and were then tested on their abilities to perform arbitrary tasks that had no intrinsic meaning to them (Brown, 1994).

Behaviorists eschewed studies of how people thought about what they experienced, and rarely tried to understand how people learned to do complex things or functioned in the real world. Watson (1913) argued that because it is impossible to validate the introspective reports of the learner, the psychological scientist should rely on external behavior. Skinner (1961) explicitly rejected such vague concepts as intellectual development or understanding, calling "mentalist" theories "purely inferential" and thus not worth pursuing. Learning was merely the induction of behavior in specific forms upon specific occasions through conditioning and reinforcement (Skinner, 1961, p. 161). Learning had occurred when rewarded behaviors were repeated.

Skinner's great faith that complex learning could be produced by presenting stimuli and immediately reinforcing correct responses led him to resurrect the idea of a teaching machine (Skinner, 1954), originally introduced during the 1920s (Pressey, 1926). The early machines were simple devices that presented factual information in small dollops, posed simple questions or fill-in-the-blank statements for students to respond to, and gave immediate feedback about correct and incorrect responses. The principles for this "behavioral engineering of teaching procedures" (Holland, 1960) included providing small discrete pieces of information to be mastered in a predetermined sequence, short responses to be learned by rote, immediate reinforcement for correct answers, many opportunities for correct performance (achieved by setting tasks at as simple a level as possible), a gradual progression of individual discrete skills intended to cumulate in a more complex performance, and use of reinforcements (rewards and punishments) for maintaining student attention and participation.

Despite thirty years of more recent research in developmental and cognitive psychology that illustrates the limitations of behaviorist views, they continue to influence education today. Programmed instructional materials, basal readers and workbook series, competency-based curriculum programs, multiple-choice testing strategies, and many teaching manuals—including some with scripts for what teachers should say and what students will respond—demonstrate the powerful hold behaviorist theories still have over curriculum.

Behaviorism's influence has been potent in education for two major reasons. First, its assumptions of predictability, its view of children as passive raw material, and its tactic of reducing tasks to their simplest parts and sequencing them in a uniform manner fit the operating principles of a scientifically managed bureaucracy like hand to glove. Second, the weakness of the teaching profession and the undereducation of teachers have invited simplistic schemes for teaching and have prevented much organized intellectual opposition to them.

A strong countervailing voice, steeped in knowledge about children and their learning and buttressed by a conviction that teachers have something to say about education has, with a few notable exceptions, been largely absent from U.S. schools. Although many individual teachers have felt that behaviorist schemes fell short of the demands of teaching and learning, the profession has been able to do little about it. Many teachers have had to "go underground," find unusual settings in which to practice, or leave teaching when they cannot succumb to the regulation of practice. As David Kearns, former CEO of Xerox Corporation, (1988) noted: "It is a baleful commentary on the nature of our schools, but the best and the brightest teachers . . . have to be 'canny outlaws' to do their jobs well. Good teachers do not fit into tidy bureaucracies, because the job of the good teacher is not to 'process' students like so many file cards, but to educate them."

Curriculum Controls

Many states and districts today continue to prescribe highly specific standardized curricula. During the 1980s, for example, teachers in Philadelphia were required to teach a curriculum that featured paced and sequenced daily lesson plans, complete with predetermined assignments, tests, and grading schemes. These were to be used irrespective of students' needs or successes. As a union representative noted, no deviations were allowed for "differences in classes, for remediation, for enrichment, for anything." The curriculum guide reflected a poor understanding of learning, breaking down basic skills like reading and mathematics into such tiny, discrete, and isolated sub-parts that students who could learn from them would have to be the exception rather than the rule. The system required massive paper-work, and it totally divorced teaching from student learning. One teacher described the situation as a catch-22: "I get contradicting messages. 'You're not on strand,' the principal says, and I say, 'Right, that's because my kids are having trouble understanding this.' And the principal says, 'That doesn't matter, you have to stay up with the curriculum.' Then two minutes later in the conference he'll say, 'You have five kids flunking math. What are you going to do about that?' And I say, 'That's why I stay in the strand until the kids know it.' And he says, 'No, you have to move on with the curriculum'" (Andrias, Kenevsky, Streib, & Traugh, 1992, p. 14).

When teachers fought the curriculum, they were accused of insubordination until the union finally succeeded in having it "unmandated." Even when the curriculum was made optional for the system as a whole, the district still required its use in high-poverty schools. As is often true, the most counterproductive approaches were enforced most rigidly in the schools serving the most disadvantaged students who most needed responsive teaching.

The Philadelphia story is not unique. Similar initiatives were launched in districts across the nation during the 1980s, and many are still in operation. In Washington, D.C., a heavily prescriptive, rigidly enforced competency-based curriculum (CBC) was introduced in the 1980s and has continued in effect throughout the years the district's performance has plummeted. Many teachers in the district are distressed by the presumption that they should not vary their teaching to meet the needs of their students. One D.C. teacher said:

Currently we are using what's called CBC, competency-based curriculum: you are given a guideline, and each day when the students come to class you're supposed to have behavioral objectives on the board and a list of instructional aids and so on. So that means that each day, you're supposed to accomplish a, b, c, whatever is on the board that day. It just doesn't work that way. They come in and check to see: "Are your goals up? Do you meet these goals this day, during this class period?" That's really unrealistic, because it depends upon how prepared the students come to class. If they come prepared with what you gave them the day before, fine. But if they haven't, man, you have to go over the material from the day before. Then you have to structure what you want to do today, and you may be way off from the goal you've set.

It makes [teaching] rigid. I don't object to having behavioral goals. I don't object to writing them on the board. But the idea that you should be able to produce, bang, bang, exactly that way every day is just unrealistic. Kids might have a question. Do you say, "Well, no, I can't answer that question right now because I have these goals that I'm supposed to meet, and I just don't have the time?" You have to deal with what they want to know when they want to know it or you're going to lose their interest.

School systems' ongoing search for a teacher-proof curriculum continues to be grounded in mistrust of teachers' capabilities to make sound decisions about how and what students should be taught. Unfortunately, a teacher-proof curriculum is also student-proof. It ignores the fact that students come to the classroom with different preconceptions, levels of understanding, and styles of learning. Detailed curriculum prescriptions have to presume that learners are passive because the alternative presumption—that students are idea producers and problem structurers whose motivations and readiness matter—would defy the precise predetermination of learning tasks. Furthermore what can be easily scripted, sequenced, and tested in a standardized fashion tends to represent only the most trivial aspects of the underlying knowledge sought.

Mandated textbooks exacerbate the problem. As Harriet Tyson-Bernstein (1988) describes in her analysis of textbook creation, the influence of interest groups where there is state adoption of texts leads to the "mentioning" problem: that is, brief references to thousands of ideas dear to reviewers but insightful analysis of none. As a consequence, the texts are so superficially written that they barely make even literal sense, and they almost never present a range of views, an analysis of ideas, a discussion of queries and controversies in a field, or the kinds of primary source data from which conclusions can be drawn. In mathematics, texts require coverage of dozens of topics each year. Students whisk through rows of problems and march quickly through chapter after chapter, applying algorithms rather than delving into concepts. Because they do not deeply understand much of what they have covered, they must be taught the same topics year after year, and many graduate with very little ability to use mathematics beyond simple operations (McKnight et al., 1987; Educational Testing Service, 1989a).

In contrast curriculum guidance in many other countries is much more lean and focused on the understanding of major ideas and the development of thoughtful performance. A recent international evaluation of mathematics and science curriculum found that U.S. curricula and textbooks cover far more topics with less depth and more repetition, and with less attention to higher-order thinking skills, than those in most other countries (Schmidt, McKnight, & Raizen, 1996). For example, whereas a typical 5th-grade U.S. mathematics text covers more than thirty topics, the Japanese curriculum framework for the first year of lower secondary school has four simple aims in mathematics: to help students (1) deepen their understanding of integer, (2) understand the meaning of equations, (3) understand functional relationships, and (4) deepen their understanding of the properties of space figures. These aims translate into only three major topics to be taught. With respect to such areas as approximation, teachers are advised to "stress an understanding of the meaning of it, and refrain from formal calculation" (Schmidt, McKnight, & Raizen, 1996; Ministry of Education, Science, and Culture, 1983, p. 37). The emphasis is on developing understanding rather than accurately applying algorithms or speeding through problems and topics. In a typical class Japanese students might spend the entire period demonstrating and discussing their different solutions to a single problem. By looking at a problem from many perspectives, examining their thinking and correcting misconceptions, they learn to think flexibly. Rather than leaving class with a set of poorly understood rules and a large number of similar problems completed by algorithm, these students come to understand many strategies for solving problems and thus are able to apply what they have learned to new situations. After years of this kind of learning the average Japanese student outperforms the top 5 percent of U.S. students in mathematics (McKnight et al., 1987).

Regulated U.S. curricula often exacerbate the coverage problem by listing hundreds of learning objectives, with related lessons and tests to be passed before the next set of objectives can be tackled, taught, and tested. Reports must be filed on the teaching and testing of these objectives. Often cutoff scores indicating "mastery" are established and used as arbiters of promotion and placement decisions.

The use of highly prescribed curricula has been most prominent in large urban school systems and in a number of Southern states with traditions of strong centralized controls. These are often places where lagging investments in education make it difficult to recruit and retain an adequate supply of well-prepared teachers. Thus low confidence in teachers' professional capabilities joins with traditions of top-down control to produce teacher-proofing tactics as a major school improvement strategy.

The evidence suggests that highly prescriptive curricular mandates do not improve student learning, especially if they effectively control teaching. A study of Chicago's Mastery Learning program is typical. It found that the program—a series of reading and mathematics units organized around hundreds of "sequential" objectives and tied to criterion-referenced tests—produced "less satisfaction, competitiveness, difficulty, and higher thought processes in [students'] learning environment" than had existed before the curriculum was instituted (Talmage & Rasher, 1980, p. 32). Teachers complained about the paperwork but even more about the program's assumption that all students would learn in exactly the same way and that the accumulation of tiny subskills would result in the acquisition of real skills. By 1981, even parents had begun to suspect that the assumptions were incorrect, and a group filed suit against the Chicago Public Schools, demanding that the program be withdrawn as educational malpractice. Indeed, although students' scores climbed on the "mastery" tests, their scores on external reading tests dropped substantially while the program was in effect. Five years later, the board rescinded the mandate.

It can be argued that the Chicago experience is a worst-case scenario. The materials were criticized by Kenneth Goodman, a past president of the International Reading Association, as poorly written, devoid of opportunities for sustained reading or for connecting language with meaning, and lacking any clear conception of linguistic development. One might therefore conjecture that if the mandate had been based on a better-designed curriculum, it would have produced better outcomes. But the problem is more deeply rooted than that. Anne Bussis (1982) describes how highly scripted test-based early reading curricula in school districts across the United States have produced the incongruous situation in which children who have mastered the measurable skills still fail to read and proficient readers sometimes cannot demonstrate mastery of "prerequisite" reading skills. Bussis remarks: "A stranger to the world of educational research, policy, and practice might legitimately wonder how we could have allowed the current situation to develop. . . . The stranger would have a good point" (p. 239). The stranger's bemusement might be answered by reference to the need for school and teacher accountability or with assurances that such incongruous situations will vanish when the perfect curriculum is found. But the stranger might continue to wonder how the problem of accommodating student difference could ever be solved legislatively and whether the perfect mandated curriculum could ever reflect the path of learning, which "more closely resembles the flight of a butterfly than the flight of a bullet" (Jackson, 1968, p. 167).

CURRICULUM GUIDANCE AND UNDERSTANDING   Many teachers' instinctive discomfort with rationalized curriculum schemes is supported by recent research on learning. This research has found that students taught to memorize bite-sized pieces of information and to apply simple algorithms are able to parrot back information on exercises that resemble the style in which the information was delivered, but these students have little capacity to use the information in novel circumstances or to connect ideas across lessons, subjects, or domains of thought. That is, they have not truly understood. Their knowledge is inert: it cannot be called upon, transformed, or meaningfully applied to problems or situations requiring synthesis or manipulation of what has been learned (Brown, 1994; Gardner, 1991; Good & Brophy, 1986; Schoenfeld, 1988).

Even more alarming, rote learning can cause students to lose confidence in the intuitive understandings of language and number with which they entered school. When repeatedly asked to memorize arithmetic facts and unthinkingly apply rules like "carry the one" or "cross out the zero," for example, children eventually become unable to reason things through, to estimate whether their answer is plausible, or to tackle a problem not already set up for them. They may actually understand less rather than more as they proceed through the curriculum applying algorithms in situations that seem senseless because they are abstracted from real experience (Gardner, 1991; Gardner & Winner, 1982; Strauss, 1982). Cognitive psychologists have found that even well-educated high school and college students often do not truly understand concepts they have supposedly learned. Although they can describe physics principles, mathematical theorems, or social science ideas in the abstract and can parrot them back as they learned them, they cannot extrapolate them to new problems. Instead they often resort to primitive misconceptions, algorithms, or stereotypes left un-corrected by their formal education (Gardner, 1991).

Conversely, students engaged in hands-on learning opportunities, projects, discussions, and research aimed at higher-order thinking are better able to remember and apply what they have learned than are rote learners. People learn best when they make connections between what they already know and what they are learning, when they can draw on their experiences and make greater meaning of them, when they can see how ideas relate to one another, and when they can use what they are learning in concrete ways (Brown, 1994; Gardner, 1991; Shulman, 1987; Darling-Hammond, 1993). Active learning strategies typically produce comparable achievement on basic skills tests but contribute more to students' problem-solving abilities, curiosity, cre-ativity, independence, and positive feelings about school (Horwitz, 1979; Peterson, 1979; McKeachie & Kulik, 1975; Soar, 1977; Dunkin & Biddle, 1974; Glass et al., 1977; Good & Brophy, 1986; Resnick, 1987a). Teaching aimed at understanding and applying ideas—once thought appropriate only for selected high-achieving students—has proved more effective than rote teaching for students across a wide spectrum of initial achievement levels, family income levels, and cul-tural and linguistic backgrounds (Garcia, 1993; Knapp, Shields, & Turnbull, 1995; Braddock & McPartland, 1993).

However, schoolwork that can be easily legislated tends to be dis-connected from experience and passively conveyed. Fascinating ideas that could be explored through biographies, debates, papers, and models are reduced to worksheets, discrete facts, and definitions to be memorized. Words that could be learned as they are read in literature or used in a student's own writing become items in decontextualized lists. Equations that could be applied in solving a scientific or mathe-matical problem become one more piece of information for students to regurgitate without understanding meaning or purpose.

Required coverage of large quantities of content can squeeze out the tasks that develop genuine understanding. Two things tend to occur: first, the sheer amount of material precludes serious inquiry into any topic or the use of strategies that support deep learning, such as having students research problems, evaluate alternative strategies, debate concepts, and write extensively about what they have found. The curriculum marches on whether students have truly understood the fundamental concepts or not. Second, content is characterized and tested at a superficial level: short-answer and multiple-choice tests allow students to appear successful without actually comprehending or later being able to remember and apply material.

The National Assessment of Educational Progress (NAEP) has long raised these concerns. The 1981 report on NAEP's reading assessments noted that "only 5 to 10 percent of students can move beyond initial readings of a text. Most seem genuinely puzzled at requests to explain or defend their points of view." The NAEP assessors concluded that "current methods of teaching and testing reading require short responses and lower-level cognitive thinking, resulting in an emphasis on shallow and superficial opinions at the expense of reasoned and disciplined thought [thus] it is not surprising that students fail to develop more comprehensive thinking and analytic skills" (p. 5).

NAEP reports have raised similar concerns about student performance on intellectually demanding tasks in writing, mathematics, science, and social studies in all the years since 1981. National data demonstrate that during the time state policymakers began to institute test-oriented accountability measures in U.S. schools, the use of teaching methods appropriate to the learning of higher-order skills decreased. Between 1972 and 1980, public schools showed a decline in the use of student-centered discussions, extended writing, and project or laboratory work (National Center for Education Statistics, 1982a, p. 83) and an increase in such techniques as programmed instruction.

The critiques of U.S. schools that emerged during the 1980s confirmed many of the effects of curriculum regulation. Ernest Boyer's study (1983) of U.S. high schools found a predominance of passive, rote-oriented learning that consisted of "fragments of information, unexamined and unanalyzed." Boyer observed: "The pressure is on to teach the skills that can be counted and reported. As one teacher said, 'We are so hung up on reporting measured gains to the community on nationally normed tests that we ignore teaching those areas where it can't be done'" (p. 90).

John Goodlad (1984) found in his massive study of more than one thousand classrooms that for the most part the curriculum appeared to call for and make appropriate only some ways of knowing and learning and not others. He found that students listen, read short sections in textbooks, respond briefly to end-of-chapter or worksheet questions, and take short-answer and multiple-choice quizzes. At the end of this one-or two-week experience, the process is launched again with the next section of the textbook. Students who have failed have no opportunity to return to their work, analyze their mistakes, and try again until they have "learned" the material (although without true inquiry into ideas, learning of this sort is still necessarily superficial). Even those who succeed at this narrow exercise have been asked only to recall information, not to analyze its credibility, assess competing points of view, or develop their own ability to "do" science or history or mathematics or literature by creating their own products.

TEACHING AND TESTING Although Gardner (1991) is probably right when he claims that no nation has fully managed to create schools that teach for understanding, international assessments reveal that U.S. schools are even less focused on this goal than are schools in high-achieving European and Asian countries (McKnight et al., 1987; Schmidt, McKnight, & Raizen, 1996). This finding is related not only to differences in texts and teaching methods but also to the fact that other countries' examinations rely on student work samples, essays, and oral examinations developed and scored by teachers, whereas nearly all U.S. testing consists of commercially developed norm-referenced multiple-choice basic skills tests. As assessment expert George Madaus concluded in an extensive study of currently used standardized tests in mathematics and science: "The tests commonly taken by students emphasize low-level thinking and knowledge. . . . These tests do not meet current recommendations of science and math curriculum experts nationwide" (Madaus et al., 1992, p. 7). When Madaus and his research team analyzed all items from the twelve most widely used standardized mathematics and science tests and textbook exams in grades 4 and 8 and in high school, they found that only 3 percent of items on mathematics tests measure high-level conceptual knowledge (the ability to generate examples and apply concepts, for instance) and only 5 percent of items measure higher-order thinking (reasoning that goes beyond simple recall and routine algorithms). The comparable percentages for science tests were higher but still under 15 percent of all items for tests and textbook exams combined. The researchers also found that the tests' conceptions of knowledge conflicted with many teachers' views of worthwhile learning and reinforced a focus on rote teaching, especially in classrooms serving predominantly minority students where test-based instruction was most extensive.

Multiple-choice tests have also severely reduced incentives for writing in school. The 1990 NAEP writing assessment found that most 11th-grade students (61 percent) are asked to write a three–page paper less than once a month and sometimes not at all. Only 8 percent are asked to write a paper of three pages or more at least weekly (Educational Testing Service, 1990; Office of Research, U. S. Department of Education, 1993). As a result, the 1990 assessment found that only 2 percent of 11th-grade students could write in an "elaborated" fashion and fewer than 20 percent could perform adequately on a task requiring analytic writing.

In the light of two decades of research, officials of the National Assessment of Educational Progress, the National Research Council, and the National Councils of Teachers of English and Mathematics, among others, have all attributed low student performance on problem-solving and critical-thinking tasks to schools' overemphasis on multiple-choice tests of basic skills (Darling-Hammond, 1991). "Because multiple choice testing leads to multiple choice teaching, the methods that teachers have in their arsenal become reduced, and teaching work is deskilled. . . . Over time and with increased testing stakes, teaching becomes more testlike" (Smith, 1991, p. 10). That is, as teachers prepare students to pass these tests, their teaching focuses on recognition of answers in artificial formats rather than the production of ideas, solutions, designs, or analyses. Test-driven teaching necessarily neglects the development of higher-order thinking and performance skills.

Testing methods influence teaching so intensely because test scores are increasingly used as arbiters of administrative decisions in U.S. schools. During the late 1970s and 1980s, policymakers and administrators began to use standardized test scores to determine student track or program placement, promotion, and graduation; to evaluate teacher competence and school quality; and to allocate rewards and sanctions. Reviving practices of the 1920s efficiency era, school managers hoped to "drive instruction" and enforce curriculum policy with tests, adding new batteries of national commercial tests, state minimum competency tests, and district curriculum tests to those already in use. Evidence from many studies demonstrates that when high-stakes decisions are attached to scores, tests can be expected to exert a strong influence on "what is taught, how it is taught, what pupils study, how they study, and what they learn" (Madaus, Kellaghan, Rakow, & King, 1979, p. 226; see also Haney & Madaus, 1986).

Many advocates of test-based policy have argued that even if tests do not measure all that we might want them to, at least they measure the foundational skills that students must build on to conquer more complex learning. However, this turns out not to be true. "Basic skills" represented on these tests are not performance abilities; they are arbitrarily defined subskills that are supposed to add up to a performance but typically do not. And as mentioned before, studies have found that teaching children to produce correct answers on multiple-choice tests of reading and arithmetic subskills does not teach them to read or solve problems and may even work against their acquisition of performance capabilities (Bussis, 1982; Kamii, 1982).

This problem has occurred with the well-known Regents curriculum and testing program in New York State. High school teachers must use syllabi and end-of-course tests developed by the New York State Education Department. Professional associations complain that some syllabi are so badly out of synch with current professional knowledge and so focused on algorithms and memorization rather than conceptual understanding that they require teaching incompatible with new professional standards. A three-course series in mathematics, for example, does not meet curriculum standards issued by the National Council of Teachers of Mathematics. One study found that the more teachers focused on producing good scores on the state tests, the more likely they were to engage in "bad mathematics" teaching (Schoenfeld, 1988).

The state's science tests are similarly criticized by teachers as tests of rote recall of isolated facts and vocabulary terms at odds with the standards developed by national professional associations. These examples from the study guide for the 1995 New York State Regents test (Raab, 1993) in biology are typical:

The circulatory system of the earthworm is most similar in structure and function to that of a

(1) Hydra

(2) Protozoan

(3) Grasshopper

(4) Human

The tissue which conducts organic food throughout a vascular plant is composed of

(1) Cambium cells

(2) Xylem cells

(3) Phloem cells

(4) Epidermal cells

The excretory organelles of some unicellular organisms are contractile vacuoles and

(1) Cell membranes

(2) Cell walls

(3) Ribosomes

(4) Centrioles

In most classrooms, the press for memorization of thousands of discrete facts like these has completely eliminated opportunities for scientific experiments or research.

Many teachers in other fields are equally unhappy with the effects of the Regents tests on their ability to teach their disciplines well. As one history teacher explained: "In our opinion, it really isn't working. When you look at how [students] get through the Regents exam, we're doing the right thing evidently, because they are getting through it. But it's the connection with history that's missing. We're from the age where we still want to see them walk out of history class and say they learned something and enjoyed it. And I don't know if that's possible."

Across disciplines, the pace of content coverage required to prepare for the largely multiple-choice tests has largely pushed out research and writing tasks that would develop students' analytic and performance skills. Most test-based curricula contain the trappings of intellectual rigor while missing the point. They fail to realize that "hard content means not just the facts and skills of academic work, but understanding concepts and interrelationships that give meaning and utility to facts and skills" (Porter, Archbald, & Tyree, 1991, p. 11). And they miss opportunities for serious learning of immediate relevance—as was evident when many students in Global Studies courses across New York State failed to learn that the Soviet Union dissolved in the early 1990s. There was no room in the predetermined curriculum to stop and discuss one of the most important world events of the twentieth century—which, after all, would not be covered on the test.

How Policy Reinforces Bureaucratization

The logic of bureaucratic education has been extended to its furthest reach in the school policies of the last twenty years. Since the early 1970s, state accountability laws have mandated procedures like management by objectives, competency-based education, specific curriculum guidelines, and related testing programs that have produced yet more reporting requirements and correspondingly more constraints on the work of teachers and administrators. Federal regulations for compensatory education, bilingual education, and handicapped education laws have increasingly prescribed educational processes and outcomes.

The education bureaucracy tends to sort children into groups for differential, but supposedly more efficient, treatment. Categorical funding has increased this tendency, classifying and segregating children by their "problems" and creating separate programs that pull children out of their regular classes to receive special services. These programs are administered as though children can be fragmented into discrete parts that can then be treated utterly separately (Klugman, Carter, & Israel, 1979). School principal Suzanne Soo Hoo (1990) described the futility of this approach after she shadowed an elementary school student whose individual education plan (IEP) dictated that he receive services from a resource specialist, speech teacher, and Chapter 1 compensatory education teacher and take part in an adaptive physical education program:

> In one day [Kelly] was asked to respond to six different adults in six different classrooms with six different sets of classroom behavioral standards. . . . One instructional period did not appear to have any relationship or relevancy to another period. . . . Like shattered glass, Kelly's learning was broken up into mini-learnings that seldom related to each other. . . . To further exacerbate the condition, Kelly is missing vital instruction back in his homeroom. He is, in fact, absent from the core curriculum. . . . Kelly had become, in a sense, a world traveler of special programs. . . . In each room he attempted to ground himself by establishing social relationships. But no one knew him very well. Often the specialists didn't remember his name. He was a phantom figure, moving in and out of [their] rooms [pp. 208–209].

A Rand Corporation study found that a large number of students experience situations like this as they are "treated" by special programs (Kimbrough & Hill, 1981). Each program label is seen as a student deficiency requiring distinctive treatment. Aside from a small number of students who do have severe handicaps, most special education students could be taught in regular classrooms, as they are in other countries, if their teachers had the preparation to teach a wider range of learners and the time and flexibility to get to know each learner well.

Another outcome of bureaucratic approaches to problem solving has been the growth of a large and costly administrative superstructure at the federal, state, and local levels for ensuring that legal requirements are carried out. Many offices and personnel are needed to manage the resulting inspections and auditing, monitoring, and reporting, and these administrative demands deflect time and dollars from sorely needed services to procedures and reporting structures. As one teacher in a city school district explained of the required IEP process for special education placements:

> There is an awful lot of time and energy wasted in our particular school. We had social workers and psychologists work all year long helping teachers on IEPs and [these professionals] didn't do any of their work at all, which is absolutely idiotic because it says in the IEPs that you are supposed to get services from the social worker and the psychologist. . . . I think the services provided have no relation, really, to the statements on the IEPs. It is very nice for formalized, bureaucratic purposes . . . but it doesn't really say anything about the quality of that service or its actual usefulness.

The goals of special programs are laudatory, but bureaucratic management has undermined program usefulness. Some experts estimate that as much as 55 percent of all the funding for special education now goes for identification, testing, administration, and other nonteaching services rather than for instruction (Rothstein & Miles, 1995). In many schools the remaining funds have supported segregated, underresourced classrooms, often staffed by untrained teachers or classroom aides and managed by IEP-defined procedures rather than by skilled diagnostic teaching. In poor rural and urban classrooms special education programs have too often stigmatized the students assigned to them without educating them more effectively.

Policy efforts to shape schooling often proceed on the presumption that legislating something is sufficient to ensure that it occurs (Horowitz, 1977). Often regulators assume that compliance is a matter of enforcement alone and does not involve problem solving and capacity building. For example, when the Office for Civil Rights sought to enforce the Supreme Court's bilingual education decree in *Lau* v. *Nichols*, "[lawyers] assumed the technology was in place when it was not. Very few districts knew how to handle the vast diversity of children coming from many different linguistic backgrounds. There were not enough trained teachers and curricular materials. For a long while, bilingual programs suffered from the fact that totally insufficient numbers of trained professionals had to work in a highly bureaucratized setting. Even today, shortages still exist. What was needed was technical assistance and professional experimentation. What took place instead was bureaucratic compliance paperwork" (Benveniste, 1987, p. 13).

Legislators also rarely consider that policies may have unintended consequences. For example, until 1994, federal compensatory education legislation required the use of norm-referenced tests for evaluating program effectiveness. As discussed earlier, these tests are now thought to impede student learning by focusing on low-level drill rather than on actual reading, writing, and mathematical competence (Commission on Chapter 1, 1992; Rotberg & Harvey, 1994).

A related policy adopted in the name of accountability is to hold back students who fail to achieve particular test scores. Substantial research has demonstrated that such grade retention ultimately results in lower achievement and higher dropout rates among the students held back (Holmes & Matthews, 1984; Shephard & Smith, 1986; Wehlage, Rutter, Smith, Lesko, & Fernandez, 1989). Although policymakers' decisions are sometimes influenced by this kind of professional knowledge—for example, New York City dropped its Promotional Gates program in the early 1990s and North Carolina repealed a law requiring minimum test scores for promotion from kindergarten—most legislators and school boards are unaware of research relating to the policies they enact or are unconvinced that it should guide their actions. In 1994, more than 2 million out of 40 million U.S. students were held back in grade, reducing both their overall learning progress and their long-run probabilities of graduating. And use of this policy is on the increase again with the enactment of standards-based reforms.

Although many schools do not know how to teach students to reach the new standards, they do know how to hold them back.

First-order solutions to problems in education are often hard for lay policymakers to resist. I am reminded of one state legislator who drafted a bill requiring schools to ensure that all of their students scored "at or above the norm" on the state's standardized tests. That such tests are designed so that only 50 percent of test takers can possibly score at or above the norm seemed irrelevant. The law would make it so. Indeed one unintended consequence of efforts to legislate learning was the "Lake Wobegon" result of standardized testing policies during the 1980s—the finding that compared to past performance, most students were scoring "above average" in nearly all states and districts as teachers taught to the tests and low-achieving students were increasingly kept out of the testing pool (Koretz, 1988).

The Accountability Dilemmas of Excessive Bureaucracy

When legislators prescribe methods that cannot achieve the desired ends, their policies become "hyperrational" (Wise, 1979). Hyperrational policies not only cause organizations to treat clients inflexibly rather than in accordance with their needs, they also undermine the development of professional standards that could better guide practice, and they impair organizational problem solving. When rules are the basis for decisions, neither individuals nor organizations are free to ask whether other strategies might not be more effective in particular circumstances. The symptoms of excessive bureaucratization include

- Lack of school-level flexibility for allocating resources—dollars, people, and time—to meet students' needs
- Lack of classroom-level flexibility for determining appropriate teaching content, methods, and materials
- Overspecialization that fragments learning and teacher-student relationships
- Increased paperwork required to communicate directives and to monitor school activities as external decisions are enforced by reporting systems

These symptoms are reported in many studies of teaching over the last decade or more (see, for example, Wolcott, 1977; Sizer, 1984; McNeil, 1986). Ironically, the major consequence of bureaucratic efforts to improve schools has been a set of accountability practices that often impede student learning. Students learn in different ways and at different rates under different circumstances, and effective teaching strategies must be flexible and adaptive to meet these needs. But because the bureaucratic model holds teachers accountable for implementing standard operating procedures (for example, covering a tightly constrained curriculum in a specific manner), teachers' knowledge about learning is actually a liability when it conflicts with these procedures (Darling-Hammond, Wise, & Pease, 1983).

Increasingly prescriptive policies created through the political process in the name of public accountability are reducing even further the schools' responsiveness to the needs of students and the desires of parents. Whether they take the form of the ridiculously cumbersome process of getting a label for a special needs child and sending him for services not useful for his learning, or the frustrating experience of marching through a mandated curriculum that is decontextualized, poorly conceived, unnecessary for some and unhelpful for others, procedures intended to create accountability increasingly create anger, frustration, and despair among parents and students. These experiences stoke the current malaise with public education and many people's desire to break loose from the system through vouchers, charters, and other means. Moreover, when practitioners must respond to complaints by reference to rules or regulations that set out how to "do" school, they have no means of solving these problems.

In the cause of uniform treatment and in the absence of choice among schooling alternatives, large numbers of students fall through the cracks when routines prevent schools from meeting their needs. Those who can afford to leave heavily regulated impersonal public schools for private schools often do. Studies show that parents originally committed to public education switch their children to private school primarily when they come to believe that their children's individual needs cannot be adequately met in the schools they attend (Darling-Hammond & Kirby, 1985). Those who cannot leave such settings are frequently alienated and ill served.

Michael Lipsky (1980) explains that a "dual accountability dilemma" operates in all "street-level bureaucracies" in which workers must make decisions responsive to the individual needs of clients while also following highly prescriptive agency procedures. He describes how efforts to exert management controls ultimately subvert the quality of services by reducing workers' accountability to clients and to professional standards of conduct. Thus, although instructional policies may be well intentioned and sometimes even well informed, the problem is that policies by their nature must be universal, operated through a bureaucratic chain of command, and implemented uniformly to produce easily measurable results. Effective teaching, however, requires flexibility, a wide repertoire of strategies, and use of judgment in complex, nonroutine situations where multiple goals are being pursued. Teachers are put in the position of having to follow restrictive policies on the one hand and trying to meet the variable needs of their students on the other. As one teacher explains, "The [district's] emphasis seems to be on following the objectives and goals, and oftentimes they forget about the children who are involved in the learning process."

Furthermore, policies that legislate practice are necessarily backward looking: they must rely on the technologies and knowledge available when they are enacted. Slavish adherence to their requirements prevents growth of knowledge and improvement of practice. Policies created by lay bodies unaware of the multiple contingencies that should influence decision making and ignorant of the possibilities for improvement in practice are bound to be inadequate and even dangerous. If medical practice were regulated by nonprofessionals through policy mandate, doctors would still be using leeches. They would have to wait for legislators to inform themselves about advances in medical knowledge and then write the new knowledge into law. Then doctors would have to apply these treatments (by now out of date) without taking each patient's unique needs into account and without adjusting practice as necessary to ensure success. This is precisely the position teachers hold in highly regulated states and districts across the United States. The dual accountability dilemma is that standardized practice is malpractice when viewed from a perspective of professional accountability. Professional teachers should be allowed to focus on doing the right things rather than doing things right.

It has taken us nearly a century to discover that, as a form of organization, bureaucracy lacks the tools to manage complex work, handle the unpredictable, or meet distinctive client needs. By its very nature, bureaucratic management is incapable of providing appropriate education for students who do not fit the mold upon which prescriptions for practice are based. As inputs, processes, and measures of outcomes are increasingly standardized, the cracks through which students can fall grow larger rather than smaller because the likelihood that each accumulated prescription is suitable for a given child grows smaller with each successive limitation upon teachers' ability to adapt instruction to students' needs. Bureaucratic solutions to problems of practice will always fail because effective teaching is not routine, students are not passive, and questions of practice are not simple, predictable, or standardized. Consequently, instructional decisions cannot be formulated on high then packaged and handed down to teachers. Nor can instructional problems be solved by inspectors who make occasional forays into the classroom to monitor performance and dispense advice without intimate knowledge of the classroom context, the subject matter being taught, the goals of instruction, and the development of individual children.

Finally, genuine accountability is undermined in bureaucracies, where authority for decisions and responsibility for practice are widely separated, usually by many layers of hierarchy. Boards and top-level administrators make decisions, and teachers, principals, and students carry them out. When the desired outcomes are not realized, policymakers blame the schoolpeople responsible for implementation; practitioners blame their inability to devise or pursue better solutions on the constraints of policy. But no one can be fully accountable for the results of practice when authority and responsibility are dispersed. Faceless regulations become the scapegoats for school failure because no person in the system takes responsibility for the rules' effects on children.

Top-down decision making retards change. Dysfunctional side effects cannot be quickly remedied while edicts hang on, immune from the realities of school life and protected by the forces of inertia and lobbies both inside and outside the bureaucracy. Yet the amount of effort and influence required to change a school system policy is so great that most teachers, principals, and parents find it impossible to deflect enough energies from their primary jobs to the arduous and often unrewarding task of moving the behemoth. Over time cynicism overwhelms problem solving, and the pressures for conformity become so strong that most principals and teachers are afraid to test the limits of the system, as federal and state policymakers recently found when they sought to offer waivers and "flexibility" from some existing mandates, and few schools applied. The end result is that the failings of the system become accepted.

Sarah Lawrence Lightfoot (1983) has observed that policy development has been hindered by "anachronistic and one-dimensional" images of teaching (p. 241). She argues that more helpful policies will focus on "images that come closest to conveying the complexities, uncertainties, and processes of teachers' lives in 'real' settings" (p. 243) and the multifaceted influences on student learning. Teachers intuitively understand this about policies although they have frequently had difficulty defending their views of the conditions needed for good teaching against the onslaught of "scientific" prescriptions.

Teachers sometimes use a verbal shorthand when they evaluate the schemes of reformers, asking whether the proponents of this, that, or another initiative "get it," that is, whether they understand the important things about teaching and learning. As the discussion in the following chapters makes clear, what policies need to "get" about teaching and learning are the things that bureaucracy devalues: the importance of connections among ideas, experiences, and people; the importance of time for deep learning; and the importance of relationships among teachers and students—the opportunities for them to create a learning community.

Notes

1. We conducted in-depth interviews with forty-six teachers in three districts in three different states to learn the effects of policies on teachers' practice. The teachers were randomly selected from lists of all teachers in each district, supplied by the teachers' associations. All of those contacted agreed to be interviewed. The sample was about evenly split between elementary (47 percent) and secondary (53 percent) teachers, with all subject areas represented. The group was representative of U.S. teachers in the early 1980s, with an average age of forty-one and fourteen years of experience. Nearly half (47 percent) held a master's degree. (Much of this research is reported here for the first time; see also Darling-Hammond & Wise, 1985).

2. Unless otherwise stated, quotations from teachers in this chapter come from the study I conducted with Arthur Wise.

## CHAPTER THREE

What Matters for Teaching

Most of all I am trying to get the children to really enjoy being in school—to enjoy learning and thinking and investigating on their own and growing to become really decent people. However, the school system probably disagrees and thinks that I should be imparting ten thousand little objectives. I do those anyway, but whether the kids remember them is questionable.

—An Elementary School Teacher

Studies of teaching (Jackson, 1968; Lortie, 1975; Clandinin, 1986) describe it as complex work characterized by simultaneity, multidimensionality, and unpredictability. In classrooms competing goals and multiple tasks are negotiated at a breakneck pace, trade-offs are continually made, unanticipated obstacles and opportunities arise. Each hour of every day teachers must juggle the need to create a secure supportive environment for learning with the press for academic achievement, the need to attend to individual students and the demands of the group, and the challenges of pursuing multiple strands of work so that students at varying places in their learning move ahead and none are left behind.

These realities contravene the bureaucratic view of teaching as straightforward work aimed at a limited number of preset and simple goals and objectives, organized into a set sequence of activities and lessons used in more or less the same fashion for all students within and across classrooms, and "delivered" to students "without regard for persons."

These different concepts of teaching have important implications for policies and their effects. Policies at odds with the realities of teaching and learning will simply not be successful. Although policymakers may think that educators implement their directives, what typically happens is much more a process of redefinition or sometimes subversion. Teachers' responses to policies depend on the degree to which the policies permit flexibility or impose constraints on their ability to meet what they perceive to be the needs of their students. As Lee Shulman (1983) observes, "Why is the juxtaposition of 'teaching' and 'policy' the statement of a problem? We are wont to think of teaching as a highly clinical, artful, individual act. Since instruction is interactive, with teachers' actions predicated on pupil responses or difficulties, it appears ludicrous in principle to issue directives regarding how teachers are to perform" (p. 488).

We must understand how teachers respond to different approaches to regulating schools if we are to develop sound education policies as well as improve teacher education and school management. Richard Elmore (1979–1980) suggests that policy studies should begin with a focus on where policy is applied rather than on policymakers' intentions. Once policy effects are understood, more productive policy can be developed through a process of "backward mapping." Questions of how to balance top-down curriculum controls and other policy guidance with school and classroom initiatives have recurred in every era of reform. These issues are about to become prominent once again as the new wave of standards-based reform washes over the education landscape.

How do teachers respond to different kinds of policy initiatives? What do they say helps and what hinders their teaching? In this chapter I draw more extensively upon the study Arthur Wise and I conducted of the effects of policies on teaching to answer these questions. The teachers we interviewed were randomly selected from two large suburban districts long known for "excellent" schools and one large urban district struggling with a host of financial and educational disadvantages.

The study was conducted during the early 1980s, when state efforts to legislate educational practice were on the rise. All three districts had begun to implement state and locally mandated accountability mechanisms focusing on more tightly prescribed curriculum and more frequent student testing. One district's Program of Studies (POS) outlined what teachers should teach in each subject. In some grades and subjects the POS allowed substantial teacher flexibility; in others it did not. In the second district several sequenced and staged curriculum packages had been developed, most prominently at the elementary level and most thoroughly in mathematics. Over the course of elementary and middle school, students had to work through several hundred specific skills in a preset order and "test out" on each of them before proceeding to the next. The third district's competency-based curriculum (CBC) featured notebooks full of sequenced topics, lesson plans, unit plans, and tests teachers were to use in each subject area.

From the teachers, we learned firsthand about the ways in which policies sometimes supported but more often impeded practice. We also learned about what matters to teachers: the importance of the *flexibility* to teach adaptively, the importance of *relationships* with students for knowing them well and motivating them, and the critical need to *focus on learning* rather than on the implementation of procedures. These are topics I examine in this chapter. Many other studies have affirmed the importance of these conditions for teaching (see, for example, Johnson, 1990; McNeil, 1986; Lee & Smith, 1994; Newmann & Wehlage, 1995). Appreciating their importance may eventually help policymakers develop strategies that support and direct but do not constrain the process of teaching and learning.

THE NEED FOR FLEXIBILITY

Despite a century of efforts to rationalize teaching, teachers continue to talk about their work as demanding and unpredictable rather than straightforward and routine. One high school music teacher put it this way: "You never know what you are going to walk into when you go into a classroom. I suppose that is what makes the job exciting, because you are doing something that is basically a little dangerous. . . . You never know what the combination of all those personalities is going to produce."[1]

Most of the teachers we interviewed (65 percent) characterized teaching more as an art than a science, suggesting that although there are important principles of good teaching, creativity and judgment are always needed.

It takes a lot of skill to deliver subject content and skills at the same time that you are dealing with different individuals and different personalities. It is a real art to be able to do both those things at once. . . . Unlike a lawyer dealing with a client or a doctor dealing with a patient, we always do our work in sets of thirty and thirty-five. You have to deal with multiple problems; if you can't do five things at once, you'd better not stay in the classroom, because you have to deal with a lot of variables all at the same time.

Consistently, studies have found that flexibility, adaptability, and creativity are among the most important determinants of teachers' effectiveness (Schalock, 1979; Darling-Hammond, Wise, & Pease, 1983). Yet policies that seek to teacher-proof instruction undermine these qualities. The multidimensionality of teaching and the vast array of differences among students are realities that prescriptions for practice cannot account for. Over and over again teachers stress that if they cannot connect with students' interests, needs, experiences, and motives, the effective teaching that leads to student engagement and learning cannot occur: "I have to consider the students' interests [and] stay in tune with what the students are thinking and doing. I could bring something into the classroom, and they wouldn't know what in the world I am talking about. If what I do does not coincide with their background, then I have lost the whole class."

Planning for Teaching

Research has shown that teachers who plan with regard to students' abilities and needs and who are flexible while teaching are more effective, especially at stimulating higher-order thinking, than teachers who engage in extensive preplanning that is tightly focused on behavioral objectives and coverage of facts. Teachers who set out to implement detailed plans based on behavioral objectives are less likely to be sensitive to students' ideas and actions (Zahorick, 1970) or to adjust their teaching strategies in response to student cues (Peterson & Clark, 1978). This decreases the amount of higher-level reasoning and incidental learning that occurs during a lesson (Duchastel & Merrill, 1977; Yelon & Schmidt, 1973; Melton, 1978). In short, teachers who most faithfully follow rationalistic curriculum schemes are least likely to teach for understanding.

Because students' prior experiences, motivations, and interests are crucial to learning, most teachers' accounts of planning focus on how they will connect their goals with students' needs rather than on how they will "deliver instruction" according to a rational planning model. When we asked teachers what they considered first when planning their work, 67 percent mentioned students first, and almost all the others mentioned students in the next breath, right behind curriculum goals. They also described how important it is to find the connections between students and subject matter:

> I think about the children I'm planning for. I think about what it is that I want them to get from the subject. I pull together whatever is needed under that subject and think in terms of the group. . . . Then I make plans to fit the child that I'm planning for.

> My main concern is what the group is like that I have that year. I don't think that I have ever taught a lesson twice in the same way in eleven years, because there is never the same group.

Even though teachers in the most highly prescriptive district made a bow to the mandated curriculum, most focused immediately on how they could vary it to meet their students' needs. One creative teacher turned the issue on its head, using the mammoth curriculum guide to provide choices for her students:

> We have a set of guides that would just choke a horse. For instance, in one subarea the material in the guide fills eight notebooks that are each four inches thick. . . . I say to the students, "These are the things that are identified in here. Now what are you particularly interested in?" And we make choices. Each of them picks out something they particularly like and they delve into that and report on it to the class.

Many teachers in our study described their planning as starting with students and looping back to them as the teachers wended their way through many other concerns:

> First and foremost I think about what will interest these students and what they are familiar with that I can compare this new idea to; I start off with things they are familiar with and lead into the thing that is

new to them. I also think about what their abilities are and what types of materials are available, then which of them the students would be most capable of handling. I try to get some variety into a lesson, perhaps changing activities two or three times during the course of the lesson to help connect with their interests.

First I think about where my kids are: what they already know and what kinds of abilities they have. What would be an interesting way to try and present the material to the children? How does this particular group learn best? Do they get a lot from teacher verbalization or do they get more from a lot of questions and a lot of student interaction? Do they get a lot more from hands-on activities? Should there be less talking and more doing? It is so different with every group, and individual students can vary from activity to activity. They may work well in one way in a science activity but need a different kind of exposure in a spelling activity. So you have to get to really know your kids and how they learn.

Connecting to Students

Teachers' insistence on attending to students' experiences, interests, and prior knowledge were once thought to result from tenderheartedness and a disregard for scientific methods. Now, however, these considerations are supported by cognitive research demonstrating that learning is a process of making meaning out of new or unfamiliar events in light of familiar ideas or experiences. Learners construct knowledge as they build cognitive maps for organizing and interpreting new information. Effective teachers help students make such maps by drawing connections among different concepts and between new ideas and learners' prior experiences (Calfee, 1981; Curtis & Glaser, 1981; Good & Brophy, 1986; Resnick, 1987a).

Nonetheless many states' teacher evaluation systems still treat teaching as the delivery of information without regard to students' thinking or their prior experiences (Darling-Hammond with Sclan, 1992). In the Florida Performance Measurement System (FPMS), for example, a scheme adopted in about a dozen states during the 1980s, teachers are downgraded if they ask any questions that "call for personal opinion or that are answered from personal experience." The coding manual states that "these questions may sometimes serve useful or even necessary purposes; however, they should be tallied here [in the 'ineffective' column] since they do not move the class work along academically" (Florida Department of Education, 1989, p. 5b).

Like many other teacher evaluation instruments, the FPMS enforces a set of uniform teaching behaviors, often trivial but easy to measure (such as "keeps a brisk pace of instruction," "manages routines," and "writes behavioral objectives"), with no regard to subject matter, curriculum, or student learning. Such evaluations often reward poor teaching and undermine good teaching. Florida's 1986 Teacher of the Year (also a runner-up in NASA's Teacher in Space program) found he could not pass review for a merit pay award under this system because his principal could not find enough of the required teaching behaviors to check off during the laboratory lesson he observed. Furthermore, the evaluation form required that the teacher be marked down for answering a question with a question, a practice forbidden by the FPMS though popular with Socrates and some other good teachers. The approach to teaching favored by the FPMS and other such instruments is distinctly ill suited to developing students' critical-thinking abilities and out of synch with most recent research on student cognition.

Such "accountability" schemes reinforce ineffective practice because they fundamentally misunderstand the experiential nature of learning and the reciprocal nature of teaching. Children need to study ideas in ways that connect to their motivations and prior knowledge, and teachers need to respond to the challenges and questions children raise (Brown, 1994). Like success in musical composition, chess playing, architectural design, and other creative fields, success in teaching involves an iterative process: teachers evaluate information about students and subjects, anticipate solutions, and then revise plans based on what actually happens in the classroom (Yinger, 1978).

Many of the teachers we interviewed explained how they not only needed to take account of students' prior knowledge and interests in planning how to approach a lesson but how they also needed to observe students' thinking during class and then adjust their plans in motion: "You can make lesson plans all you want," commented one teacher, "but if for some reason you start something and it is not working, you have to change it right on the spot. You have to adjust to the kids." Another teacher described why she does not follow the highly detailed lesson plans her district requires:

How are you going to predict what kids are going to say or what they are going to understand or ask you? It is just so ridiculous. You need to know what you are going to present and then go from there. A lot of days you think you are going to present something and the kids are not ready for it, so you chuck it. Or they may really get into something and take extra time so something else has got to go.

Feeling the Effects of Curriculum Prescriptions

Teachers reported that curriculum prescriptions influenced their work in different ways, depending on how specific the guidance, how rigidly enforced, and how high the stakes for students. Requirements were least troubling when they were general enough to allow teacher responsiveness or when they were not strictly enforced by administrators. Teachers who were offered broad-gauge direction through a curriculum guide, with plenty of room to develop the ideas to fit their students, were comfortable with district guidance. This situation occurred most often in the most affluent district and in the subject areas least affected by standardized testing: that is, social studies, science, and the arts rather than reading and mathematics. Where curriculum guidance was broad and general, teachers felt there was a benefit to having some common direction as long as it was expressed in a way that allowed for creativity and flexibility in the classroom.

Where curriculum was highly prescribed, most teachers were uncomfortable, although they dealt with their discomforts differently. Some teachers treated the district requirements as a paperwork game. As one teacher put it, "A lot of the goals of the school district can be taken care of by putting some words on paper and then going ahead and doing things the way you want to." Another concurred: "I find writing [the goals] out to be busy work, but that's what they want, and if that keeps them happy, they can have it."

A very few teachers (under 10 percent of our sample) liked having a high degree of guidance so that they would have less independent thinking and planning. One teacher reflected the views of Franklin Bobbitt quoted in Chapter Two when she explained her pleasure with the curriculum guide this way: "[Curriculum] is planned by the system. We are required to do certain things and teach certain skills, and that makes it easy because we know what is required of us." Throughout the interview, this teacher's concerns for curriculum were limited to coverage; they never extended to student learning. However, most teachers felt their effectiveness would be impaired if curricular guidance told them exactly what they were required to do each day for every lesson or what materials they could use. Teachers limited to specific texts or working under intrusive programs like the urban district's competency-based curriculum felt that the curricular mandates reduced their ability to adapt their teaching to students. Most rejected these constraints in one way or another:

> I went into one school for an interview, and they set down a rigid pattern so that every teacher teaching a certain subject would cover a certain page a certain day and another page another day. If somebody were that rigid with me, I would say no. Anybody who's had any experience of teaching knows that you may cover a certain topic one day and find you need to follow it up the next day, whereas other topics that you think will call for five days may call for three. You're not always sure with each individual class, and if I were kept to that rigid constraint, I wouldn't be teaching, and then I'd get out.

> Before when you were teaching the children, if the children had certain needs and you couldn't meet them with specific materials that were county approved, like the basal reader or whatever, you could branch off and use other materials. But in the school I just transferred out of, the principal said you could not use anything but this one reading series. I felt like I couldn't meet the needs of the children. . . . [This school district] used to preach meeting the individual needs of the children, which I believe in very much, but now it seems they're so concerned with "back to basics," they hinder good teaching at times.

> Well, right now we are under a program called CBC, and their concern is that all teachers are following those guidelines. [It's] difficult because it does interfere with your teaching. I admit I do not always abide by that. When I see that it doesn't fit with the needs of a particular class, I close my eyes to it.

A few of the teachers we interviewed felt so strongly about their goals for teaching and learning and their need to focus on children that they overtly "bucked the system."

> There is no way I will teach to the POS. To me they are asking you to teach some ridiculous things, things that are not necessary at the

particular grade level, such as driver's license forms and job applications in the 7th grade. [It's silly] to have to stop your schedule to teach to those things.

There was a time when area supervisors were supposed to be able to walk into the room and see these goals up and around the room. I am not about to string [behavioral objectives] up around the wall. No one has questioned me on it yet, and if they do, I'll tell them to write them and put them up. I have more important things to do.

I told them I wasn't going to follow their precise goals and techniques, because I had set my own goals, keeping the children in mind, and then I made sense to them of what I was doing.

Most teachers operating under tightly mapped systems saw themselves as creative saboteurs, always looking for ways to insert more interesting projects, more creative work, and more connections to students' own experiences as they traveled the highly constrained routes prescribed by the curriculum guide. They described their detours with the sort of secretive relish that accompanies the thrill of liberties taken behind closed doors:

We have a book that tells you in this year you're supposed to teach this, this, this, and this. So it's pretty much laid out for you, but I allow the students the advantage of branching off if they want. I allow them to cut out news articles that we talk about occasionally. I allow them to branch off with questions they might have.

A lot is prescribed by the school system. There isn't a lot of freedom to vary from these guidelines, but I've oftentimes varied from them and just decided to accept the responsibility if someone should question me.

Such subversion of a poorly designed curriculum raises the level of teaching somewhat—but not enough. Too often the curriculum is so overwhelming and the press of content coverage so severe that teachers feel unable to pursue ideas that derive from students' interests or to deal with anything in depth. Their focus is deflected from educating students to covering the curriculum: "Everything is prescribed by the school system. I am not supposed to teach anything that is not prescribed. . . . I have never figured out yet how they sit in the central office and just keep handing us these prescribed units. I don't know where you are supposed to get the time to teach them because you are supposed to cover everything else, plus."

Teachers in such highly constrained settings feared for students' welfare and for their own future as professionals. They felt their effectiveness was impaired when they were required to use methods that proved inappropriate for some students, to present material that was beyond the grasp of some and below the grasp of others, to sacrifice students' internal motivations and interests in the cause of "covering the curriculum," and to forego the *teachable moment,* when students were ready and eager to learn, because it happened to fall outside of the prescribed sequence of activities. These teachers also objected to the ways in which highly prescriptive curricula inevitably trivialized instructional goals and reduced learning to memorizing lower-order skill bites that failed to stimulate and challenge students' aptitudes for thinking and doing. As one teacher put it:

> I have no objection to some enunciation of goals or objectives, but to assume that people are going to learn if all of us adopt these particular techniques seems to me to be absolute idiocy. . . . If students were encouraged to think on their own, to analyze a situation, and to develop the alternatives, one would be much better off than trying to say, "In this situation one does this." For technical kinds of things, one can always look it up somewhere. The point is, how does one express oneself, how does one write, for example, as opposed to knowing exactly how a gerund is used.

Another described how her efforts to make meaning for students were made more difficult by curriculum prescriptions: "The schedule demands x number of minutes for this and that, so you can't always teach an integrated core. I like a core curriculum where you can really integrate everything. I think it has more meaning to kids. I have only been able to do that one year. I had to have special permission, and that was the best year I ever had."

These teachers' accounts describe the unintended consequences of overly specific curriculum prescriptions: compartmentalization and dumbing down of the curriculum to those kinds of learning most easily atomized, neglect of students' needs and interests, and lack of time for more intellectually challenging modes of instruction. When teachers need special permission to teach as reformers now urge, the pursuit of curriculum reform will obviously require a great deal more than exhortation or bottom-up change.

THE IMPORTANCE OF RELATIONSHIPS

Many special features of teaching work make relationships important. Children and teachers do not choose one another; furthermore, teachers cannot succeed unless students are willing to put forth effort to learn and unless the entire group is working productively. David Cohen (1996) notes that teachers' dependence upon students for the production of learning makes teaching intrinsically risky. These risks are increased when teachers aim for more ambitious learning rather than settling for rote work, which is more easily controlled. To manage these risks, teachers need both high levels of skill and school structures that allow the extended time and close sustained relationships with students that can leverage motivation and commitment (Darling-Hammond, 1996).

As Lortie (1975, p. 137) observed, extracting work from immature, conscripted workers requires that teachers "forge bonds which will not only ensure compliance but . . . generate effort and interest in learning jobs." So it is not surprising that teachers feel their first order of business must be the development of interpersonal ties and a shared sense of purpose within the group. Researchers have often noted that teachers, especially in the elementary grades, devote substantial energy to creating a stable community within the classroom (Cusick, 1979; Jackson, 1968; Janesick, 1977; Lortie, 1975), one governed by group goals and by the strength of relationships.

I'm trying to get them to learn certain things that I want them to learn, but in doing so I realize that if I cannot get a good relationship with these students, so that we can have trust between one another and they can feel comfortable in the classroom asking questions, then I'm not going to teach them anything.

My very first objective is to create a good relationship in the classroom, because I very firmly believe that you can't do anything with the students until they believe in you, until you have some kind of a feeling for who you are working with and what their abilities and feelings are. Another goal that I like to achieve is the ability to think. They may not remember five years from now how many members there are in the

House of Representatives or some other facts that I will teach them about government, but hopefully they will have developed some skills for how to think, how to know what is fact and what is opinion, how to sort it out in their minds, how to be presented with some facts and come to a conclusion.

Most of the teachers we interviewed resisted extensive curriculum prescription because they understood that the most powerful learning occurs when students are ready and when something connects to their own experience and needs. Teachers saw the creation of those connections as the primary job of the teacher. Nearly all (84 percent) said the most important attributes of good teachers include an ability to relate to and motivate students and to adapt teaching to student needs. Knowing students well was viewed as critical:

I think with children one of the things you have to do first is to get to know them. Even with those you find a little bit hard to like at first, you have to find something that you really appreciate about that child so that you can really teach them, because if you don't you're not going to get anyplace.

Individual kids' needs, awarenesses, and differences are part of understanding the whole teaching process. Whether you have a kid sitting in the front row because he has a visual problem and you have to have an auditory contact, a kid back there who doesn't speak English, a kid who has parents who are breaking up, a kid over here who has just been in a fight with somebody outside the classroom, or a kid who has physical handicaps, it all depends on the situation. . . . There are all types of problems and, of course, the more you know, it puts you in a better situation.

Asked to remember a teacher who made a difference to them, the teachers in our study recalled teachers who knew and reached out to them and made learning intellectually engaging. Many recalled teachers who made a difference in their lives by helping them to feel worthwhile. They valued the fact that these teachers taught *with* regard to persons:

One teacher conned me by making me take a special geometry test. She said, "You know, you are not doing well in this class, and I may put you in a special section." She made me take a special test, and for some reason I got a hundred on that test, and I felt, "Hey, I can do this!" It wasn't until later that I realized that the test was designed so that I could pass. Teachers like that, you see, conned me into learning. They felt a responsibility for me. They thought I had some potential. They looked for it. [They] are the ones I appreciated the most.

My 6th-grade teacher had the ability to take what were considered to be the worst children in the building and just turn them out—make them feel good. They turned out to be contributors to society rather than the problems that everybody predicted that they would turn out to be. I remember the way she would pull them aside and talk to them in a soft tone. She would give them opportunities to participate in things. She never abused them; never made fun of them. She tried to make them see their worth.

Others recalled teachers who used active teaching strategies that caused students to inquire, discover, and apply knowledge: an English teacher who asked students to write essays in the style of the authors they studied, a math teacher who asked for real-world applications of concepts, a social studies teacher who brought history alive through drama and debate. However, these emphases on engagement in active learning and connection to students are the features of teaching least valued by policies that prescribe curriculum divorced from students' interests and that organize students' and teachers' time together in ways that attenuate personal connections.

In order to create strong relationships and a functional working group, teachers must minimize outside interruptions and distractions while maximizing control over student involvement and securing enough time with students to have an effect. Yet rational management models devalue these concerns when they pass students off from one teacher to the next, fragment instruction with pullout programs that interrupt class time, and require curricula that fail to build connections among ideas and between ideas and students. Elementary teachers, especially, struggled consciously with these issues: "Teachers feel like the day is so broken up because of the children going out for so many different things. If they go out for speech or a special program like Title I and if they go out for band or anything else, the day is terribly broken up. It's hard to teach the group."

Teachers also strongly emphasized the importance of creating an insular community with shared goals and interests:

> Have you ever heard that concept "close the door and teach?" This is something that teachers always talk about with a faraway look in their eyes. If you are able to do that then there aren't very many things that will affect you negatively. Once you are not able to do it, it all goes downhill in a hurry. You have got to cloister yourself in there with the students and do that thing that you do.

A FOCUS ON LEARNING RATHER THAN PROCEDURES

Most teachers in our study felt that their views of good teaching were at odds with those of their school districts. The large majority (79 percent) described concerns for children and for learning as central to good teaching, but only 11 percent felt their school districts shared this view. Most (75 percent) felt that their school districts, reflecting the behaviorist learning theories described in Chapter Two, were more concerned with implementing specific teaching techniques tied to precise objectives and with diagnosing student deficiencies. Teachers saw themselves as differing from their school districts in the extent to which they viewed students as active participants or passive recipients in the learning process, the extent to which they saw student concerns as central or peripheral to the choice of learning goals and activities, and the extent to which they saw teaching as focused on student development or the identification of deficiencies.

Covering the Curriculum

Teachers' sense of conflict was heightened where they were subject to curriculum packages with hundreds of behavioral objectives to be covered in sequence at each grade level. In some of these curricula each discrete skill or learning segment had to be tested before going on to the next, and then the scores had to be recorded along with lists of skills taught and the date they were taught. These tests were added to state- and districtwide annual testing (which included reading and mathematics test batteries at almost every grade level, along with periodic tests in other subjects and various aptitude tests for placements in programs and tracks). One common complaint was the amount of time deflected from teaching to the administration of procedures and tests viewed as more useful to administrators than to teachers and students.

> So much of the teacher's time is spent in things other than teaching: record keeping, the rigid Program of Studies, the pre-and post-testing. . . . And there is this massive record system to keep tiny little bits of it—when it is presented, when it is mastered, when it is re-taught and reinforced and posttested. It is just mammoth. Then that is to go onto a computer. We have that in the office. But they have not yet been able to get the children down on a computer.

Teachers emphasized that instruction with the goal of getting students through these tests distorted the teaching and learning process, failing to support the careful student assessment needed for adaptive teaching:

> [The system] is just pulling out the weaknesses of the child, and I'm concerned with much more than the weaknesses of the child. . . . In many instances when we are teaching children we find that although they have done poorly on a diagnostic test, the reason for this poor performance is not a lack of skill. You need to watch the student well enough to find out why he performs as he does. My relationship with this child is much more than communication through one test.

Indeed many teachers felt that systems that marched students through the sequential testing of hundreds of discrete objectives entirely missed the point of the learning process:

> Getting a kid interested in learning and keeping him interested is probably more important than doing checklists of goals and objectives on each kid for each content area.

> I am constantly being asked to define my goals, my way of achieving those goals, and my way of evaluating to see if I have achieved those goals. They seem to be very interested in that, and I get the impression that really that is all they are interested in. But it couldn't be true. There must be some human beings up there, too.

Finally, many felt that their districts' curriculum mandates paid more attention to getting through specific procedures than to teaching students to think. One middle-grades teacher reflected the views of many of her colleagues when she stated that the required elementary math curriculum in fact interfered with students' ability to understand mathematics:

> There is too much emphasis on "do this, do this, do this" rather than on the thinking process, which kids haven't learned, although they certainly have the ability. Not only is everything I'm supposed to cover prescribed for me, but there are tests given. So if I felt I might take a little freedom [to focus on problem solving], there wasn't time because the kids were tested, and from this testing it was determined where they were going.

A middle school teacher in another district described a similar problem:

> The 4th- or 5th- or 6th-grade teacher is . . . busy covering this program of studies. . . . In math the teacher will cover this area for two weeks and then this area for two weeks and this area and then this area. [As a result], the kid never gets it all together. So when the kid gets in 7th and 8th grade, he hasn't got the basics. Furthermore, nowhere in that program of studies did I see the word "problem solving" or "thinking." That's what's missing, and the teacher doesn't have the time to say, "Let's give them a lot of problems to teach them to think on their own, not swallow this rigid course outline." That's what's wrong with the students I'm seeing, even the above average students. [The Program of Studies] contains so much that you cannot possibly cover all of it. What would be nice would be a program of studies [that] would give the teacher some flexibility to put that enrichment material in.

It is telling that in the words of this teacher and many others across the three districts, thinking and problem solving were no longer part of educational basics; they had become "enrichment material."

Teaching children to think and covering the curriculum were frequently described as at odds. The mathematics curriculum just mentioned, for example, presented several problems. First, the required skills sequence was often out of synch with conceptual learning.

Students were to learn to add and subtract with two-digit numbers in one grade but were not to move to three-digit numbers until much later, making it difficult to teach the concepts involved in place value and addition in a thoughtful fashion. Second, the sequence of timed tests required students to memorize arithmetic facts in the early grades rather than to reason about mathematics. This strategy undermined their genuine understanding of number relationships and handicapped them with shaky conceptual foundations for their later learning. Third, the speed with which units and facts were to be covered and the way they were to be taught and tested left little opportunity for work with manipulatives or for extended problem solving. As a result, as often happens, the curriculum actively discouraged thinking and the development of understanding.

Sometimes a lockstep curriculum makes it impossible for students to advance in their understanding. For example, one curriculum we heard about required computer-administered tests of each skill, and nothing further could be taught until each skill test was passed. Teachers found this approach limited learning for both slower and faster students. One noted, for example: "I have some children who are still on the same level they started on in September. And if they try three times then that's it. After the third time, you're not supposed to frustrate them, so now they're stuck in that category and they won't be able to get out." The approach also created a problem for students who *could* pass the tests:

> What they have done is put down every objective they want every child to learn from kindergarten through eighth grade. There are volumes of objectives—absolute volumes of objectives. Each child has to pass the objective at this level before he can pass the next objective. I had the top 5th and 6th graders, so I had to [test] everything they were supposed to have passed. I spend absolute hours testing these kids, and I have lost a lot of math teaching time. As the system operates now, I would throw it out. . . . It is expensive and [the district's] study shows that it makes no appreciable difference. Well, it if takes that much time and money and makes no difference, then I say throw it out.

Though the system impaired teaching and learning, it gave administrators a sense of control. The objective in this case was to construct computerized records of each student's "mastery" of every one of hundreds of subskills, records that school principals and central office administrators could call up by classroom and school. From the perspective of administrative accountability, the system was Bobbitt's dream come true. From the perspective of teachers, however, it was a major deflection of classroom time and effort and a frequent obstacle to student learning.

Teaching to the Test

In Chapter Two I described how, by the 1980s, standardized testing had become a powerful force in shaping life in classrooms. The teachers in our study confirmed that teaching to the test can take the place of more thoughtful learning. They reported losing valuable time for teaching to the demands of testing programs. Comments that "the standardized tests given so frequently during the year take away from the time when I can be teaching students" were a constant refrain. As tests were becoming more and more important for making decisions in the three districts, the stakes for performance went up and so did the time spent explicitly preparing for tests:

> In 3rd grade the children take the Cognitive Achievement Tests and also the Iowa Test. We have to spend a month or so in preparation for administering the test, not covering any particular content, but showing the children how to color in the circles and keep their place . . . so by the time the test happens, the children have had enough practice with sample questions and how to turn the page and how to keep their place that they are not frightened by the test. But the actual test time takes a whole month, too, so you're spending a lot of time in preparation and in the giving of the test that you could be spending teaching.

> In the line of work I'm in right now I have an awful lot of testing I have to do and that concerns me sometimes. At the end of school I spent five weeks testing children. They were tired of testing; I was tired of testing; and I felt like I wasn't doing any teaching.

In our sample, 60 percent of the teachers reported that the emphasis on testing had affected their own teaching, and 95 percent reported that standardized testing had affected other teachers. Those least affected were teachers in subjects like music, art, gym, and vocational education, where standardized testing had intruded little, but even these teachers were keenly aware of their colleagues' concerns. In addition to chewing up time for teaching and making teachers feel pressured, the effects of testing fell into three categories: changing curriculum emphases, teaching students how to take tests, and teaching students for the test.

Teachers often described how teaching to the test caused them to lose the teachable moments when students are interested in an idea and want to pursue it. They also lost opportunities to take more comprehensive views of their students' abilities: "[When] certain things are going to be on the test, you have to limit branching off into areas that may interest the students more. [Testing] limits what you can do and how you interact with the kids. It limits your time. Your attention is shifting from the student to 'will he pass this test?'"

Teaching to the test, teachers said, means more than just preparing students to understand the format or "tricks" of multiple-choice tests. It also means emphasizing the kind of knowledge represented on a test in precisely the form it appears on that test—in other words, teaching for simple multiple-choice responses and deemphasizing subjects, skills, and forms of performance not tested. Teachers felt the losses most affected the higher-order learning skills they valued:

> I've changed my teaching behavior. I do not use as many essay tests as I did before because I try to give them things which they are apt to meet on standardized tests. I feel that it is hurting the children rather than helping them because they don't have to write their own sentences.

> We've been more or less pressured from the top down, starting with the superintendent and supervisors and principals. Therefore you teach to the test. You need to teach the format of tests so that they understand the kind of test that they are going to take. You teach similar types of problems that they are going to be faced with.

> I feel I spend more time testing than teaching. It has eliminated time to do what a lot of [people think] are frills. I do less science. I have always been very strong on science, but you have got to meet the standards of those tests, [which are] basically in math and reading.

Because they do not see what the tests measure as "real learning" or what they do to prepare for the tests as "real teaching," teachers who are asked to drill students for the tests are deeply resentful:

We almost stopped the curriculum for a period of time to teach specific skills. Sometimes I kidded my colleagues that I felt like a prostitute because I was doing these kinds of things which were supposed to be on the standardized tests but they were so directed that [they] changed the content, the approach, and the coursework that we were doing.

There is a great deal of pressure on a teacher to meet the criterion of these tests. The ex-principal I was under was making the teachers take the SRA test and rewrite it and present it to kids before they had to take it so they would do well on the test, and I resent that kind of thing completely.

Teachers are sick and tired of testing. They are so tired of that SRA testing and the POS testing and all the other testing that they have to do every nine weeks. They have had it up to their eyebrows. They really are tired of it because they have to teach to the test, which is something that they don't want to do.

Despite policymakers' presumption that teachers should use standardized test results to gauge their teaching effectiveness, only 12 percent of teachers in our sample found the results useful. Over two-thirds (69 percent) said they gauged their effectiveness from what they observed about how well students were learning and from direct student feedback. Another 26 percent used their own classroom measures of achievement. Most teachers (78 percent) felt the standardized tests fail to measure important aspects of teaching and learning, including achievement in such academic areas as writing and problem solving and growth in important areas of social and emotional development such as the ability to work with others.

In addition most teachers suggested that test performance depends less on what students actually know and can do and more on students' "testwiseness": whether the student understands the test format and test maker's thinking; whether the student can represent his knowledge in the particular way the test demands; whether her experience base matches the cultural assumptions underlying the test; whether he is having a good day, had enough to eat, or slept the night before; whether she is fearful of tests, and so on. For all these reasons and others, the teachers continued to frame their goals for themselves and for students in terms of connecting to students personally, helping them learn to use their minds in more powerful ways, and contributing to their ability to become worthy people and succeed later in life, even when those were not the aspects of teaching that were tested.

Some teachers were not subject to the pressures of tightly managed curriculum and testing plans, but most (57 percent) experienced tensions when they tried to reconcile their education goals with those of their school districts. These tensions typically resulted in conflicts with administrators, feelings of being overwhelmed by excessive demands, or a continual sense of guilt at not being fully able to serve two masters. Most teachers tried to accommodate district requirements, at least superficially, but preserved what they felt was important for students even when that seemed an act of defiance.

> There is tension in myself when I ignore the things that they tell me that I am supposed to do, but . . . there is also the feeling that I think that I am right.

> I'm not defiant. I turn in my list of objectives and things that I am required to do. I don't say "this is silly." I do those things. [However], I sometimes feel that the way I teach is not honored.

> I find myself playing a game at times, because when I am observed I do what they are looking for. In the meantime I still may be using techniques that I feel are best going to suit my students.

Other research has found similar effects of rationalistic curriculum policies. Zancanella (1992) found that middle school teachers in Missouri experienced disturbing conflicts between their teaching goals and those of a mandated curriculum associated with a state test. Flinders (1989) and Hawthorne (1992) found that high school English teachers who felt pressured by district- and state-mandated material to neglect the development of in-depth understanding tried to negotiate for additional student time and to bring students into curriculum decisions when possible.

These examples reveal teachers' dual accountability dilemma (Lipsky, 1980) that I described in Chapter Two: teachers feel accountable to the school system for implementing prescribed procedures, and they feel accountable to students for helping them become successful learners. They see these accountabilities as different. Most of the teachers in our study leaned toward a professional view of accountability: they felt their primary accountability was to students and parents (76 percent), but they also felt accountable to the principal or the school (62 percent). One teacher said, for example, "Well, I would say teachers are accountable to the parents and children, first—to the community. Then, on the other hand, teachers are accountable to the individual school and the system. Those accountabilities are different. Ideally, I believe the people living in the community should be the people who determine whether the school or the individual teacher is measuring up to what they want."

RESPONSES TO BUREAUCRATIZATION

As I mentioned in Chapter Two, the imposition of additional constraints on what is taught and how was the single most frequent reason these teachers gave for considering leaving teaching. They felt further bureaucratization of teaching might fatally impair their effectiveness and their intrinsic satisfaction with teaching:

> If they started tightening up any more as far as more testing, meeting more requirements . . . if it got any more standardized and routinized, if they told me that I couldn't do some of the things that I do in the way of interacting on a human level in the classroom, I would leave in a minute.

> If I can't be innovative and stay within the confines of the policy but use my own discretion and my own initiative, that would make me leave the school system.

> If they try to come in and force me to teach something that may not be applicable to my individual situation, then I would have to go back to something else.

> I think if they dictated how I was going to teach every kid I might tell them goodbye.

> I think that any more controls . . . in this school system would just about tilt it for me.

The fact that these answers came so readily to teachers' minds suggests that these teachers were already wrestling with their feelings about standardizing policies. Many of them observed that they knew of others who had already left teaching for these reasons. Their comments recalled the criticisms of Mary Dodge and Ella Flagg Young early in the twentieth century:

> What is happening is that a lot of the really good teachers have been frustrated and they're dropping out of the profession. . . . The morale is low. The motivational level for the teachers is low.

> [Teachers are discouraged] because we have a school system dictate everything to [us]. . . . [Y]ou have to stick so closely to what they say that you can hardly bring your innovative ideas into the classroom.

Virtually all the teachers said that having enough professional autonomy and discretion to teach flexibly was important to them. Most teachers associated the "right amount of autonomy" with sufficient control over instructional strategies to address students' needs and interests. When asked what policies they considered helpful, teachers generally described not policies but helpful conditions or people— often a principal who protected their autonomy and buffered them from unreasonable central office demands:

> I think our principal allows us as much freedom as she can. I look at the curriculum guide, but I do not model my program after that and she doesn't insist that we do. . . . There is not a lot of pressure as there is in some schools to follow it in a certain way. She does give the teachers a lot of freedom in how they teach and what they see as important, and that's probably why I feel comfortable teaching in [this] school.

> I have a fantastic principal who really cuts down on any amount of paperwork that he can for the teachers.

> The first [helpful policy] that came to my mind is that this past year we got a new principal whose policy is to respect you as a professional, to give you support, generally to respect who you are and let you do what he knows you are able to do. That procedure . . . is the most helpful.

Interestingly, teachers generally could not think of any specific policies that would help them do their jobs. What they felt they needed were supports and protections from the unhelpful demands of current policies. Detailed prescriptions for practice, it turns out, not only constrain teacher decision making but also undermine the knowledge base of the profession and its ability to recruit and keep talented people. As Sykes (1983) notes:

> Administratively mandated systems of instruction not only hinder teachers' responsiveness to students but over time discourage teachers from learning to be responsive, from developing sensitivity to individual differences, and from broadening their repertoire of approaches. Ultimately such systems become self-fulfilling prophecies: routinized instruction, and the attendant loss of autonomy, makes teaching unpalatable for bright, independent-minded college graduates and fails to stimulate the pursuit of excellence among those who do enter. Over the long run, then, the routinization of instruction tends to deprofessionalize teaching and to further discourage capable people from entering the field [p. 120].

We too found that professionally oriented teachers are those most troubled by edicts that ask them to focus on rules and reporting systems rather than students. As one explained:

> I feel sorry for any teacher who is interested in teaching. It is going to be much worse in the years to come. For those who like the record keeping, and there are plenty of them—pathetic teachers but great record keepers—this will be a way of moving . . . up the ladder. It won't help the good teachers. It will help the people who teach by the book because it is safe and it doesn't require any imagination.

In sum the policies that had recently been adopted in the three districts we studied had had important effects on classroom practices, but they were not always the ones intended. Some teachers felt able to ignore the policies or adapt them to their own ways of working. Others, however, experienced discernible negative effects: for them, the policies reduced the amount of time for teacher-student interaction and made it harder to focus on student concerns, interests, and ideas. The policies also influenced the quality of and time for teaching. Instruction was more hurried, more focused on the narrow content and limited format of tests, and less likely to include what the teachers called "real teaching"—projects, discussions, and activities that could probe ideas and student interests more deeply and develop skills as they would be used in real settings.

THE POLICY PROBLEM

The concerns of the teachers in our study are precisely those that current school reform efforts are seeking to address, yet many policies unwittingly set up greater prescriptions, which actually undermine the goals they seek. Few policymakers have undertaken the geological dig necessary to reverse the bureaucratic mandates that have piled up over the last hundred years. As a consequence, teachers and students find themselves trapped in catch-22 situations where they are asked to respond to new goals for schooling but are simultaneously caught in a web of rules, regulations, structures, and directives that directly and indirectly make it difficult, and in some cases impossible, to achieve those goals.

Although there is a recognition among reformers that public education is becoming overregulated and that the teaching occupation has become steadily less attractive to many talented college students, many reform proposals nonetheless continue to introduce overly intrusive constraints as they also propose greater teacher participation in decision making. With one hand states are passing laws that pay lip service to bottom-up school reform, and with the other hand they are enacting tighter controls on curriculum, texts, tests, and teaching methods.

These contrary impulses reflect the two competing theories of school reform currently at work across the country. One theory focuses on tightening the controls: more courses, more tests, more prescriptive curricula, more regulations, and greater enforcement through systems of rewards and more sanctions. The other seeks to build local capacity through stronger teacher education and the development of schools as inquiring, collaborative organizations. Without such professional structures, school-level decision making will be entrusted to many who are unprepared to exercise that responsibility wisely, and school reform will be defeated by the inabilities of those who must carry it out. The basis of professional decision making—that is, shared knowledge and a commitment to use it on behalf of stduents—is quite weak in public schools. Over many years the definition of *professionalism* has been turned on its head. Rather than using the term to connote a high level of knowledge applied to practice that aims to serve the needs of clients in intellectually honest ways, most school systems use it to mean unquestioning compliance with system directives. Evaluation criteria stress good-soldiership and conformity with district policies over knowledgeable advocacy and use of appropriate teaching practices.

In addition state, district, and school policies have often been remarkably uninformed by knowledge about teaching and learning. Quite often, education agency staff as well as lay school board members have developed and enacted policies that reflect little or no knowledge of existing research about the effects of the mandated strategies on teaching, learning, student success, or the functioning of schools. Many of these policies are directly or indirectly harmful to student learning. This occurs because there are few strong vehicles for ensuring that educators—including principals, superintendents, and other education agency officials—know about teaching and learning research and how to use that research skillfully to inform their decisions or to guide their recommendations to legislators who have policymaking authority. The lack of professional knowledge in many education bureaucracies and the remarkable propensity of both legislatures and education agencies to act without adequate knowledge or consideration of the effects of their actions seriously complicate the lives of students, parents, teachers, and other educators who are trying to support learning.

As policymakers and educators now seek to turn the giant ocean liner that is the nation's public education system, they must decide whether they want to further bureaucratize or professionalize teaching. These different objectives have very different implications for the kind of teaching force that will be attracted to education and the kind of teaching that will be possible. In a recent assessment of the demands of teaching for understanding, David Cohen and Carol Barnes urge a "new pedagogy for policy" (1993). By this they mean that policymakers must provide greater opportunities for teachers to learn how to enact reforms aimed at more complex and challenging learning goals. To this I would add that policymakers and educators need to develop also a *new policy for pedagogy.* This new policy must support the conditions under which teaching for understanding can occur, not as a subversive activity but as a regular part of all children's schooling.

Note

1. As in Chapter Two, unless otherwise noted, all quotations from teachers are from the study described earlier.

## CHAPTER FOUR

Teaching and Learning for Understanding

The relative absence in schools of a concern with deep understanding reflects the fact that, for the most part, the goal of engendering that kind of understanding has not been a high priority for educational bureaucracies.

—Howard Gardner, *The Unschooled Mind* (1991, p. 8)

Whatever our twentieth-century education system has produced, it is increasingly clear that it has not developed a widespread pedagogy for understanding, one that provides students with opportunities to test and apply their ideas, to look at concepts from many points of view, and to develop proficient performance. Students taught for understanding can evaluate and defend ideas with careful reasoning and evidence, independently inquire into a problem using a productive research strategy, produce a high-quality piece of work, and understand the standards that indicate good performance. They demonstrate that they understand by using what they have learned to solve problems they have not encountered before.

It is not that today's students are incapable of doing these things. It is that they have rarely been asked to do so. Teaching matters. How it matters was vividly illustrated in two letters to the editor published side by side in the *New York Times* on November 6, 1991 (p. A24). Written by two students in response to then President Bush's proposed school choice plan, the letters argued that choice was not the issue. The first was from a European student:

> As a student who attended a high school that offered a European education and now attends an American university, I can see the difference between the knowledge acquired by American and European students. American students . . . seem to have been bombarded with facts and figures that they were forced to memorize. European students are taught the same subjects, but instead of memorizing them, they are forced to understand them. This may seem a small detail, but as a result of the difference in teaching, European students have a better understanding of the subjects taught. They are more likely to remember the facts because what is understood lasts longer than what is memorized. Critical thinking, analysis of subjects in depth and research techniques are skills that I and other European-educated students learned in our high schools but have to learn again at our American universities.

The second was from a high school student in Madison, Wisconsin:

> I believe that the main reason we rank at the low end in education is that we are primarily taught to memorize text until we reach 10th or 11th grade. As a student in the 11th grade, I am only now being asked to think logically to solve problems. It would have been much easier and a lot more useful if our elementary and middle school teachers had begun to explain why certain equations worked and taught us how to discuss poems or a speech. . . . I cannot remember a teacher ever asking us about our feelings about an event or about the effects of historic decisions. If we do not know how to analyze a problem, how are we ever going to compete in the real world? The problems we are going to face are not all going to be written down in a textbook with the answers in the back.

Teaching for understanding is not wholly absent from U.S. schools. It was sometimes found during the 1930s, 1960s, and early 1970s in classrooms that attempted curriculum reforms. It can be found today in some classrooms, particularly in affluent communities and college towns where teachers are well prepared and parents demand intellectually engaging education. It can be found in progressive private schools that serve wealthy students and public alternative schools that serve poor ones. It can be found in good preschools, which have remained more grounded in understanding of learning and development than most public grade schools have. It can also be found in some programs reserved for "gifted and talented" students and in some courses labeled "honors" or "advanced placement." And it can increasingly be found in those schools that are restructuring for new forms of teaching and learning.

Most exciting and most difficult is the work of schools that are tackling the issues of excellence and equity together, creating new learning environments that model a spirit of inquiry, inclusiveness, and interdependence with students who represent the wide array of cultures, languages, ethnicities, and socioeconomic backgrounds that is America today. In the past, most school systems responded to greater student diversity by separating newcomers from the mainstream through pullout programs and more rigid tracking mechanisms. Rather than effectively educating the different groups, however, this strategy has created competition for scarce resources and a highly stratified, increasingly segregated, and sometimes hostile environment. Over time, this approach has worsened intergroup tensions and reduced and eroded community stability.

Instead of stratifying and rationing curriculum in response to diversity, a growing number of schools are working to create intellectually challenging programs that are enriched by diverse perspectives and responsive to a variety of approaches. Some of these schools are connected to networks like the Coalition of Essential Schools, Accelerated Schools, the School Development Program, the National Network for Educational Renewal, and other school-university partnerships. Other schools are experimenting with applications of ideas like Howard Gardner's multiple intelligences theory (1983) and Ann Brown's reciprocal teaching theory in Community of Learners settings (1994). These initiatives are striving to address the problems experienced by earlier reforms that were unable to maintain a dialectic between students and subjects—pursuing teaching for disciplined understanding and supporting diverse learners at the same time. Many of these schools are reaching challenging learning goals with students who are normally written off as well as with students who normally do well at the less ambitious learning demanded by most schools.

What do these restructured schools do? And how do they manage to do it? In this chapter I first describe some of these places. Then I outline the shared features research suggests are responsible for their success. I also describe the policy implications of each major feature of their work.

SCHOOLS THAT WORK

In 1986, Wheeler Elementary School in Louisville, Kentucky, was considered a "good" school with "traditional top-down management, an orderly, strict environment; respectable test scores; and an experienced staff . . . [where] teachers worked diligently in self-contained classrooms . . . relying heavily on basal readers, detailed curriculum guides, and drill-and-practice worksheets" (Whitford & Gaus, 1995, p. 19). Though the school had a good reputation from years gone by, teacher and student morale was poor, teachers were isolated, and many students were not successful: a substantial number failed to be promoted each year.

Today, after six years of restructuring, Wheeler Elementary is a very different place. Children are actively engaged in their learning. They run a daily school news show, author and illustrate their own books and reports, maintain journals of their learning, engage in science investigations, play chess, use CD-ROMs, and debate current events and mathematical problems. Faculty provide activities in each of the seven areas of intelligence outlined by Howard Gardner, arguing that this variety helps students experience success daily. Grade-level failures have been eliminated, achievement has climbed, students are motivated and engaged, and teachers feel more efficacious than ever before. Team teaching, shared planning time, and participation in a shared management committee spur continual improvement. Parents are involved in decision making and in classroom life.

Teachers at this school feel they have learned a lot about how to teach their students well, and they describe results that are self-sustaining:

> These kids just love school. When we were off for election day, some didn't want to be off. We don't have as many behavior problems because we do so many things. They are constantly moving along. I think it's [the curriculum] being thematic, too, and connecting into current events.

> I guess the main difference I see is in the kids. The kids enjoy coming to school. The intrinsic motivation to learn is very high. Kids are

stopping me in the hall now and saying, "What are we going to learn in math today?" What we're doing is meeting the expectation [that things should be interesting]. We can't sit children in desks today and expect them to just absorb what we say. They have to be involved in learning [Whitford & Gaus, 1995, p. 32].

The catalysts for these changes included activities and structural changes that influenced teachers' knowledge and perspectives about teaching: reorganizing the school into five multiage teams of 88 to 120 students and four to five teachers each; instituting shared planning time, which created new conversations about children and teaching; learning together at the Gheens Academy about child development, thematic curriculum development, and shared decision making; and developing a process for inside-out change that required teachers to decide what they would undertake and how, rather than being told what to do. As principal Charlene Bush recalls: "During that first year, I remember thinking, if [the staff development leaders] would just tell us what to do, I know we'd do a great job. But they never did tell us. We finally realized that it was up to us. We'd been given an opportunity, but we had to initiate something. It became something we believed in, something we internalized, rather than something someone else believed in" (Whitford & Gaus, 1995, p. 26).

Teachers at Keels Elementary School in Columbia, South Carolina, agree that their participation in learning and problem solving dramatically improved their school. Located near a military base and serving a highly transient group of low-income students of color, the school was nearly slated for closing fifteen years ago when its population changed and performance declined. After four years of restructuring its practices, Keels now produces extraordinary levels of academic success for its students and serves as a model for many surrounding schools (Berry, 1995). Although fewer than half of the students entering Keels meet the state's "readiness" standard in kindergarten, by the end of 1st grade over 90 percent meet state standards in reading and mathematics. PTA meetings are now standing room only, and there is a waiting list of families who live outside the attendance zone requesting transfers into the school.

Supported by a progressive principal who engaged teachers in decision making and launched conversations about research and practice, faculty eventually identified and introduced their own initiatives. These included cooperative learning in heterogeneous classes, whole language instruction and hands-on work in mathematics and science, social studies projects such as studies of the stock market, computer-based learning applied to such programs as Writing to Read and Reading Recovery, parent education workshops and home visits, and after-school programs including tutoring and supervised homework sessions. Students are involved in peer teaching and in decision making about school discipline and extracurricular events. Faculty are now developing performance assessments and portfolios in science. Teachers plan collaboratively and conduct peer observations, helping one another learn new practices. The Writing to Read classroom exemplifies what learning is now like at Keels:

> A sign proclaimed: "This is a Risk-Free Environment." In one corner of the room, a group of students were working a lab experiment where traits of plants were being investigated and students were classifying, sorting, and measuring. These students were finishing up a 3-week unit on seeds, stems, and leaves. . . . [They] wore visors with the word "scientist" inscribed on top. . . . Other students were writing about what they were learning. Those students wore visors with the word "author" inscribed on top. [Teacher] Sandra McLain deftly reads and critiques Constance's work and says to her in a resonant voice, "You just about have a science book written." Constance joyously responds with a "YES!" In other corners of the room, a child reads sitting on a bean bag chair and next to him another child "meets an author" on audio-tape. Across the room there are three computers where students brush up on phonemes. Sandra noted "the more they write the more they learn" [Berry, 1995, p. 122].

Because school staff researched and adopted each initiative, they now have a commitment to their work that drives their continual press to improve. The further they stretch and the more they realize about what students can do, the higher their expectations for both themselves and their students. These staff comments are typical:

> At the first day of school we give them things they can do. . . . [I]n fact the first two words we make sure they can read are "I can" and "we can." With every skill we teach, we use the visual, the auditory, and the kinesthetic. We write words, make up sentences, draw pictures. We push them into being complete readers. One way we do this is by cutting the junk and fluff out of reading programs, like all the pages in the workbooks.

Before I thought they just needed to know the basics in science. . . . I do not believe this anymore. . . . We are in the first stages of [restructuring the science curriculum]. We are wedding basic science building blocks with major math principles. Students are learning to sort, graph, weigh, measure, and predict. They are learning about data and constructing hypotheses, all in the first grade. I did not learn this until high school! [Berry, 1995, p. 121].

Over and over again, those who are recreating schools experience the surprises of success once thought impossible. In Philadelphia, teachers working in charter schools that are small learning communities housed within large high school buildings feel they have a new lease on their professional lives and their students' futures. Team teaching, working with the same students for several years, sharing planning and decision making, and having the opportunity to invent curriculum have enabled these teachers to boost attendance and academic achievement:

Finally, I can teach students in ways that allow me to engage with them, and other faculty, and hold onto them for their entire secondary school experience.

When we meet as a team and talk about students, we can brainstorm on how to handle problems. It makes a great deal of difference when I can say to that student, "Well your other teachers said *this* about you." We're working as a team and the students *know* that. . . . Those meetings are really valuable. We discuss what we can do *for* students.

I always thought of myself as a good teacher, but not always so creative. I have never enjoyed teaching as much as I do now. I am learning from my colleagues in the charter and, the most amazing thing, I never thought my students wanted to see themselves as students! We would all give the class away to the most disruptive students. Now the students tell Charlie to "shut up and let us learn" [Fine, 1994, pp. 6–8].

In these Philadelphia schools, high school parent involvement has ceased to be an oxymoron. Once there was something to connect to, parents were glad to be involved. As one said: "When [my son] was first in the charter, I thought 'something new again.' But then I saw him flourish, and the teachers took such an interest in him, and in me.

They called me, and we worked together. The charter has given me something to connect to. Through it I became interested in the school. I feel like it is my school now, too" (Fine, 1994, p. 8).

Although many existing schools are restructuring their work, educators, parents, and community members are also launching new schools that apply reform principles from the start. The Foundations School in Chicago, for example, was established in 1992 by teachers who wanted to operate "a teacher-directed, child-centered, ungraded, and multi-age public school that worked for teachers and children" (Hill & Weaver, 1994, p. 55). One founder was award-winning teacher Lynne Cherkasky-Davis. Like many other deeply committed teachers who are at the forefront of restructuring schools, Cherkasky-Davis had long been achieving exceptional success working with "at-risk" students in a traditional inner-city school. Even in that school, her classroom was described as

> A purposeful maelstrom of activity. . . . Kids read constantly, at home and at school, selecting their own books and sharing them with parents, classmates, and teacher. Children take a tremendous amount of responsibility, keeping attendance, publishing their own books, editing each other's work, moving about the many learning centers. Parents are involved, reading books to their children every night, and visiting the classroom often to assist. . . . Kids work with fourth-grade reading buddies, they exchange correspondence with their pen-pals. All this, by the way, occurs among children whom no one expects to be able to read or write [Hill & Weaver, 1994, p. 56].

This classroom-level success—against the odds and in an unsupportive environment—was not enough for Cherkasky-Davis. She explains that she joined with some colleagues to launch a school because "I was running my whole-language, developmentally appropriate kindergarten with only the nod of the principal, the sneer of colleagues and the questions of 'my parents.' I needed something more. I needed more support, a network from which I could learn, colleagues who thought like I did and would share strategies" (pp. 57–58).

Increasingly, educators like Cherkasky-Davis are taking the lead in creating schools that work for teaching and learning. In New York City the work of a hardy band of teachers who began reinventing schools in the 1970s has now grown into networks of dozens of schools. One of the first of these schools, Central Park East Elementary School, was launched in 1974 by a few teachers seeking to implement open education ideas in East Harlem. Deborah Meier, the teacher who led this enterprise, recalls:

> One of our primary reasons for starting the school . . . was our personal desire for greater autonomy as teachers. We spoke a lot about democracy, but we were also just plain sick and tired of having to negotiate with others and worry about rules and regulations. We all came together with our own visions—some collective and some individual—of what teaching could be like if only we had control. Ours was to be a teacher-run school. We believed that parents should have a voice in their children's schooling, and we thought that "choice" itself was a form of power. We also believed that we could be professionally responsive to parents and that, since the school would be open to parents at all times and the staff would be receptive, there would be plenty of opportunity to demonstrate our responsiveness [1987, p. 37].

Central Park East (CPE) was hugely successful and soon had long waiting lists of parents seeking admission for their children. Students in multiage classrooms taught by a band of creative teachers worked on arts and science projects, read extensive literature and wrote in every genre, and explored communities and cultures through biographies, field trips, and interdisciplinary research. Within ten years CPE grew to four schools in the same neighborhood—three elementary schools and a high school. A follow-up study of CPE graduates after the school's twentieth year found that the school's effects were extraordinary and long lasting. Among its initial students, most of whom read below grade level at entry, 89 percent of whom were African American or Latino, and most of whom were low income, 95 percent went on to receive high school degrees, and 66 percent went on to college, some of them to Ivy League schools. By comparison only 67 percent of the same cohort of New York City students graduated, and only about half that number went on to college, even though as a group they were whiter and richer than the CPE students (Bensman, 1994).

During the 1980s, teachers around New York City launched many other small alternative schools committed to finding a learner-centered, democratic form of education. A group of new small high schools featuring greater personalization, long-term relations between adults and students, authentic instruction and assessment, and a common, non-tracked curriculum has been so successful that it has become a launching pad for the creation of nearly one hundred similar schools. (These high schools' unique organizational features are described more fully in Chapters Five and Six.)

Large-scale research, too, is beginning to confirm the positive effects of school restructuring on student achievement. A recent study of 820 secondary schools nationwide found that those that had undertaken greater levels of restructuring aimed at personalized attention and longer-term relationships between students and teachers, a common curriculum offering higher-order learning for all students, team teaching and collaborative teacher planning, and parent and student involvement produced significantly greater achievement gains between grades 8 and 10 and grades 10 and 12 than those that maintained traditional practices (Lee, Smith, & Croninger, 1995). Not only did students of differing achievement levels all attain substantially higher gains than those in traditional schools, the range of achievement between high- and low-achievers was also narrower. Factors that appear to make a substantial difference include common curriculum experiences and high expectations for all students (that is, course offerings are narrow and tracking is minimized, therefore students take similar courses with strong academic content), an emphasis on active learning and authentic instruction, and forms of organization that allow teachers to work together and take collective responsibility for students.

Despite these and many other existing proofs of school restructuring success, widespread reforms tend to falter because many policymakers and practitioners do not fully understand what the changes entail or appreciate the fact that any serious change will affect all the other "regularities of schooling" (Sarason, 1982). For school reform to succeed in the long run, policymakers and educators need to act on a shared understanding of what meaningful learning is, what it requires, and how it can be supported.

CONDITIONS FOR UNDERSTANDING

Securing greater student learning will ultimately depend on our developing more skillful teaching and more supportive schooling. Otherwise the outcome of raising learning standards will be greater failure rather than higher levels of accomplishment. That some schools have learned to teach effectively is proof that others can do so as well. But few will learn from these pioneers' successes unless this society consciously shifts its view of standards for education. We must stop thinking that standards exist primarily as selection devices to distinguish among students for allocating educational benefits and start thinking of them as aids to student development.

Quite often Americans seem to believe that standards for education have been raised if more people fail to meet them. This view is obvious in schools and colleges where discussions about raising standards devolve into tactics for making admissions policies more selective rather than for improving the quality of education offered. It reflects an underlying belief that performance is a function of innate ability rather than the processes of schooling. It also reveals how little confidence we have in our ability to teach powerfully enough to produce high levels of learning for most students. It is this ability that we as a nation need to develop for the twenty-first century.

Students who think and perform well nearly always have had a qualitatively different schooling experience from students who have not developed these abilities. Fortunately, those who have not yet been asked to understand and perform at high levels can learn to do so at any stage in their education once they experience teaching that is intensely focused on developing thoughtful performance. There are a number of different requirements, however, for such ambitious teaching to succeed.

In my own teaching I have found that one key to student development is providing clear standards and criteria for performance on specific tasks, linked to lots of feedback about work in progress and continual opportunities for students to revise their work in response to this feedback. Students also need access to examples of high-quality work that they can use as models. The process of revision in light of feedback and exemplars that represent very explicit standards is an important aspect of teaching for understanding. Initial grumbling about high expectations turns to satisfaction with high levels of accomplishment when students are motivated and enabled to go far beyond their entering levels of ability by serious opportunities to develop competence and the scaffolding to help them learn how.

When faced with learning demands that stretch them to the edge of their developing capacities, students must also have access to substantial coaching to support their progress and to ensure they will be motivated to succeed rather than intimidated into failure. Clear standards must be coupled with sustained supports. Teachers must work in settings structured to enable close, continual relationships. Personalization is not just "nice" for students; it is essential for serious teaching and learning. In addition, complementary goals and supports must be present throughout the entire school environment—and, ideally, understood and supported in the home—if the habit of understanding is to be developed across domains and disciplines. Lone ranger teaching cannot enable students to become competent thinkers and decision makers as well as constructive human beings.

There is no single silver bullet that will produce these conditions for understanding in schools. Curriculum, teaching, assessment, school organization, governance, and professional development must all work together around a common set of understandings about how people learn, grow, and develop. In the rest of this chapter I describe nine key features of environments that support the kinds of meaningful learning seen today in successful restructured schools, and I spell out each feature's implications for school policy:

- Active in-depth learning
- Emphasis on authentic performance
- Attention to development
- Appreciation for diversity
- Opportunities for collaborative learning
- Collective perspective across the school
- Structures for caring
- Support for democratic learning
- Connections to family and community

No one of these features alone can ensure that students will be both challenged and supported in their learning. Schools must weave these strands into a tightly interknit tapestry if they are to support both competence and community.

Active In-Depth Learning

Active learning reflects the old saying "I hear and I forget; I see and I remember; I do and I understand." Active learning aimed at genuine understanding begins with the disciplines, not with whimsical activities detached from core subject matter concepts as some critics of hands-on learning suggest, and it treats the disciplines as alive, not inert. Schools that teach for understanding engage students in *doing* the work of writers, scientists, mathematicians, musicians, sculptors, and critics in contexts as realistic as possible, using the criteria of performance in the disciplines as standards toward which students and teachers strive.

In addition to the research I cited earlier on active inquiry learning conducted during the curriculum reform era of the 1960s and 1970s, several recent studies have confirmed that achievement on both performance tasks and traditional tests is enhanced by active learning. In a study of more than two thousand students in twenty-three restructured schools, Newmann, Marks, and Gamoran (1995) found much higher levels of achievement on complex performance tasks in mathematics and social studies for students of all backgrounds who experienced what these researchers termed "authentic pedagogy"— instruction focused on active learning in real-world contexts that calls for higher-order thinking, consideration of alternatives, use of core ideas and modes of inquiry in a discipline, extended writing, and an audience beyond the school for student work. In addition, a recent analysis of data from the 1988 National Educational Longitudinal Surveys found that students in restructured high schools where "authentic instruction" was widespread experienced much greater achievement gains on conventional tests. The researchers note that "an average student who attended a school with a high level of authentic instruction would learn about 78 percent more math between 8th and 10th grade than a comparable student in a school with a low level of authentic instruction" (Lee, Smith, & Croninger, 1995, p. 9).

To engage students in critical thinking and production, tasks should represent real performances in the field of study (not bite-sized pieces of work that are several steps removed from an actual performance): for example, student can design, conduct, and analyze an experiment rather than just list the steps of the scientific method; write or interpret a piece of literature rather than merely identify the topic sentence in a paragraph; develop and test a hypothesis rather than complete a canned laboratory experiment. Students can keep a garden and observe the results; raise animals and study their growth; conduct research about local environmental conditions; write and produce a newspaper from a historical era; develop and argue a famous case in moot court; build a house to scale; or mount an artistic performance. A morning at the Bronx New School in New York City provides a host of examples:

In one classroom, a group of 4th and 5th graders makes preparations to spend the day at the Brooklyn Bridge, guided by their teacher, a visiting architecture professor, and his students from a local college. . . . The group has a meeting before leaving to discuss some architectural information they will be investigating. . . . In the other 4th and 5th grade, there is a map of a recent class trip to Van Cortlandt Lake. A group of children examines the water in the terrarium and checks the "pond critters" they are keeping alive as part of their study of ecosystems. . . .

The children [in the 2nd/3rd grade class] . . . have just finished their morning meeting, where they discussed the termination of their two major studies before the end of the year: the Egyptian study and the science projects on human and animal habitats. . . . Observing the room while the children work on their projects, one sees many charts, graphs, maps, and lists where children report what they know, and want to know, about particular subjects. . . . The tables are clustered to accommodate three or four children at a time. Two girls are discussing the length of the Nile and making labels of the Lower and Upper Nile. Three others are gluing and supporting a paper pyramid until it dries. Other children are writing stories or reports about what they have learned. Some are looking up the exact length of the Nile River to design an accurate key for their map. Adults and children work together, and all are clearly engaged in their tasks [Darling-Hammond et al., 1993, pp. 31–35].

Active contextualized learning can also occur through computer simulations, such as the hypermedia-based Jasper project developed at Vanderbilt University. One of a growing number of video-computer simulations that create realistic contexts for problem solving, Jasper requires students to analyze data and apply knowledge of geography, mathematics, and earth science as they tackle such problems as saving someone stranded in the wilderness.

Just creating interesting tasks for students is not enough, however. Work that results in deep understanding has at least three features: it requires the use of higher-order cognitive functions, taking students beyond recall, recognition, and reproduction of information to evaluation, analysis, synthesis, and production of arguments, ideas, and performances. It asks students to apply these skills and ideas in meaningful contexts, engaging them in activities they have real reason to want to undertake. And it builds upon students' prior learning but presses toward more disciplined understandings. Whereas starting and ending with students' immediate interests does not create deeper understanding, careful use of standards and scaffolding can push students from intuitive understanding and interested engagement to more intellectually principled and technically skilled performances.

APPLICATIONS IN MEANINGFUL CONTEXTS   Among members of the nationwide Coalition of Essential Schools the metaphor for active learning is "student-as-worker." The objective is to enable students to act on their own knowledge in purposeful ways. As Sizer (1992) explains: "Displaying knowledge can be done with relative ease by a passive student. *Use* requires the student to be a fundamental part of the process" (p. 85). Similarly, in Community of Learners classrooms, students act as researchers, taking responsibility for learning about various aspects of a larger topic so that they can then teach the rest of the class (Brown, 1994). The need to teach the material to others triggers more active engagement and deeper learning than would sitting passively while the teacher tells, the learner listens, and a test is taken. Students are typically expected to plan and structure an area of inquiry, to incorporate and integrate academic learning into practical activities, and to produce their own work—ranging from portfolios of artwork to experimental designs and finished reports. The point is to provide opportunities for learning that is "active, strategic, self-conscious, self-motivated, and purposeful" (Brown, 1994, p. 17). Because human beings are innately driven to make meaning from our environment, we learn and perform best when the meaning of our work is apparent. Thus academic conventions—including the "basics" of arithmetic facts, spelling, and text decoding—are learned in more powerful ways when embedded in meaningful activity.

Apprenticeships are one way to immerse students in an area of study so they come to understand its many parts and develop practical skills through tacit modeling as well as explicit formal teaching. Typically, apprenticeships allow students to learn increasingly complex tasks in progressive stages. Apprentice experiences can be structured through community service and internship opportunities outside the school and through peer tutoring arrangements where students learn from their older or more expert peers in multiage classrooms. Gardner (1991) argues that apprenticeships may be the means of instruction that builds most effectively on the ways most young people learn best, combining experiential and formal learning with personalized guidance:

[Apprenticeships] permit aspiring youngsters to work directly alongside accomplished professionals, hence establishing personal bonds as well as a sense of progress toward an end. Frequently they also feature interim steps of accomplishment, with workers situated at different levels of the hierarchy, so that a learner can see where he has been and anticipate where he is headed. Apprenticeships often are highly motivating; youngsters enter directly into the excitement that surrounds an important, complex undertaking, where the stakes for success (and the costs of failure) may be high. Finally, apprenticeships embody centuries of lore about how best to accomplish the task at hand, and this lore can be invoked or exemplified at the precise moment when it is needed, rather than at some arbitrary location in a lecture, text, or syllabus [p. 124].

Regardless of the vehicle, extended in-depth learning requires substantial blocks of time devoted to deep immersion in an area of work and study. For example, a core principle of the Coalition of Essential Schools is that "less is more," that understanding some things well is more important than encountering a great many things without understanding them. Experiences in taking on problems and developing skilled performances enable students to think and solve problems in other settings. Gardner, Torff, and Hatch (1996), too, argue that in the ongoing battle between *breadth* and *depth,* emphasis should be placed on the latter:

[O]nce individuals are comfortable in the crucial symbol systems of reading, writing, and reckoning, we discern no necessity to place a special premium on one subject as opposed to another. . . . Far more important, in our view, is the experience of approaching with depth *some* key topics or themes in the broadest disciplinary areas—math and science, history and philosophy, literature and the arts. Students need to learn how to learn and how to probe deeply into one or another topic. Once they have achieved these precious insights, they are in a position to continue their own education indefinitely. And if they have not mastered these lessons, all the facts, factoids, and mandated tests will not save their souls [p. 50].

Developing students' understanding requires both the time for extended in-depth learning and the skillful guidance of a teacher who constructs scaffolding for key ideas, anticipates misconceptions or stereotypes, and designs learning experiences that build on students' thinking and reflect the standards for inquiry in the discipline.

A PRESS FOR DISCIPLINED UNDERSTANDING   Students need more than engaging tasks to develop real expertise, however. To reach high levels of proficiency in any sphere of activity, they need to engage in continued practice and refinement of performance over a sustained period of time on a piece of work that is complex enough to represent the many kinds of knowledge and skill that must come together to produce accomplished performance.

A mark of real expertise is the ability to understand interrelationships in an area of study and to apply insights and skills to a range of situations. The more expert someone is, the more flexible she is in the application of her understanding to a variety of circumstances within the domain. Thus students should engage in different kinds of thinking—written analyses of their own and others' work, reflective journals, quantitative and qualitative studies and products, and oral presentations—because this variety allows them both to tap existing strengths and to develop others, creating a flexible repertoire of thinking and performance strategies.

As students apply what they are learning through research and case studies, models and demonstrations, discussions and designs, they should be called upon to analyze the results of their efforts in a systematic fashion against some standards and exemplars. As they assess their own work and that of others, they should see and analyze examples of good performance and talk about what makes them good, so that they come to internalize standards of performance. Students must have the chance to continually revise their work so that it comes ever closer to meeting the standards. This is a key condition for learning that is rare in most classrooms although it is well understood as essential for developing prowess in sports, music, and other performing arts.

I am distinguishing here between the kind of development needed to produce whole products and performances and the bite-sized "competencies" that characterized the competency-based education initiatives of the 1970s and that are reemerging in some places today as one interpretation of "outcomes-based education." These reductionist views of performance offer such student objectives as "identifies the short a sound," "adds two-digit numbers with regrouping," and "lists the steps of the scientific method," rather than more meaningful goals such as "reads fluently with understanding," "reasons well mathematically," and "develops and tests hypotheses."

In the context of valued performances, standards can be a centerpiece for conversations about purpose and goals. Teachers and students can ask why are we doing this and what are we aiming for? Students need opportunities to make choices that enable them to start from what they know and care about, but they also need shared standards and requirements to ensure that they ultimately develop disciplined habits of mind and skills in each field of study.

POLICY IMPLICATIONS OF ACTIVE IN-DEPTH LEARNING The policy implications of these conditions for active in-depth learning are at least fourfold. First, curriculum guidance must focus on core concepts and allow for in-depth inquiry rather than demanding the superficial coverage of massive amounts of factual information. Second, assessments must look for evidence of understanding and not only for recall and recognition of information. Third, structures for learning—designations of courses and allocations of time—must allow extended blocks of time for teachers and students to work together around meaningful problems in ways that are as authentic as possible. Fourth, teacher evaluation systems must recognize teachers for skillfully managing activity-based learning rather than for using only lecture and recitation models.

A compartmentalized curriculum delivered in forty-two-minute class segments devoted to the coverage of large quantities of information does not easily support understanding of that information. As Gardner, Torff, and Hatch (1996) observe: "If we wish to teach for understanding, we have to accept a painful truth: it is simply not possible to cover everything. Indeed, the greatest enemy of understanding is 'coverage.' Only to the extent that we are willing to choose certain topics as worthy of exploration, and then to devote the time that is needed to explore these topics in depth and from multiple perspectives, is there any possibility that genuine understandings will be widely achieved" (p. 49).

It is a major problem that current curriculum policies and U.S. state and local curriculum guides from California to New York often enforce superficial teaching by their insistence that much specific material be covered and by their failure to sort the crucially important from the decidedly trivial. Despite the productive and important efforts of professional associations such as the National Council of Teachers of Mathematics to construct new curriculum standards, the current reality is that most U.S. schools exist in a coverage culture that must be transformed if students are to be supported in developing deep understanding and useful performance skills.

Furthermore, teaching that enables active learning is substantially different from the teaching models that undergird many teacher evaluation and staff development systems. Most teacher evaluation instruments rate teachers against an expectation of "frontal teaching," in which teachers present information verbally and maintain control of students by keeping them quiet and in their seats. However, teachers who set up active learning tasks that engage students in purposive work spend substantial time moving through the classroom to work with individuals and small groups, noting their accomplishments and needs, and directing students to new tasks or resources as appropriate. In a study of teacher evaluation, my colleagues and I found that supervisors who walked into such classrooms would often suggest that they come back with their checklists on a day when the teacher was "really teaching," that is, standing up in front of the room giving a lecture (Wise, Darling-Hammond, McLaughlin, & Bernstein, 1984). Similarly, a study of the implementation of California's new curriculum framework in mathematics found the inquiry-oriented teaching desired by the framework was difficult for teachers to enact in districts that employed direct instruction models as the basis for managing and supervising teaching (Darling-Hammond, 1990b). When rigidly enforced, such models require transmission teaching, which cannot meet the goals of active in-depth learning.

Emphasis on Authentic Performance

Virtually all babies learn to talk with little difficulty within the first several years of life. They discover that speech has a purpose, and they listen, theorize, try out sounds, and use feedback to figure out how to communicate about what concerns them. By the age of four or five, most have mastered a vocabulary of thousands of words and use it effortlessly. However, if we taught babies to talk as most skills are taught in school, they would memorize lists of sounds in a predetermined order and practice them alone in a closet. Their acquisition of these sounds would be tested and graded periodically, but they would receive little practice in real-world contexts or feedback on their efforts.

After four or more years of study, they would probably speak about as fluently as most foreign language students do when they graduate from high school—that is, far less easily and knowledgeably than today's entering kindergartner does.

Authentic performance is critical to the development of competence. Thus meaningful performances in real-world contexts need to become both the stuff of the curriculum and the focus of assessment events. These, in turn, should become so closely intertwined as to be often inseparable. In Essential Schools, as in schools in many other countries, exhibitions of performance are culminating events that demonstrate student learning through products like mathematical models, literary critiques, scientific experiments, dance performances, debates, and oral presentations and defenses of ideas. When prepared through constant critique and coaching, these exhibitions motivate intensive effort and high levels of understanding (Sizer, 1992; Darling-Hammond, Ancess, & Falk, 1995).

Similarly, in Arts Propel classrooms (found in Pittsburgh and elsewhere), "domain" projects enable students to work on practices central to a discipline, like rehearsing a piece of music or writing a scene of a play, acting alternately as producers, perceivers, and reflectors on their own work and that of others. *Process-folios* help students keep track of and reflect on their work from initial efforts through critiques, refinements, and finished pieces (Gardner, 1991).

THE IMPORTANCE OF AUDIENCE   Exhibitions, projects, and portfolios provide occasions for review and revision toward a polished performance. These opportunities help students examine how they learn and how they can perform better. They are often expected to present their work to an audience—groups of faculty, visitors, parents, or other students—to ensure that their apparent mastery is genuine. Providing opportunities for others in the learning community to see, appreciate, and learn from student work, such presentations also signal to students that their work is important enough to be a source of public learning and celebration. Presentations and performances develop important life skills in students and also, because they are living representations of school goals and standards, revitalize and reenergize those objectives. As Ann Brown (1994) observes: "Audiences demand coherence, push for high levels of understanding, require satisfactory explanations, request clarification of obscure points. . . . There are deadlines, discipline, and most important, reflection on performance.

We have cycles of planning, preparing, practicing, and teaching others. Deadlines and performance demand the setting of priorities—what is important to know?" (p. 8).

Planning, setting priorities, organizing individual and group efforts, exerting discipline, thinking through how to communicate effectively with an audience, understanding ideas well enough to answer the questions of others—all these are tasks people engage in outside of school in their life and work. Good performance tasks are complex intellectual, physical, and social challenges. They stretch students' thinking and planning abilities and use student aptitudes and interests as springboards for developing competence.

The power of these extended, applied learning experiences is suggested by the effects of extracurricular activities like drama, debate, Model Congress, or the school newspaper, where such authentic performances are most typical. Some participation in such extracurricular activities has been found to be highly correlated with academic achievement (National Center for Education Statistics, 1995b) and a better predictor of later life success than class rank, grades, or standardized test scores (Skager & Braskamp, 1966).

MULTIPLE CRITERIA   The criteria used to assess performances should be multidimensional. They should represent the various aspects of a task and be openly expressed to students and others in the learning community, not kept secret in the tradition of content-based examinations (Wiggins, 1989). For example, a research report might be evaluated for its use of evidence, accuracy of information, evaluation of competing viewpoints, development of a clear argument, and attention to conventions of writing. When work is repeatedly assessed, the criteria help guide teaching and learning by placing teachers in the role of coaches and students in the role of performers and self-evaluators.

A major goal is to help students develop the capacity to assess their own work against standards, to revise, modify, and redirect their energies, taking initiative to promote their own progress. Such self-directed work and self-motivated improvement is required of competent people in many settings, including a growing number of workplaces. Assessment strategies like portfolios take the concept of progress seriously—making the processes of product refinement and improvement a central aspect of the task and its evaluation. Thus they also allow students the opportunity to see, acknowledge, and receive credit for their growth, regardless or their level of initial competence.

One of the earliest state initiatives to create assessments that support performances of understanding was Vermont's portfolio system in writing and mathematics. Because of broad teacher and parent involvement in standard setting and assessment development, this portfolio system has taken root in schools with positive effects on instruction (Koretz, Stetcher, & Deibert, 1992; Murnane & Levy, 1996a, 1996b). California, Connecticut, Delaware, Kentucky, Maryland, and New York are among the other states that have also begun to use performance-based assessments that require students to solve mathematics problems, analyze and use historical documents, conduct and critique science experiments, and write and communicate in many genres. Early studies are attributing substantial writing achievement gains to these new assessments, no doubt in part because the neglect of writing by earlier multiple-choice tests has left much room for improvement(Koretz, Stetcher, & Deibert, 1992; Murnane & Levy, 1996a; Appalachia Educational Laboratory, 1996; Whitford & Jones, in press).

These performance-based assessments are criterion referenced rather than norm referenced, which means that they are structured to evaluate how well students have learned important knowledge and skills rather than to rank order students against one another. Norm-referencing technologies for test construction measure curriculum poorly; in the effort to construct a bell-shaped curve, they discard items to which too many, too few, or the wrong subsets of test takers know the answer, whether these items represent important performance expectations or not. In contrast criterion-referenced assessments measure students' progress against standards of content and performance. Such assessments may ultimately support schools' efforts to emphasize understanding and progress, particularly if the assessments acknowledge the varied types of real-world competence students have to offer.

POLICY IMPLICATIONS OF EMPHASIS ON AUTHENTIC PERFORMANCE To support performance development and to support adaptive teaching, current norm-referenced multiple-choice standardized tests will need to be replaced by criterion-referenced performance assessments that are developed and used by educators for state, district, and local purposes. The new assessments will need to pose tasks that are good representations of higher-order thinking as well as basic skills and provide information that illuminates *how* students are thinking and learning as well as *what* they know and can do.

Attention to Development

When students are engaged in active learning around meaningful tasks, they are experiencing teaching that supports their cognitive development. However, many schools seem bent on ignoring development. As Tracy Kidder (1989) remarks: "The problem is fundamental. Put twenty or more children of roughly the same age in a little room, confine them to desks, make them wait in lines, make them behave. It is as if a secret committee, now lost to history, had made a study of children and, having figured out what the greatest number were least disposed to do, declared that all of them should do it" (p. 115).

Developmentally attentive schools start from the presumption that the school should be user-friendly. School work should build upon children's normal developmental dispositions so that student and teacher energy can be turned to the pursuit of important learning rather than wasted on an adversarial process of unnatural behavior management. In user-friendly schools and classrooms teachers select intrinsically motivating activities that enable students to master their environment, are appropriate to students' stages of growth, and address common curriculum goals. Activities alternate between relatively short periods of whole-group instruction and longer stretches of work time when students engage in different tasks suited to their readiness and needs.

Teaching and learning are reciprocal, with learning experiences continually reshaped by students' changing needs and understandings. Teachers interact with individuals and small groups of children, asking questions, jotting down notes about what students say and do, what they understand and misunderstand, what they seem ready to try. Teachers guide students to the activities they need to undertake as well as enabling them to pursue the areas in which their abilities are highly developed, thus blending challenge and satisfying performance for each student.

Students' interests are both indicators of readiness and engines for propelling exploration and learning. However, taking student interests into account should not be confused with letting students do whatever they want. Development—whether cognitive, physical, social, or emotional—both enables and is enabled by educational experiences. Interests are shaped and encouraged as well as seized upon. The goal is that children "should will what they do; they should act, not . . . be acted upon" (Édouard Claparède, quoted in Piaget, 1970, p. 152).

This distinction is crucial for productive learning. A few years ago my son experienced the contrast between developmentally grounded and developmentally ignorant education when he moved from a Montessori kindergarten to a typical public school 1st grade. In the first setting students moved from task to task working individually and in small groups—sitting on rugs while assembling puzzles and completing writing tasks, working in gardens and at computer stations, experimenting with water and measurement in a science corner, reading quietly on pillows in the book corner. Class meetings provided common time for social learning and content studies in science and social studies. Skill work occurred individually and in small groups based on students' readiness. A balance between chosen work and required work allowed teachers to encourage students' interests and talents while addressing areas of need. In the second setting students sat for hours at cramped desks in enforced silence completing assigned workbook pages. Group lessons were determined by the basal reader and curriculum guide rather than by students' needs. The work was boring and, by any measure of their developed abilities, unnecessary for most of the children, as well as instructionally ineffective. An elaborate scheme of rewards and punishments was used to sustain these uncomfortable behaviors.

As my son's skills had developed beyond the demands of the required 1st-grade curriculum, I was surprised when he came home one day and told me, "Mom, 1st grade is too hard." When I asked him what was hard about it, he replied, "My teacher told me I need to learn to sit like a rock." Like his two sisters before him, who had also encountered inappropriate early childhood classrooms in another school system, my son returned to Montessori school in those early years. He reentered public school in 3rd grade, when he could survive the conventions of a setting focused more on the enforcement of procedures than the learning needs of children.

In order for teachers to build upon readiness and nurture further growth they must have keen skills of observation and a substantial knowledge base about learning and development so as to recognize what students are thinking and what they are ready to learn. Without such knowledge, "the teacher cannot properly understand the students' spontaneous procedures, and therefore fails to take advantage of reactions that appear to him quite insignificant and a mere waste of time" (Piaget, 1970, p. 69). Strong teacher preparation is the foundation for developmentally attentive teaching.

HONORING THE REAL BASICS   Policies, too, affect the extent to which developmentally informed practice is possible in schools. Since the 1970s, a growing number of state and local policies have demanded earlier and earlier teaching of "basic" academic skills as they are reflected on standardized tests, pushing out the hands-on discovery methods that have characterized early education. Developmentally appropriate activities often seem frivolous to behaviorists, who would rather see students engaging in highly structured drill-and-practice on letters and numbers as they sit at desks than see them crouching before blocks, standing at easels, or acting out stories. However, much research has found that play has important cognitive as well as social and emotional payoffs (Kamii, 1982; Piaget, 1970). As children at play imagine and work through situations, emulate adult activities and behaviors, create things, and use what they know in authentic if imaginary contexts, they are hypothesizing, trying out ideas, practicing, and applying their knowledge and skills.

Other research indicates that children's visual and perceptual development allows most of them to begin to learn to read easily around the age of seven. Prior to this time, only a relatively few children have the visual acuity to focus comfortably and accurately on print for long periods of time. As a consequence most European schools emphasize play, the arts, and social learning until students are seven, when they learn to read quickly, easily, and with more universal success. The distinctly American desire to speed development produces substantial parent and teacher anxiety and high levels of reading failure when it overrides processes of physical development by asking five-and six-year-olds to do something their visual ability makes difficult for many of them.

A large-scale test of some of these developmental propositions took place during the 1970s in the province of North Rhein-Westphalia in what was then West Germany. Legislators' desires to induce readiness and to speed learning led some to propose replacing traditional play kindergartens that encouraged active and concrete learning with academic kindergartens that would teach children basic skills in more structured ways. An important decision was then made to test this proposition with careful longitudinal research (something that almost never happens in U.S. education policymaking). The effects of fifty academic kindergarten programs were compared with those of fifty play kindergartens over a five-year period. Teams of researchers from two different universities, using different research methods, found that the outcomes were strikingly different but not in the direction expected. At the age of ten, children who had attended play kindergartens were better adjusted socially and emotionally in school; were more cognitively advanced in reading, mathematics and other subjects tested; and excelled in creativity, intelligence, "industry," and oral expression (Ewert & Braun, 1978; Tietze, 1987; Winkelmann, Hollaender, Schmerkotte, & Schmalohr, 1979). The studies concluded that the effort to override developmental considerations had not succeeded, and the academic kindergartens were discontinued.

In the United States the opposite has occurred. Hands-on learning in the early grades has been replaced in many schools by desk-bound learning conducted with basal readers and workbooks, and curriculum packages that emulate standardized tests. Play corners, blocks, picture books, easels, and sand tables have disappeared from many classrooms as teachers have been directed to teach for the tests. Young children are asked to learn in ways that are inappropriate for them and ineffective for nearly anyone. Pushing students to work in artificial ways on tasks for which they are not ready leads to high rates of failure, unhappy children and teachers, and increasingly punitive environments. As a consequence of developmentally insensitive curriculum and test-based promotion and placement policies, retention rates in kindergarten and 1st and 2nd grades have skyrocketed, readiness tests have proliferated, and the more affluent parents have begun to hold their children out of primary school until a later age to give them a greater advantage in meeting the inappropriate expectations they are likely to encounter (Shepard & Smith, 1986; Elkind, 1988; Bredekamp, 1987).

ORGANIZING SCHOOLS AROUND DEVELOPMENT   Attention to child development also makes a tremendous difference in how schools function as organizations. James Comer's highly successful School Development Program (Comer, 1988)—which transformed failing inner-city New Haven schools to among the most successful in the city—illustrates how building a shared base of knowledge about child development among parents, teachers, and other school staff can create settings in which children flourish. Comer's team helps practitioners and parents understand what children need for healthy development and then helps them work together to change policies and practices to provide these conditions. The schools involved find that students begin to succeed as educators and parents build stronger relationships with one another, create more opportunities for students to develop competence, and replace punishments with strategies for proactively teaching positive behaviors (Comer, Haynes, Joyner, & Ben-Avie, 1996; Comer, Haynes, & Hamilton-Lee, 1989).

The benefits of developmental attentiveness do not stop after the early years. In a recent review of research on the education of early adolescents, Braddock and McPartland (1993) argue that many well-known adolescent difficulties are not intrinsic to the teenage years but are related to the mismatch between adolescents' developmental needs and the kinds of experiences most junior high and high schools provide. When students need close affiliation, they experience large depersonalized schools; when they need to develop autonomy, they experience few opportunities for choice and punitive approaches to discipline; when they need expansive cognitive challenges and opportunities to demonstrate their competence, they experience work focused largely on the memorization of facts; when they need to build self-confidence and a healthy identity, they experience tracking that explicitly labels many of them as academically deficient. Many students who entered middle school feeling good about school leave persuaded that they do not count and cannot learn (Carnegie Council on Adolescent Development, 1989).

Teenagers who stay in more nurturing settings where they encounter less departmentalization, fewer teachers, and smaller groups experience higher achievement, attendance, and self-confidence than those who enter large impersonal departmentalized secondary schools (Wehlage, Rutter, Smith, Lesko, & Fernandez, 1989; Bryk, Lee, & Smith, 1990). As Braddock and McPartland (1993) explain: "A positive human relationship between a student and teacher contributes to student learning because the student's desire to earn the respect and praise of a favorite teacher can be a powerful source of social motivation. . . . Moreover, students who do not feel a direct human attachment with school personnel are more likely to have poor attendance or to drop out than individuals who perceive themselves to be part of a caring school community" (p. 140).

Developmentally attentive secondary classrooms allow students to work in ways that support their needs for affiliation and autonomy. Curriculum approaches allow for social interaction and student initiative as well as opportunities to illustrate competence in a variety of ways. Strategies like writers' workshops and independent research projects allow students to start from whatever their initial skill levels may be and progress with coaching to new levels of accomplishment.

Collaborative work allows students to learn from the modeling of peers. Internships address adolescents' needs to develop autonomy and self-responsibility as well as specific skills in areas of personal interest.

POLICY IMPLICATIONS OF ATTENTION TO DEVELOPMENT   At least two kinds of policies are needed if most schools are to be more developmentally attentive. Teacher and administrator education and licensing policies that ensure a foundation of knowledge about learning and development are most important. From this base a wide range of decisions in schools and classrooms are likely to be better made. Although many states have begun to require more extensive preparation of teachers, others like New Jersey, Virginia, and Texas actually reduced their teacher training requirements in the 1980s and now require little or no study of child development even for early childhood and elementary teachers (Darling-Hammond, 1992; Darling-Hammond, Wise, & Klein, 1995). Few states require secondary school teachers to know much about adolescent learning and development and even fewer require school administrators to be knowledgeable in these fields. As a consequence of states' uneven licensing and program approval policies, many educators simply do not know enough about child development to make good judgments about teaching practice.

In addition curriculum policies should encourage practices that acknowledge the wide range of variation in normal development, rather than using artificial norms to govern presentation of material and promotion through the grades. Curriculum guidance should allow teachers enough latitude to help students connect to concepts in the ways and at the times most appropriate for them, with supports available for those who need additional help. Such acceptance of developmental differences should not replace vigilance when students are not learning appropriately but should provide greater clarity about how to support learning and when to activate special efforts.

Appreciation for Diversity

Contemporary intelligence theory (Sternberg, 1985a; Gardner, 1983) confirms what is obvious when we look at human accomplishments—that people possess a complex mix of intelligences that are developed over time in cultural contexts and used in various ways. Traditional schools have often sought to deny or subordinate intellectual diversity to the demands of narrowly drawn standardized curricula, but restructured schools support classrooms that buzz with a variety of approaches and with activities that allow students to increase their strengths and to struggle productively with areas they find difficult. Successful teachers use a wide range of teaching strategies in a reciprocal process demanding intimate knowledge of students and how they think (Darling-Hammond, 1990c). They know that students may find the initial inroads to understanding the American Revolution, for example, by writing a newspaper article that reports key events of the time, researching the art or music of the era, evaluating tax policy and the balance of trade, or framing a debate between proponents of independence and colonial loyalty.

At the Key School in Indianapolis, students have an opportunity each day to develop each of the seven intelligences Gardner describes: logical-mathematical, musical, spatial, interpersonal, intrapersonal, bodily, and linguistic. Teachers look for ways to identify and build upon student strengths by addressing students' use of visual, verbal, auditory, and tactile senses and by using deductive and inductive approaches to learning. This provides pathways to success for students who in traditional classrooms would be marked for failure, yet it does not avoid the need to develop skills across all areas (Gardner, 1991). When students start from the strategies they find comfortable, they can achieve successes in learning that ultimately enable them to expand their repertoire of skills and approaches.

THE BENEFITS OF DIVERSITY   In contexts where multiple intelligences are respected, heterogeneity is a plus, not a problem. Learner-centered schools structure classrooms to use differences among students as the basis for shared student expertise and cooperative learning. David Hirschy, a physics teacher at the highly successful International High School in New York City, describes how he first understood this in his work with limited English proficient students:

It became apparent that many of the techniques that I used in teaching, when applied to limited English proficient students, simply didn't work. There were students who just didn't understand when I spoke to the class. There were students who had extensive science preparation in their native countries, and there were students who had very little formal education. The attempt to have all students arrive at the same place at the same time was impossible. Now the truth is that it is impossible with native English speakers also. It just isn't as obvious. . . . Heterogeneity is not a problem to be solved. In fact when embraced, it is a positive force in the classroom [Hirschy, 1990a, pp. 16–17].

Hirschy's use of collaborative activity-based teaching strategies enables students to learn the same things in different ways and to share with one another the insights each has derived. When students know different things and are variously adept at different aspects of a task, they become resources for one another. As Ann Brown (1994) explains:

Traditionally school agendas have aimed at . . . decreasing diversity. This tradition is based on the false assumption that there exist prototypical, normal students who, at a certain age, can do a certain amount of work, or grasp a certain amount of material, in the same amount of time. In [Community of Learners], although we assuredly aim at conformity on the basics—everyone must read, write, think, reason, etc.—we also aim at nonconformity in the distribution of expertise and interests so everyone can benefit from the subsequent richness of available knowledge. The essence of teamwork is pooling expertise. Teams composed of members with homogeneous ideas and skills are denied access to such richness [p. 20].

Planned diversity in knowledge and skills is consonant with the new forms of organization that are emerging to replace bureaucracies. Rather than creating strict divisions of labor that assume that knowledge resides at the top of the hierarchy and each person performs his job independently as specified from above, new organizations are creating teams that require distributed expertise among the members of the group. Individuals' different knowledge bases contribute to a more thoughtful and complete analysis of problems and solutions.

EMBRACING PERSPECTIVES   Finally, an appreciation for diverse experiences and perspectives enhances both the power of students' thinking and their range of vision as social members. To be full and complete, inquiry about important problems and questions must cross community and cultural boundaries as well as disciplinary and departmental ones. In fact, the basis of the earliest universities was that they brought together scholars from all over the known world. They sought to create ways to share diverse perspectives from various geographic areas, cultures, and disciplines as the basis for developing knowledge and finding truth. The same ideal of knowledge building—of creating powerful shared ideas from the integration of diverse experiences of the world—undergirds the concept of multiculturalism in today's curriculum.

A multicultural approach to education explicitly includes a range of experiences, views, and representations of human thought in all aspects of the curriculum, from literature and the arts through science, mathematics, and technology. It not only gives students a sense of inclusion (Banks, 1993), it also develops their ability to appreciate multiple perspectives, which is an important aspect of cognitive and social functioning and one of Piaget's indicators of higher stages of cognitive development. A multicultural approach can help students develop an analytic frame for life in a democracy, seeing problems and ideas from many vantage points and appreciating the many views that social life comprises.

CONNECTING TO EXPERIENCE   In addition, as I have pointed out, we have increasing evidence that academic achievement is related to teachers' ability to connect curriculum to learners' experiences and frames of reference. In schools that teach diverse learners well the connection is drawn in many ways: by using autobiographies and family histories as a starting point for lessons, engaging in neighborhood studies, sharing individual students' linguistic and cultural knowledge with the class, including multicultural content in selections of topics and materials, and using parent conferences to solicit knowledge about students to inform teaching. Drawing such connections helps students build on what they know as they expand their horizons. It also models education as democracy by seeking participation, connections, and contributions from all students.

A recent study of academically challenging teaching in high-poverty classrooms (Knapp, Shields, & Turnbull, 1995) found that teachers' efforts to connect learning to students' experiences and backgrounds were strongly related to student achievement. In the 140 classrooms studied, both low- and high-achieving students learned most in mathematics, reading, and writing when teachers emphasized conceptual understanding, complex problem solving, advanced skills and performances, discussions of alternative solutions and points of view, extended writing, and student-generated ideas and products rather than restricted skills practice. The researchers found that "teachers who took active, constructive steps to connect learning to students' backgrounds were much more likely to have chosen meaning-oriented approaches to the teaching of reading, writing, and mathematics. This finding is not surprising. Indeed, it is partially true by definition. That is, by focusing on meaning, teachers build a bridge between children's knowledge base and their academic learning experience. By connecting instruction more closely to children's home experiences, teachers can achieve higher levels of engagement" (pp. 772–773).

Working with student differences within common settings is precisely what bureaucratic specialization of tasks has sought to avoid. Schools have hoped to make learning and teaching easier by homogenizing classrooms through tracking and ability grouping, age grading, and segregation of "special needs" children. However, a substantial body of research now shows that reducing diversity is not always beneficial for learning and that multiage, multilevel classrooms can be extremely successful for all kinds of students (for a review see Anderson & Pavan, 1993).

Meanwhile, much research has also found that tracking—the separation of students into separate instructional strands with differentiated curricula based on presumed or tested ability levels—decreases learning opportunities for low-track students without substantially increasing them for high-track students (for reviews, see Oakes, 1985, 1989; Slavin, 1990). Although many people favor tracking, some for experiential reasons, research shows that schools that have minimized or eliminated tracking generally do better with high-and low-achieving students alike (Lee, Bryk, & Smith, 1993; Hoffer, 1992).

Tracking in U.S. schools is more extensive than in most other countries, which do not usually group students by presumed ability or achievement prior to high school. And although many countries do have two-tiered high school systems (separating academic and vocational studies), they operate even then from a presumption that effort rather than ability is the most important determinant of learning. Although tracking in the United States has been justified on the grounds that it allows schools to better meet students' needs, students in lower tracks receive a much less challenging curriculum that accounts for more of the disparities between what they and other students learn than does their entering ability level (Dreeben, 1987; Lee & Bryk, 1988). They achieve less than students of similar aptitude who are placed in an academic program or an untracked setting (Gamoran, 1990; Gamoran & Mare, 1989; Hoffer, 1992; Lee & Bryk, 1988). In addition, because these groupings tend to stratify students by race, class, and ethnicity, they impede the growth of democratic learning communities.

To acknowledge the shortcomings of tracking is not to ignore the fact that there are often good reasons for differentiated course taking based on students' prior experiences as well as their interests and talents, especially as they enter high school. The principle schools should follow, however, is that students should be offered access to the same intellectually challenging coursework for most of their school careers and that different course taking should be based on what they actually know, are willing to tackle, and want to learn, rather than on presumptions about what they can or ought to learn.

POLICY IMPLICATIONS OF APPRECIATION FOR DIVERSITY   Although the disadvantages of tracking are increasingly well known, the benefits of heterogeneous classrooms are attainable only when teachers are prepared to teach in ways that use diversity to advantage, employing reciprocal teaching and cooperative learning strategies skillfully. This prerequisite implies policies that support a stronger knowledge base among teachers, so they can master this more demanding pedagogy, and that support curricula allowing multiple teaching strategies. It also implies policies that support the heterogeneous grouping of students rather than those that segregate programs as a function of categorical funding streams and placement requirements (as discussed in Chapter Six).

Opportunities for Collaborative Learning

A visit to a 3rd-grade classroom in New Rochelle, New York, one of a growing number of urban suburbs, reflects the U.S. norm in 1996.

> Coming from homes that range from housing projects to elegant colonials, the students present a range of experiences and learning needs. About one-third are African American or Latino; two speak languages other than English at home; and two receive special education services for part of each day. These distinctions are meaningless here, however. The class hums like a well-rehearsed orchestra as students move to the middle of the room for meeting time. To prepare for a story-writing assignment, they brainstorm ideas about how to make their group-work productive. The teacher skillfully guides the discussion and writes their ideas on the board: "Let everyone share their ideas." "We cooperate and work together." "Sometimes we have to compromise."
>
> She reminds them to make a web of their ideas so that they can figure out how to put them in order. The children hurry back to their

desks, clustered together in groups of 4, and begin work immediately. "You have to get everyone's ideas," one tiny girl reminds a young boy at her table. Everyone is hard at work, heads leaning toward one another as they offer and record their thoughts. Some run to the bookshelf for dictionaries and other books that provide the research they need. In a typical group, children take turns suggesting sentences, querying each other's suggestions, recording, noting spelling and punctuations, and editing the work. The teacher moves from one group to the next, checking, questioning, prodding, nudging. The students need little help. They are already seasoned writers and collaborators. It is no wonder that students in this class score at the top of the district each year on assessments of reading and writing [National Commission on Teaching and America's Future, 1996, p. 22).

Collaboration between and among students and faculty is at the core of schools where diversity enhances learning, just as it is in the new work environments where teams pool knowledge. Collaboration allows both children and adults to verbalize and sharpen their thinking as they teach one another (Slavin, 1995). As teacher David Hirschy explains:

> Collaboration, a combination of individual and small group work, and an environment in which variety is expected allow us to capitalize on differences. The benefit to the slower student is having a model in the classroom and assistance from peers. The advanced students learn to meet high expectations in an atmosphere where variety is expected and to expand their responsibility to include others. . . . Groups are [important] because students need to use language to learn language. They need to talk with each other. They need to read instructions. They have the opportunity to repeat, to review, and to listen. . . . The focus is on students learning rather than on me teaching. . . . The goal is for students to assume responsibility for their own learning, and to discover how they learn best [1990a, pp. 18–19].

TALKING FOR LEARNING   Whereas traditional classrooms tend to be still but for the sound of teacher talking, learning-centered classrooms feature student talk and collective action. To those accustomed to the individual learning situations in which a teacher or text is the stimulus and absorption of material is the process, cooperative learning may look disconcerting. In fact, however, outside the classroom most learning is social: people learn in families, playgroups, and workgroups everything from how to behave under specific circumstances to how to read, cook, and operate a computer. Social learning lends multiple methods to the process of making meaning. Interactions with peers or more advanced "teachers" (who may themselves be students) provide an audience for trying out ideas, thinking out loud, and getting feedback.

As Vygotsky (1962) observed, when children use language they are not only verbalizing their internal thinking processes but also aiding their conceptual development. Talking is a vehicle for learning. Deborah Meier (1995) has stated that teaching is not talking and learning is not listening; instead it may be in fact that "teaching is mostly listening and learning is mostly telling" (p. xi). Teachers learn from watching learners as they work; students learn by articulating what they know. Opportunities to talk give learners access to the pre-existing knowledge structures embedded in language, so that they have ready-made concepts and cognitive structures at their disposal when they are ready to use them (see, for example, Corbett, 1971).

This basis for whole language approaches to reading and writing holds equal power for the learning of mathematics, science, and other subjects. Organized into groups to share ideas, learners may test solutions to mathematical problems; collectively design experiments, arguing about variables of possible relevance and strategies for evaluating their effects; or take turns teaching what they have learned about a topic to the rest of the group.

Reciprocal teaching (Palincsar & Brown, 1984) was explicitly designed to capitalize on students' *zones of proximal development.* Each zone stretches from the student's current level of competence to a level requiring greater understanding, which he can shortly reach with the help of other people and learning aids. When students work in groups, their many overlapping zones of development help provide fortuitous insights and pathways to others in the group. "Because thinking is externalized in the form of discussion, beginners can learn from the contributions of those more expert than they. . . . Collaboratively, the group, with its variety of expertise, engagement, and goals, gets the job done" (Brown, 1994, p. 11).

Because it is so important to externalize thinking to promote understanding, cooperative classrooms are intentionally designed to foster communities of discourse. Discussions take place at classroom meetings, small- and large-group forums, and individual conferences. One teacher gives this specific instance of how such discourse provokes learning:

When a math problem is discussed at a classroom meeting, many strategies for learning will often be presented. Sometimes one person's strategy will open up an understanding for another. For example, at one meeting Hugh explained how he does multiplication by engaging in repeated addition. This was the only way that Manuel, who had been having a terrible time grasping the concept, seemed to be able to understand it. Although many of us had tried to help Manuel before, it wasn't until he heard and saw a fellow student's explanation that he was finally able to make the connection [Lieberman, Falk, & Alexander, 1994, p. 7].

The possibilities for peer teaching created by collaborative learning settings also support multiage and multilevel groupings of students. Contrary to conventional wisdom, classrooms deliberately organized to include a span of developmental levels can be more supportive to learning than single-age or single-level classrooms. They allow younger or less-developed students to learn social behaviors and academic skills from more expert peers; they allow older students to develop self-confidence and to demonstrate and deepen their competence. Arrangements that keep students with the same teacher for more than one year, give students a better chance to learn classroom norms and develop at their own pace and teachers a better chance to know students and their families. Research shows that the teaching and grouping strategies used in such settings help schools avoid tracking, labeling, and retaining students who need more time than others to develop in certain areas, and increase these students' eventual success (Anderson & Pavan, 1993).

Finally, multilevel groups enable students who are newer to certain tasks to learn more effectively, because they can see models of more skilled performances and undertake mini-apprenticeships with more experienced peers. More expert students learn more deeply when they teach what they know to others. And in a classroom that attends to a range of performances, intelligences, and interests, virtually every student has something to contribute that she is particularly knowledgeable about and something to learn from others that she did not know.

POLICY IMPLICATIONS OF OPPORTUNITIES FOR COLLABORATIVE LEARNING
Although heterogeneous collaborative settings can be extremely successful when they are well managed, orchestrating this kind of learning

takes planning, insight, and skill. Without careful structuring and guidance, groups can go awry. Some students may dominate. Others may appear to shirk or coast. Initially, students—like adults—have difficulty allocating and managing work. Therefore structuring cooperative learning demands knowledge of collaborative teaching strategies as well as an understanding of learning and development (Slavin, 1990; Cohen, 1986). In addition, supports for specific kinds of skill learning are still needed, and a blend of individual and collective activity must be arranged.

Like many other changes that enhance successful learning, the shift to collaborative learning depends on changes in policies. We need policies that on the one hand do not assume a single approach to school organization and on the other hand support a stronger base of teacher knowledge for this more complex kind of practice.

A Collective Perspective Across the School

On the first day of middle school, most students move through six or eight teachers' classrooms, trying to "psych out" each teacher's philosophy of education and view of what counts. One may demand painstaking adherence to the way in which facts and definitions are presented in the textbook; another may ask for critical thinking; still another may emphasize neatness and proper use of conventions. The basis for grading is often mysterious. "I give a zero if your name is not on the paper," says one. "I look for your independent opinion," says another. The norms of interaction also differ. Some teachers exhibit care and respect for students; others are demeaning or even cruel. Some create democratic classrooms, but others believe their role requires an authoritarian stance. Over the course of this day—and indeed over their entire school careers—students have to make sense of an inconsistent potpourri of varying standards, which are often largely tacit to boot. A typical U.S. student encounters about sixty teachers before he graduates from high school, each of whom has different ideas about what matters and what counts. It is no wonder that students are often confused about what schools are trying to achieve and that they spend more effort trying to figure out how to get by than how to develop deep understanding or high-quality performance.

SHARED NORMS   Research on extraordinarily successful schools has found that in contrast to those with individualistic norms, these schools have forged a sense of mission, a shared ethos, and common norms of instruction and civility (Coleman & Hoffer, 1987; for a review see Lee, Bryk, & Smith, 1993). Although such strong cultures may be easier to forge in elite private academies and Catholic schools, where they were discovered early on by researchers, some public schools have also created a sense of character and strongly shared commitments and have been equally successful at creating powerful learning for a wide range of students (Darling-Hammond, Ancess, & Falk, 1995; Hill, Foster, & Gendler, 1990).

Schools that are restructuring spend a great deal of time thinking through what they value, how they will know if they have achieved it, and what they must do to create connected learning experiences that will enable students to reach school goals. Essential Schools, for example, often engage in a process of "planning backwards" (McDonald, 1993) in developing their graduation requirements, asking, first, what kind of graduate do we want? Then, how do we get there? And finally, how will we know when we have arrived? This process results in both clarity of purpose and a shared view of what students ought to know and be able to do as a result of their education.

When common goals and commitments motivate school life, learning becomes more powerful because it is cumulative rather than disjointed. Students and teachers work toward habits that are practiced, reinforced, and supported until they become second nature. Rather than switching mind-sets several times each day and many times over the course of a school career, students can concentrate on developing their abilities, and teachers can collaborate with one another in helping them do so.

POLICY IMPLICATIONS OF A COLLECTIVE PERSPECTIVE ACROSS THE SCHOOL Policies that support the development of a collective perspective in schools include those that call upon each school to develop shared goals, standards, and assessments and enact them in collective practices. If each school is to develop a collective perspective, state agencies must delegate substantial responsibility for shaping instruction to local schools, so that staff and community members can argue through strategies and reach a strong consensus about how to proceed. It makes sense to hold schools accountable for results only if they have the opportunity to develop effective means. This process of debate, central to the work of successful restructuring efforts, is a necessary basis for collective action. If on the one hand all decisions are made externally, there is nothing to discuss within the school, and the grounds for shared action and accountability are removed. If on the other hand all referents for practice are internal to the school, there is little learning opportunity or creative tension to press for change. Schools' efforts to develop unifying practices are ignited by occasions for inquiring into school life and outcomes. School quality review processes in states like New York and California, for example, foster self-studies of schools and periodically send teams of practitioners to visit in the role of critical friends (see Chapter Eight). When site-based management and shared decision making occur alongside school reviews that take an outside-in look at practice, the juxtaposition produces a creative tension that energizes teachers', administrators', and community members' efforts toward ongoing inquiry and improvement.

Structures for Caring

Relationships matter for learning. Students' trust in their teachers helps them develop the commitment and motivation needed to tackle challenging learning tasks. Teachers' connections to and understanding of their students help those students develop the commitment and capacity to surmount the hurdles that accompany ambitious learning. Key to teacher-student connections are continuing relationships and mutual respect, conditions best supported in small school units.

CONTINUAL RELATIONSHIPS IN PERSONALIZED SETTINGS   For teachers to come to know the minds and hearts of students well and for students to develop real expertise, teachers and students must have extended time together. The importance of this continuity and closeness is seen in the result of the relationships between coaches and athletes over the years it takes to develop a team or between musicians and their teachers who study together for years to develop high-level performances. Success depends as much on the strength of these relationships—on coaches' intimate understanding of their students' emotional makeup and the motivation they activate by the commitment they have made—as on knowledge of students' learning styles and technical skills.

Unlike schools in many other countries where teachers often stay with their students for multiple years and multiple subjects, U.S. schools typically pass students off to different teachers for each grade and each subject and also for counseling and special programs. Just as teachers begin to know their students reasonably well, they must pass them on to someone else who must start all over again trying to figure out how they learn.

In contrast Japanese teachers stay with their students for at least two years. As one principal explains, "The first year you look and listen; then in the second year the real learning can begin" (Sato, 1994, p. 12). German teachers keep the same students for two to four years through 10th grade. A German principal who, like most European school heads, also teaches, explains: "We don't lose several weeks each September learning a new set of names, teaching the basic rules to a new set of students, and figuring out exactly what they learned the previous year; and we don't lose weeks at the end of the year packing students back up. Most importantly, teachers and students get to know each other—teachers get to know how each student learns, and students know which teachers they can go to for various kinds of help. The importance of this is incalculable" (Ratzki, 1988, p. 14).

In addition, because teachers in other countries serve as counselors, they know their students from a personal as well as an academic perspective. And because they work in teams, they can help each other solve problems related to individual students and to teaching. These arrangements turn out to be much more effective for learning— especially the intensive learning demanded by high standards—than the assembly-line strategies used by U.S. schools.

Learner-centered schools in the United States are creating new structures for organizing the work that students and teachers engage in. As I describe in the next chapter, these structures create more time each day and week for in-depth work as well as greater possibilities for long-term relationships. Evidence shows that better outcomes are achieved by "personal-communal" school models : smaller schools fostering common learning experiences; opportunities for cooperative work and continual relationships; and greater participation of parents, teachers, and students (for a review see Lee, Bryk, & Smith, 1993). A recent study of 820 high schools in the National Education Longitudinal Study database found that schools that had restructured to personalize education and develop collaborative learning structures for adults and students produced significantly higher achievement gains that were also much more equitably distributed (Lee & Smith, 1995). Their practices included keeping students in the same home-room or advisory group throughout high school, establishing smaller school units through school-within-a-school structures, forming interdisciplinary teaching teams, giving teachers common planning time, involving staff in schoolwide problem solving, involving parents, and fostering cooperative learning.

For more than thirty years studies of school organization have consistently found that small schools (with enrollments of roughly 300 to 600) promote higher student achievement, higher attendance, lower dropout rates, greater participation in school activities, more positive feelings toward self and school, more positive behavior, less violence and vandalism, and greater postschool success (Haller, 1992, 1993; Fowler, 1992; Howley & Huang, 1991; Howley, 1989; Green & Stevens, 1988; Lindsay, 1982, 1984; Oxley, 1989; Pittman & Haughwout, 1987; Garbarino, 1978). These outcomes are also found in settings where students have close sustained relationships with a smaller than average number of teachers throughout their school careers (National Institute of Education, 1977; Gottfredson & Daiger, 1979). Teachers can work for longer periods of time with smaller total numbers of students either by teaching a core curriculum to one or two groups of students rather than a single subject to several groups or by teaching the same students for more than one year. Schools in which students remain with a cohort of their peers also foster a sense of community and a set of continuing relationships that are important to learning and to the affiliations needed to sustain trust and effort. Trying is closely linked to the existence of structures and relationships for caring.

Deborah Meier (1995), the former principal of Central Park East Secondary School, explains why small schools work better for students and teachers:

> Small schools mean we can get to know a student's work—the way he or she thinks. . . . This requires seeing children over time. It means passing them in the hall before and after we have taught them, knowing their other teachers well, seeing them in many different settings and guises and thus developing a broader repertoire of ways to approach them. This close knowledge helps us demand more of them; we can be tougher without being insensitive or humiliating. It also means we know their moods and styles—who to touch in a comfort-

ing way and who to offer distance and space in times of stress. It means that every adult in the school feels responsible for every kid, and has insights that shared can open up a seemingly intractable situation to new possibilities. Knowing one's students matters, including—and perhaps especially—those who are hardest to know [p. 111].

New small high schools launched in New York City and Philadelphia in the last several years have already demonstrated that they produce greater engagement and academic success than the comprehensive high schools they are replacing (Darling-Hammond, Ancess, MacGregor, & Zuckerman, in press; Fine, 1994). Organizing people so they can create a community is essential to eliciting their commitment.

MUTUAL RESPECT Environments that attend to students as individuals also help heighten the probabilities that school relationships will be characterized by respect and caring rather than by demeaning interactions, threats, and sanctions. One of the principles of the Coalition of Essential Schools is that the tone of a school "should explicitly and self-consciously stress the values of unanxious expectation ('I won't threaten you, but I expect much of you'), of trust (unless it is abused), and of decency (the values of fairness, generosity, and tolerance)" (Sizer, 1992, p. 208). Such values become more plausible when teachers and other school staff know students well enough to base expectations on firsthand knowledge, when trust can be buttressed by shared experience, and when decency can be reinforced through the power of communal norms.

Milbrey McLaughlin (1994) reports that in the five years of research in secondary schools conducted by the Center for Research on the Context of Teaching, "students' expressions of 'invisibility' were chorus and refrain" in a majority of schools: "'Nobody knows my name.' 'Nobody cares if I show up or not.' 'I had to introduce myself to my math teacher at back-to-school night.' . . . Students told us 'the way teachers treat you as a student—or as a person actually,' counted more than any other factor in the school setting in determining their attachment to the school, their commitment to the school's goals and, by extension, the academic future they imagined for themselves" (p. 9).

In far too many schools, relationships between staff and students are characterized by mistrust manifested in authoritarian treatment, demeaning statements, and a plethora of petty rules that no one could fail to offend sooner or later: no hats, no entering the building before

8:20 A.M., no use of the library before or after school, no talking during lunch, no talking during class, no talking in a language other than English, no use of bathrooms during class time, no use of bathrooms between classes, and on and on. Detentions, suspensions, and withheld privileges are handed out for offenses large and small, especially to "lower-status" students. The first day of school in many places is spent describing the many ways students can be punished rather than making them feel welcome in this place where they must spend so much of their time. Students wonder aloud why adults could not just remind children how to behave. "Just tell me if I'm doing something wrong," pleaded one young boy at a school I visited.

This is not to say that real problems do not sometimes occur that require serious attention and appropriate consequences. However, they are less frequent where adults understand how to use students' normal drives toward affiliation and competence to engender positive attachments and self-responsibility (Ginott, 1970; Glasser, 1990; Faber & Mazlish, 1995). Authoritarian systems that rely on heavy-handed sanctions ultimately increase the level of student alienation and misbehavior and reduce possibilities for addressing problems constructively (Dornbusch, Ritter, Leiderman, Roberts, & Fraleigh, 1987). Many dozens of studies have confirmed that motivation, positive behavior, and learning are enhanced by strategies that support students' natural drives toward competence, self-esteem, and self-responsibility, but that reliance on extrinsic rewards and punishments ultimately undermines learning and psychological development because it reduces risk taking, willingness to tackle challenging work, the quality of performance, and the development of intrinsic motivation and self-discipline (Lepper & Greene, 1978; Lepper, 1981; Deci, 1976; Kohn, 1993).

The middle ground between permissiveness and authoritarianism is *authoritative* practice. Authoritative treatment sets limits and consequences within a context that fosters dialogue, explicit teaching about how to assume responsibility, and democratic decision making. Children and youths raised in authoritative homes and schools—environments characterized by warmth, discourse that encourages autonomy, and demands in the form of high expectations—are psychologically healthier and more prosocial in their behaviors than those raised in either authoritarian environments or permissive ones (Baumrind, 1967; Dornbusch, Ritter, Leiderman, Roberts, & Fraleigh, 1987).

Authoritative schools and households allow students to make choices and decisions, to take responsibility for the natural consequences of their actions, and to see things through. When problems occur in such environments, an honest effort to understand what happened is the first step in any exchange. Then decisions can be made about appropriate next steps: whether a parent should be called, a counselor involved, or a consequence devised. When a student needs parental support, counseling, and problem solving, the issues underlying his behavior can be addressed early rather than ignored. When a consequence is appropriate, it can be developed to respond to the real problem and to teach responsibility. For example, students who litter or deface property can be assigned to school beautification efforts. Students who cut class can spend time making up work with their teacher rather than being suspended. In these ways students are pulled further into the arms of the school rather than being pushed out. This makes it clear that the student has a responsibility to learn and that the school is deeply invested in ensuring that learning occurs.

In productive environments students and faculty often receive conflict resolution and mediation training so that conflicts do not escalate and can be resolved by negotiation rather than punishment (which by itself cannot teach new behaviors). Students participate in developing school rules so that they see the rules as fair. Once they have greater ownership in obeying the rules, they typically become willing participants and enforcers rather than violators. Often the students having the most difficulties are given the most responsibility as trained peer mediators, and they become helpful and constructive leaders when given a productive outlet (Glasser, 1990).

Although there are certainly some large schools that work closely with students in these ways, they are rare. In large impersonal institutions where employees carry difficult case loads and relationships are not sufficiently strong to allow firsthand knowledge of people, it is easy to come to believe that elaborate rules and sanctions are the only way to survive and maintain control. Every rule is a response to something that went wrong at least once or to a theory that it will surely go wrong if not prevented. Large schools often convey the message that they need to defend themselves *against* students; they cannot afford to be *for* students. In contrast, consider Deborah Meier's description of how rules are forged at small democratic schools like Central Park East Secondary School:

> Issues of behavior, school management, and student/teacher relations occupy our attention. We spent a good deal of time debating student

"dress codes," mostly shall they or shan't they be allowed to wear hats. But even this issue was argued on terms that allowed students to join us. People brought in articles about the impact of clothes and raised issues about the importance (or not) of worrying about how others see us and whether our informality would make it harder for kids to shift to more formal ways of dressing in more formal workplaces. The opponents of dress codes eventually won, but supporters occasionally still submit interesting pieces of evidence for their side [1995, p. 110].

Authoritarian schools pursue control through imposed rules. Authoritative schools pursue mutual respect for democratically made decisions.

POLICY IMPLICATIONS OF STRUCTURES FOR CARING   The process of engaging school members in discourse and decision making builds thoughtfulness and respect that translate into positive social learning. Developing more humane and psychologically healthy schools requires school structures and strategies that allow for the enactment of caring and the teaching of caring. These depend in turn on policies that strengthen educator preparation, promote personalization of schools so that greater intimacy and understanding are possible, and establish a curriculum that develops respect and empathy. As Meier observes:

> If we want children to be caring and compassionate, then we must provide a place for growing up in which effective care is feasible. Creating such intimate schools is possible even in an existing system of large buildings if we create smaller communities within them. . . .
>   Caring and compassion are not soft, mushy goals. They are part of the hard core of subjects we are responsible for teaching. Informed and skillful care is learned. Caring is as much cognitive as affective. The capacity to see the world as others might is central to unsentimental compassion and at the root of both intellectual skepticism and empathy. . . . Such empathetic qualities are precisely the habits of mind that require deliberate cultivation—that is, schooling [1995, p. 63].

The need to develop trusting and respectful relationships between and among adults and students in order to foster learning overlaps with democratic education's goals of helping students to learn decision-making skills and to understand and respect the rights and views of others. Ultimately, the task of developing healthy schools is the task of fashioning education as democracy.

Support for Democratic Learning

At some level, Americans understand the importance of public education to democracy—the necessity for all children to have at least a minimal education, learning the rudiments of citizenship and a means of making a livelihood. However, the more fundamental need is to prepare people for active participation in social decisions and for a productive shared life with fellow citizens. Few seem troubled by the fact that U.S. schools rarely enact democratic life within their boundaries, that they are more often authoritarian than participative and more frequently segregative by social class, race, and culture than integrative. That the only social institution charged with teaching children for democracy does not teach democratically should be a matter of grave concern for us all.

Democratic education is deeply social—an education that as John Dewey (1916) suggested, enables a person "to live as a social member so that what he gets from living with others balances with what he contributes. What he gets and gives as a human being, a being with desires, emotions, and ideas, is not external possessions, but a widening and deepening of conscious life—a more intense, disciplined, and expanding realization of meanings" (p. 360).

ACCESS TO DEMOCRATIC PARTICIPATION If schools are to be agents of democracy, they must provide access to knowledge that enables creative thought and access to a social dialogue that enables democratic communication and participation. Yet both are denied students in most large bureaucratic schools that segregate students into rigid tracks, consign many of them to a passive, deadening curriculum, minimize personal relationships among adults and students, and substitute predetermined procedures for participation in deciding what school should be.

Recent critiques of bureaucratic schooling have noted the dysfunctional consequences of emphasizing external rather than internal controls, management rather than engagement of teachers and students (McNeil, 1986), and compliance achieved through coercion rather than ownership (Glasser, 1984). Such practices establish a single official knowledge, allow only one voice, undermine autonomy, and silence diversity and difference (Apple, 1990; Greene, 1992), thus preparing students to accept inequality and authoritarianism. Many classrooms, especially those serving low-track students, are organized for conformity and compliance rather than democratic thinking: they are characterized by a noninvolving autocratic atmosphere and few opportunities to deliberate, think critically, express and examine views, or engage in decision making (Goodlad, 1984; Oakes, 1985). Meanwhile a small number of high-track students receive high-status knowledge and the skills required for higher education and for positions of power and leadership. High-track classes are organized for student independence, engagement, and critical thinking, the skills necessary for effective participation in democracy. But all students, not just a "talented tenth," need access to these skills.

Education for democracy requires more than equal access to technical knowledge. It requires access to social knowledge and understanding forged by participation in a democratic community. How people are grouped for teaching and learning and for participation in decision making is important, what they are asked to participate in is important, and how they are asked to participate is important. In *Democracy and Education,* Dewey (1916) stated that "a democracy is more than a form of government; it is primarily a mode of associated living, of joint communicate experience" (p. 87). He spoke of the building of and extension of associations as one of the ways by which we should evaluate social modes of life, including schools. Given that a society is an association with shared interests and that all of us belong to a wide variety of societies of different kinds, we can gauge the worth of these associations by asking, first, "how numerous and varied are the interests which are consciously shared?" and, second, "how full and free is the interplay with other forms of association?" (Dewey, 1916, p. 83). How integrative are these associations? How much do they strive to make connections with other groups' perspectives and sets of interests? Dewey also declared that "in order to have a large number of values in common, all the members of the group must have an equitable opportunity to receive and to take from others. There must be a large variety of shared undertakings and experiences. Otherwise, the influences which educate some into masters educate others into slaves. And the experience of each party loses in meaning, when the free interchange of varying modes of life experiences is arrested" (p. 84).

A communication that is, in Dewey's words, "vitally social or vitally shared" is one that allows each person to experience the perspectives of another and by that connection to develop understanding and appreciation for that person's experience and understanding of the world:

> There is more than a verbal tie between the words common, community, and communication. [People] live in a community in virtue of the things which they have in common; and communication is the way in which they come to possess things in common. . . . Not only is social life identical with communication, but all communication (and hence all genuine social life) is educative. To be a recipient of a communication is to have an enlarged and changed experience. One shares in what another has thought and felt and in so far, meagerly or amply, has his own attitude modified [pp. 4, 6].

Seeking out the perspectives of others helps us avoid what Edmund Gordon and colleagues (1990) call "communicentric bias: the tendency to make one's own community the center of the universe and the conceptual frame that constrains thought" (p. 19). Just as early astronomers' belief that the earth was at the center of the universe constrained knowledge about the realities of the universe, making Copernicus's ideas appear threatening and divisive, so a reluctance to seek out multiple perspectives constrains understanding of what is real and what is possible in our social life.

Democratic education demands a "Copernican shift" (Dewey, [1900] 1956) in worldview, a chance to seek richer truths in more varied contexts, to more fully understand each other, and ultimately to create more vitally social communities. Appreciations of other perspectives are the foundation for the broader *shared* perspective that allows us to form communities and societies. Paradoxically, it is only by acknowledging the legitimacy of diverse points of view that we can begin the work of forging a common point of view that takes account of others.

POLICY IMPLICATIONS OF SUPPORT FOR DEMOCRATIC LEARNING   Democratic schools seek to create as many shared experiences and as many avenues of discourse for diverse groups of students as possible. Because they avoid blanket tracking, such schools not only provide a more equal education with greater learning opportunities and markedly better outcomes (Fine, 1994; Lee & Bryk, 1988; Darling-Hammond, Ancess, & Falk, 1995) but also respond to the need all

people feel to find a place in which their experiences can be acknowledged and affirmed. A democratic pedagogy (Glickman, in press) supports freedom of expression, inclusion of multiple perspectives,
opportunities to evaluate ideas and make choices, and opportunities
to take on responsibility and contribute to the greater good. Because
democracy must be lived to be learned, democratic classrooms can be
developed only in inclusive organizations that encourage broad participation of students, parents, teachers, and community members.

The policies that encourage schools to accommodate diversity in
classroom learning will also support democratic learning if practitioners are prepared to develop discipline policies and construct pedagogies that allow for student participation. It is worth noting here that
changes in policies that categorize and track students can have multiple beneficial effects, supporting many aspects of learner- and learning-centered schooling. However, the success of such changes is only as
probable as the strength of educators' preparation for complex, responsive forms of practice.

Connections to Family and Community

Finally, schools need to build connections to families and communities as a means of deepening the relationships that support child development and of acquiring the knowledge about students needed to
teach responsively. James Comer (1994) explains the relationships
needed for healthy child development this way:

> A child develops a strong emotional bond to competent caretakers—
> usually parents—that enables them to help that child develop . . . in
> social, psychological, emotional, moral, linguistic and cognitive areas
> [that] are critical for future academic learning. The attitudes, values
> and behaviors of the family and its social network strongly affect such
> development. A child whose development meshes with the main-
> stream values encountered at school will be prepared to achieve at the
> level of his or her ability. In addition, the meshing of home and school
> fosters development: When a child's social skills are considered ap-
> propriate by the teacher, they elicit positive reactions. A bond devel-
> ops between the child and the teacher, who can now join in supporting
> the overall development of the child [p. 2].

Where there are gaps in the developmental preparation of the child or significant differences between the norms and expectations of home and school, disjunctures result that can lead to school failure. However, if schools are able to reach out successfully and become partners with families, teachers and parents can create common ground for child development that bridges differences and creates mutually supportive practices in the home and school.

Though it is important for parents to be represented on decision-making committees and involved in setting school direction, what parents most need and most want are closer connections to the learning process for their individual child. In many restructured schools, faculties build parent support for and understanding of classroom work through frequent parent conferences, reviews and displays of students' work, and involvement in classroom activities and school workshops, all of which include parents in their children's development and the work of the school.

When parent engagement extends beyond the bake sale and when students and their work are at the center of the conversation, teachers and parents can focus together on how children are learning. Both can offer observations about students' strategies, paces, and styles of learning; their different strengths and experiences; the ways they express what they know; and the kinds of teaching strategies effective for them. When teachers' insights are supported by parents' insights, teachers can more easily connect students' experiences to curriculum goals.

In a growing number of schools authentic assessment practices support stronger communication with parents. For example, assessments like the Primary Language Record (PLR) formally elicit parents' knowledge about their children (Darling-Hammond, Ancess, & Falk, 1995). In interviews parents are asked what each child reads, writes, and talks about at home and what changes or developments the parents have noticed. Samples of the child's work stimulate further conversation about what the child is doing and learning. As parents reflect and report on the child's literacy behaviors in response to the teacher's focused questions, they become more conscious of how literacy develops and of their role in supporting it. Teachers in turn gain more knowledge about the child and his or her family context. Teacher Alina Alvarez from PS 261 in New York City describes her experience with the process this way:

As part of my PLR work, I interviewed the parents of all the children in my class. I always thought I had respect for parents, but I was amazed at how much I could learn from them about their kids in general and about their literacy development in particular. . . . I [also] gained a heightened awareness of and respect for their backgrounds and cultures. I learned to listen to parents differently and to help them develop a positive, sometimes different, perspective on their child by reflecting back to them what they already know. This has enabled me to develop a partnership, rather than a one-sided relationship in which I am the expert telling them what I know [Darling-Hammond, Ancess, & Falk, 1995, pp. 186–187].

Similar insights occur when parents and teachers meet to examine students' portfolios and when families are involved in students' exhibitions of their work. The resulting conversations enable teachers to better understand family contexts and enable parents to view their children in new ways and to appreciate the school's efforts and goals (Darling-Hammond, Ancess, & Falk, 1995).

Finally, schools can connect with the community through continuing educational programs for adults, student internships with local businesses, collaborations with community-based recreation and youth service organizations, and partnerships with health care and social service agencies. These activities integrate some of the different parts of students' lives, so that students feel rooted in the community and the school at the same time and nurtured in communities of caring (McLaughlin, Irby, & Langman, 1994). Other organizations can complement and reinforce a school's efforts and often can create certain bridges to homes and families that are difficult for schools to establish. In these times when neighborhoods are less communal than in the past and especially in highly stressed locations, explicit efforts to build community are needed to keep students connected to education and connected to their futures.

REFORM AND POLICY CHANGE

Teaching and learning for understanding does take place in some U.S. schools and could take place in all of them if they organized their work in ways that we now know improves students' motivation and achievement. Successful schools feature in-depth, active learning, emphasis on authentic performance, attention to development, appreciation for diversity, opportunities for collaborative learning, a collective perspective across the school, structures for caring, support for democratic learning, and connections to family and community.

However, these traits will not be universal in our schools until school policies change. Policies do not support teaching for understanding when they require passive learning of reams of facts and bits of skills, require standardized teaching for students who differ in how they learn and how much they have already learned, prescribe time blocks for teaching irrespective of subject matter or teaching method, prevent teachers from learning about students as individuals, assess students with multiple-choice norm-referenced tests and teachers by how well their students do on these tests, set school practices from the top down, allow glaring inequities in resources for education, and fail to invest in teacher learning.

None of the reforms described in this chapter are easy; nor can they be undertaken one piece at a time, because changes in any one aspect of schooling affect all the others. That is why focusing schools on children rather than on the demands of schedules, course guides, and procedures requires a Copernican shift in the worldviews of educators and policymakers alike.

Traditional assumptions about how people learn and behave are not easily replaced by new ones that posit multiple intelligences, intrinsic motivation for competence, and construction of ideas. Long-standing structures are difficult to transform, as are the habits of work they have created. All of these changes require more knowledge and skill, more willingness to act collectively, and more commitment to a common set of goals than traditional schooling demands. A romantic rush of enthusiasm alone is not enough to sustain the hard work needed.

Many restructuring initiatives have begun with experiments in governance like school-based management and shared decision making intended to encourage bottom-up initiative and ownership of change. These are important starting points, but they must be supported by structures that help schools develop a capacity to innovate and learn from their collective experience. In the next chapter I describe how successful schools that have developed all the qualities discussed here are able to organize themselves to sustain this kind of work. Then I turn my attention to the systemic changes needed to grow up these kinds of schools in every community.

## CHAPTER FIVE

Structuring Learner-Centered Schools

The kinds of changes required by today's agenda can only be the work of thoughtful teachers. . . . To find time for thoughtful discussion we need to create schools in which consensus is easy to arrive at while argument is encouraged (even fostered) and focused on those issues of teaching and learning close to teacher and student experiences, rather than on procedural rules and processes, building-wide disciplinary codes, detention policies, filling out forms and checklists, scheduling, etc. . . . This continuing dialogue, face to face, over and over, is a powerful educative force. It is our primary form of staff development.

—Deborah Meier, *The Power of Their Ideas*
(1995, pp. 108–109)

Behind the scenes in schools that have successfully restructured are new kinds of relationships and conversations among teachers, principals, and other staff, supported by new organizational structures that allow all these individuals to work together in ways very different from those they once used. The subtle effects of these supports can be sensed in a school that privileges learning for students and teachers, although much probing is needed to understand how they operate.

Despite the diversity of American life and inequities arising from local control of schools, many observers have noted how much alike most schools are. In the typical school the office is the first thing one sees, the quietest and best-outfitted part of the school, a forbidding place with its long high counter separating the office staff from others who enter. The next sight is a glass-enclosed trophy case and a bulletin board of announcements about meetings, sports events, and rules to be followed. Long clear corridors of egg-crate classrooms are broken by banks of lockers and an occasional tidy bulletin board. Classrooms look alike, teachers' desks at the front of each room commanding the rows of smaller desks for students. The teachers themselves work independently, their time and efforts managed by periodic bells that structure classes and duties and by the announcements boomed by the loudspeaker. Occasional faculty meetings ensure that further announcements are shared. Otherwise teachers make their way through the day largely isolated from colleagues.

Schools that are successfully reinventing teaching and learning look quite different. The office is often difficult to find, stashed away in a corner, full of desks and curriculum materials that mark working spaces for both teachers and administrators. Students and parents enter the office comfortably with questions and announcements of their own: the place belongs to them too. Symbolically, office, hallway, and classroom walls are plastered with student work: writing, designs, models, and artwork are everywhere along with notices of conferences, workshops, and other learning events. Classrooms usually have clusters of desks or tables; the teacher's desk often sits at the back. Handmade models of planets or skeletons hang from the ceilings. Graphs and charts, explanations, questions, and classroom constitutions written by students adorn walls. Wooden cubbies provide a home for students' things. Teachers frequently work in teams and visit one another's classrooms. Teacher workrooms host planning meetings throughout the day. Classes and hallways are busy but more relaxed than in traditional schools, because class periods are longer, classes change infrequently, and announcements over the public address system are rare. Most communication occurs during faculty teams' and committees' regular meetings and through the collectively compiled school newsletter.

Equally important, largely invisible organizational features make teaching for understanding possible by structuring teachers' and students' work together more productively. In particular, schools that reach diverse learners effectively have restructured accountability and assessment, the organization of learning groups, decision-making processes, and staffing approaches. Without these structural changes, the practices described in the previous chapter would be impossible to develop and sustain over time.

MORE THAN CHARISMA: STRUCTURES FOR SUCCESS

There is a tendency to dismiss high-performing schools—especially those that succeed with poor and minority students—as the anomalous results of charismatic leaders or bands of unusual teachers. This view suggests that successful schools cannot become widespread, and it obscures the lessons these schools offer about structures that support student success. Although there is no one cookie-cutter approach to school reform, no packaged program that can be adopted off the shelf, common features of successful schools have emerged from recent research. In this chapter I describe the structural features of these schools. They include a collective set of goals, commitments, and practices enacted throughout the school; small continual learning groups for students and teachers, shared governance coupled with teaching teams, time for teachers to collaborate and learn together, and a rich array of learning opportunities for all members of the school community (for reviews see Lee, Bryk, & Smith, 1993; Newmann & Wehlage, 1995; Darling-Hammond, Ancess, & Falk, 1995; Murnane & Levy, 1996a).

Although each school creates approaches that make sense in its local context, as this chapter illustrates, these approaches are always the result of active deliberation among teachers, parents, and students about their goals and needs. Explicit goals for student learning and shared, schoolwide values are the framework for restructuring. They help maintain a press for ambitious teaching and academic achievement along with keen attention to students and their needs. Each school has created ways to know students well and to engage in ongoing inquiry as a basis for continual improvement.

The approaches of successful restructured schools exhibit striking parallels with the organizational strategies of "high-performance, high-involvement" corporations that have decentralized power, knowledge, information, and rewards (Lawler, 1986; Wohlstetter, Smyer, & Mohrman, 1994). Both kinds of organizations reduce specialization and develop teams that give workers more authority, greater opportunity to learn, and enhanced capacity to succeed. Some have compared the workings of these schools to the operations of businesses that use W. Edwards Deming's Total Quality Management principles (Schmoker & Wilson, 1993), due to the schools' emphasis on teamwork, investment in ongoing training, "constancy of purpose," and collaborative decision making based on data collected by team members. It is not, however, that most restructured schools are deliberately implementing Deming's principles. Their work began long before TQM had become a buzzword or a passing fad. Rather, businesses and schools that are becoming learning organizations are operating from the same principles about human performance and motivation that psychologists have affirmed for decades: that most people are motivated much more by the opportunity to make a difference and the satisfaction of doing well than by extrinsic rewards and sanctions, that information about performance and outcomes enhances learning, that a sense of efficacy grows when people are able to control and influence their work, and that collaboration improves performance.

What about the incentives found in restructured schools? What keeps this work going? What inspires teachers to do so much more than the system seems to expect of schools generally and of those serving low-income students of color especially? What inspires students to work harder and attain more than their peers in other schools? Are these just the extraordinary actions of irreplicable folks? As I describe here, incentives that speak to the fundamental motives of teachers and students are built into these new organizational structures. The incentives for teachers are the opportunity to achieve greater rewards by doing well with students and continually learning from one another. The incentives for students are the opportunities to be cared for and to become competent. These incentives are available because new structures give teachers much greater time with students and control over students' overall school experience, which gives students a greater likelihood of success. The new structures also give students much greater opportunity to be known and to learn well.

The combined result of publicly appraised learning goals, a set of well-developed structures and participatory processes for achieving these goals, and deeply embedded incentives for maintaining them is a highly effective system for learner-centered accountability—one that ensures that students make progress in their learning and do not fall through cracks in the schooling process.

Scaling up New-Model Schools

That common strategies for restructuring schools can succeed and spread is demonstrated by the experience of a rapidly expanding group of small alternative schools in New York City. These schools began as a handful of success stories during the 1980s and now number well over one hundred. They are leading the process of redefining public education through their individual and collective efforts, sometimes in partnership with and sometimes at odds with the New York City Board of Education.

A number of studies conducted by the National Center for Restructuring Education, Schools, and Teaching (NCREST), at Teachers College, Columbia University, have documented the work and outcomes of many of these schools, detailing the high success rates of students who would have been labeled at-risk in traditional schools and analyzing the structures and practices that support this success (Ancess, 1995; Darling-Hammond, Ancess, & Falk, 1995; Darling-Hammond et al., 1993, Darling-Hammond, Ancess, MacGregor, & Zuckerman, in press; Lieberman, Falk, & Alexander, 1994; Snyder, Lieberman, Macdonald, & Goodwin, 1992). The discussion in this chapter draws substantially on these studies.

I focus here on the organizational arrangements created by the earliest of these schools. These structures have been used as models for many other reformed schools and have proved to be robust, producing similar success for other schools in New York and elsewhere.

The story begins with a remarkable cross-school collaboration. In the 1980s, a group of restructured schools holding similar values joined together to create the Center for Collaborative Education (CCE), a network that sponsors cooperative work on school renewal, professional development, and community education. Some of the original schools, like Central Park East, had been started from scratch. Others had been "regular" public schools that reshaped themselves to create more learner-centered settings. All became affiliated with the nationwide Coalition of Essential Schools as well as with their local network. Like many such teacher-to-teacher and school-to-school networks, CCE helps teachers and principals expand their knowledge and their vision for education, engage in shared problem solving, and gain the moral and financial supports needed to continue the tough work of urban school reform.

In 1992, this network, which then numbered thirty schools, took on the task of reconfiguring the buildings of two large failing high schools so that they could eventually house groups of smaller schools and other social service organizations. Existing schools helped to birth twelve new ones in this Coalition Campus Schools Project. The network also helped the new schools develop curriculum and school policy, secure space and supplies, and negotiate with the board of education. In return, working with the new schools offered the established schools a means of reflecting on and improving their own practice.

The first batch of six new schools was launched in 1993, serving many of the 9th-grade students at the Julia Richman High School—the 2,400-student comprehensive school being replaced—and other students from across the city. As the recruitment process worked out, a greater proportion of the new schools' students were eligible for special education and Chapter 1 compensatory education assistance than had been true in the old comprehensive school. Nonetheless, within the first year—despite all the problems of finding space, recruiting students, hiring staff, and overcoming innumerable bureaucratic hassles—the new schools had demonstrated they could engender more student engagement and much less academic failure than had their predecessor. As one indicator of success, for example, the new schools registered an average attendance rate for their 9th graders of 88.5 percent by December 1993 as compared to an attendance rate of only 66 percent for 9th graders at Julia Richman High School the year before, a statistic related to the former comprehensive school's dropout rate of over 60 percent (Darling-Hammond, Ancess, MacGregor, & Zuckerman, in press).

By spring of 1996, the partially reconfigured Julia Richman campus included four small high schools plus a medical clinic. It also includes the Ella Barker K–8 school, an infant-toddler nursery, a teen parent resource center, and a professional development institute. (Two of the new schools plus several "old" ones moved into the site. The other new schools are housed at a variety of other sites.) Meanwhile, a second campus in the Bronx is following suit. Thus the project is beginning to reconceive the structure and function of large school buildings as well as the nature of high schools.

This work is part of a much larger citywide initiative in which the New York City Board of Education launched more than fifty small new-model high schools between 1992 and 1995. In 1995, the Center for Collaborative Education took on the even more ambitious task of creating an additional fifty new schools in partnership with three other reform organizations, as part of Walter Annenberg's multimillion-dollar challenge to recreate schools in several cities across the nation.

These combined initiatives have created an environment in which local community districts in New York City, along with community-based organizations and groups of educators, have launched or restructured literally hundreds of schools. These reformers are nudging U.S. education into the twenty-first century by reinventing schools as small personalized communities of learners in the very city where schools as large impersonal bureaucracies were perfected one hundred years ago.

EVIDENCE OF SUCCESS   Among the "older" schools begun in the 1980s, the results are striking: serving primarily low-income students of color and recent immigrants, the high schools produce graduation and college-going rates of over 90 percent, and the elementary schools produce high levels of academic attainment as measured by their early grades' progress and the placements of their students in programs for the "gifted" and in selective high schools when they reach later grades.

Because the results obtained by these schools so confound the prevailing assumptions about schooling and urban youth, it is especially important to understand how they succeed. In the remainder of this chapter, I focus on four of the high schools: Central Park East Secondary School, International High School, Manhattan International High School, and the Urban Academy.

Central Park East Secondary School (CPESS) was created in 1985 in part to provide a high school compatible with the elementary school experience of many of Central Park East Elementary's students. Eighty-five percent of the students in grades 7 to 12 were from Latino and African American families, living mostly in the neighboring East Harlem community; 60 percent qualified for free or reduced-price lunch; and about 25 percent were eligible for special education services. Had these students attended a neighborhood comprehensive high school, their chances of graduating within five years would have been about 50 percent, and their chances of going to college would have been less than half that. Yet every one of the first class of graduates in 1991 was accepted to postsecondary education, more than

90 percent of them to four-year colleges. Graduation and college-going rates have remained over 90 percent in the years since.

International High School (IHS) in Queens, which accepts only recent immigrants who score below the 20th percentile on New York City's language achievement battery, produces similar success. In 1992, International served 459 students from fifty-four countries who spoke thirty-nine languages and represented a wide range of native and English language proficiencies. Over 75 percent were Latino, Asian, or black children; 75 percent also qualified for free or reduced-price lunch. Through active, collaborative, interdisciplinary instruction, IHS enables students to learn English while engaged in rigorous academics. Like CPESS, International was founded in 1985 and has had graduation and college admissions rates exceeding 90 percent since its first graduating class in 1988. In the past three years International has helped to launch two new schools serving similar populations of students, one in Manhattan in 1993 and one in Brooklyn in 1995. Only three years later the first of these already has a strong record of academic success. The other is off to an auspicious start.

The Urban Academy in Manhattan serves students who generally have dropped out of or experienced failure in other high schools. The school is designed to personalize coursework and advisement to the greatest extent possible, and it, too, produces success for students for whom failure had been the norm. Serving mostly low-income and minority students, many of them once at risk of dropping out, the school sees more than 90 percent of its graduates accepted to college.

COMMON COMMITMENTS   It is noteworthy that the CCE schools, both elementary and secondary, have achieved success using similar organizational features and educational commitments, even though they do so in diverse ways. Each school has arrived at different manifestations of twelve principles they all hold in common. The principles emphasize the following characteristics: (1) *school purposes* ("helping young people learn to use their minds well"), (2) high and universal *academic standards,* (3) *interdisciplinary, multicultural curriculum* focused on powerful ideas, (4) *small size and personalization,* (5) commitment to a goal of *student-as-worker* and *student-as-citizen,* (6) *performance-based assessment* aimed at clearly stated competencies, (7) *respectful tone and values* that emphasize unanxious expectation and decency, (8) *family involvement,* (9) *shared decision making,* (10) *commitment to diversity* among students and staff, (11) selection of the school by *student choice,* and (12) administrative and budget targets featuring a *reduced student load and shared planning time for teachers* and a *budget comparable to that of other schools.*

These shared commitments are enacted through a set of organizational arrangements that provoke collective accountability and assessment of student learning according to shared standards; learning groups organized for personalization and continuity; decision making structured for maximum participation and shared access to knowledge and information; and staffing managed so that most staff attend to teaching, the organization's core work, and take responsibility for continual direct work with students.

Restructuring Accountability and Assessment

One notable feature of these schools is the extent to which they have worked through a collective set of beliefs and goals for learning that is represented in graduation standards and performance exhibitions evaluated by groups of teachers. They have used national professional standards and their own collective knowledge to develop curricula that reflect widely touted reform ideals. Together and separately, the schools have evaluated the implications of the National Council of Teachers of Mathematics (NCTM) standards for their mathematics curricula, developed whole language approaches to literacy development, and created inquiry-oriented science and social studies curricula.

Designated as New York State Partnership schools to work as demonstration sites with the New York State Department of Education, the schools have been freed from many state regulations and authorized to create their own accountability systems. The innovative curriculum and assessment efforts of several of the original CCE schools served as exemplars for the state's initial rethinking of its of curriculum and assessment practices (New York State Council on Curriculum and Assessment, 1994). Portfolio and performance assessment models from CPESS, International High School, and the Urban Academy are serving as the first entries in the state's new Assessment Collection, a computerized database that provides examples of authentic assessments to school districts across the state.

At CPESS, students' intellectual development is guided by five "habits of mind": the abilities to weigh and use evidence, to see and understand differing viewpoints, to see connections and relationships, to imagine alternatives, and to assess implications and effects. These intellectual habits permeate the entire curriculum and the evaluations of student work. They are incorporated in the assessment criteria for the required graduation portfolio, which specify the kind of work that must be presented in fourteen curriculum areas ranging from science and technology to ethics and social issues, and from school and community service to mathematics, literature, and history.

Over two or more years students complete science experiments, research reports, literary critiques, mathematical models, artwork, videos, and other pieces of work as part of the portfolio. After many revisions this weighty collection is evaluated by a graduation committee composed of teachers from different subjects and grade levels, an outside examiner, and a student peer, who examine all fourteen entries and hear the student's oral defense of seven. Passing is not pro forma. Portfolios are rigorously evaluated and often sent back for more work; students learn what it takes to develop a piece of work that meets the standards of inquiry in a field and the standards of written and oral discourse demanded by committee members. They get feedback and revise and revise and revise; they internalize the standards; they develop the capacity for sustained effort and ambitious work (Darling-Hammond, Ancess, & Falk, 1995). As one recent graduate, now in college, described the effect of the portfolio on her current abilities: "It's worth all the work you do in 12th grade. It prepares you for college. The outcome is that we're able to tell somebody what we think. We can think critically, go in-depth, and research things on our own. We can express our viewpoint and back it up."

In like fashion, students at the Urban Academy must demonstrate their competence to teachers, students, and outside examiners in six areas: an original science experiment, a mathematical application, a literary discussion, a social science research paper, an artistic critique, and a creative work. They must also demonstrate that they have made positive contributions to the school community and to the community at large and have met a high standard of participation in class work, that they have maintained a record of independent reading, can negotiate library searches, and are proficient in the use of computers.

At both CPESS and the Urban Academy, because staff from all grade levels serve on graduation committees, the committee meetings are a moment of truth in which all the members of the school community can see the fruits of their labors. There is no escaping what has worked, what has not worked, and what needs more work. Lower-grades teachers are much more aware of what they need to do to prepare students to succeed on their portfolios. Upper-grades teachers can evaluate how to support students' next efforts and how to strengthen instruction and coaching overall. Staff also get feedback on their standards as applied to student work from external reviewers—college teachers, assessment experts, and others—who meet to review the work and discuss whether it reflects high standards.

The assessments stimulate a high level of curricular coherence around goals and standards and also supply examples of high-quality work. The public exhibition of student work brings focus to the educational experience and becomes a concrete vehicle for staff collaboration and development. Use of the standards strengthens shared goals and values and the sense of the school as a coherent entity with common direction.

CPESS teacher Edwina Branch notes that "developing standards for portfolios makes teachers think about what they're doing in their classrooms." She feels she and her colleagues have strengthened the curriculum to meet the standards, and she constantly uses the portfolio scoring grid, based on the five habits of mind, as a way to talk to students about the criteria they should be applying. Branch describes how

> Teachers pushed each other to answer why are we doing this? and what do we want kids to get out of it? [Assessment] is understood to be something we need as an entire school. . . . I can't imagine right now trying to teach without thinking about assessment all the time. It's easier to be in your own little world and not be accountable to anybody. It's much easier for me to be in this room doing what I want. But it's not the best thing for the kids, and it's not really the best thing for my teaching [Darling-Hammond, Ancess, & Falk, 1995, p. 54].

Faculty find that the assessment processes raise schoolwide questions for them to work on: What must the school do to help students produce work of depth and quality? What must happen in classes and in advisories, resource rooms, and elsewhere? Do new courses or other supports, such as writing labs, need to be invented? Deborah Meier notes that the process of working through portfolio requirements, standards, and evaluations motivates improvement of teaching across the entire school. By tackling the question of graduation standards with authentic examples of student work as the focus of the conversations, "we've created a school that's more collective in its practice" (Darling-Hammond, Ancess, & Falk, 1995, p. 63).

Schoolwide processes of defining standards, making student work public, and taking responsibility for developing high-quality performance are all part of developing an accountability ethic and standards of practice.

Restructuring Learning Groups

Ambitious learning requires school structures that provide time for the more complex teaching and relationships that give serious ongoing assistance to learners. It is ludicrous to expect secondary school teachers who see 150 students daily in forty-two-minute segments for a single semester or year to come to know the minds of any of them particularly well or to tackle difficult sustained work with them. Teachers are not to blame for this state of affairs, although they typically are exhorted to do things such as attending to the individual needs of students that the organizations they work in make impossible. The master schedule—indeed the master of all possibilities in schools—must change before schools and teachers can support serious teaching and learning.

STRUCTURES FOR LEARNING   At CPESS and a number of other new schools that have adopted the same organization, students are grouped within "houses" of four to five teachers and seventy-five to eighty students each. They remain with the teachers and students in their house for two years, until they "move up" to the next division (the three divisions serve students in what would traditionally be grades 7 and 8, 9 and 10, and 11 and 12).

In grades 7 to 10, each teacher is responsible for two subject areas—math and science or social studies and English—which are taught together in two-hour blocks of time to two groups of students each day. Teachers also counsel students and take care of certain governance responsibilities. As I describe in the next chapter, this practice is made possible by a redesigned approach to staffing and scheduling. As a result of reorganizing teacher work, class size averages 18 students and the total student load per teacher is 36—in contrast to the 150 or more common in most high schools.

At International and Manhattan International High School, staff are divided into several clusters of four to six teachers each. For each interdisciplinary cluster, a team of teachers takes complete responsibility for a group of about sixty-five to seventy-five students each term. These groups of students are in turn divided into "strands" of about twenty-five students who spend all day with each other during that term. Teachers within each cluster plan, write, revise, and update the curriculum together and take full responsibility for managing the strand's entire instructional day. Because they are attached to teams, guidance counselors have a lower per-pupil load and stronger connections to both teachers and students. The team makes decisions about scheduling, curriculum, teaching strategies, discipline, and grading. During their four years at International, students take two cycles with the same teachers.

IHS teachers developed this arrangement after discovering that the performance of students in the first interdisciplinary cluster they tried was significantly better than that of students in the regular courses because of the more intensive, focused attention the cluster students received. Several years later, after careful deliberation, the entire faculty decided to convert to the cluster approach, concluding that this arrangement increases teacher responsibility for students as well as teacher control over the conditions of teaching and learning. As teacher David Hirschy (1990b, pp. 15–19) explains: "Our new schedule has given us confidence that we, as teachers, can affect the learning environment of the students we serve in real and concrete ways. The shift toward students sharing and learning from each other, rather than teachers teaching, has been facilitated. Our role has been expanded to include planning and designing the learning community in which we work each day. It has demonstrated that, given time and real decision making power, teachers can exercise careful and visionary judgment."

Faculty at International insist that in all aspects of the school it is important that students and teachers engage in similar experiences: collaborative work, shared decision making, portfolio assessment. Moving teachers into interdependent teams gives them an experience working in groups that enables them to work more effectively with students who are themselves working in groups. Teacher Steve Lindberg explains: "The teachers are now working in the same ways that the students are. The students in most classes work in groups [and] rely on each other to do things. There's responsibility. When people aren't working up to par, the group suffers. When people do very well and support each other, then the group goes well. . . . The idea that in groups, people are responsible to each other as they learn, that people can rely on others, is one of the core values of the school."

The much smaller Urban Academy serves one hundred students who come in with varying academic backgrounds and course-taking needs from schools they have left or dropped out of. The school's small size and the students' varied backgrounds make formal teaching teams less necessary and common structures for student course taking less possible. Urban Academy has fluid structures that feature frequent team teaching and regular teacher visits to one another's classrooms. Teachers design the instructional program by discussing together how their expertise can be combined with local college courses to create a program that will meet the school's graduation proficiencies and students' needs.

At all these schools, reductions in class size and load and the creation of shared planning time for teachers are a result of resource allocation decisions that decrease specialization of functions and administrative overlay. Although teachers teach within their disciplinary fields, less specialized staffing arrangements and more joint work among staff across fields help them to develop knowledge about students that is usually absent in highly departmentalized settings. In addition teachers' intensive work with students for much longer periods of time establishes fruitful teacher-student alliances.

Within these schools' personalizing structures, curriculum and teaching are organized to access information about students' experiences, concerns, interests, and views. Students conduct oral histories, develop family trees, write narratives about their experiences, and talk and write about their interests, goals and aspirations. These activities give teachers information about where their students are coming from and where they are going. In contrast to traditional schools, which presume that knowing students is irrelevant to teaching them, these schools consciously create strategies aimed at understanding students in order to help them learn.

STRUCTURES FOR CARING   Rather than asking guidance counselors who manage caseloads of two hundred or more to address the "personal" needs of students, most restructured schools put advising into the hands of teachers, who are given time to work intensely with a small number of students. In all of these schools, staff members, including administrators, take responsibility for "family groups," or "advisories," small groups of students, typically twelve to fifteen in number, who meet several hours each week with a staff member to discuss personal and academic issues, to get help on homework or exhibitions, and to plan for the future. The advisory period is used as a study time and as an opportunity for quiet reading and writing; for discussion of health, social, and ethical issues; and for one-on-one and group advising and counseling.

The adviser is the advocate and expert for each student in the group, meeting frequently with each student's parents or other family members and with other teachers to ensure communication about the student's needs and progress, to "tap the family's expertise" (Central Park East Secondary School, n.d.), and to guide the student through courses, exhibitions, and graduation requirements. The focus of this work is academic as well as personal. Advisers work with students for more than one year, take them on college trips and field trips, call them at home if they are late or absent, and meet with parents to look at student work and talk about concerns. This ensures that parents, teachers, and students are all working with the same understanding of goals and processes and that there is a high degree of mutual effort.

Students feel well attended in this arrangement. As several at Manhattan International describe their schooling experience: "Teachers know about the students. When you don't understand something, they know when you need help." "The teachers know us. They talk with our parents about our problems, our personality. They give us counsel." "[Teachers] know you. They see if you're working, and if you're good friends with other students. They see if you're behaving well. They ask if you have problems."

Restructuring Decision Making

As teachers develop standards and assessments and work closely with students to meet school goals and objectives, they continually learn what is necessary to produce success for their students both individually and collectively. Acting on what one has learned requires the authority to make decisions, and these teachers have it. All the restructured schools discussed here are faculty run, through a variety of committees focused on education issues and through work units (teams and houses) focused around groups of students. These structures provide means for continually surfacing and solving issues and problems.

As Mohrman and Wohlstetter (Mohrman, Wohlstetter, & Associates 1994) note, work that is complex, uncertain, and group oriented is often best accomplished when employees involved in service delivery are also directly involved in planning, allocating resources, and controlling performance. This idea confronts Frederick Taylor's notion that planners and doers should be separated and work should be guided by detailed directives from the top of the system (see Chapter Two).

GOVERNANCE   Because these restructured schools are deliberately small, governance engages every teacher. The schools are structured for democratic decision making rather than representative governance or merely advisory input. This point is critical: everyone has a voice, and everyone hears the other voices. Thus ownership of practice and the development of shared ideas are possible. In contrast, because large schools find it difficult to manage universal participation, they typically use representative forms of governance, such as school-based decision-making councils, that involve a small number of faculty in decisions, leaving out and sometimes alienating the others (Lieberman, Darling-Hammond, & Zuckerman, 1991). Democratic participation enables small schools to make more than incremental changes in practice with the full endorsement and engagement of all faculty members; such democratic decisions are critical to lasting change.

Both the elementary and secondary schools associated with the Center for Collaborative Education have deeply rooted faculty governance systems. They operate in the context of strong shared norms and values (each school's version of the twelve CCE principles) that teachers use as touchstones when hiring colleagues, developing evaluation systems, engaging in peer review, making curriculum decisions, setting standards for assessing student and teacher work, and deciding on professional development. Shared norms and values provide the coherence that enables decentralized schools to operate responsibly. Because most public schools have not had the opportunity to work through a set of shared convictions, that will be a necessary first step toward shared decision making.

Faculty governance occurs at both the school and team levels. In addition to schoolwide councils, teachers also serve on teams and committees that communicate ideas horizontally and vertically and ensure participation throughout the organization. These strategies maximize individual participation as they maintain a whole-school perspective, an important balance that requires attention in all participatory organizations.

Decisions that reside in teaching teams or other workgroups are either made within a framework established at the school level (as a curriculum decision grounded in the school's consensus about curriculum goals might be) or returned to the school council for final approval (as a staff hiring decision might be). At CPESS, decision making occurs in both divisionwide and schoolwide meetings. School committees interview and hire staff, plan and implement professional development, and manage other functions that cut across the concerns of house and division teams. Smaller groups of staff often work on specific issues, bringing them back to the whole staff when policy decisions must be made. This gives all staff the chance to participate in the final decisions and maintains coherence and unity of purpose in the work of the school. At the Urban Academy, which is small enough to function as a committee of the whole, ad hoc committees and workgroups have changing membership to reduce the territoriality that can emerge when subgroups remain static. This policy also increases opportunities for people to develop shared perspectives and to learn from one another.

Student and parent involvement in governance is also common. Both parents and students are involved in school-level decision making at CPESS. At the Urban Academy, International High School, and Manhattan International High School, student representatives from each advisory meet regularly to discuss schoolwide issues of concern and make recommendations. At the Urban Academy, students have a say in the hiring of new teachers after attending demonstration lessons taught by the candidates.

At International and Manhattan International High Schools, each teacher serves on one of several decision-making committees dealing with staff development, personnel functions such as staff hiring and peer evaluation, curriculum, or parent involvement. A coordinating council includes the school's administrators, union representative, PTA president, student association president, and a representative of each of the teaching clusters. Their participation supports vertical and horizontal communication throughout the school. Teachers at International see this democratization as a key to transforming classroom teaching: "There is a relationship between the management style of a school and the learning style in the classroom. When the management style is authoritarian, the learning style in the classroom is authoritarian and teacher driven. When we change the management style to a more democratic, collaborative style, it becomes a model for learning in our classrooms" (Defazio & Hirschy, 1993, quoted in Darling-Hammond, 1996, pp. 167–168). The Manhattan International teacher contract makes explicit the responsibilities created by shared decision making: "We firmly believe in the school based management and shared decision making model of school governance and that all members are co-participants in such a governance body, with the understanding that they intend to abide by staff decisions, and take responsibility for the school's work, its outcomes and daily practices."

TEAMS It is significant that teachers' primary work units in restructured schools are organized around shared groups of students rather than around subject matter as traditional high school departments are. Working as a team, teachers can be responsible for student welfare rather than for delivering content lessons to students passing by on a conveyer belt. Team structures allow decentralized decision making that leads to greater accountability for student welfare and learning rather than greater fragmentation of teaching.

A very strong feature of the organizational design at CPESS is that all teachers work on two kinds of teams: one focuses on a shared group of students and their needs and the other on curriculum planning. First, within each house, a math/science teacher, a humanities teacher, and a resource room teacher or counselor share a common group of students for two years. These teachers meet for seven hours weekly during planning and lunch time. Second, while students are participating in community service activities, each teacher meets with a discipline-based curriculum team one morning a week to plan curriculum across divisions and houses. The two-team structure focuses teachers both on learning standards and on learners, and it ensures that information is widely shared throughout the organization.

COLLECTIVE DECISION MAKING AND PEER REVIEW The schools' teams have substantial freedom in enacting curriculum, but decentralized authority does not mean unfettered individual autonomy. Instead teachers have greater collective authority coupled with greater professional accountability. Major curriculum decisions are collectively made by teams or by the entire faculty, as are many decisions regarding how students will be supported and evaluated in their work. Teachers must hash out the issues until they agree. At CPESS, assessment of graduation portfolios serves as a major forum for creating a collective perspective. At the Urban Academy, twice monthly schoolwide curriculum meetings and weekly staff meetings are used to plan curriculum, look at individual students and their needs, examine how well the school is achieving its intentions, and share specific classroom practices and problems.

The teachers see themselves as giving up individual autonomy in order to gain collegial feedback and more success for their students. As a teacher at Manhattan International High School puts it: "[My colleagues and I have] had to work together on curriculum, look at each other's work. We're forced to be more collaborative. So there's kind of a loss of freedom to some extent. But I think it's compensated for by the lack of isolation and the feedback you get. With feedback, there's growth. Here you can't hide. It's kind of hard at first, but it's good for you."

At both International and Manhattan International all faculty members serve on peer evaluation committees for their colleagues. They observe others' teaching and are observed in their own classrooms, develop a portfolio of their work and respond to others' portfolios, engage in self-evaluation, and prepare and receive written evaluations of teaching. The school funds courses, conferences, and other professional development teachers may need to improve performance in particular areas. Peer evaluation committees are empowered to grant tenure and to recommend continuation or dismissal. These decisions are taken seriously and are far from pro forma. Not all teachers are invited to stay. At International, administrators also evaluate each team as a whole, and staff respond to an annual questionnaire in order to evaluate the principal. All these functions expand knowledge and information across individuals and teams as they also press for accountability.

SHARED KNOWLEDGE AND INFORMATION   To make responsible decisions, workers in any organization must have a steady flow of information about their work and its outcomes and continual opportunities to build their knowledge. At least five features of these schools support decentralized information and shared knowledge.

First, *team planning and teaching* allow teachers to share knowledge with one another. Work structures take advantage of distributed expertise as teachers fill in gaps in one another's base of knowledge and experience. Team members help one another plan what they will do in their classrooms, serve as sounding boards for ideas, and add disciplinary and pedagogical expertise. In an interdisciplinary model of teaching, teachers need to expand their expertise in the areas in which they have less training and experience. Through team planning, teachers more experienced in social studies support those more experienced in English language arts, and vice versa. Mathematics and science teachers make the same interchange. Maintaining distributed expertise is a consideration both in hiring decisions and in team formation.

Similarly, schools in many European countries routinely prepare teachers to teach in more than one subject area and organize their work in teaching teams that support continual learning within and across content areas. Such opportunities for developing greater shared knowledge are not found, however, in traditional U.S. secondary school settings. Even though over one-third of all teachers teach at least some courses outside their area of preparation (National Commission on Teaching and America's Future, 1996), these out-of-field assignments are typically not supported by team planning that would consciously build teachers' knowledge.

Whereas curriculum teams allow teachers to share disciplinary knowledge, house teams help teachers share knowledge about students and integrate instruction. For example, humanities teachers and math/science teachers may work together to integrate geometric studies of pyramids into a unit on ancient Mayan civilization. And students' advisers can easily share information about students' concerns and progress within the context of team meetings, without having to chase down seven or eight different teachers with different schedules as they would in a traditional high school.

Second, *cross-group structures for planning, communication, and decision making* form a web of horizontal communication throughout the school. Cross-team planning and learning occur through schoolwide staff meetings (conducted at least weekly in all of the schools), shared governance, and assessment events such as schoolwide faculty reviews of exhibitions and portfolios.

Third, *professional development* is built into the schedule and tied to ongoing homegrown innovations so that teachers learn by doing as they collectively construct new practices. For example, CPESS teachers have learned a great deal about students, teaching, and learning from their deep engagement in creating and continually revising the portfolio system, by linking this work to staff development and subjecting students' work and teachers' judgments to further scrutiny by

outside reviewers. When teachers at International developed a port-
folio-based peer evaluation strategy for themselves, they learned a
great deal about how self-reflective learning works. Because they saw
the advantages of building collections of work and reflecting on them
in groups, they ultimately began to use portfolio and peer review
strategies for their own students.

Fourth, the schools continually share *rich information about students, families, and classroom work* through vehicles like narrative report cards, student and teacher portfolios, class and school newsletters,
and widely distributed meeting notes. Information about what teachers are doing and how it is working is available everywhere throughout the school. In contrast, communication in traditional schools
usually deals with logistics and procedures (bus schedules, meeting
dates, new guidelines) or presents limited proxy data about learning
(grades, test scores) rather than concrete examples of student and
teacher work. Furthermore, communication is usually managed from
the top rather than through a dense schoolwide web of discussions
among teachers, students, and parents.

Finally, *highly visible shared exhibitions of student work* make it clear
what each school values and how students are doing. Not only are student products extensively displayed throughout the school but teachers also collectively create assessments and evaluate student learning
within and across classrooms. These practices spread information
about student learning and classroom teaching. As teachers look at
the work of their own students they learn much more than they could
from standardized tests about what is working as they had hoped and
what is not. As they look at the work of other teachers' students, they
have a window into the curriculum and teaching strategies used in
other classrooms.

Aggregated data about student performance are also regularly available and discussed. At International, for example, every staff member
has access to all measurable information about the performance of all
students. Thus every team knows student pass rates for in-school and
college courses, Regents Competency Test scores, attendance rates, suspensions, college acceptance rates, dropout rates, and faculty attendance rates along with other in-school academic progress indicators.
Data are broken down by individual course or team where appropriate and included in an end-of-year evaluation report.

Shared information about how students are achieving can motivate greater accountability. One cluster team at International High

School, for example, was disturbed that its students showed higher levels of incompletes at the end of a cycle than other clusters' students. In response to this information they assigned themselves as mentors, one to each student who had an incomplete, working on their own time with former students to help them complete the work so that they could pass (Ancess, 1995).

In addition the process of developing and evaluating performance assessments with other teachers enhances teacher learning not only about students but also about teaching and learning more generally (Darling-Hammond & Ancess, 1994). It sharpens their ability to think in a curricular way, to understand the scaffolding needed to produce high-quality performances, and to develop strategies that will help their students achieve the standards embedded in complex tasks.

INCENTIVES FOR TEACHERS AND STUDENTS

Traditional schools provide few incentives to support the efforts of teachers who want to come to know the needs of their students well, who are willing to look for the answers to the knottiest problems of teaching and learning, and who want to work with the students for whom attainment in education is especially risky and labor intensive. Instead bureaucratic schools' incentives encourage teachers to depersonalize and standardize instruction so as to comfortably handle large numbers of students in short blocks of time; to use pedagogical strategies that are as simple, self-contained, and routine as possible; and to avoid teaching the neediest students by moving to higher tracks or transferring out to more attractive schools as they gain seniority. Schools that serve low-income and minority students are especially heavily sanctioned environments.

In the education world, status generally accrues to staff who teach high-tracked students or who teach in schools with economically and educationally advantaged student bodies. So new teachers and those with less clout are assigned the task of working with students who need the most help to learn well. These students and their teachers also receive fewer resources at both the classroom and school levels (Darling-Hammond, 1995). Unlike professions where the most capable practitioners gain status and rewards from working on the most difficult problems, teaching gives the greatest benefits to those who handle the easiest cases. Furthermore, monetary incentives favor those furthest away from teaching. Substantially higher pay can be acquired only by leaving the classroom for administration. Salary hikes for professional learning cease after a teacher reaches a certain education and experience level. Within schools little time is granted for professional development and few motivations exist for changing practice.

In the successful schools described here a very different set of intrinsic and extrinsic incentives and supports operates for teachers and students.

Incentives for Teachers

Teachers in restructured schools continually describe the intrinsic rewards that derive from their increased success with students as the most powerful factor that keeps them engaged in the intensive work of transforming their pedagogy and reforming their school organizations. Their reports are consistent with several decades of research indicating that the opportunity to be effective is the single most powerful motivator for entering and staying in teaching and for triggering commitment and effort (Rosenholtz, 1987). A number of specific incentives support these intrinsic rewards.

REDUCED PUPIL LOADS   Smaller pupil loads that allow for greater personalization enable teachers to be more successful and are a key incentive for teachers to teach in restructured schools. Across the four schools discussed here, teachers work with as few as thirty-six students at one time and no more than seventy-five, half or less of the traditional load. That the CCE schools are deliberately creating new incentives in this area is explicit in the teacher contract developed by Manhattan International High School in its first year of operation. The contract states, in part, that "in return for smaller class size and smaller total student rolls, teachers will work with students in classes, family groups, clubs, teams, tutorials, seminars, projects and coaching individual students. . . . All faculty, in their roles as family group advisors, are expected to keep families informed of student work, progress and other concerns."

When these closer relationships pay off in greater success with students, teachers are doubly rewarded for their work.

TIME FOR SHARED WORK   Time for new faculty roles is built into the schools' regular schedule. Each school does this differently but manages, through block scheduling and creative student programming, to create several-hour blocks for joint teacher planning, staff development, and faculty governance. At some schools, teachers meet for a half day each week while students are engaged in community service activities. On some days, students begin and end earlier than usual in order to free up additional hours for staff meetings. At International High School a "clubs" period for students provides a full afternoon once a week for faculty development. This time is used for staff-guided learning and shared decision making, not for training determined by someone else or transmission of administrative directives, which traditionally absorb faculty meeting time.

OPPORTUNITIES FOR OWNERSHIP AND INVENTION Teachers in these schools are committed both to their schools and to the change process because they value their roles in developing the innovations they are undertaking. They have gained greater autonomy by agreeing to operate collectively. Within jointly set and agreed-upon parameters, they have tremendous opportunity to invent their own practice and to shape the school's work. Such opportunities are incentives for effort.

School codirector Paul Schwarz notes that "the teachers at CPESS feel as though they own the school because of the governance structure. They don't mind the extra time they have to put in because they are invested. It's like how the bodega owner feels about stocking the shelves and sweeping the floor, versus the McDonald's worker." Faculty members confirm this view. Teachers talk enthusiastically about the work they are engaged in and the substantive changes they continually initiate rather than about extra chores they feel they are forced to take on. Teachers who previously worked in traditional high schools frequently talk about being reborn, reenergized, and renewed by a chance to work in an environment that enables them to be so much more effective and creative.

The greater control over their own work that staff gain from their participation in decision making is a powerful incentive to remain in the school and in the profession as well as to continue the work of change. The psychology of positive action—of doing rather than being done unto—is important for developing self-efficacy and for motivating purposeful effort.

SUPPORT FOR INDIVIDUAL INTERESTS AND LEADERSHIP Rather than operating hierarchical career structures in which teachers must leave teaching to participate in other activities, all of these schools offer teachers the work variety that enables them to use and develop their talents in individually satisfying ways. For example, teachers can participate in research projects or develop courses and areas of study ranging from the use of video or computer media to applications of mathematical modeling techniques.

Teachers are known for their areas of expertise and are encouraged to lead and contribute to curriculum initiatives and related school projects based on their interests. They also find leadership opportunities in their schools' many committees and teams. Some leadership tasks are compensated with modest stipends or extra time; others are not but bring the rewards of collegial appreciation and self-efficacy. Teachers are actively encouraged to take leadership in the profession as well. They present at conferences and create study groups. They share their expertise with other schools and faculty in the CCE network. Grants sometimes support the professional development work that teachers engage in within their schools or with other faculties interested in learning about the curriculum strategies or assessments they have developed.

A number of teachers from these schools have left to start new schools in New York City. They undertake these challenges knowing they are supported by a collegial network that will help them learn and problem solve in their new roles.

INTERNALLY DEVELOPED STANDARDS AND ASSESSMENTS   The power of schoolwide standard setting and highly public assessment strategies is that they convey valued ideals in a concrete way, they provide occasions to recognize and celebrate student and teacher work, and they make clear the areas where more work is needed. For faculty the publicness of the process is an incentive to prepare students well for the exhibition; an additional incentive is the gratification that comes from student success.

Peer review processes for faculty form another set of powerful incentives. When faculty observe and assess their own and each others' work, not only do they gain insights into teaching and develop shared standards of practice but positive peer pressure also results from making teaching public and talking about it regularly.

Incentives for Students

Students describe the incentives that come from being cared for and having clear attainable goals to aim at along with plenty of supports to ensure their success. These supports result from redesigned work structures that create extended time for students to be with teachers and for teachers to care.

STANDARDS AND SUPPORTS   Managing high academic standards so they serve as incentives rather than disincentives for students is a delicate business. A combination of high standards and high supports is essential to creating the motivation to work until success is achieved. The standards carry stakes: students cannot graduate until they receive passing scores on all their portfolios, and graduation committees enforce the standards by requiring revisions when work is not up to par. Especially in the first years of this graduation system, a number of CPESS students did not graduate in June but had to work through the summer and sometimes into the following year to reach the standards. At the same time, supports to meet the standards are present: teachers continue to work intensively with students until they succeed. If this were not the case, the standards might persuade students simply to give up.

Former CPESS teacher Jill Herman (now director of a new school) remarked that sometimes the metaphor "teacher as coach" could more accurately be "teacher as nag." "I've had kids who will come and say, 'Look Jill, you yell at me. You make me sit down. I want you to make sure that I do this'" (Darling-Hammond, Ancess, & Falk, 1995, p. 55). Students commented often about their teachers' availability and desire to make sure students succeed. As one said fondly of her adviser, "She bothers me. She gives me the 'what to do' and I have to do it. And if I don't understand something, she's there, just her and me, and she'll explain it to me in a one-on-one."

CARING   As Urban Academy teacher Nancy Jachim has found, one challenge a school faces is negotiating the tensions of the competing agendas of caring and academic rigor so that these agendas serve each other: "The teacher's agenda is curriculum. Students have a different agenda. If the teacher connects with the students, the students will accept the school values. They will achieve. The student's agenda is to relive the parenting experience—caring, personal contact. [Our] students need the caring and attention. . . . They are slouching toward success, not pursuing it ardently" (Darling-Hammond, 1996, p. 183).

In all of these schools, students voice over and over again how important it is to them that they are cared for. The attention they receive and the doggedness with which teachers pursue their futures with them—taking them on trips to college campuses, coaching them through exhibitions, meeting with their parents—are the incentives that secure their commitment to work hard and to achieve. Because the schools are structured to allow teachers to care for students effectively, students develop trust, and students begin to believe that accomplishing the school's goals will be important to their later success. This faith then fuels the effort that teachers need from students to produce learning.

HOME-SCHOOL CONNECTIONS   Another set of incentives for students derives from the tight connections forged between teachers and parents that allow both to better understand the student's experience and to create mutually reinforcing incentives at home and school. Because advisers tend to meet with parents several times a year and to talk with them much more frequently than that, needed supports can readily be identified and established, and problems can be worked through before they become crises. Sometimes solutions can be worked out when students' schoolwork is suffering because of an after-school job or babysitting responsibilities at home. Sometimes the exchange of information simply makes it easier for parents and teachers to acknowledge students' efforts and work with students toward the same ends. When teachers secure the interest and involvement of parents, the incentives around the student begin to work synergistically.

Strong parent-teacher connections are also important for bridging the wide cultural gulf that sometimes separates U.S. schools, as Eurocentric institutions, from minority communities that have experienced a history of exclusion (Ogbu, 1992; Comer, 1988). Finding common ground with parents can reduce cultural conflicts that create competing psychological incentive structures for students. International and Manhattan International High Schools work especially hard at this task, calling parents frequently; holding workshops for parents to help them learn English, deal with immigration issues, and complete college applications; publishing newsletters in multiple languages; and arranging for translators at PTA meetings. Parents speak appreciatively about how the teachers "keep after" their children, meeting with and calling parents so that students are not allowed to fail.

Some students have parents who are absent, ill, or unavailable; others live in foster care, with other relatives, or on their own. Teachers of students whose parents are unavailable try to connect with another supporter or advocate for the student. Where none exists, teachers or school directors sometimes take on this role themselves. There is a strong commitment to ensuring that no student has to confront school and adolescence without support.

CHOICE, PARTICIPATION, AND AUTONOMY   Because they are alternative schools, all the schools discussed in this chapter operate as schools of choice. None uses choice to cream the best students from among those who apply: some admit only students who have failed elsewhere; all explicitly seek an economically, ethnically, and educationally diverse student population; give first preference to neighborhood children in their high-poverty communities; and will often accept a low-achieving student who needs their support over a high-achieving student who does not. However, choice is important to the schools' success; it allows them to be more educationally adventurous, because parents and students have consciously selected the nontraditional teaching and organization they offer, and it creates strong bonds among student, parent, and school.

As Central Park East founder Deborah Meier explains, "We work harder where our loyalties are tapped and where we believe we have some power, if only the power to make a move. [Choice] creates conditions that reinforce a sense of membership in a community, a quality that parents, teachers, and youngsters are missing in most areas of their lives today" (1995, p. 101). The act of choosing creates a new dynamic for the relationship between student and school—one in which free will rather than coercion is the operant variable.

Choice also operates in the schools' curricula, as students have frequent opportunities to choose the topics for projects they will undertake, to pursue internships in fields of interest, and to select college courses. Students join in shaping their own learning, participating in parent-teacher conferences, the curriculum development process, and classroom decision making as well as school governance. Visitors to one of these schools are likely to be greeted and briefed by students, and students frequently participate in teams that represent the schools at conferences and meetings. Students participate in portfolio reviews and on graduation committees for their peers, and they engage in ongoing self-evaluation as well. For developing adolescents who need both autonomy and affiliation, the opportunity to be heard and to be taken seriously is a major incentive to commit to the school environment.

Finally, much of the work students undertake is intrinsically interesting, and the opportunity to display their competence in public exhibitions that include parents as well as teachers and outsiders is highly motivating. Work that is engaging and that builds a sense of accomplishment operates as an incentive. As a member of the first graduating class at Central Park East Secondary School put it, "This environment gives us more standards. It makes us stand up straight. It makes us look at ourselves in the mirror and feel proud of our accomplishments" (Darling-Hammond, 1996, p. 185).

Incentives and structures that take account of students' needs to be cared for and to participate in shaping their own work are as important as those that take account of teachers' needs for knowledge, information, and authority in managing their work. In applying the ideas of high-involvement, high-performance organizations to schools, it is most productive to think of students and teachers as coworkers, undertaking together the task of creating ambitious teaching and powerful learning.

## CHAPTER SIX

Staffing Schools for Teaching and Learning

The fact is that one of the major factors maximizing the gulf between educational goals and accomplishments has been the way resources have been defined. . . . There is a universe of alternatives one can consider and if we do not confront that universe, it is largely because we are committed to a way of defining who should be in the classroom.

—Seymour Sarason, The Culture of the School and the Problem of Change (1982, pp. 275, 284)

The schools described in the previous chapter provide an environment for teaching and learning that would be the envy of most educators, students, and parents. Class sizes are small; teachers work intensively with smaller numbers of students for long periods of time; students know their teachers well and can go to them with problems and triumphs; parents talk and meet with teachers frequently; teachers have large blocks of time each week to plan with their colleagues, build curriculum, make decisions, observe one another, and work with students and parents. As a consequence of this personalization, the schools are safer, more communal, and more successful in providing the cognitive, social, and emotional supports students need to learn.

But how can restructured schools afford to do these things? Doesn't this kind of school environment cost more than other schools and more than the U.S. public would ever be willing to spend? Isn't this kind of education simply out of reach for most communities? The answer to these questions would be yes if schools tried both to maintain their existing structures and to buy more teacher time and reduce class sizes. Because restructured schools are designed from different premises, however, they do not cost more than traditional schools.

In restructured schools in New York City, for example, total per-pupil expenditures are usually equivalent to those in large comprehensive schools, for a number of reasons. First, large schools often hire a greater number of administrative personnel (who are more expensive than teachers) as well as support staff who manage paperwork. One study found that nearly twice as much of a school's tax levy staffing allocation was used for supervisory and clerical staff at large comprehensive high schools as at small alternative schools (Public Education Association, 1992). Traditional schools also receive greater levels of categorical funding for such programs as special education, compensatory education, and bilingual education, partly because they label more students and serve them in more segregated settings than do the alternative schools even when their student populations are similar. Large schools are also more likely to maintain programs that qualify for vocational education and other federal funds. Furthermore, due to their higher violence and vandalism rates, large schools spend much more than smaller schools for the out-of-formula costs of security guards, metal detectors, and plant maintenance (Public Education Association, 1992).

In addition the high absenteeism and dropout rates of New York's neighborhood comprehensive high schools leave them with many fewer students to educate than their resource allocations would suggest. It is not unusual for a school to have only 60 or 70 percent of its enrolled students actually in attendance and to graduate only half. If one were to calculate costs per graduate, most of the large comprehensive high schools in central cities would cost at least twice as much per pupil as the more effective alternative schools.

Restructured schools operate differently, investing in the front lines of teaching and learning and in the core relationships between classroom teachers and students rather than in an elaborate administrative apparatus and a bevy of nonteaching specialists who sit at the periphery of classroom life. They use their resources of time, staff, and dollars more productively and effectively than do large traditional schools.

The remainder of this chapter describes in detail how current staffing practices in most schools result from assumptions about efficiency and effectiveness that are no longer tenable. Data from other countries and from restructured schools reveal alternative staffing methods that cost no more than schools are already spending but result in much more successful learning environments. In the last part of the chapter I discuss the specific policy changes needed for U.S. schools to adopt the staffing policies that restructured schools are using to both students' and teachers' advantage.

ALLOCATING RESOURCES WITHIN SCHOOLS

To understand how resources are used, colleagues and I studied a typical New York City comprehensive high school with an enrollment of 3,380 students, a suburban high school of about 1,600 students, and several smaller high schools associated with the Center for Collaborative Education.[1] We also reviewed research on restructured elementary schools to examine how they use resources under different organizational models. We found there are at least three organizational principles, similar to those found in high-performance businesses, that guide the resource allocations of highly productive schools.

First, the Taylorist divide between planners and doers is minimized or eliminated. This means that nearly everyone teaches and everyone plans. Most resources are devoted to core classroom teaching rather than to nonteaching functions or pullout services. This practice reduces pupil-teacher ratios *and* permits more shared time for practicing teachers.

Second, staff are organized in teams, each of which is responsible for an entire piece of work, in this case, for a group of students. Use of such teams creates a simpler work organization that demands less complex coordination than traditional bureaucracies require and encourages pooling of subject matter expertise and knowledge. Instead of having a layer of planners who oversee the work of a layer of supervisors and coordinators who oversee the isolated work of individual "doers," work is structured to allow direct communication among workers, who function collaboratively. Rather than sitting on the side, specialists are incorporated into teams. In restructured schools, teachers with counseling or special education expertise are regular members of teaching teams; they teach a class of students *and* help other teachers on their team learn how to work more effectively with special students.

Third, students and teachers engage in fewer separate classes per day and those classes extend for longer periods of time. Rather than schedule eight classes per day of 42 minutes each, restructured schools create three to five class periods of 70 to 120 minutes each. As in a college setting, students take four or five courses at a time rather than seven or eight, studying each one more intensely. This approach reduces teachers' overall pupil loads and number of different preparations without reducing instructional time. The smaller pupil loads make more teacher time available to students and more professional learning time available to teachers.

The Traditional Urban High School

The large comprehensive school we studied is considered a relatively good one. It serves a diverse population that includes a substantial middle class and does not have a high rate of violence and vandalism. Nonetheless, when we collected our data in 1994–95, a pupil-adult ratio of 13.7:1 translated into average class sizes of 33 to 34. Teachers saw 167 students per day on average and had very little joint planning or meeting time with other teachers.

Class sizes are large because over 40 percent of staff are primarily nonteaching personnel: one principal, nine assistant principals, eleven guidance counselors, thirteen secretaries, ten school-based services specialists (social workers, psychologists, and the like), and seventeen security guards are employed along with twenty-two nonteaching school aides, fourteen paraprofessionals, and three librarians. (In this analysis and those that follow, food service workers, janitors, and bus drivers are excluded as they are allocated through another process and formula.) "Big School" administrators and supervisors have little contact with students in a teaching or advising capacity. Their time is consumed by paperwork and by the task of coordinating the fragmented work of all of the other personnel.

As Table 6.1 shows, of the 247 adults hired by the traditional large comprehensive school, only 143 (58 percent) are full-time teachers. Some of these teachers perform additional compensatory time roles, acting as safety, security, and discipline deans and as supervisors of attendance, scheduling, office activities, and other administrative tasks. The time needed for these roles deducts the equivalent of thirteen FTE

	Big School (Traditional High School)	Small School 1 (International High School)	Small School 2 (Central Park East Secondary School)
Total students	3,380	460	450
Instructional staff[1]	230	45	44
Principal/director	1	1	1.5
Assistant principals	9[2]	2	0
Guidance counselors	11	4	0
Secretaries	13	1	1
Librarians	3	0[3]	0.5[4]
School aides	22	2	4
Paraprofessionals	14	6	4
Lab technician	1	0	0
Compensatory time	13 FTEs	0	0
Full-time teachers	143	29	33
Security guards	17	Site host provides	1[5]

Table 6.1.   Comparison of School Staff Allocations.

Note: Food service workers, janitorial and maintenance workers, bus drivers, and school-based services excluded.

[1]Excludes staff working on special grants.

[2]Six of these assistant principals are department heads who teach two periods each day.

[3]A teacher serves as librarian when not teaching classes.

[4]A librarian is shared with another school in the building

[5]The building has three security guards serving three schools. One is allocated to this school.

(full-time equivalent) teachers from the teacher ranks and thus from time allocated to teaching. Though important in the context of a large complex organization needing lots of coordinating and reporting, most of these jobs are not necessary in smaller more personalized environments. By the time nonteaching staff and nonteaching duties are factored into the equation, only 33 percent of adult time is left for teaching at this traditionally managed school.

Similarly, Cooper, Sarrel, and Tetenbaum (1990) found that only 32 percent of instructional staff time is spent teaching in regular high schools as compared to 60 to 85 percent of staff time in elementary schools, intermediate schools, and alternative high schools. Moreover, the nonteaching time in traditional high schools is not spent on collaborative planning and curriculum work as it would be in other countries. Despite the fact that so little of the total staff time is used for teaching, teachers have only one preparation period daily, and it is not organized for joint planning or staff development. Teachers meet collectively for at most one forty-five-minute staff meeting per week.

Equally important is the way that the large traditional school we studied organized students' and teachers' time. The students' day consists of eight forty-two-minute periods with four minutes of passing time between each one. Teachers teach five periods a day and are assigned noninstructional tasks like lunch duty and hall duty for one period a day on a rotating basis. They spend 17.5 hours each week in classes with students (Exhibit 6.1). Because of their large pupil loads, this means teachers have on average only 6.2 minutes per week to spend with each student they teach.

The Suburban High School

Our analysis of an affluent suburban high school outside New York City found many similar features. Although the school is smaller (1,600 students) and spends substantially more money per pupil, teachers' and students' school lives are largely the same as those of their city counterparts except for smaller class sizes, averaging around twenty-three to twenty-five, close to the national average. In 1994, 62 percent of staff were involved in teaching, although not all were full-time teachers, and 38 percent were assigned to a variety of non-teaching duties. The latter personnel included six administrators, nine department heads, eight guidance counselors, thirteen secretaries, and five psychologists and social workers.

Teachers still taught five classes daily, most carried a total student load of 120 or more, and they had little or no shared planning time. Students still saw seven or eight teachers daily in forty-two-minute periods and had few chances for extended relationships with staff. Although this schooling experience was a somewhat gentler one, it did not secure highly personalized relationships between students and teachers, nor did it allow teachers to work together to improve the quality of their teaching.

Restructured High Schools

In contrast restructured schools spend most of their funds on classroom teachers and organize their schedules to give teachers more time with the same students and with each other. At International High

Teacher Schedule

	Monday	Tuesday	Wednesday	Thursday	Friday
8:05 A.M. 8:47 A.M.	Planning	Planning	Planning	Planning	Planning
8:51 A.M. 9:33 A.M.	Class	Class	Class	Class	Class
9:37 A.M. 10:23 A.M.	Duty	Duty	Duty	Duty	Duty
10:27 A.M. 11:09 A.M.	Class	Class	Class	Class	Class
11:13 A.M. 11:55 A.M.	Lunch	Lunch	Lunch	Lunch	Lunch
11:59 A.M. 12:41 P.M.	Class	Class	Class	Class	Class
12:45 P.M. 1:27 P.M.	Class	Class	Class	Class	Class
1:31 P.M. 2:13 P.M.	Class	Class	Class	Class	Class

Student Schedule

	Monday	Tuesday	Wednesday	Thursday	Friday
8:05 A.M. 8:47 A.M.	Class	Class	Class	Class	Class
8:51 A.M. 9:33 A.M.	Class	Class	Class	Class	Class
9:37 A.M. 10:23 A.M.	Class	Class	Class	Class	Class
10:27 A.M. 11:09 A.M.	Class	Class	Class	Class	Class
11:13 A.M. 11:55 A.M.	Lunch	Lunch	Lunch	Lunch	Lunch
11:59 A.M. 12:41 P.M.	Class	Class	Class	Class	Class
12:45 P.M. 1:27 P.M.	Class	Class	Class	Class	Class
1:31 P.M. 2:13 P.M.	Class	Class	Class	Class	Class

Exhibit 6.1.   Traditional School Sample Schedules.

School, for example, the principal, assistant principals, and all other staff work with students in advisories. Guidance counselors are attached to teaching teams and work with students in classes, seminars, and group sessions. The librarian is a classroom teacher who teaches classes and works with the school's media resources. Full-time teachers constitute 67 percent of the staff as compared to only 58 percent at the traditional comprehensive high school (Table 6.2).

Central Park East Secondary School (CPESS) offers a model with even less specialization: there are no guidance counselors, attendance officers, assistant principals, supervisors, or department heads. There is one art teacher, one foreign language teacher oversees the work of others hired on hourly contracts, and a librarian is shared with another school in the same building. The school codirectors teach classes themselves and have responsibility, as do all teachers and other professional staff, for counseling students in advisories. Virtually everyone at the school works directly with students, and full-time teachers constitute 73 percent of all staff.

Teachers at both alternative schools have significantly smaller pupil loads than Big School teachers and significantly more shared planning

	Big School (Traditional High School)	Small School 1 (International High School)	Small School 2 (Central Park East Secondary School)
Full-time teachers as percentage of staff	58 percent	67 percent	73 percent
Percentage of adults teaching or working with advisories[1]	68 percent	100 percent	87 percent
Ratio of students to adults	13.7:1	10.2:1	10.0:1
Average class size	33.4	25	18
Average pupil load[2]	167	75	36
Teacher minutes per pupil per week[3]	6.2	13.6	33
Joint planning/staff development time for teachers[4]	45 minutes/week	6 hours/week	7.5 hours/week

Table 6.2.   Selected Comparisons of Resource Use.

[1]Includes paraprofessionals working in classrooms.

[2]Number of students teacher is responsible for at any one time.

[3]Load to time ratio: The number of students a teacher sees to the amount of teaching time each week.

[4]Excludes personal planning time.

time. At International, interdisciplinary clusters organize classes that are seventy minutes long and average twenty-five students each. Classes are offered four times per week, so students get as much instructional time as in other schools, but teachers teach fewer courses. This gives them fewer total students, fewer preparations, and more time to engage students in active learning and groupwork in the classroom. Average pupil load is seventy-five, less than half that of teachers at Big School, and teachers have at least twice as much time per pupil (an average of 13.6 minutes per student per week).

At CPESS, teachers in grades 7 to 10 teach two interdisciplinary classes (math/science or humanities) that meet for nearly two hours daily, four times per week. With class sizes of eighteen, this results in a total pupil load of thirty-six, less than one-fourth the load of a teacher at Big School. Advisories of about fifteen students each meet for about three hours per week and often comprise the same students teachers are working with in class. This method of organization results in extensive staff time with individual students: an average of thirty-three minutes per student per week. In the Senior Institute (the CPESS equivalent of grades 11 and 12), teachers give students even more personal attention: they teach two classes and conduct five hours of advisory each week and then spend the remainder of their time coaching students one-on-one on portfolio work. In addition to their in-school coursework, Senior Institute students take courses at local colleges and complete internships at work sites.

Shared time for planning, professional development, and governance is much more extensive in the restructured schools. At International, cluster teachers share seventy minutes of planning time daily and have a half day each week for staff development and collective work while students are in clubs (Exhibit 6.2), amounting to a total of six hours of shared time each week.

At CPESS, teachers meet once a week for a full morning with their disciplinary teams while students are engaged in community service placements (Exhibit 6.3). They meet with other house teachers twice a month during an extended lunch and planning period and with the total staff twice a week. Altogether, these teachers average seven and one-half hours a week for joint planning in addition to five hours weekly of personal planning time.

Through a combination of staffing choices (nearly everyone teaches), role designations (teachers take on a broader array of responsibilities), scheduling practices (block schedules with longer

Teacher Schedule

	Monday	Tuesday	Wednesday	Thursday	Friday
8:00 A.M. 9:10 A.M.	Class	House Group	Planning	Class	Class
9:15 A.M. 10:25 A.M.	Planning	Seminar	Class	Planning	Planning
10:30 A.M. 11:40 A.M.	Class	Planning	Class	Class	Class
11:45 A.M. 12:55 P.M.	Lunch	Class	Staff Development	Lunch	Lunch
1:00 P.M. 2:10 P.M.	Class	Lunch	Staff Development	Class	Class
2:15 P.M. 3:25 P.M.	Free	Free	Staff Development	Free	Free

Student Schedule

	Monday	Tuesday	Wednesday	Thursday	Friday
8:00 A.M. 9:10 A.M.	Class	House Group	Class	Class	Class
9:15 A.M. 10:25 A.M.	Class	Seminar	Class	Planning	Planning
10:30 A.M. 11:40 A.M.	Lunch	Lunch	Lunch	Lunch	Lunch
11:45 A.M. 12:55 P.M.	Class	Class	Clubs	Class	Class
1:00 P.M. 2:10 P.M.	Class	Class	Clubs	Class	Class

Exhibit 6.2.   International High School Sample Schedules.

Teacher Schedule

	Monday	Tuesday	Wednesday	Thursday	Friday
8:00 A.M. 9:00 A.M.	Planning	Planning	Planning	Planning	Advisory
9:00 A.M. 10:45 A.M.	Class	Humanities team meeting	Class	Class	Class
10:45 A.M. 1:00 P.M.	Class	11:30 A.M. House meeting (2 times a month)	Class	11:30 A.M. Meetings, planning, lunch	Class
1:00 P.M. 1:45 P.M.	Lunch	Class	Lunch	Class	Staff meeting
1:45 P.M. 3:00 P.M.	Advisory		Advisory		
3:00 P.M. 4:30 P.M.	Staff meeting				

Student Schedule

	Monday	Tuesday	Wednesday	Thursday	Friday
8:00 A.M. 9:00 A.M.	Spanish	Spanish	Spanish	Spanish	Advisory
9:00 A.M. 11:00 A.M.	Humanities	Community service 9:00 A.M.–12:00 noon	Humanities	Humanities	Humanities
11:00 A.M. 1:00 P.M.	Math/science	Gym/lunch	Math/science	Gym/lunch	Math/science
1:00 P.M. 1:45 P.M.	Lunch	Class	Lunch	Class	Free
1:45 P.M. 3:00 P.M.	Advisory		Advisory		

Exhibit 6.3. **Central Park East Secondary School Sample Schedules.**

periods and fewer classes), and curriculum decisions (a core curriculum with no tracking), these restructured schools marshall their resources to enable more intense and intimate work between and among students and teachers.

Restructured Elementary Schools

Similar gains in shared time among teachers and personal attention to students have been achieved in elementary schools that have reduced class size by reducing the number of specialists and nonteaching staff and increasing the number of classroom teachers. Such schools have restructured their staffing patterns by "pushing in" special teaching expertise to teams and classrooms rather than "pulling out" children for fragmented special services. Many have also created shared planning time for teaching teams by using student clubs, "specials" (art, music, and physical education), and local recreation services, or by creatively banking time—adding instructional time on some days in order to free up an afternoon on another day each week.

At Hefferan Elementary School in Chicago, teachers teach four full days of academic classes each week and spend the fifth full day planning together with their multigrade teams as students rotate to "resource" classes in music, fine arts, computer lab, physical education, library science, and science lab (Miles, 1995). At Ashley River Elementary in South Carolina, teachers have eighty minutes each day for planning, including significant shared time with their grade-level teams. Meanwhile, class sizes have been lowered by reducing the number of specialists and counseling positions; now 75 percent of staff are classroom teachers. At Quebec Heights Elementary in Cincinnati, Ohio, teachers have found five and a half hours a week to plan together and have lowered pupil-teacher ratios to 15 to 1 by reducing specialization, creating multiage clusters of students and teachers, integrating special education teachers into cluster teams, and eliminating separate Title I classes to reduce the size of groups for all students (Miles, 1995).

In these schools and others these strategies are further supported by policies that place teachers with the same students for two or more years and that create teaching teams with distributed expertise. These practices often reduce failure rates and reduce referrals for special services because they result in greater knowledge of the child and family situation, more time to build useful teaching strategies for individual students, and more opportunities to gain advice from colleagues (Lieberman, 1995; Darling-Hammond et al., 1993). In all the schools discussed here, evidence shows that students are learning more than they did in traditional school structures as each child gets more individual attention and as teachers continually develop their expertise.

Figure 6.1 illustrates these principles. It shows how, in an elementary school of six hundred students, it is possible to reduce class size from twenty-five to sixteen students and increase teachers' joint planning time from less than four to at least ten hours per week by increasing the proportion of classroom teaching staff. In this example, classroom teachers increase from under 50 percent to over 80 percent of total staff as nonteaching professional staff are recruited back into the classroom and pullout teachers and specialists are infused into teaching teams. Each team consists of seven teachers serving one hundred students and including teachers with expertise in the arts, counseling, and the education of special needs students. Key administrative supports remain—including a principal, secretary, bookkeeper, and social worker for the school and a lead teacher and media and computer specialist for each cluster of three teams at the primary and intermediate grades. Teams members can organize their time to take advantage of each other's different talents for different activities and can draw upon each other's expertise in their collective planning. Classwork no longer needs to be fragmented by an array of pullout programs. The two lead teachers—one for the primary grades and one for the upper grades—have half their time released from teaching to facilitate planning and to cover other teachers' classes while those teachers visit and observe one another. As a result teachers have greater opportunities to learn from one another and students receive greater sustained attention from their teachers. The system as a whole takes greater responsibility for student learning (National Commission on Teaching and America's Future, 1996).

None of this is to argue that overall funding does not make a difference. The schools I have described also benefit from the fact that their very committed teachers donate large quantities of materials, personal resources, and time beyond that for which they are paid. And affluent suburban schools make available many services and opportunities that restructured schools and others in New York City have not been able to provide for their students, including up-to-date computers and curriculum materials and after-school academic and recreational services. So although it is highly useful to learn how

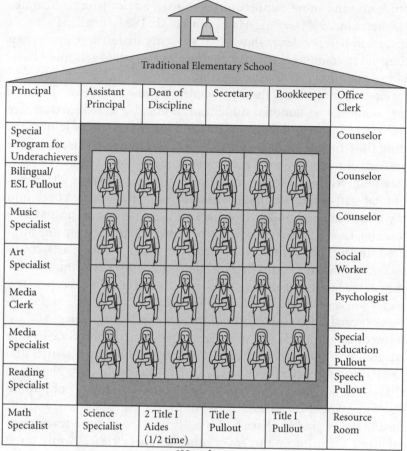

Traditional Elementary School

Principal	Assistant Principal	Dean of Discipline	Secretary	Bookkeeper	Office Clerk
Special Program for Underachievers					Counselor
Bilingual/ ESL Pullout					Counselor
Music Specialist					Counselor
Art Specialist					Social Worker
Media Clerk					Psychologist
Media Specialist					Special Education Pullout
Reading Specialist					Speech Pullout
Math Specialist	Science Specialist	2 Title I Aides (1/2 time)	Title I Pullout	Title I Pullout	Resource Room

600 students
24 classroom teachers
26 other staff
Class size = 25
Teacher time = 3.75 hrs./week

**Figure 6.1.   Traditional and Redesigned
Elementary School Structures Compared.**

Source: National Commission on Teaching and America's Future, 1996, p. 106.

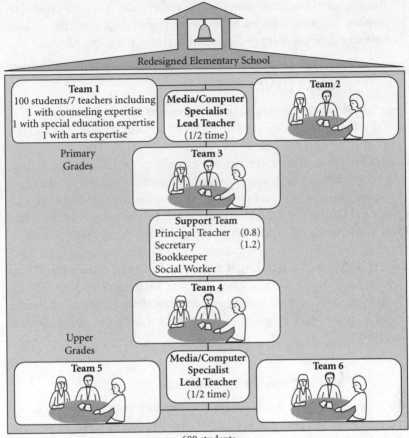

Redesigned Elementary School

Team 1
100 students/7 teachers including
1 with counseling expertise
1 with special education expertise
1 with arts expertise

**Media/Computer
Specialist
Lead Teacher**
(1/2 time)

Team 2

Primary
Grades

Team 3

Support Team
Principal Teacher   (0.8)
Secretary   (1.2)
Bookkeeper
Social Worker

Team 4

Upper
Grades

**Media/Computer
Specialist
Lead Teacher**
(1/2 time)

Team 5

Team 6

600 students
43 teachers (FTE)
7 other staff (FTE)
Class size = 16
Teacher time = 10 hrs./week

reallocations of resources can make a difference, it is also crucial to remember that a foundation of adequate resources is essential. (Issues of resource distribution are discussed further in Chapter Seven.)

A NATIONAL VIEW

What these restructured schools do is possible nearly everywhere. Nationally, the ratio of total staff to pupils in schools is about 1:9 and the ratio of instructional staff to pupils is about 1:13. (This number includes building administrators, supervisors, curriculum specialists, and other certified personnel as well as classroom teachers and aides.) However, the ratio of teachers to pupils is considerably larger at 1:18 (National Center for Education Statistics, 1994a, pp. 89, 93, 95), and class size averages about twenty-four, reaching thirty-five or more in some cities. These averages include some much smaller special education classes and much larger regular education classes (National Center for Education Statistics, 1994b; Picus & Bhimani, 1994). Clearly, schools have changed considerably since the days when one could imagine Mark Hopkins at one end of the log and the student at the other.

Staffing and the Use of Time

What do all the people who are not classroom teachers do? According to the U.S. Department of Labor, in 1986, more than 21 percent of elementary and secondary school employees were engaged in administrative and support functions and 58 percent were engaged in teaching and other professional specialties. The remaining 21 percent were engaged in service, maintenance, and transportation activities. Thus, excluding service workers, school systems employ approximately 1 administrative staff person for every 2.5 instructional staff persons; furthermore, only about three-quarters of these instructional staff actually take on the responsibilities of classroom teaching.

The number of administrative staff in school systems nearly doubled between 1955 and 1985, while the number of teachers increased at only half that rate (National Center for Education Statistics, 1982b, 1987). Much of the growth was in the number of program officials and clerical staff in central and area offices and the number of non-teaching staff within schools (aside from school principals, whose numbers did not increase). By 1993, individuals classified as teachers made up only 52 percent of all staff, a steep decline from the 70 percent of staff who were teachers in 1950 (National Center for Education Statistics, 1994a, 1995a). Of the 52 percent classified as teachers, about one-fifth were not assigned to classroom teaching. Administrative and support staff made up about 30 percent of the total, and principals and other instructional staff made up the remainder (see Figure 6.2).

In contrast, teachers constitute more than three-fourths of all public education employees in Belgium, Japan, and Italy and more than 60 percent in most other countries (Organization for Economic Cooperation and Development, 1995). These countries, rather than build up large external offices for inspecting, monitoring, and controlling teaching, invest more of their resources in supporting the efforts of

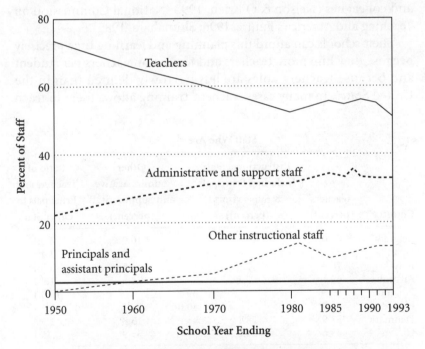

**Figure 6.2.   Staff Employed by Public Schools
(in Full-Time Equivalents).**

Note: Plotted points are school years ending
1950, 1960, 1970, 1981, 1985 to 1991, and 1993.

Source: National Center for Education Statistics, 1993a, pp. 148–149; 1995a, p. 89.

better-paid, better-prepared teachers who are given the time and responsibility for managing most of the work in schools. It is because U.S. schools have invested in a relatively smaller number of lower-paid, less well prepared teachers, directed and augmented by large numbers of administrators, supervisors, and specialists, that the United States far surpasses other countries in the share of nonteaching staff it employs in its schools (see Table 6.3).

Teachers in most of these other countries have broad professional roles that engage them in many aspects of school functioning. They generally teach groups of students only about fifteen to twenty hours out of a forty-to forty-five-hour workweek. During the remaining time, they engage in preparation, joint planning, curriculum and assessment development, school governance, their own professional development (including study groups, observation of other teachers, research, and demonstration lessons), and one-on-one work with students, parents, and colleagues (Nelson & O'Brien, 1993; National Commission on Teaching and America's Future, 1996; Shimahara, 1985).

Their schools can afford this planning and learning time precisely because they hire more teachers and fewer nonteachers per student and because teachers' roles are less narrowly defined than in the United States. In many cases teachers' training allows them to teach

		Staff Who Are		
Country	Teachers (percent)	Instructional Staff Including Principals & Supervisors (percent)	Other Administrative and Support Staff (percent)	Ratio of Teachers and Principals to Other Staff
Belgium	80.0	10.0	10.0	4.0:1
Japan	77.4	—	22.6	3.4:1
Italy	76.4	7.3	14.5	3.5:1
Australia	69.1	7.1	28.6	1.9:1
Finland	60.8	39.2		1.55:1
France	60.0	40.0		1.5:1
Denmark	57.9	28.1	15.8	1.3:1
U. S.	43.6	24.2	33.9	0.75:1

Table 6.3.   International Comparisons of Instructional and Other Staff.
Source: Data © OECD, *Education at a Glance: OECD Indicators,* 1995. Reproduced by permission of the Organization for Economic Cooperation and Development. (This adaptation of the data has also been published in *Using What We Have to Get the Schools We Need: A Productivity Focus for American Education,* 1995, p. 44.)

multiple subjects to the same students rather than a single subject over and over again to different students. Moreover, their schools do not hire specialists to supervise, write curriculum, and run special programs. Instead teachers develop curriculum and manage school affairs. They also serve as guidance counselors for their students. Trained to meet a broad range of learning needs, they do not send special needs students off to pullout classes. And they become more effective because the more ways in which they know their students—over several years as counselors as well as teachers, for example—the more they can adapt instruction to meet student needs. As Nancy Sato (1994) explains, Japanese teachers "cannot imagine hiring a separate counselor, because a major aspect of their role as teacher is that counselor role. They wonder how one can teach students without forming a strong, trusting relationship first. And, once that bond is formed, then they are the best people to serve in the counselor role" (pp. 8–9).

Teachers in other countries often share a workroom in which they spend their breaks and meet regularly to work on curriculum, assessment, and school management together. Japanese and Chinese teachers offer demonstration lessons to each other, intensively discussing the nuances of specific concepts, how they might be presented, what kinds of questions students might have, and what kinds of questions teachers should ask to elicit student interest (Stigler & Stevenson, 1991). German teachers hold "curriculum conferences" within the school to develop class materials and look at student work (Ratzki, 1988). These school structures assume that teachers must see students whole and continually consult with one another to make wise instructional decisions.

In contrast, as I have discussed, the teaching job in the United States is designed as piecework. Teachers instruct large groups of students for most of the day. "Regular" teachers teach standard material to "regular" students. "Special" children are periodically sent off to "special" teachers. Teachers and students have limited time together, teachers do no joint planning, and curricula and materials are designed by others. When this approach is not effective, more special programs, and thus new slots in the bureaucratic matrix, are created.

In this assembly-line conception of teaching, relationships matter little. Policymakers see little need for collegial consultation and planning, for close work with individual students and parents, or for substantial professional development. Thus teachers have little time allowed for these activities. Most U.S. elementary teachers have three or fewer hours for preparation per week (only 8.3 minutes for every hour in the classroom), and secondary teachers generally have five preparation periods per week (13 minutes per hour of classroom instruction) (National Education Association, 1992).

As Figure 6.3 vividly illustrates, it is possible to provide students with larger numbers of teachers and give those teachers time for collegial work if resources are allocated differently. For example, like schools in some other parts of Europe, public schools in Zurich, Switzerland, provide an intensely student-focused educational environment with virtually the same numbers of students and dollars per pupil as the typical U.S. school district of Riverside, California. According to one estimate, in 1986–87, Zurich invested its dollars in twice as many teachers and ten times as many doctors and nurses per pupil by operating with much smaller administrative staffs and running much smaller, more personalized schools (roughly one-fifth the size of U.S. schools on average). In contrast Riverside's administrative and support staff, numbering more than 1,000, nearly equaled its teaching staff and far surpassed the modest administrative staff in Zurich, numbering only 113 (Cheeseboro, 1990). With comparable school expenditures, Zurich's 2,330 teachers earn about 50 percent more than the average for U.S. teachers (Nelson & O'Brien, 1993). The Swiss teachers are also better prepared, more involved in professional decision making, and better supported with time for collegial work than those in most U.S. schools.

Organizational and Funding Strategies

Another difference between U.S. schools and those in many other countries lies in the number of administrative layers between schools and the governmental agencies that fund and administer them. In many other countries a central ministry sends funds directly to schools and manages the lean accountability system—largely composed of curriculum frameworks, assessments, and periodic school reviews—that guides their work. In the United States, schools report at the least to school district central offices, to state education departments, and to the federal government. In most big cities they also report to area offices that sit between the central office and the schools. In many states they also report to regional units that sit between the state department and districts. Thus they report to at least three and more likely four

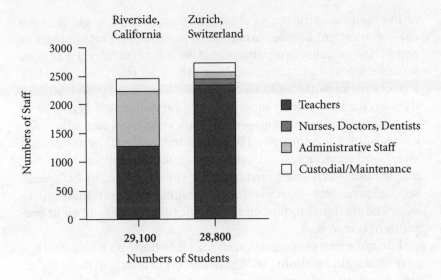

	Riverside, California	Zurich, Switzerland
# of teachers	1,223	2,330
# of nurses, doctors, dentists	9	119
# of certified administrators	142	0
# of classified administrative and office personnel	863	113
# of custodial/maintenance staff	228	167
# of school sites[1]	37	138

Figure 6.3.   Comparison of Riverside, California, and Zurich, Switzerland, School Districts.

[1]Plus 200 kindergarten sites.

Source: Cheeseboro, 1990.

or five major administrative levels. Funding all these levels increases the dollars spent on the management of schooling rather than its conduct. The many programs administered at each level also have separate reporting requirements and offices, so that the typical U.S. school district organizational chart looks like a honeycomb with all its boxes for the assistant superintendents and directors of a large set of specialized core functions—elementary education, secondary education, adult education, pupil personnel services, staff personnel services, food services, research and development, finance and facilities, and the like—and additional boxes for the coordinators of "special service" programs—special education, bilingual education, compensatory education, migrant education, health services, dropout prevention, and so on.

I do not mean to suggest that all such functions are unnecessary or that all should be abolished. There are important functions for restructured districts and state agencies to carry out even when more decisions devolve to the school level. Nor are these observations meant to cast blame upon hard-working agency staff who are doing the jobs set out by the current structures in the only ways those structures allow them to be done. Categorical approaches to program funding and regulatory mandates from legislatures have created the administrative management needs these agencies are required to assume. What I am arguing is that legislative strategies and administrative strategies must be changed in tandem while a new paradigm for organizing districts and state agencies also takes hold.

In recent years superintendents in some school districts have begun to restructure district functions and to reduce central office staffing in ways that build school-level capacity and offer district-level leadership focused more pointedly on improving teaching. For example, District Superintendent Anthony Alvarado, of New York City's Community School District #2, has made professional development the central focus of management and the core strategy for school improvement for his diverse multilingual district of 22,000 students. The belief governing the district's efforts is that students' learning will increase as educators' knowledge grows.

Alvarado has reduced central office functions to the essentials, sent most office staff back to schools, created more functional work units, and focused the attention of all managers on improving teaching. All available discretionary resources, a share now reaching about 3 percent of the total district budget, are invested in professional development for teachers and principals. The investments, which are paying off in rapidly rising student achievement, are funding the Professional Development Laboratory, a project that sends teachers for three-week visits to the classrooms of expert teachers engaged in practices the visitors want to learn; instructional consulting services that allow expert teachers to do sustained work with groups of teachers within schools; cross-school visits and peer networks designed to bring teachers and principals into contact with exemplary practices; and ongoing study groups and intensive summer institutes that focus on core teaching strategies and on learning about new standards, curriculum frameworks, and assessments. There is close careful scrutiny of teaching at every level and continual pressure and support to improve teaching quality (see Elmore, in press). In the long run such district restructuring will be as important as school restructuring to the creation of more productive schools.

ENVISIONING ALTERNATIVES TO TODAY'S BUREAUCRACY

Many of the diseconomies described earlier in this chapter result from the underlying logic of bureaucracy, which seeks to (1) make decisions hierarchically, thus requiring cadres of decision makers above the level of the school and classroom; (2) specialize functions, thus requiring great numbers of specialized personnel and large investments in the coordination of functions; and (3) manage work through the detailed specifications of procedures, thus requiring monitoring of processes and results through elaborate reporting systems. These aspects of bureaucracy increase complexity both vertically (through the extended hierarchy) and horizontally (through extensive specialization), making it difficult for parts of the system to connect to one another, for employees to know how what they are doing relates to what others are doing, and for students to have their needs addressed holistically.

Work Structures and Administrative Demands

Figure 6.4 shows how most U.S. schools are organized to allow specialization by grade level, by subject area, and by special program areas. Teachers work in separate cells in the matrix, which grow increasingly small after the primary grades in terms of the amount of

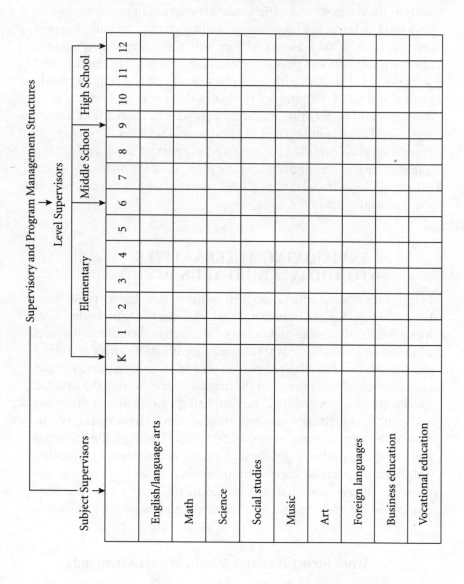

Supervisory and Program Management Structures

Level Supervisors

Subject Supervisors

	K	1	2	3	4	5	6	7	8	9	10	11	12
			Elementary				Middle School				High School		
English/language arts													
Math													
Science													
Social studies													
Music													
Art													
Foreign languages													
Business education													
Vocational education													

Program Supervisors and Staff →

Guidance counseling																	
Compensatory education																	
Special education																	
Bilingual education/ESL																	
Gifted and talented education																	
Drug abuse prevention																	
Pregnancy prevention																	
Dropout prevention																	
Etc.																	

Figure 6.4. Bureaucratic Management of Teaching.

Source: © Organization for Economic Cooperation and Development (1995).

Education at a glance: OECD indicators. Reproduced by permission of the OECD.

student life they cover. Teachers typically have time and opportunity to relate only to the other teachers in their cell and to the supervisors assigned to cover rows or columns in the matrix. Students have to negotiate each cell separately, moving from one teacher to the next, accommodating different settings, expectations, and groups of peers, and making sense of the whole more or less on their own. Adding new ideas for teaching and learning to these vestigial structures simply will not work. Many districts are currently trying to "do reform" without changing the underlying features of school and district organization. The resulting frustrations and clashes of effort are reducing the old system's capacity to do even the limited schooling it knows how to do well and are also impeding reformers' efforts to undertake new strategies (Darling-Hammond, Ancess, MacGregor, & Zuckerman, in press). If new approaches to managing schools are to take hold, the old logic must be replaced by a new one that better accomplishes the goals and functions bureaucracy has tried to serve.

The outcomes of organizing teaching and learning in large highly specialized organizations are counterproductive for both teachers and students. For example, many of the typical problems in urban high schools occur because teachers do not have time to address the many academic and personal needs of the 150 or so students they see each day, because personal attention is difficult to sustain in a school of 2,000 or 3,000 students, and because students' needs, interests, and aspirations do not fit comfortably into the institution's regimens. Student responses to this impersonal environment range from alienation expressed as violence, vandalism, truancy, early pregnancy, and dropping out to underachievement, anomie, and disengagement from school.

Rather than humanizing the educational experience to prevent some of these problems, the bureaucratic solution is to create new offices, job titles, and programs that seek to compensate for the effects of an ill-designed system. It establishes separate offices and staffs—each with its own hierarchy, paperwork, and reporting requirements—to deal with school security, teen pregnancy prevention, dropout prevention, truancy, drug abuse prevention, compensatory education, and so on. The assumption appears to be that carving up students into little pieces that correspond to programs will somehow solve their corresponding problems. But when student maladaptation results from an ill-managed and dehumanized system of schooling, simply adding more programs can have little positive result. Yet the bureaucratic juggernaut rolls on.

When the problems are not solved, still more offices are created to meet the increased "need" for services. As each row and column of the matrix conducts its separate business at the top of the organization and as teachers work in their separate cells at the bottom, the tasks of oversight, communication, and coordination grow ever more unmanageable. Thus bureaucracy feeds on the fruits of its own labor, and resources for schools and classrooms are drained away.

The people who work in bureaucracies are often as frustrated as those who need their services, and they know that their organizations badly need restructuring. For example, when New York City began launching dozens of new high schools, school founders and board of education officials had to coordinate the separate efforts of a high schools division, an alternative schools division, several local school boards, and separate departments in charge of leasing, renovating, purchasing, hiring, and legal matters, all operating more or less independently. When innovation is attempted, diffuse authority and inadequate communication mechanisms cause snafus at every turn. To better use resources and support good work, boards of education need to decentralize those functions that can better be handled by schools and create integrated functional district-level teams for the conduct of functions that remain centralized.

Similarly, when districts manage curriculum and instruction separately from hiring, evaluation, and professional development, the core ideas about what matters in teaching and learning are likely to be disconnected across areas. Policies and practices accrue willy-nilly over time as boards, superintendents, and assistant superintendents come and go with their distinctive ideas. Even when substantive coherence is attempted, it is difficult to enforce. Heroic efforts at reporting and meeting and coordinating take place among administrative and supervisory personnel in districts and schools, but much of the enterprise remains conceptually unglued.

A new logic for building organizations will need to confront the following fundamental assumptions of bureaucracies, whose effects I have been documenting throughout these chapters.

- The assumption that tasks will be performed most efficiently when jobs are highly specialized, broken down into small components and routinized so workers need limited knowledge for each assigned task

- The assumption that organizations are most effective when managed from the top down, divorcing both frontline workers and their clients from major decisions

- The assumption that knowledge residing at the top of a bureaucracy can be codified in rules and procedures so that the workers need relatively little skill except in following orders

New Alternatives and Professional Knowledge

Although the flaws in these three bureaucratic assumptions are now obvious, the solutions have been less so. Many states and districts have begun to decentralize decision making and expand teachers' roles. However, few have recognized the critical link between the knowledge base of educators and the success of new strategies. Consequently, the results of efforts to share decision making, create more inclusive instructional groups, and restructure teaching schedules and curriculum have been extremely uneven. Success has occurred where educators have had the opportunity to develop the knowledge and skills they need to enact more complex practices; where educators have lacked requisite knowledge, unintended but inevitable failure has followed reform attempts.

A high degree of teacher knowledge and effective, personalized school settings are closely interrelated. It is because many U.S. educators have received relatively little preparation for understanding learning processes, student development, and adaptive teaching that special programs and offices have proliferated. Because the teaching job has been viewed as the implementation of routines for "normal" students, most teachers have not been prepared to handle "special" students—those who learn poorly from lecture and recitation strategies, who do not speak fluent English, who develop at different rates or in different ways than others their age, or who have minor learning difficulties such as visual or perceptual problems. In fact *most* students fit one or more of these descriptions, and because "regular" classrooms are often too rigid to adapt to their learning needs, an increasing number of them do poorly or are placed in special education and remedial programs. Inflexible curriculum systems and teachers' inadequate knowledge that lead to referrals of students out of the regular classroom require the hiring of more specialists, which paradoxically reduces funding for the teacher development and smaller classes that would allow regular teachers to meet a greater range of student needs.

In Boston, for example, a recent study found that 30 percent of students are identified for special education, bilingual education, or Chapter 1 programs, and 40 percent of teachers teach these students in pullout classes (Miles, 1995). Consequently, despite a teacher-to-pupil ratio of 1:13, most regular Boston classrooms average twenty-three students and some are as large as thirty-four. Miles observes:

> Using so many teachers outside regular classrooms means that all students, except those receiving completely separate education, spend the bulk of their time in larger instructional groups. In addition Boston, like many school systems, has needed to develop administrative systems to monitor and coordinate the various teachers and service providers working with special students. This process diverts even more resources from the regular classroom, gradually making them larger. So, ironically, the very action designed to lessen the demands on teachers, referring a student outside the regular classroom, may increase them. . . . The pattern is self-perpetuating: the more schools designate specialists to respond to diverse learning needs, the less resources and pressure exist to help teachers in the regular classroom develop these skills [pp. 479–480].

Since the 1970s, the proportions of funds and school staffing resources devoted to special educational programs have grown astronomically. An analysis of school spending in New York State between 1979 and 1992 found that the most dramatic area of expenditure increase was for students designated as disabled. Spending for teaching of children with disabilities accounted for 5 percent of total budgets in 1980 and 13 percent in 1992. Meanwhile expenditures for teaching "regular" students dropped from 54 percent to 49 percent of the total. In that same period, spending for pupil personnel services (school psychologists, counselors, and the like) and other nonteachers also grew at a substantially faster rate than other categories of staff salaries (Lankford & Wyckoff, 1995).

Some states, like New York and California, are creating new licensing categories and endorsements to encourage more teachers to gain knowledge of how to teach special needs students. New standards for teachers from the National Board for Professional Teaching Standards and related licensing standards from the Interstate New Teacher Assessment and Support Consortium expect all teachers to have greater knowledge of how to teach learners with special needs, including new

English language learners and those with learning disabilities. And some colleges and school districts are offering professional development that helps teachers become much more effective with diverse learners. These programs help teachers learn to practice in the ways described in the last two chapters: how to collaborate with one another in studying children; how to use varied learning approaches; how to use assessment and peer tutoring strategies for more intensive and individually focused instruction; and how to focus systematically on core ideas and critical content, using graphic, verbal, and visual representations to make ideas accessible to a wide range of learners (Joint Committee on Teacher Planning for Students with Disabilities, 1995).

By supporting such teacher learning, schools can make it possible for nearly all students to succeed in more intimate mainstreamed settings. The more knowledgeable and skilled each teacher becomes, the less fragmented schools need to be.

POLICIES FOR PRODUCTIVE RESTRUCTURING

If schools are to find the financial means and organizational capacity to make significant change, major reallocations of resources and authority must be made from central offices and peripheral programs to classrooms and the support of teacher learning.

To foster personalized settings, funding policies that encourage the building of large schools because they are supposedly efficient need to be replaced by policies that encourage the building of schools with optimum sizes of about 300 to 600 that are actually more efficient and effective. Another option is to build multiuse sites that accommodate several schools that share space for such facilities as gymnasiums, athletic fields, and libraries and such services as health care and day-care centers.

To ensure that teachers are prepared to work with a range of diverse learners, licensing standards will need to demand greater knowledge about learners and learning on the one hand and support preparation for more cross-disciplinary teaching on the other. As in Germany, teachers might be encouraged to prepare in two disciplinary fields rather than one so they can offer greater expert curricular coverage along with more personalization of teacher-student relationships.

Time for ongoing professional development and collaborative work must be structured within schools. If even half of the professional staff currently working outside the classroom were recruited back to classroom teaching, every teacher could have at least ten to twelve hours per week of collective planning time. Salary schedules offering knowledge- and skill-based pay would be incentives for teachers to develop multiple areas of expertise and would support flexibility and expansion in job roles (Conley & Odden, 1995). Each team of teachers should contain the distributed expertise needed to serve students well within and across groups.

To allow more intensive, focused approaches to learning, states and districts must loosen rigid time requirements for the teaching of specific subject areas and reduce the number of instructional mandates that have accrued over time. New York State, for example, not only requires specific coursework in mathematics, English, spelling, reading, writing, social studies, history, geography, government, global studies, economics, science, art, music, health, hygiene, physical education, foreign language, and occupational education but also requires instruction on the topics of Flag Day, drug and alcohol abuse, the dangers of driving, bicycle and traffic safety (thirty periods), the humane treatment of animals and birds (weekly), fire prevention (monthly), fire drills (at least twelve a year), the conservation of natural resources (last Friday in April), and much more (New York State Education Department, 1990).

In order to invest greater resources in classroom teaching, states and districts also need to repeal overly prescriptive staffing regulations. For example, in addition to its staggering array of curriculum, program, testing, and reporting mandates, New York State has regulations that require districts to hire guidance counselors, a director of physical education, a health coordinator, a full-time principal, a specified number of certified school library media specialists and certified assistants, a district treasurer, and a tax collector. Interestingly, there are no requirements for hiring a minimum number of teachers (New York State Education Department, 1990).

Furthermore, teachers in New York City, as in many other districts, must be supervised by principals or assistant principals, who must be released for all or specified portions of their teaching loads based on the number of people they supervise. Teachers may not supervise other teachers; thus peer review processes are precluded, and review requirements lead to a further proliferation of nonteaching staff. Although alternative schools are not subject to all these staffing regulations, in traditional schools, staffing units must be used for the categories for which they are allocated and approved by the central board. This can sometimes mean reducing funding for teaching to protect administrative positions. For example, New York City's 1994–95 "Allocation Guidelines" advise that the "allocation for Assistant Principals, Special Education . . . must be used for the purpose intended and scheduled" and the school "must continue to budget fully for that position even if they are not funded fully for that position" (New York City Board of Education, 1994).

Such staffing patterns are deeply embedded. When a mentoring program to allow veteran teachers to assist beginning teachers was introduced in New York State, the administrators' union sued the state, arguing that the program violated requirements about who could supervise teachers. The state ultimately ruled against the union, arguing that it was difficult to see how it could be harmful for teachers to help their novice colleagues. Ultimately, each of the regulations governing allocations of staff will need to be evaluated and many of them eliminated for schools to have the flexibility to restructure teaching in more productive and professional ways.

There are good reasons for some such requirements and for the ones found in state and regional school accreditation procedures. They set a floor of educational opportunities for all students in a society that leaves much education funding to the whims of local taxpayers. Although this function remains critically important, the way it is currently pursued relies on bureaucratic presumptions about school organization and staffing that are now outdated. Attempts to tightly specify school inputs have not equalized resources among schools— although they have constrained educators' imaginations about how resources might be more effectively deployed. As I argue in the next two chapters, it would be preferable for accreditation and funding strategies to ensure the full and equitable funding of a curricular entitlement that supports professional standards of practice and high standards of learning for all students, rather than to specify the particular configuration of inputs schools should provide.

In this era of school redesign, we should no longer seek to dictate all the educational approaches local schools must follow. Instead, in our press for higher performance and greater equality, we should ensure that schools have clear goals coupled with adequate resources that can form a solid foundation for local decision making about how best to teach. The task ahead is to marshall local energy with state supports and leadership in a synergy more conducive to innovation and equity than current prescriptions for practice on a base of unequal resources now allow.

Note

1. This chapter reports findings from a study I conducted in 1994–95 with the assistance of Peter Robertson and Lori Chajet through the National Center for Restructuring Education, Schools, and Teaching at Teachers College, Columbia University. We collected budget and staffing data and conducted interviews with key staff at four schools—two traditional and two restructured high schools—to understand how they allocate people and dollars to the various tasks of schooling.

## CHAPTER SEVEN

Creating Standards
Without Standardization

*What the best and wisest parent wants for his own child,
that must the community want for all of its children. Any
other ideal for our schools is narrow and unlovely; acted
upon, it destroys our democracy.*

—John Dewey, The School and Society ([1900] 1956), p. 3)

What would the best and wisest parent want for his
own child? And how can it be enacted for all the children of the community? How can a society develop and support its schools so that
good teaching is widespread rather than reserved to only a few?
Throughout this book I have argued for efforts that build the capacity of schools and teachers to support more powerful learning. Better-
supported teachers working in better-organized schools will certainly
make a difference. But this does not mean a system is no longer
needed or that existing policies can be ignored. What teachers can accomplish is profoundly influenced by the environments in which they
work and the expectations for schools in the society as a whole. Even
if schools were more sensibly managed and more equitably funded,
we would still have to answer the question of what kind of learning
they would undertake. This chapter outlines one answer.

One lesson of change, according to Michael Fullan (1991), is that
neither centralization nor decentralization works; that is, just as wide-

spread school change cannot occur solely by policy mandate, neither can it occur by school invention alone, without supports from the policy system. If school-level reforms continue only by waiver and exception, they will surely evaporate in a very short time, long before good schooling spreads to the communities where it is currently most notable by its absence. And if policies do not address questions of education goals, systemwide capacity, and equity, the outcomes of bottom-up efforts will be inadequate to the needs of a democratic society. Neither a heavy-handed view of top-down reform nor a romantic vision of bottom-up change is plausible. Both local invention and supportive leadership are needed, along with new horizontal efforts that support cross-school consultation and learning.

If some system is needed, the question is how much system and of what kind? What should the system seek to do? And how should policies be framed to accomplish these goals? I argue in this chapter that standards for student learning, linked to standards for teaching and schooling, are core elements of an education infrastructure that can support a genuine right to learn. These standards could provide a basis for curriculum and assessment policies, resource allocations, supports for professional learning, and occasions for teacher and school inquiry that create pressure and encouragement for change. Although standards and tests cannot by themselves drive classroom practice, well-constructed standards that articulate a strong professional consensus can encourage reforms that bring to life in our schools the notion of a right to learn.

THE POTENTIAL OF STANDARDS TO MOBILIZE CHANGE

A coherent view of curriculum, assessment, and teaching is at the core of any vision of more effective education. Education standards have become a major policy vehicle in part because they can reflect changes in goals, including, for example, the major shift in the kind of learning our society desires of young people, which in turn requires a major shift in teaching and schooling. Depending on how they are fashioned and used, however, standards for learning can either energize or kill reform.

Recent efforts to create standards for students have focused on *content* and *performance* standards that outline what students should know and how they should demonstrate their understanding. Content standards might suggest, for example, that middle school students be able to write a persuasive essay. Performance standards would then articulate evaluation criteria and provide illustrations of what a good essay includes (for example, a clearly stated opinion supported by reasons and evidence, an explanation and refutation of opposing points of view, and appropriate use of writing conventions). Many professional associations and states have begun to fashion curriculum frameworks structured around such content and performance standards and indicators. In some cases, especially in mathematics, states and localities have made considerable use of professionally developed standards as they develop curriculum.

The fundamental premise of today's standards-based reform is that challenging education goals and contemporary knowledge about how people learn can be incorporated into practice when standards guide decisions about curriculum, teaching, and assessment. The power of standards as tools for guiding practice can be seen in other countries' schools and in the professions that have built a strong knowledge base that is acknowledged as the foundation for professional decisions.

In most European and some Asian countries, goals and objectives for curriculum are developed by educators working through their state, provincial, or national ministries of education. These curriculum frameworks are slim documents that outline core concepts to be treated in each field. They are typically linked to systems of assessments, also developed and scored by teachers, that are used at key junctures in the educational process, especially near the close of middle school and of high school. The assessments are generally performance based. They evaluate students' learning through essay and oral examinations, reviews of in-class student work, research papers, interviews, and portfolios of student work. Sometimes students choose the tasks or areas in which they will be examined. Often they defend their work before jurors who probe their thinking and press for deeper understanding.

Teachers are involved in examining their own students and those in other schools. Because assessments are scored by teachers and tied to ongoing classroom work, the process of assessment informs practice and helps develop shared standards among faculty and students across the educational enterprise as a whole. In addition teacher preparation supports the development of teaching skills associated with these goals, and inspection systems also support the standards. Although it would be misleading to characterize these systems as flawlessly tidy, many strive for a thoughtful approach to curriculum and for coherence among the few areas in which they influence schools.

Standards of practice are also used in many professions. They guide the work of architects in constructing sound buildings, accountants in managing finances, engineers in assembling space shuttles, and doctors in treating patients. Professional standards also guide the training and licensing of professionals in these fields. These standards are not prescriptions; instead they reflect shared norms and knowledge about underlying principles of practice, the effects of various techniques, and decision-making processes.

Educators in the United States have much less experience than these other groups with the development and use of professional standards. Because teaching in the United States has been managed as a bureaucratic rather than a professional enterprise, vehicles for developing and transmitting standards—such as professional associations, standards boards, and accrediting agencies—have traditionally been weak or nonexistent. Instead implicit and unexamined standards exist by default. They are the aggregations of decisions made by textbook makers, test publishers, individual state agencies, legislatures, and school boards, often uninformed by professional knowledge, shared ideals, or consensual goals for education. Teachers are rarely involved in the professional activities of standard setting, curriculum development, or assessment.

Although there is much agreement among educators and policymakers on the need for schools to aim for much more useful and challenging learning, disagreements exist over how standards should be defined and how they should be pursued and evaluated. In some views, curriculum standards should be the basis for national or state tests linked to rewards and sanctions for students, teachers, and schools and intended to drive change from the top down. In other views, standards developed by professional associations should be tools for inquiry, used to inform state and local policies and to energize schools' efforts to rethink practice. I argue that standards for student learning can be most useful when they are used as guideposts, not straitjackets, for building curriculum, assessments, and professional development opportunities, and when they are used to focus and mobilize system resources rather than to punish students and schools.

In this chapter I describe why and how I believe standards-based reforms could help learning, particularly if policymakers use standards in ways that take into account the contexts of schools and the preconditions for change. I argue that useful approaches to standards-based reforms should use government policy sparingly and encourage extensive involvement of the education profession and local communities. State guidance should be "designed as a shell within which the kernel of professional judgment and decision making can function comfortably," orienting teachers and schools "toward collectively valued goals without mandating specific sets of procedures" (Shulman, 1983, p. 501). Policies should be based on an understanding of how change actually occurs and on an appreciation of how government can support good work without getting in the way.

POLICY AND THE REALITIES OF CHANGE

Policymakers need to understand that policy is not so much implemented as it is reinvented at each level of the system. What ultimately happens in schools and classrooms is less related to the intentions of policymakers than it is to the knowledge, beliefs, resources, leadership, and motivations that operate in local contexts. These are among the factors that produce what Richard Elmore (1983) has called "the power of the bottom over the top."

Telling schools to change has never worked to produce markedly different teaching over many decades of efforts at curriculum reform. The transmission curriculum has hung on tenaciously even when structural changes have occurred (Cuban, 1990; Tyack & Tobin, 1994). Studies of change efforts have found that the fate of new programs and ideas rests on teachers' and administrators' opportunities to learn, experiment, and adapt ideas to their local context. Without these opportunities, innovations fade away when the money stops or enforcement pressures end (Berman & McLaughlin, 1978; McLaughlin, 1987; Fullan, 1991). Because policies "cannot mandate what matters most" (McLaughlin, 1990), they must alter the conditions for local learning if they want to achieve their goals.

In addition policymakers need to understand that their intentions will land in an environment already cluttered by geological layers of prior policies and local conditions that may be hostile to the desired changes (Darling-Hammond, 1990a). Policymakers must build capacity for and commitment to the work required rather than assuming that edicts alone will produce the new practice they envision. The more policies impose inflexible constraints, the less possible and likely it is for innovation and learning to occur.

Lessons from Previous Curriculum Reforms

Despite impressive attempts to expand the reach of engaging, intellectually demanding instruction, neither bottom-up nor top-down reforms of the past have had much reach or staying power. The efforts of progressive educators in the 1930s demonstrated both the success of school-level reforms and their failure to change the system. And federally sponsored curriculum reforms in the 1960s demonstrated how consensus about learning could be created at the top of the system without widely influencing the field.

A major reason for these failures was the process by which changes were sought in schools beyond the initial experimental sites. Early "implementers," who had had the opportunity to become deeply engaged in the process of school invention, developed the commitment and capacity to undertake new practices. Later on, however, practitioners were expected to enact these complex new ideas without struggling through a process of questioning and developing their own appropriate practices. Reform ideas are often passed on as dicta or mandates, a thin listing of new things to do, conveyed with little discussion or rationale. Thus many of the practitioners involved in the second and later stages of reform never really understood what the initiatives were about.

Perhaps the most important finding from the Eight-Year Study of progressive schools in the 1930s (see Chapter One) was that the most successful schools were distinguished by the process of inquiry staff undertook together rather than by the content of the particular reforms they developed. Their success came from their search for shared goals, which they used to guide curriculum and organizational decisions (Chamberlin, Chamberlin, Drought, & Scott, 1942). Teachers and administrators reported that it was the collective thinking stimulated by this process that engendered the vitality, willingness to change, and conviction to continue that changed the life of their school (Aiken, 1942).

Such commitment and a schoolwide capacity for collective problem solving are essential to any serious change. Because practices that take learning seriously affect all the core technologies of schooling, new practices threaten all the "regularities" of schools (Sarason, 1982). When teachers today try to develop more challenging instruction and attend to the individual needs of students, their efforts bump up against traditional schedules, discipline policies, grading and promotion procedures, and virtually everything else that defines the current schooling enterprise. When schools are able to recognize the extensive changes needed for this learner-centered teaching to succeed, new instructional practices can lead to transformation of other existing conditions of schooling. Without such recognition, reforms become diluted or are pushed off to special programs for small numbers of students. If the whole school does not evolve to support the demands of more challenging instruction and more learner-centered practices, the changes are strangled. Practitioners claim, honestly, that "we tried it and it didn't work."

Similarly, it can be argued that the reforms of the 1960s were successful in articulating the big ideas underlying a curriculum of understanding and enacting them in powerful ways in the schools where teachers worked as partners in invention (Elmore, 1996). The initiatives of that time were developed by some of this nation's most prominent curriculum scholars and learning theorists, including Joseph Schwab, who developed the Biological Sciences Curriculum Study (BSCS), and Jerome Bruner, whose Man: A Course of Study (MACOS) extended a curriculum of understanding into the social sciences. Related efforts were launched by the School Mathematics Study Group (SMSG Math), the Physical Sciences Study Committee (PSSC Physics), and many others.

These efforts all met with the same fate. The top-down curriculum reform worked in those schools that were also directly involved in bottom-up work on the ideas and practices embodied in the curriculum programs. This participation in the inventive process made serious change possible. As the curricula spread, however, teachers elsewhere were expected to implement approaches they had had no role in developing. Without deep understanding or commitment to the ideas, they were unable to bring them off successfully, and the reforms died out.

Despite a tremendous investment in development and a massive flurry of adoption activities, the reforms withered on the vine, soured by the inability of most teachers to implement the kind of challenging instruction the reforms envisioned and starved of local support for the kind of teaching and learning they sought. The limited payoff from these enormous investments demonstrates that reliance on top-down curriculum reform as a means of changing schools is a strategy with serious flaws. School change is a much more complicated affair than introducing a different curriculum. It rests on the capacities and willingness of teachers and administrators to comprehend and undertake multiple desired changes and also on the support or resistance offered by the community in which changes must root if they are to survive.

In the postmortem analyses of the 1960s reforms, researchers discovered that teachers' curriculum translations were so varied as to negate the concept of a common curriculum. For example, a BSCS study revealed that teachers teaching the same lessons from the same course versions to classes of similar ability levels taught so differently that "there really is no such thing as a BSCS curriculum presentation in the schools" (Gallagher, 1967, p. 17). Then came the finding from Harvard's Project Physics course and others that students' ultimate achievement and attitudes were not solely a function of the curriculum. Instead they were strongly related to teachers' values and classroom behaviors and to the resulting social learning climate in classrooms (Rothman, Welch, & Walberg, 1969; Walberg & Rothman, 1969). Finally, researchers discovered that the processes of curriculum implementation and school change—that is, the ways in which schools and school districts set out to engage these new ideas—strongly influenced outcomes (Carlson, 1965). The manner in which change is introduced and supported influences the attitudes, knowledge, ability, and political will of those attempting implementation (Fullan, 1991). And the dispositive factor in curriculum reform is ultimately what teachers know, believe, and are able and willing to do.

The flawed belief that reforms can simply be replicated elsewhere once they have been developed in demonstration sites is one key to the unhappy history of curriculum change. The process of change is inherently constructivist. Any reform that is merely implemented will eventually recede rather than taking root. Each school community must struggle with new ideas for itself if it is to develop the deep understanding and commitment needed to engage in the continual problem solving demanded by major changes in practice. As Fullan (1994) observes, it is impossible to achieve ownership in advance of learning something new. "It is only when greater clarity and coherence is achieved in the minds of the majority of teachers that we have any chance of success" (p. 4).

Transformations that stick also require the involvement of parents and students and the commitment of central offices (which will otherwise continue to develop competing policies). However, because most school systems do not know how to manage the intensive engagement with ideas and people required to enact broad policy change, they typically adopt only the superficial trappings of reforms—those features they can absorb with comfort without threatening the status quo.

Déjà Vu All Over Again

Research findings on the fate of the 1960s curriculum reforms are already being reiterated in studies of current efforts. For example, with little information or professional development available, teachers striving to use California's new mathematics framework have had difficulty learning to teach in the new ways it calls for. One teacher commented to a researcher, "My biggest hurdle to doing all these new methods . . . is my knowledge of what I've done all these years." Another asked repeatedly, "Still, how do you teach problem solving? I do not know" (Darling-Hammond, 1990b, p. 239).

In addition, reformers rarely consider how new ideas will lodge in local contexts with their variable levels of resources, distinctive community ideas, and preexisting policy constraints. When schools do not have the fiscal resources or curriculum tools to enact reform goals and when community members are suspicious about the goals and tactics of new curricula, new ideas cannot succeed. Furthermore, as mentioned earlier, policies do not land on fresh ground; they land on top of other policies, many of which are not conducive to the strategies needed for enacting the new ideas.

In the case of the California mathematics framework, for example, researchers found that teachers' efforts were confounded by the state's multiple-choice basic skills testing program, which was at odds with the goals of the new framework, and by many districts' use of direct instruction models for classroom control and teacher evaluation. One teacher noted that "teaching for understanding is what we are supposed to be doing . . . [but] the bottom line here is that all they really want to know is how are these kids doing on the tests. . . . They want me to teach in a way that they can't test, except that I'm held accountable to the test. It's a Catch 22" (quoted in Wilson, 1990, p. 318).

In addition, the case studies found that supervisory models such as the Achievement for Basic Skills (ABS) program and Madeline Hunter's Instructional Theory into Practice approach also required tactics at odds with the framework's goals. These approaches presume a teacher-directed classroom featuring tightly structured content presentations, independent drill-and-practice, and frequent questioning and testing at a low cognitive level. In contrast, the framework presumes students will engage in in-depth problem solving, extensive discussion of ideas, cooperative learning, and complex time-consuming assessments of understanding. As one teacher said of the tensions between the new framework's goal to teach students to think and the strict pacing system and testing required by the mandated ABS program: "I don't know how well [the ABS test] measures their understanding of concepts. . . . It's hard. . . . [The students] are not used to thinking, and there isn't enough time to let them sit there and figure it out" (quoted in Peterson, 1990, p. 293).

Teachers sense the contradictions between the way they are required to teach under old systems and the way they need to teach to be successful in the new system, but neither states nor school districts have been prepared to deal with the conflicts their policies have posed. Teachers' efforts to learn a difficult new pedagogy are undermined by curriculum guides, teacher evaluation systems, and testing programs reflecting contradictory images and standards for teaching. As Brian Rowan (1996) comments: "Misaligned standards can result from an incremental approach to change, in which standards in one area are reformed while others remain unchanged. But misaligned standards can also result from invalid theories of performance. For example, policy makers can hold a faulty theory of teacher performance and design a system of education standards consistent with this faulty theory" (pp. 211–212).

Getting It Right

Coherence clearly counts. When parts of the policy system conflict with one another, the whole enterprise lurches about like a carriage pulled by horses dashing off in different directions. When schoolpeople are continually asked to work in self-contradictory contexts, they must either become cynical or adopt an Alice-in-Wonderland attitude—"if you don't know where you're going, any road will get you there." After a while, they cease trying to make sense of things.

The obvious need for sensible reinforcing connections among the influences on teaching, learning, curriculum, assessment, evaluation, and funding has led to proposals for "systemic reform" that have informed much policy work in the 1990s (Fuhrman, 1993; O'Day & Smith, 1993). Even among those who believe that greater coherence in the cause of more empowering forms of learning is a worthy goal, however, there is substantial disagreement about how best to achieve it. A key area of disagreement is the extent to which systemic reform ought to try, as reformers did at the beginning of the twentieth century, to design and mandate the specifications for schooling from the top of a government system and the extent to which it ought to establish key parameters and supports but delegate strategic and technical decisions to schools, communities, and the teaching profession.

FINDING THE RIGHT ROLE FOR GOVERNMENT   Part of the task of developing more constructive supports for schools is understanding what the best roles are for government and for local practitioners, parents, and professional associations. We now know some things about what governments are good at and where their intervention is likely to be counterproductive. In general, higher-level agencies are needed for allocating and reallocating resources in equitable ways, for addressing gross abuses of authority or law, and for supporting learning across institutions and jurisdictions. They can spread knowledge by funding and disseminating research and demonstration projects, and they can help widely dispersed people and institutions work with one another, thus offsetting parochialism and inefficiencies in service delivery. Recently, networks have become another strategy for accomplishing these important tasks when bureaucracies have failed.

However, governments are not good at specifying precisely how funds should be spent, how resources should be configured, or how educational treatments should be conceived and delivered. As Tom Green (1983) notes:

> Public policy is a crude instrument for securing social ideals. We would not use a drop-forge to quarter a pound of butter or an axe to perform heart surgery. Public policy is the drop-forge or the axe of social change. It is not the knife or scalpel. That is to say, public policy deals with gross values. It . . . is not the fit instrument to secure all our desires. For example, even if we knew what is needed to make every school excellent and every teacher a paradigm of wisdom in the care of children, it would remain doubtful that we could express this knowledge in public policy and thus secure the good we seek. . . . Minimizing evil is a proper aim of public policy. Maximizing good is probably not. The latter assumes that we may shape the axe into a scalpel [pp. 322–323].

It is useful to divide responsibilities between those that must be centrally administered and those that by their nature should not.

Wise (1979) offers a useful distinction between equity and productivity concerns in this regard. The former generally must be resolved by higher units of governance because inequalities "arise out of the conflicting interests of majorities and minorities and of the powerful and the powerless. Because local institutions are apparently the captives of majoritarian politics, they intentionally and unintentionally discriminate. Consequently, we must rely upon the policymaking system to solve problems of inequity in the operating educational system" (p. 206). However, productivity questions are intrinsically more difficult because they arise not out of a political impasse but from the fact that the appropriate use of teaching knowledge is highly individualized while policies are necessarily standardized. Varying student circumstances make it impossible to effectively regulate methods of teaching. It is because public policy cannot act as an effective arbiter of such teaching decisions that it is important to ensure teachers' professional competence.

This analysis suggests that states should undertake policies that

- Create a political consensus around education goals and adopt high-quality standards that embody these goals.
- Ensure adequacy and equity in the allocation of resources.
- Develop and enforce meaningful standards of competence for professional staff.
- Build local school capacity through professional development and the support of organizational learning across schools.

Meanwhile governments should delegate decisions about teaching and learning processes and specific curriculum strategies to local schools and professional associations, which can better determine the needs of individual learners and incorporate advances in knowledge. Professionally developed standards can create a lens for examining local school practice in light of appropriate norms (Elmore, 1996). Such use of standards can create the discourse needed to support improvement within schools as it also develops an external presence for accountability.

As a nonhierarchical alternative to the top-down–bottom-up view that places policy people at the top and schoolpeople at the bottom, we might imagine a set of concentric circles beginning with the student, the teacher, and the school and eventually encompassing the community, the school district, and the state (see Figure 7.1.) This image allows for a simultaneously inside-out and outside-in view of schooling influences. Productive tension and learning can occur as faculty interact with one another and with students and families within schools and as schools interact with community concerns, external standards, and professional networks. These influences are multidirectional; every part of the enterprise informs and affects every other.

Each part of the system pursues accountability as shared goals, norms, and values are translated into *policies*, organizational *structures* are created to make the policies work, *processes* that guide work are employed within these structures, *feedback and assessment* mecha-

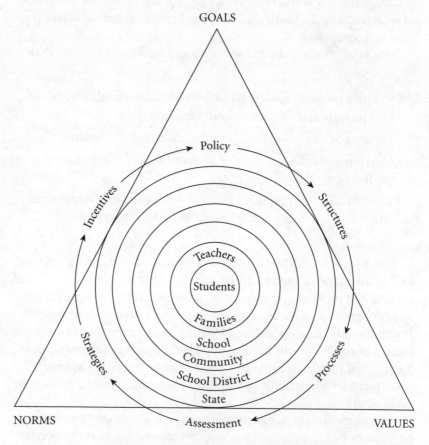

Figure 7.1.   A Model of Accountable Policy.

nisms are established to identify needs and progress, *safeguards* are created to ensure that harmful practices do not occur, and *incentives* are designed to promote productive practices. For children to be well served, these aspects of school, district, and state efforts must work together and focus on both the demands of learning and the needs of learners.

SUPPORTING THE WORK OF CHANGE   If policymakers want to design policies that can work to change instruction so it supports greater student understanding, their theories must account for the ways in which teachers' knowledge, beliefs, and contexts influence their teaching. In particular policymakers need to understand how human beings learn to do things differently (Elmore, 1996), so that they can structure reforms in ways likely to change practice.

What teachers already know and believe about subjects and students, what they have had the opportunity to learn about pedagogy, and what the structures of schools enable them to do are all critical variables in the change process. Policymakers who want teachers to succeed at new kinds of teaching must understand that the process of change requires that teachers have time and opportunities to reconstruct their practice through intensive study and experimentation.

This means that policies should, first, create extensive *learning opportunities* for teachers, administrators, parents, and community members, so that the complex practices envisioned by ambitious standards have a chance to be studied, debated, tried out, analyzed, retried, and refined until they are well understood and incorporated into the repertoire of those who teach and make decisions in schools. These opportunities must be collaborative rather than individualistic, involving groups of educators, parents, and others inside and across schools who interact regularly around problems of practice, engage in joint problem solving, probe the meaning of their experiences, and provide each other with moral support in the difficult process of reform.

Second, policies should allow for widespread *engagement* of a school's constituencies in the process of considering, developing, and enacting changes. Communities must have a substantial role in constructing their own reforms. As I discussed earlier, when people are asked merely to implement ideas handed down to them by others, these ideas are bound to be poorly understood and mistrusted unless people have an opportunity to create adaptations that will be valued and appropriate in the local context. Success comes when reformers provide those who must create change with the leadership that enables them to take charge of their own reform process rather than be smothered under prescriptions for implementation.

Third, policies should recognize the need for *simultaneous change* in all the regularities of schooling that influence the possibilities for successful teaching. This means rethinking the entire array of policies from school funding to teacher education to school accreditation to collective bargaining rules that hold the current regularities of schooling so firmly in place.

Finally, policies should be constructed to maintain the delicate balance between external standards that press for improvement and the school autonomy that is the engine for internal change. I argue that this can best be achieved by developing *professional standards* for learning, teaching, and schooling and using these standards to guide *school inquiry* processes that stimulate engagement, learning, and renewal within schools.

TOWARD STANDARDS-BASED REFORM THAT SUPPORTS INSIDE-OUT CHANGE

Proponents of standards and assessments as levers for systemic change believe such standards can provide a focal point for raising student performance across the nation. The National Council on Education Standards and Testing (NCEST) argued in its 1992 report that "in the absence of demanding content and performance standards, the United States has gravitated toward having a de facto minimal skills curriculum. The many state minimum competency tests, the lower level skills orientation of most textbooks, and state and local policies that do not adequately promote quality are examples of this minimal approach. . . . Such low expectations shortchange students and ill-serve the country. Yet as long as today's low standards remain in place, the performance of the majority of students is unlikely to improve substantially" (p. 12).

Proponents of national standards have viewed coherent guidance at the upper reaches of government as a necessary starting point for local consistency in planning and management (O'Day & Smith, 1993). Such standards would consist of statements of what students should know and be able to do, incorporated into documents like curriculum frameworks to guide other education policies such as those concerning teacher preparation, curriculum materials, and assessments. The vision is that "when fully implemented, this model of content-driven systemic reform would be a uniquely American adaptation of the educational policies and structures of many of the world's highly developed nations. It would marry the vision and guidance provided by coherent, integrated, centralized education policies common in many nations with the high degree of local responsibility and control demanded by U.S. tradition" (O'Day & Smith, 1993, p. 252).

Given the messy state of education governance and politics in this nation, the relative scarcity of professional vehicles for guiding school decision making, the conflicting policies to which school practitioners must respond, and the forces that have allowed commercially developed texts and tests to set standards, the argument for standards-based systemic change starting from clear definitions of curriculum goals is an appealing one.

Others, however, worry that standards and tests could overspecify curriculum and teaching so that communities would have no voice and teachers no room to address diverse student and community needs and interests. They argue that, given the nature of knowledge and the diversity of human experiences and paths to learning, it is not plausible to decide from places far from schools and classrooms exactly what, how, when, and in what way ideas ought to be taught and student understanding tested (Clune, 1993; Sizer, McDonald, & Rogers, 1992).

Opponents have raised a number of further concerns and issues: that national or state standards would override the local involvement in standard setting necessary for creating serious conversation about educational aims and for developing commitment to difficult changes (Sizer, 1991, 1992); that national standards and tests would necessarily narrow curriculum, just as some state and local tests already have in the United States and as examinations have in other countries (Madaus, 1992, 1988); that new tests would demonstrate how much disparity in achievement exists but would do nothing to ameliorate unequal learning opportunities and by creating new hurdles might exacerbate unequal education and employment opportunities; and that standards-based reform might ignore the more difficult and fundamental aspects of school improvement. One critique argued that the NCEST report "puts its faith in tests, maintaining that tests and standards 'can be the cornerstone of the fundamental, systemic reform necessary to reform schools.' Moreover, its specific proposals for national action are largely limited to tests and standards. Most of the remaining and more difficult aspects of school improvement, such as professional development and family and community supports are left for states and localities, and the report offers no specific proposals for dealing with them" (Koretz et al., 1992, pp. 1–2).

All these concerns point to the knotty issues that must be worked out to ensure that new standards spur greater accomplishments rather than merely reify existing failures. As with all policy ideas, the devil is in the details, and it is in a carefully nuanced approach to inside-out and outside-in change that standards, combined with supports for local schools, are likely to work.

Developing Educationally Useful Standards

Confidence in standard setting as a strategy for reform was initially sparked by the success of the National Council of Teachers of Mathematics' self-initiated, profession-led effort to write curriculum standards during the 1980s. The NCTM experience differed in important ways from the standard-setting activities later undertaken by the federal government. High school teacher Bill Fernekes explains that "NCTM not only garnered a tremendous amount of money to develop the standards, but they did it in a way that was intelligent, by saying they were going to take their time with the effort, develop the standards, and then work through their professional organization to spread the word. . . . [T]his hasn't happened through a top-down mandate. It has occurred through professional organizations and through publicity of those standards, done in a broad-based way" (Lockwood, 1993, p. 12).

NCTM also developed companion standards for teaching and teacher development, asserting that teachers' knowledge and skills are as important as any form of curriculum guidance. This work has been used as a source for new standards for teacher certification and licensing. And the dynamic nature of the NCTM standards is reflected in the fact that they are already under revision. Good standards always advance knowledge and therefore evolve as knowledge grows. They are not lodged in concrete as government edicts tend to be. The NCTM standards model the possibility that professional standards can be tools for rethinking practice rather than regulations that constrain it.

The standards have provided a useful and much-used set of ideas against which local educators are testing out their practices and plans.

Across the country, supports for this process have been provided by NCTM, schools of education, and teacher-to-teacher networks. The standards are organized around general constructs, learning goals, and areas of study. They offer a compass for change, not a blueprint. For example, some of the fourteen standards for grades 9 through 12 describe overarching goals—mathematics as problem solving, communication, reasoning, and connections—and others outline important content—algebra, geometry, functions, and so on. Within each area, the standards outline a half dozen key abilities for students to develop, such as the ability to "use tables and graphs as tools to interpret expressions, equations, and inequalities" (National Council of Teachers of Mathematics, 1989, p. 150) or the ability to "use simulations to estimate probabilities" (p. 171). Each set of standards is accompanied by a discussion of the rationale for the centrality of the skills outlined, along with examples of the kinds of work students might undertake to foster and demonstrate their understanding.

These standards are clear enough to help teachers develop curricula pointed in a common direction, but they are not so voluminous and prescriptive as to require superficial content coverage or to limit teachers' inventiveness in bringing ideas to life for their students. The standards differ from some others in that they illuminate the structure of the discipline and the goals of teaching and learning but they do not prescribe when and how students must learn specific pieces of content. Thus they are permeable to teachers' efforts to develop curriculum adapted to their own students' progress, interests, and needs.

NCTM's experience illustrates how curriculum standards that articulate professional knowledge and allow for professional judgment can be helpful tools for informing state and local curriculum building, teaching practice, and assessment development. Well-conceived and well-constructed standards in other fields may help local educators reshape classroom practices as they incorporate contemporary knowledge about teaching and learning into their work. However, producing such standards is easier said than done.

Most of the more recent standards development efforts have been launched governmentally. The results have varied greatly in their quality, the extent to which they develop a conception of curriculum that reflects current understandings about learning, and the extent to which they represent a consensus among scholars and practitioners in the field. The same variability is found among state standards-writing initiatives. Some thoughtfully articulate curriculum goals that will advance student understanding; others rehash the stuff of current textbooks or provide too little guidance to be useful.

Many existing standards documents do not encourage teaching for understanding. Like traditional curricula and textbooks that suffer from the "mentioning" problem (see Chapter Two), they outline hundreds of bits of information for students to acquire at various grade levels in each subject area, creating expectations for content coverage that render impossible the in-depth study students need to understand and apply ideas. In the social sciences alone, the 1993 draft standards for geography, world history, and U.S. history, civics, and government outlined more than one thousand performance indicators for students at each benchmark grade level. Many were laundry lists of facts to be identified, described, or defined. In geography, for example, 4th graders are expected to be able to describe the physical characteristics of Earth's biosphere, atmosphere, lithosphere, hydrosphere, and Earth-sun relationships; explain volcanic eruptions; draw a map of the world from memory; predict population patterns; and do more than three hundred other things. In history these same 4th graders were to "describe the tradition of crusading warfare and the increasing ethnic polarization of the Iberian peninsula circa 1350–1500" and "explain the success of the Avis dynasty in Portugal . . . in reasserting monarchical authority," along with more than three hundred other pieces of information. In high school, teachers are asked to complete hundreds of tasks from the geography and history frameworks and then fit in sixty-nine content standards with over three hundred performance indicators for civics and government. These indicators call on students to "list," "identify," and "explain" more often than to "weigh," "evaluate," or "apply" the hundreds of facts, ideas, and beliefs they are expected to acquire.

The thousands of pages of standards statements produced by such combined efforts stand in stark contrast to the slim seventy-page framework that embodies all of Japan's national curriculum guidance or the comparably sleek volumes of many other countries. Some U.S. standards documents are less a representation of disciplined thinking about the central purposes and core concepts of the disciplines than they are an accumulated grab bag of the pieces of information various committee members brought to the table. The undisciplined breadth of these standards has quickly come to represent a curriculum for exposure (Porter, 1989) rather than a curriculum for understanding, exacerbating the existing problem of a curriculum so stuffed with pages, chapters, and facts to cover that it marches past students without their grasping the main ideas or developing the essential skills they need to function as educated people.

Other sets of standards, especially some early state efforts, have been criticized for the opposite reason—for expressing learning goals in statements so vague and general as to be meaningless ("students will learn to think critically," for example). Neither extreme is helpful for educators. If standards are to support effective teaching, they must find a *medium grain* form of expression, articulating important educational ideas sufficiently clearly to convey meaning but avoiding overspecification in order to give teachers room to make curriculum meaningful to their students.

Curriculum Frameworks and the Enacted Curriculum

The same principle of disciplined clarity should apply to curriculum frameworks developed to communicate standards to schools. A fair amount of confusion in the standards debate has occurred because people use the term *curriculum* very differently. Some use it to mean the guidance inscribed in documents sent to schools to outline what is to be studied. Depending on policymakers' or curriculum writers' intentions, this might be fairly lean or extremely detailed. However, teachers and other curriculum developers generally use the term *curriculum* to encompass all the arrangements a school makes for students' learning and development, including the sequence, format, and content of courses; student activities; teaching approaches; and the ways in which teachers and classes are organized (Victoria Ministry of Education, 1988, p. 8). In this view, curriculum is the lived experiences of students and teachers in classrooms (Snyder, Bolin, & Zumwalt, 1992), not the pieces of paper that make up the curriculum guide, textbook, or syllabus. Curriculum resources have certain "potentials," but the teacher ultimately enacts curriculum as she uses materials along with other ideas and resources to construct experiences with students (Ben-Peretz, 1975). Thus teachers and principals develop curriculum when they work through courses, lessons, assignments, and school support systems, whether or not their efforts are shaped by a curriculum guide from the district, state, or other source.

Many states are seeking to develop *curriculum frameworks* embodying new content and performance standards to provide direction for schools and districts as they construct curricula that meet the needs of their students. The framework documents are not themselves curricula but "the bridge between standards at one end and what happens in the classroom at the other. Ideally, frameworks provide, as the dictionary suggests, a basic structure of ideas. They spell out the essential skills and understandings to be developed, and some of the major themes and questions to be explored" (Gagnon, n.d.). They also articulate performance criteria that show vividly what students should be able to do at different benchmark points along the school continuum. But they do not constrain teaching methods, mandate specific texts, or outline daily lesson plans. These methods, texts, and plans are properly the province of teachers, who need flexibility in selecting strategies that will work for their students.

> A curriculum framework is not a manual to be looked into on Monday morning. In practice, teachers produce their own manuals, to remind them what to say and do when they close the classroom door. A good state or district subject matter framework is nonetheless a powerful help to teachers' daily work. By definition, it should be an easily read map of ideas. Clearly expressed, the ideas suggest a range of alternative next steps that teachers may choose for themselves, free to bring their students along by any paths they think best. Moreover, teachers can improvise with confidence, because the frame, the map, is always there to return to for the next stage of the journey [Gagnon, n.d.].

Standards and frameworks should identify the fundamental concepts and relationships that structure a discipline and describe a common core of expectations for students: that they communicate and write effectively, understand certain mathematical principles, use scientific tools of inquiry, and so on. However, there must also be room for schools to teach what is important to the people in them. Many areas of study will necessarily differ by community. Marine biology may be of greater interest to students in coastal areas, and farming and forest life may be of greater relevance to students in upper Wisconsin. Extended study of public transportation systems may engage children in New York City, and students in New Mexico might study desert wildlife. A curriculum that enables all students to learn must allow for differing starting points and pathways to learning so that students are not left out or left behind, for different strategies that meet varying learning styles and needs, and for the prospect that students' demonstrations of their knowledge will reflect contextual differences that vary widely in a country as large and as diverse as the United States.

Even in countries much smaller than the United States, curriculum and assessment decisions are quite localized. In the former West Germany, there were eleven state ministries of education setting separate examinations for each state. Schools in Great Britain have traditionally had the opportunity to select among at least eight regional assessment programs. In France, twenty-three separate academies set the *brevet de collège* examinations and the baccalaureat exams for each academy (Koretz et al., 1992, p. 7). Although there is a national curriculum, it is not highly constraining. French educators contrast the plight of U.S. teachers, whom they perceive as enslaved to standardized textbooks, with the situation of French teachers, who are expected to develop their own classroom curricula in response to their local contexts and students' needs (Bouvier, 1995).

In addition to the diverse examination systems these countries maintain, schools and students may often choose which two or three examinations they will take out of an array of thirty or more offered (Madaus, 1992). Within examinations, students frequently have choices about the essay questions they will answer, the books and ideas they will bring to bear, and the ways in which they will approach performance tasks. In these ways, examinations are adapted to student and teacher interests and local contexts.

There are important social, political, and educational reasons for supporting such diversity. Sizer, McDonald, and Rogers (1992), for example, argue for local involvement in standard setting in this way: "Much in the fashion of Aristotle, who claimed that essence is necessarily intertwined with experience, we believe that standards cannot exist apart from experience. To answer the question, 'What is good enough here?' one must refer to images of *good enough . . .* and in the process, one should not stray too far from where *here* is" (pp. 6–7).

Finally, some argue that states should create a tightly specified curriculum that outlines in great detail what is to be taught each year, in invarying scope and sequence, so that transient students will be able to pick up with the curriculum wherever they go (see, for example, Hirsch, 1996). However, this rationale is flawed because it ignores the role of the learner in the learning process. Even students who stay in one place learn at different rates and in different ways. Although general curriculum guidance of the sort offered in other countries can be useful in helping teachers build on the work of their predecessors, lockstep curriculum programs, as I have described throughout this book, have not benefited U.S. students, holding some children back when they are ready to move ahead and failing to educate those who do not learn in the manner the curriculum dictates.

To be effective, teachers must meet students *where they are,* not where an idealized curriculum guide imagines they should be. This is particularly important in a nation with high rates of immigration and mobility, where students continually enter and exit classrooms as their families move among various states and countries and thus different school districts. If teachers are to succeed, they must have the flexibility to teach what students need to know based on what they have learned before. Teachers must also be free to use material that allows them to connect what must be taught with what students can understand. Curriculum guidance that overly prescribes content and methods prevents teachers from constructing the necessary bridges between students' experiences and learning goals.

Standards and frameworks are likely to be most useful when they focus on a relatively small set of truly important core ideas and on preparing students to inquire successfully into new areas of study, to find and use information so that they can analyze and generate ideas, and to produce ideas and products so that they have the tools to continually educate themselves for the world they will live in. Christine Gutierrez, an outstanding high school teacher in Los Angeles and a member of the National Commission on Teaching and America's Future, argues that externally set standards should account for about 50 percent of curriculum space and teaching time, leaving the other 50 percent for teachers to create work that builds on students' interests and experiences and addresses their specific learning needs. At least some of this work should be jointly developed and assessed by teachers across the school, so as to establish the collective goals and norms of practice that make school a coherent, reinforcing experience for students.

The Locus of Standard Setting and Assessment

At their best, curriculum standards embody a general aim and vision for changes that must still be worked through in more specific terms in the schools. This working through is educative in itself as it stimulates inquiry into practice. Local engagement in standard setting is important for several reasons: first, because contexts vary and hence good practice must also vary; second, because ownership and involvement are critical components of the change process; and finally, because learning how to practice differently requires active engagement in constructing the intellectual foundations upon which one's practice will rest. It is for this last reason that progressive educators have always insisted that teachers must be trained to be curriculum developers rather than only curriculum implementers. Teachers must learn how to look closely at their students and think deeply about curriculum goals and the varieties of pathways to learning if they are to teach in ways that make the connection between students and subjects. They can profitably use curriculum ideas developed by others, but they must construct the specific curriculum enacted in their classrooms with their own students in mind.

If teachers are to focus on essential goals rather than a cacophony of competing directives, state and federal policymakers will need to restrain themselves from thinking that the only strategy for change is to enact an ever-increasing pile of mandates from the top, creating regulatory gridlock and intellectual chaos in the schools that must reconcile these conflicting impulses. As Fullan (1994) suggests of federal standard-writing efforts to date: "Current systemic reform initiatives may ironically actually increase [schools'] overload and incoherence problem. What looks like clarity at the top may contribute more clutter at the bottom. There is no reason to assume that the systemic reform debate to this point has added one iota of clarity to the confusion faced by the majority of teachers" (p. 4).

Although coherence is an important goal, it is most important that it be achieved by each school for itself, at the local level where students and teachers must make sense of the educational environment and construct an integrated approach to learning. This kind of local coherence is possible only if educators are encouraged to use resources such as standards and frameworks as tools for informing their own curriculum building rather than as mandates to implement unthinkingly.

MULTILEVEL STANDARD SETTING   The presumption of hierarchical intelligence—that is, the notion that higher levels of government will always create better ideas to guide local decisions—has long been a problem for policymaking in education. This assumption has created much of the regulatory gridlock schools now experience. It is an assumption that competes with ideals about local control, decentralization, and diversity and that has been increasingly brought into question by the lessons restructuring businesses have learned about the importance of encouraging frontline inventiveness.

The presumption that national standards will always be superior to state and local initiatives has already proved to be unwarranted. Some local work has incorporated more serious consensus building, better-grounded views of teaching and learning, and more sophisticated thinking about teaching and assessment than some of the federally sponsored standards efforts have. Many states and localities have been concerned that their own efforts will be held hostage to less thoughtful conceptions of teaching, schooling, and the disciplines if these efforts must be certified against national standards rather than evaluated on their own terms.

At the same time, local work can also be shoddy. It can be poorly informed, unaware of contemporary teaching knowledge and conceptions of disciplinary knowledge, constructed hurriedly, and developed without adequate input. There is no guarantee that what is invented locally will always be of high quality, and little sense in asking every local practitioner (many of whom are already overloaded) to reinvent the wheel on his or her own.

The trick, then, is to figure out how all parts of the system can come to value quality and to share knowledge. Because our field still knows little about how to structure curriculum to support the success of a wide range of learners at much more intellectually ambitious tasks, it is important to encourage different approaches and to learn from those that work. Schools that are succeeding at the dual tasks of raising expectations and helping diverse learners to meet them should be studied and understood as grist for ongoing work on standards and school improvement. Their approaches should inform the standard-setting work of states and national organizations, just as their practice may be informed by the efforts of these other bodies.

At present, the practices of extraordinarily successful schools are typically not understood or honored by those who create standards, tests, and curriculum in state agencies and publishing houses. Schools like Central Park East and International High School, for example, maintain their success only because they receive waivers from state curriculum and testing requirements. Meeting these requirements would force them to lower their standards and engage in less instructionally useful practices. Those at the front lines of inventing more successful schools have little access to the bureaucrats who regulate from offices far away, and who, in turn, typically believe they have little to learn from the real-world work of teachers and students. If the system is ever to learn how to support successful practice where it exists and grow it in other places, the assumption of hierarchical intelligence must be suspended. Government agencies should take on as their own obligation learning about what allows good schools to succeed and what effects agency actions have on school practices. The policy system must learn to be less arrogant and more bilateral so that its work is informed by the wisdom of good practice and its efforts do not override those of good schools.

There are ways to construct policy that provides leadership as it also develops local capacity to make good decisions and leaves room for those decisions to be made. Education policymakers have tended to use only a limited array of the tools potentially available to them, relying more heavily on mandates or ineffectual inducements for change than on strategies that legitimize professional guidance and transform the incentives that operate within schools (Elmore & Fuhrman, 1993).

One way to stimulate continued healthy debate and experimentation is to encourage multiple versions of standards and have them reviewed by bodies with expertise in the appropriate disciplines and in curriculum and teaching, assessment, and schooling. (For one example of how this might be done, see Cohen, 1995.) As in the European contexts described earlier, diverse sets of high-quality standards and assessment options might be preferable as sources of intellectual leavening for states and local districts that are creating curriculum frameworks, so long as each set was informed by research and professional knowledge about how students learn to reason, understand, and apply their knowledge.

States seeking to use new student standards to improve curriculum, teaching, and assessment should seek policy strategies that encourage schools to consider professionally developed standards as touchstones for their own development of curriculum and assessments. At the same time, states should focus their frameworks and assessments on the small but powerful set of core knowledge and skills that are at the heart of schools' central purposes: the ability to think, communicate effectively, use mathematical and scientific ideas well, understand social systems, and acquire resources to frame and solve problems. If governments can resist the temptation to prescribe everything, and if they create processes that allow local participation in standard setting and assessment development, they can help schools develop the capacity to use standards wisely and teach more effectively.

LOCAL PARTICIPATION IN ASSESSMENT   Ultimately the work of enacting new standards is intensely local and directly tied to the work that teachers and students do together. As David Cohen (1995) notes, the chief use of standards is to focus attention on student work, "and it is student work that we want to improve, not standards or scholars' ideas about standards" (p. 755). Real improvements will come about not because standards have been written by committees but because the standards come alive when teachers study student work, collaborate with other teachers to improve their understanding of subjects and students' thinking, and develop new approaches to teaching that are relevant and useful for them and their students.

Teachers' hands-on work creating curriculum and assessments and setting standards is part of their own learning process and a major motivator for change. "Translating an idea into action and experiencing its consequences counts for much more [than simply having a new idea] and constitutes the basis of personal (as opposed to 'academic') knowledge and learning. . . . If significant change is to occur, it requires a quality of experience that supports personal exploration, experimentation, and reflection" (Bussis, Chittenden, & Amarel, 1976, p. 17).

Curriculum and tests that are designed, imposed, and scored entirely externally can never play this important role in school improvement, because they deny teachers and students the opportunity to be a part of the process of wrestling with the standards. Teachers' understandings of students' strengths, needs, and approaches to learning are not well supported by external testing programs that send secret secured tests into the school and whisk them out again for machine scoring that produces numerical quotients many months later. To learn to teach differently, teachers must be involved in designing and evaluating assessments, just as teachers are in other countries around the world. This involvement builds knowledge about what constitutes successful performance, how well students' work reflects standards for good performance, and ultimately, what kinds of practices support student success. As Peter Senge (1992) has observed of organizational learning in general, "making continual learning a way of organizational life . . . can only be achieved by breaking with the traditional authoritarian command and control hierarchy, where the top thinks and the local acts, to merge thinking and acting at all levels. This represents a profound shift from a predominant concern with controlling to a predominant concern with learning" (p. 2).

It is for this reason that the locus of assessment development and scoring is as important as the nature of the assessment tools and strategies. An assessment system in support of improved teaching and learning will include both state- and locally developed assessments that are constructed and evaluated by teachers to inform their teaching as well as to inform their publics. In schools that are developing more authentic assessments of student learning, especially when these are schoolwide exhibitions or portfolios, teachers' engagement in evaluating student work proves to be a powerful vehicle for professional development because it helps teachers look directly at the effects of teaching on learning.

Looking at student work with other teachers and discussing standards in very explicit ways also helps develop shared definitions of quality. Evaluating work collaboratively rather than grading students in isolation helps teachers make their standards explicit, gain multiple perspectives on learning, and think about how they can teach to produce the kinds of student work they want to see. Where teachers do this, changes in teaching and schooling practices almost invariably occur—especially for those students who have been less successful at schoolwork (Darling-Hammond, Ancess, & Falk, 1995; Kornhaber & Gardner, 1993). Changes in practice also occur when teachers from different schools convene to score assessment tasks together. As one account describes the conversations of Vermont teachers who gather in the summer to evaluate portfolios: "Often heated, the discussions focused on what constitutes good communication and problem-solving skills, how first rate work differs from less adequate work, and what types of problems elicit the best student work" (Murnane & Levy, 1996b, p. 263).

As teachers see how students approach tasks, they learn about their teaching. A 4th-grade teacher from rural Vermont, put it this way: "Through the scoring I find my own personal weaknesses in what I am doing with my children. By seeing so many portfolios and listening to Jill [the leader of the 4th-grade math scorers] I find lots of avenues that I can bring back to my children" (Murnane & Levy, 1996b, p. 264).The more information teachers obtain about how students perform, the more capacity they have to rethink their pedagogy, and the more opportunities they create for student success.

In addition, when schools wrestle with standard setting, the collective struggle to define directions, to evaluate progress, and to map backward into new curriculum and teaching possibilities can create an engine for schoolwide change that is absent when assessment is entirely externalized. For example, when teachers at Hodgson Vocational-Technical High School found students unprepared for the demands of the new senior project they had developed, they began to integrate research skills into their courses, give students more practice in oral and written communication, and plan professional development days to address the issues that had surfaced, such as integrating mathematics across the curriculum and teaching special education students more effectively (Darling-Hammond, Ancess, & Falk, 1995). In addition, where parents and community members are involved in looking at and evaluating exhibitions of student work, their involvement in and greater understanding of what schools are trying to accomplish can support the classroom and schoolwide changes required for sustained reform (Sizer, McDonald, & Rogers, 1992; Darling-Hammond, 1993).

As I describe later, mixed models that include prominent roles for both states and localities in developing and implementing standards and assessments that count can support local change and also stimulate widespread rethinking of education goals.

Using Assessment to Promote Learning

For some, the appeal of national or state standards and tests is that they would provide the basis for new design specifications for schools and a trigger for rewards and sanctions for students, schools, and districts that would motivate students and teachers and drive reform (Tucker, 1992; Hornbeck, 1992). These proposals assume that schools can be made to improve by offering students and teachers rewards for high test scores and penalties for low ones. Supplying concrete goals along with carrots and sticks is the presumed answer to underperformance. This approach, however, has failed wherever it has been tried. A more productive approach would use assessments to guide investments in school and teacher learning linked to changes in practice.

CARROTS AND STICKS OR CAPACITY BUILDING   There is some truth to the notion that standards that count can redirect schools' focus. There is ample evidence that what is evaluated does tend to be emphasized in organizations. The reason the rewards-and-punishments approach ultimately fails, however, is that it offers incentives for schoolpeople to do things that they do not know how to do and that the system does not encourage, and it offers no support for educators to build their knowledge and capacity for change. Given the dramatic inequalities in funding, staffing, and knowledge that exist among U.S. schools, punishments like failing students, firing teachers, or taking over schools are not likely to produce success where it does not now exist.

New Jersey's takeover of failing schools provides a vivid example. After twenty years of fighting court-ordered school funding reforms that would have corrected the gross spending disparities between poor, largely black city school systems and wealthy suburban ones, the state took over two low-funded, low-achieving city districts, promising to turn them around. Three years later, when achievement had not improved, the state's representatives pointed to inadequate funding as the reason for their failure. Finally, a state court insisted again that the state equalize spending for these schools. This will not guarantee better performance, but it will launch a process of rebuilding that should have begun two decades earlier. "Beating the dog harder" (Clune, 1993) is an inadequate strategy for meaningful reform.

The carrots-and-sticks approach is similar to the Theory X described in management literature. Theory X assumes "(1) that the average human has an inherent dislike of work and will avoid it if he can, (2) that people, therefore, need to be coerced, controlled, directed, and threatened with punishment to get them to put forward adequate effort toward the organization's ends and (3) that the typical human prefers to be directed, wants to avoid responsibility, has relatively little ambition, and wants security above all" (McGregor, 1960, pp. 49–50). This view is at odds with contemporary research that indicates that workers derive satisfaction from doing their jobs effectively; they are motivated by opportunities for learning, growth, and responsibility; their productivity and job satisfaction are increased by opportunities to work with others toward the attainment of shared goals; and their effectiveness increases with concrete feedback about the results of their work (Deming, 1986; Senge, 1990a). It is this latter view that undergirds policy proposals aimed at increasing the knowledge of school staff and redesigning schools so they can use more effective practices.

Furthermore, research in businesses has found that rewards and sanctions schemes linked to discrete performance measures often ignore system problems, heighten internal competition, and boost the measures of immediate interest at the expense of broader goals.

Organizations with such incentives often experience long-term failure due to goal displacement, reduced cooperation, and inadequate attention to collective learning and problem solving (Deming, 1986; Senge, 1990a; de Geus, 1988).

THE EFFECTS OF TEST-BASED ACCOUNTABILITY SCHEMES The standards-and-sanctions approach to school reform suffers from similar shortcomings. More than a decade's worth of evidence shows that simply setting test score goals and attaching sanctions to them does not result in greater learning—and sometimes produces destructive side effects (Darling-Hammond, 1991; Jaeger, 1991; Madaus, 1991; Shepard, 1991). In many states and school districts test-based sanctions have created incentives for schools to keep out or push out the most educationally needy students. Large numbers of students have been retained in grade so that their scores look better, placed in special education so that their scores will not count, denied admission, or pushed out of schools in order to keep average scores up (Allington & McGill-Franzen, 1992; Darling-Hammond, 1991; Gottfredson, 1986; Orfield & Ashkinaze, 1991; Smith, 1986; Walker & Levine, 1988). These strategies lead to lower levels of student learning and higher dropout rates in the long run even though test scores appear to improve (Carnegie Council on Adolescent Development, 1989; Holmes & Matthews, 1984; Shepard & Smith, 1986; Mann, 1987; Massachusetts Advocacy Center, 1988). As a study of test-based "accountability" in one large city found: "Student selection provides the greatest leverage in the short-term accountability game. . . .The easiest way to improve one's chances of winning is (1) to add some highly likely students and (2) to drop some unlikely students, while simply hanging on to those in the middle. School admissions is a central thread in the accountability fabric" (Smith, 1986, pp. 30–31).

Schools that take students who have been pushed out elsewhere and keep low-achieving students from dropping out are actually penalized in the accountability game. All the incentives press toward controlling the population of those served, a game that works best for the most powerful players, until troublesome clients can be pushed out of the system entirely. Similar outcomes have occurred in medicine. In one state that decided to rank cardiac surgeons based on the outcomes of their surgeries, many doctors began to turn away the most difficult cases or to refer them to physicians in other states because these cases might detract from the doctors' outcome measures (Bumiller, 1995).

Simplistic incentives like these go straight to the periphery of the issue: they result in the appearance of improvement without the reality, leaving larger social problems in their wake.

Focusing on testing without investing in organizational learning is rather like taking a patient's temperature over and over again without taking the necessary steps to promote greater health. Equally important, such policies heighten existing incentives for talented staff to opt for school placements where students are easy to teach and school stability is high. Capable staff are less likely to volunteer to teach where many students have special needs and performance standards are more difficult to attain when they risk losing rewards or incurring sanctions. This compromises even further the chances for education of disadvantaged students, who are already served in underresourced schools by a disproportionate share of inexperienced and underqualified teachers. Applying sanctions such as a removal of registration, punishment of staff, or denial of diplomas to schools and students with lower test score performance penalizes already disadvantaged students twice over: having been sent to inadequate schools to begin with, they are punished again for failing to perform as well as other students who attend schools with greater resources and more capacity.

AN ALTERNATIVE APPROACH TO STANDARDS AND REFORM　An alternative approach to reform uses standards and assessments as means of giving feedback to educators and as tools for organizing student and teacher learning, rather than as a sledgehammer to beat schools into change. The different effects of the two approaches can be seen in Kentucky and Vermont—states that have taken distinctive approaches to reform.

Both states set out in the late 1980s to create performance-based assessment systems that would allow more thoughtful evaluation of student learning on more challenging and authentic measures. However, Kentucky's system was framed by a punitive accountability structure that proposed rewards for schools whose average scores improved by specific ratios each year and sanctions for those whose scores did not improve to the level specified in the statute (Kentucky Legislative Research Commission, 1990, p. 21). Vermont's system was launched with the goal of measuring and reporting student learning, and using the results to focus attention on how instructional improvement should be pursued. The wide involvement of educators in designing and implementing the assessments and a more appropriate use of stakes have made it a powerful tool for improving teaching (Murnane & Levy, 1996b).

Kentucky's experience illustrates how a good idea for improving curriculum and student assessment can be undermined by a bad idea for accountability. The state legislature's decision to use performance-based assessments to rate children and to allocate high-stakes rewards and sanctions to schools led to many decisions that made the system more costly and less useful for improving instruction than it could have been. One central decision was that because of their high-stakes uses, the tests would be developed, managed, and scored by external contractors. This keeps the costs of the system extremely high—over $100 million by one estimate (Wheelock, 1992)—and eliminates the potential learning that teachers could get from scoring student work. This may be one reason why studies are finding that Kentucky teachers have not integrated assessment into their instructional practices (Stufflebeam, in press).

Nonetheless, the new assessments themselves—a combination of short and long extended tasks and portfolios—began as a dramatic improvement over previous tests and, prior to the implementation of the sanctions scheme, were found to be influencing instruction in positive ways, especially in encouraging much more extensive and higher-quality student writing (Stufflebeam, in press; Appalachia Educational Laboratory, 1996; Whitford & Jones, in press). However, once rewards and sanctions had to be accommodated, the state eliminated some of the portfolio work and reinstated multiple-choice questions in order to boost scoring reliabilities quickly, even though this diluted the most instructionally valid and powerful aspects of the assessments.

Evaluations have found that the Kentucky accountability index has many shortcomings that undermine its ability to measure school quality. These include problems with validity and reliability, the arbitrariness of the plan's expected improvement levels, its failure to take into account differences in student populations and community conditions, and its failure to evaluate the same students over time. The use of cross-sectional rather than cohort analyses of performance means that annual scores are often an artifact of changes in the population of students taking the test rather than changes in the quality of teaching they experience. For example, one two-hundred-student middle school with a reputation for excellence found itself on the "merit school" list one year and, with a small change in enrollment, on the "deficient" list the next, without having undergone any change in teaching quality or school practices (Whitford, 1996). Of nine schools on the "sanctions" list in 1996, five had been "in rewards" two years earlier (Whitford & Jones, in press). Educators in many schools, particularly small schools and those with large numbers of disadvantaged students or high turnover rates, feel victimized by the accountability system because it does not measure the actual progress of their students (Appalachia Educational Laboratory, 1996; Stufflebeam, in press; Whitford & Jones, in press).

Reports from the field also suggest that educators' anxiety about school performance is passed on to students who increasingly experience pressure and sanctions as teaching is increasingly focused on test-related drills, which are becoming narrower as the tests become less authentic and less performance oriented (Whitford & Jones, in press). Some evidence suggests that, because of these pressures, increased scores are a result of better test taking rather than genuinely improved learning (Hambleton et al., 1995). The accountability index, notes one researcher, "proved to be a dysfunctional part of the Kentucky reform" (Stufflebeam, in press).

These findings suggest that policymakers may often be framing the relationship between assessment methods and stakes in an unproductive way. Rather than limiting the range of assessments because of the stakes they have attached to them, perhaps they should limit the stakes to those that can support educationally productive assessments. When assessments are created that produce improvements in teaching and learning, we should ask whether stakes that undermine these beneficial influences are warranted and defensible.

Vermont's experience illustrates a very different approach, in which a smaller number of performance assessments at a few key developmental points are used to inform educators about student progress. The state assessments include both "on demand" performance tasks and portfolios that are used throughout the school year so that teachers and students can learn from assessment results and continually improve their work. In this mixed model some tasks are standardized and others are open to choices made by teachers and students about the topics, genres, or strategies they wish to pursue. The state assessments also provide models for the assessments developed in local schools. The primary goal is to use assessments and reporting systems to create rich longitudinal information about students' work and progress that supports thoughtful analysis of what is working well and what needs additional attention.

Vermont's writing and mathematics portfolios, developed by teachers across the state, include both "uniform tests" that involve all students in responding to common tasks, and locally selected work samples that reflect particular kinds of work to be represented in the portfolios. Teachers convene to assess these portfolios for 4th- and 8th-grade students, working in moderated scoring sessions that teach them how to evaluate the student work in comparable and reliable ways. As reliabilities in scoring have increased, the results have been reported annually for each district, with detailed examples of the kinds of work Vermont students are accomplishing across seven dimensions of mathematics performance and five dimensions of writing performance. District reports include extensive information about the community, school spending and other resources, and such things as the percentage of faculty participating in assessment-related professional development activities. Districts hold "school report nights" to talk about the results, and schools display students' work to the community at large, using the portfolios to describe to parents what and how their children are doing.

The portfolios are valued by teachers and parents because they promote extensive reading, writing, and mathematics problem solving, and they provide detailed, concrete information about students' progress that can be used to guide and improve teaching from day to day. The process of building portfolios promotes classroom dialogue about standards for good work and helps both students and teachers learn to evaluate work and revise it until it reaches high standards. Teachers are learning how to develop and evaluate assessments and how to teach toward the new standards through the work of seventeen teacher-to-teacher support networks that sponsor professional development sessions and summer institutes across the state.

Both learning and risk taking are strengthened by opportunities for evaluating results once a safe environment for innovation has been created. Former Vermont education commissioner Richard Mills confronted early on the question of whether to attach high-stakes rewards or sanctions to assessment results. He rejected the idea, knowing that it "would alienate teachers and jeopardize the most important goal, improving teaching in Vermont's public schools" (Murnane & Levy, 1996b, p. 275). Nonetheless, the assessments do count: they are important because they are widely reported and discussed and because they are credible to teachers, parents, and community members, who believe they measure important abilities in authentic ways. The state's involvement of large numbers of teachers and community members in designing and discussing the assessments and its widespread reporting of results produce a medium-stakes environment for the assessments that has proved productive.

Recent evidence indicates that the assessments, along with the professional development opportunities associated with them, are positively affecting instruction and stimulating school improvement (Murnane & Levy, 1996a, 1996b; Koretz, Stetcher, & Deibert, 1992) as they promote teacher learning. This thoughtful use of student standards and assessments holds promise as a foundation for genuine accountability—the kind that ultimately works for students rather than primarily for politicians.

CREATING GENUINE ACCOUNTABILITY

Accountability is achieved when a school system's policies and operating practices work both to provide good education and to correct problems as they occur. An effective accountability system is designed to increase the likelihood of successful practices, ferret out harmful practices, and provide internal self-correctives—feedback, assessments, and incentives—that support continual improvement.

Assessment data are helpful in this regard to the extent that they provide relevant, valid, and useful information about how individual students are doing and how schools are serving them. But this is only a small part of the total process. Accountability encompasses how a school system hires, evaluates and supports its staff; how it makes decisions; how it acquires and uses the best available knowledge; how it evaluates its own functioning; and how it safeguards student welfare.

If new standards are to result in greater student learning, rather than greater levels of failure, our accountability policies need to

- Ensure that teachers and other educators have the knowledge and skills they need to teach effectively to the new standards.
- Help schools evaluate and reshape their practices.
- Put safeguards in place for students who attend failing schools.

Standards for Teaching: Ensuring Professional Accountability

When students are expected to achieve higher standards, it stands to reason that educators must meet higher standards as well. They must know how to enable students to master challenging content and how to address the special needs of different learners. Therefore high and rigorous standards for teaching are a cornerstone of an accountability system that focuses on student learning. As I describe in Chapters Eight and Nine, current ad hoc approaches to teacher recruitment, preparation, licensing, hiring, and ongoing professional development must be reshaped so that all students have access to teachers who can teach in the ways new student standards demand.

Standards that vividly describe good practice are beginning to inform new teacher assessments and approaches to professional development. Among them are three sets of standards that outline a continuum of professional development beginning with teacher education and moving through initial licensing to accomplished practice. They include (1) standards for the approval of teacher education programs developed by National Council for Accreditation of Teacher Education (NCATE), (2) related standards for beginning teacher licensing developed by a consortium of more than thirty states working with the Interstate New Teacher Assessment and Support Consortium (INTASC, 1991), and (3) standards for advanced teacher certification that have been developed by the National Board for Professional Teaching Standards.

These professional standards and assessments capture the kind of teaching that produces substantially more powerful learning for students, and they help teachers work toward more effective practice (Darling-Hammond, Wise, & Klein, 1995). Like teachers who have been engaged in developing assessments for students, teachers who have participated in performance assessments developed by the National Board and INTASC find the experience offers powerful professional development because the assessments are authentic measures of teaching, they are directly focused on the nexus between teaching and learning, and they examine the progress of real students toward valued learning goals. (Chapter Nine discusses this topic further.)

States can make a substantial difference in the teaching students experience by incorporating these standards into accreditation of teacher education, performance-based licensing systems for beginning teachers, and incentives for the continued acquisition of teaching skill through National Board certification.

Standards for Schools:
Developing Organizational Accountability

Quality teaching depends not just on teachers' knowledge but on the environments in which teachers work. Schools need to offer a coherent curriculum focused on higher-order thinking and performance across subject areas and grades, time for teachers to work intensively with students to accomplish challenging goals, opportunities for teachers to plan with and learn from one another, and regular occasions for teachers to evaluate the outcomes of their practices.

If schools are to become more responsible and responsive, they must find ways—as other professional organizations do—to actively design more productive approaches and to make evaluation and assessment part of their everyday lives. Just as hospitals have standing committees of staff that meet regularly to look at assessment data and discuss the effectiveness of each aspect of their work, so schools must have regular occasions to examine their practices and effectiveness. And just as lawyers, doctors, psychologists, and other professionals consult with one another to solve problems on behalf of their clients, so teachers must have opportunities to share knowledge with colleagues on behalf of their students.

School-level accountability can be supported by *school quality reviews* like those now under way in California, Illinois, and New York. In these reviews, an expert team of local practitioners and state education department staff spends a week in a school to examine teaching and learning and create an "evidence base" about school practices. This becomes the foundation for continual work on school improvement. Because it focuses on teaching and learning rather than paperwork and procedures, the process has proved to be an extremely effective strategy for serious change.

Information about student achievement must also be part of evaluating school effectiveness. To be useful, this information must look at the *progress* of individual students rather than at average school scores, which do not take into account students' different starting points or changes in the population of students taking a test. Moreover, assessments must be useful measures of critical thinking and performance skills, going far beyond the multiple-choice tests that ignore many of the abilities today's standards require.

Standards for the System: Creating Safeguards for Students

A system for diagnosing and remedying the sources of school failure is an essential component of an accountability system that works for students. Most current intervention strategies—including inspection systems, sanctions schemes, and school takeovers—have failed because they have ignored teacher and school learning and the systemic causes of school failure. When there are serious shortcomings in schools' practices and outcomes, states should involve expert teams in evaluating the root causes of school failure, such as the qualifications of personnel, students' access to high-quality teaching, and the nature of the curriculum, administrative strategies, organizational structures, and resources. Once the causes are identified, state, district, and school together should develop a plan to correct them. Remedies could range from supplying intensive professional development to restaffing, changing programs, or closing the school. Schools should have expert technical assistance to support their efforts to change. If they cannot do so successfully, however, they should be closed and their buildings used to house new schools created by educators who know how to design them for greater success.

If policy changes are needed to implement a remedy or to ensure that the identified problems do not regularly recur (in that school or in other schools), then the state and local district should also assume responsibility for developing new policies that better support school success and protect students' entitlement to high-quality education. A genuinely accountable system recognizes that school problems can be caused as much by district and state policies such as unequal funding, hiring and assignment of unqualified personnel, and counterproductive curriculum policies as they are by conditions within the school. Thus the responsibility for correcting school failings must be shared. In a system of shared accountability, *states* would be responsible for providing sufficient resources, for assuring an adequate supply of well-qualified personnel, and for adopting standards for student learning. *School districts* would be responsible for distributing school resources equitably, hiring and supporting well-qualified teachers and administrators (and removing those who are not competent), and supporting high-quality teaching and learning. *Schools* would be accountable for creating a productive environment for learning, assessing the effectiveness of teaching practice, and helping staff and parents communicate with and learn from one another. *Teachers and other staff* would be accountable for identifying and meeting the needs of individual students and for meeting professional standards of subject matter teaching. Together with colleagues, they would continually assess and revise their strategies to better meet the needs of students.

Together, standards for student learning, for teaching, and for schooling could stake out the intellectual bases for a policy framework that presses for more thoughtful and caring education for all students. However, if these standards are to avoid becoming yet another set of mechanistic management tools, they must allow for local participation and invention. In the remainder of this chapter I illustrate how this can be done. I describe New York State's efforts to develop a new approach to policy that might accomplish both of these goals: teaching for understanding and encouraging local participation in reform.

INSIDE OUT AND OUTSIDE IN: CURRICULUM REFORM IN NEW YORK STATE

With its long tradition of extensive regulation and top-down controls, New York State education is in many ways a prototype of the bureaucratic schooling system of the twentieth century. However, the state's recent efforts at policy redesign represent the initial inklings of a new policy paradigm aimed at building local capacity and stimulating change through a judicious combination of standard setting and deregulation. The difficulties encountered in this process also illustrate the growing pains to be anticipated in the course of fundamental change.

In the early 1990s, Commissioner of Education Thomas Sobol and the New York State Board of Regents launched a set of school reform initiatives explicitly aimed at reaching more challenging learning goals for all students through a process of "top down support for bottom up reform." In contrast to traditional regulation of schooling procedures, these efforts started with questions of learning. As Sobol (1992) continually reminded educators: "The heart of the process is teaching and learning. What should be taught and what should be learned? How is it best taught and how is it best learned? What must teachers do and what material and human support do they need in order to be most effective? What must students do and what material and human support do they need to learn most effectively? In the end, the business of schools is still schooling, and we must pay more systematic and sustained attention to how we do it. Focus on teaching and learning" (p. 17).

New York's *New Compact for Learning,* the state education department's reform blueprint, began with the precept that "all students can learn" and promised to "focus on results," "provide the means," and "provide authority with accountability" (New York State Council on Curriculum and Assessment, p. vii). The goal, since carried forward by commissioner of education Richard Mills, is to encourage schools to focus on improving outcomes rather than on implementing procedures—on doing the right things rather than on doing things right. It is a challenging strategy to pull off in an extraordinarily regulated environment.

The State Context

The state's syllabus-based Regents examination system, the only one of its kind in the United States, evolved out of the same historical traditions as similar systems in England, Australia, and Canada, and more closely resembles systems in these and some European countries (in form though not in the nature of the examinations themselves) than those in other U.S. states. High school students take examinations in a wide range of courses that are guided by state syllabi. Those that pass a prescribed array of courses and at least eleven tests receive a Regents diploma (currently about 35 percent of graduating students). Others must pass at least six lower-level exams to receive a local diploma. Because the two different sets of examinations are tied to different curricula, the examination system encourages early tracking of students into the separate courses required by the two-tiered diploma system.

The system's strengths are that the examinations are connected to curriculum, which could in theory enable the exams to be standards based; teachers are involved in scoring the examinations; and some teachers are involved in developing the examinations, although they are a small handful when compared to the numbers of teachers who participate in the development of similar examinations in other countries.

System weaknesses include the fact that few of the examinations demand critical thinking, analysis, extended writing, or other performances and the quantity of tests has proliferated as their quality has declined. Students can complete the Regents curriculum without ever writing a paper of more than a few pages, reading a primary source in history, doing a research project, or designing a single science experiment. The curriculum is so tightly prescribed there is little room for addressing student needs or more ambitious learning goals. Because of these shortcomings, most private schools and some wealthy public school districts refuse to offer a Regents diploma, believing they can create a richer curriculum experience without these constraints. The state university system has found the Regents exams increasingly unhelpful in university admissions and placement decisions, and university trustees have passed resolutions urging that the exams be replaced with more performance-based assessments and portfolios of work (State University of New York, 1992, 1994).

The Regents action plan passed in the early 1980s increased the number of mandated tests but did little to increase system capacity to improve learning. Studies found that the state accountability system, which evaluates and sanctions schools based on student test scores, has led to greater numbers of students being retained in grade and identified for special education (Allington & McGill-Franzen, 1992) and to greater rates of dropouts and pushouts (Smith, 1986). By 1992, New York had slid to forty-fifth out of the fifty states in its high school graduation rate, graduating just over 64 percent of its high school students in four years (Feistritzer, 1993).

Meanwhile other research has documented how teaching to the rote-oriented state tests undermines the quality of teaching and learning in classrooms (Schoenfeld, 1987; Harris & Sammons, 1989; Price, Schwabacher, & Chittenden, 1992). Although many students fail the tests, those who pass do not appear to learn more effectively than students had before the tests were installed. On independent measures of achievement New York students perform below the national average and increasingly less well than others in the region (Feistritzer, 1993; National Center for Education Statistics, 1993b). Meanwhile, over the course of the decade, New York State schools grew more unequal in their funding and more racially and economically segregated, with schools serving low-income and minority students offering significantly fewer opportunities to learn (Berne, 1994). The proportion of unqualified teachers increased dramatically, especially in cities and in low-income schools (Darling-Hammond, 1996). The theory that high-stakes testing would drive systemwide reforms of resource allocations and teaching quality did not pan out. The tests pushed vulnerable students out of school without improving their educational opportunities one whit. By the early 1990s, the majority of schools found themselves struggling to meet changing social demands and student populations within a highly constrained system that prevented needed change.

First Steps: Encouraging Local Innovation

An invitation to schools to request waivers of state requirements brought hundreds of petitions for permission to redesign courses and modify Regents examinations with alternatives promoting research and project work and allowing a greater range of students to tackle upper-level courses. Several dozen more school districts banded together under the auspices of the state education department to create new performance-based options to replace selected portions of Regents examinations. The state approved waivers and options based on the evidence offered that the alternatives would meet or exceed state standards. A palpable excitement about school renewal began to sweep the education community, but it was coupled with a deep-seated skepticism about whether the state would stay the course and follow through with serious overhaul of its own policies.

Next Steps:
Rethinking Curriculum and Assessment

In 1992, the Regents appointed the New York State Council on Curriculum and Assessment, comprising educators, parents, and business and labor representatives, and charged it with developing a plan for implementing the *New Compact*. In contrast to some states' short-lived commissions that issued plans after a few months and then disbanded, the New York council worked for three years to plan and launch a new system that could energize school renewal. The council, which I chaired, oversaw the development of standards and curriculum frameworks written by teacher committees, and created a plan linking the frameworks to the development of a new assessment system for students, professional development for educators, a school quality review initiative for schools, and reforms in school financing (New York State Council on Curriculum and Assessment, 1994).

In combination these initiatives could construct a foundation for shared accountability that rests on a tripod of standards for student learning, standards for teaching, and standards for school delivery—standards that create shared responsibility for ensuring that students have the opportunity to learn as the *New Compact* envisions (see Figure 7.2). They also represent a shift in the state role from prescribing classroom practice to building local capacity through infusions of knowledge, resources, and flexibility: "Because there is no 'one best system' that can prove equally effective for all students, the state cannot attain its goals by imagining and enforcing a set of methods by which they will be achieved. Instead, it must set directions, provide supports, monitor results, and ensure safeguards so that neither children nor schools are allowed to 'fall through the cracks'" (New York State Council on Curriculum and Assessment, 1994, pp. 3–4).

The curriculum frameworks start with goals for what students should know and be able to do that are translated into content and performance standards aimed at in-depth understanding and applications of knowledge. The frameworks integrate discipline-based and interdisciplinary content with life and workplace skills: the abilities to manage resources, access and use information, take responsibility and initiative, work cooperatively with others, work with systems and technology, and frame and solve problems productively (Secretary's Commission on Achieving Necessary Skills, 1991). By describing learning outcomes rather than teaching inputs (specific courses, texts, or syllabi), the frameworks allow schools and teachers many different ways of meeting the goals.

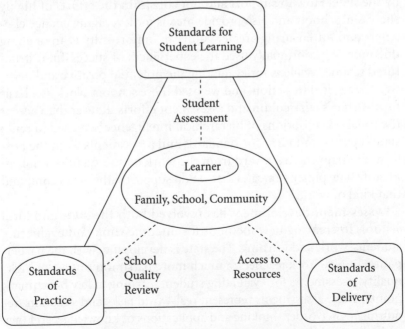

Figure 7.2. Foundations for Accountability.

This focus on results rather than requirements represents a major shift in curriculum thinking, which once relied on lists of activities or topics neither justified in terms of their goals nor prioritized in terms of their relative importance for illuminating central ideas and relationships within a discipline. It is hoped that this insistence on thinking about what we ultimately want students to understand and be able to do will encourage schoolwork that focuses on the essentials of performance rather than on getting through particular procedures that bear uncertain relationships to the development of competence.

Like those who have worked on similar processes in other states, I can attest to the difficulty we had finding an appropriate middle ground between standards that are little more than vague hand-waving and those that are laundry lists of facts and skills with no unifying conception or prospect for developing understanding. Frameworks were written and rewritten many times as we gradually found a way to focus on important goals of learning and their representation in performances of understanding.

It was equally difficult to maintain a balance between historical impulses toward overprescription and countervailing pressures for deregulation from schools who were finding their reform efforts constrained by the state. How to support and not constrain the efforts of highly successful schools and also provide means for leveraging change elsewhere and for ensuring greater equity in opportunity is an ongoing dilemma. We continually used the experiences of successful restructured schools as a lens for evaluating the potential positive and negative effects of state action, and we used these schools' work as a basis for the state's curriculum and assessment efforts. Rather than accept the usual presumptions of hierarchical intelligence, we tried to build state capacity and ideas for standards and assessments from the bottom up, mapping backward from the work of successful schools to identify state policy strategies that would support rather than confound that kind of work.

Assessment development has involved both the state and local schools in creating new methods for documenting and evaluating students' work and learning. The state is developing, with the participation of New York teachers, a much more parsimonious set of high-quality assessments for evaluating student learning at key benchmark points. These assessments represent real-world tasks and situations requiring higher-order thinking and applications of knowledge, and they provide multiple ways for students to demonstrate their knowledge and skill, including written and oral examinations, performance tasks, projects, and documentation of their work.

Each state assessment includes both "on-demand" and "curriculum-embedded" components. This means that although some parts of an assessment still occur on designated testing days, other parts involve students in research, experimentation, reading, writing, and problem-solving tasks that occur within the classroom over many days. In this way, achievement of more challenging learning goals through extended work can be assessed; teachers can use assessments as feedback for their teaching; and diverse learners have more opportunity to show what they know. Many learners—including those whose first language is not English, those with special education needs, those who learn and perform best in modalities other than written ones, and those who simply do not do their best work on high-pressure timed tests—will be able to develop more competent performances when they are allowed to do so over a period of time that permits reflection, use of different learning modes, and revision. Some assessments are designed to give students a choice of topics and strategies. This strategy allows assessment to fit different contexts but maintains common performance standards.

Many local schools and districts are also developing portfolio systems for keeping track of student learning in ways that inform teaching and learning and reflect local goals and values. A key consideration is that assessment should be intrinsic to the teaching and learning process rather than a punctuation mark at the end of a year-long experience unguided by knowledge of what students are thinking and how they are doing. The New York State Council on Curriculum and Assessment (1994) stressed that "curriculum, instruction, and assessment must be interrelated and interconnected. . . . Assessment must be embedded in the teaching and learning process, rather than 'delivered' out of context at discrete testing moments throughout a student's career. It must be dynamic, rich with information about student potentials as well as progress, and be motivating to students, teachers, and schools as it illuminates compelling goals along with means for reaching them" (p. 11).

A new performance-oriented series of Regents examinations, including on-demand and curriculum-embedded components, is intended to support a unified (rather than a two-tiered) system of curriculum and assessment, allowing for designations of levels of competence from "basic" to "distinguished." Districts will also be able to choose state-approved options, such as Advanced Placement or Pacesetter examinations or locally developed options. In this way state standards can be maintained as local choices are encouraged.

Pilots of these assessments in English language arts, mathematics, science, and technology have shown high levels of validity and reliability (Pecheone, Falk, & Darling-Hammond, in press). Equally important, students and teachers report that the assessments support teaching and learning. These comments about the examinations from students are typical:

> I get to actually write and spell instead of filling in those blanks. Filling in the blanks is not helping you to read and write.
>
> I liked all the writing because it explained me.
>
> I liked the tough problems because it made me think and got my mind on the right track.
>
> It really tests if you understand math, not if you can just fill in a circle.
>
> I liked the real life situations because we will really use them.

Teachers commented that the assessments, which provided several pathways into a task, allowed struggling students to show what they could do and that advanced students also found the assessments engaging because they were challenged to think and show their performance without an item-induced ceiling limiting their work. Teachers from all over the state mentioned how much participating in and scoring the assessments taught them about teaching and learning:

> The test really modeled good practice! It made me look at what I am doing for the class as well as for the individual children. The extended task helped me organize what I do; it made doing report cards a "piece of cake" because I had so much information about my students. It really showed me clearly the strengths and weaknesses of my students [an elementary school teacher].
>
> The test gave me a look at myself as a teacher. I thought I was teaching math before, but this test made me realize that I need to make things real and practical [an elementary school teacher].
>
> The really important part of the exam was that students were able to show their work. This made me see how they were thinking. It gave

me a chance to see what I need to do in my teaching. I thought I was teaching math before but now I see how much more I need to do. For example, explaining how they got their answers was really hard for them to do [a middle school teacher].

There was a lot of research involved in this. It made me see that we need to focus more on helping them learn how to research [a middle school teacher].

The project was so motivating that everyone came to school early to work on it. It served as a most powerful learning experience. It raised some really important questions for me about evaluation. I had difficulty in trying to evaluate their performance because the students put in tremendous effort but they started out with so little skills and understanding that they couldn't perform up to the criteria of the assessment. We all realize from this that we can no longer keep teaching unrelated skills. Both my students and I enjoyed this performance task and we all learned a lot from it [a high school teacher].

These kinds of teaching epiphanies are a primary purpose of the new assessment system, which should help teachers better understand their students and their own teaching as it also informs students, parents, and the public about performance.

The major supports for attaining the new standards are twofold: *an infrastructure for professional learning,* including participation in assessment development, access to curriculum resources, and new standards for teacher licensing and evaluation, and *opportunity-to-learn standards* enacted through a school quality review process that examines whether and how school practices enable students to meet the new learning goals. The most difficult work lies ahead, but a framework for pursuing it has begun to emerge.

Professional Learning Opportunities

The kinds of reforms called for by the *New Compact* require major investments in practitioners' knowledge about curriculum, teaching, assessment, learning, and school organization. Just as teachers have been isolated from one another, unable to share their questions and knowledge, schools, too, have been islands of practice, unaware of the ways in which they deal with many of the same dilemmas. Although local invention can provide a powerful engine for change, it needs fuel to get started, and schools need pipelines for the exchange and infusion of ideas.

A restructured state agency can nurture networks that enable schools and teachers to share what they are doing with one another. In contrast to the trickle-down theory of knowledge dissemination embedded in the bureaucratic model, these strategies build a horizontal web of opportunities for practitioners to learn from one another, like the teacher networks launched in Vermont and California to support curriculum and assessment reforms. Rather than serving primarily as the seat of syllabus writing, the New York education department too is beginning to serve as a facilitator for sharing ideas across communities.

A computer-based database, the Assessment Collection, contains prototypes of performance tasks, exhibitions, portfolios, and documentation protocols. The state pilot assessments are widely circulated so that teachers can use them with their classes, evaluate student work together, and develop their own assessments to address the goals of the new curriculum frameworks. Curriculum and assessment materials are being placed on-line through the Internet. As the new frameworks are complete, the department encourages practitioners to send in curriculum materials, samples of student work, assessment tools, and descriptions of teaching strategies that can be assembled to provide colleagues with a broader repertoire of ideas.

Similarly, as individual districts developed options for new performance assessments, the state education department convened practitioners to share their designs with one another, to learn more about how to strengthen their work, and to improve the overall caliber of both state and local efforts. Importantly, these efforts were as educative for state staff as for local practitioners. The learning was multidirectional. Gradually, schools and teachers across the state became partners in reinventing their schools, and the state helped to develop practice by supporting experimentation and learning.

At this writing, the Regents are considering a major overhaul of teacher education and licensing requirements to ensure that entering members of the profession are prepared to practice in the ways the state's learning goals require. They have proposed to begin requiring professional accreditation of schools of education for the first time. This would stimulate major redesign of teacher preparation programs, provoking them to consider the implications of student standards for teacher training, to attend to knowledge bases about learning development and diversity, and to work collaboratively with schools on teacher development. New York's participation in the Interstate New Teacher Assessment and Support Consortium is another potential support for its efforts to develop new teacher licensing standards and examinations. Incentives currently under consideration for teachers to participate in advanced certification through the National Board for Professional Teaching Standards would reinforce these efforts by providing powerful learning opportunities and recognition for veteran teachers who develop accomplished teaching.

The most difficult task is focusing the efforts of a loosely coupled infrastructure for professional development. The work of various districts, universities, teachers centers, BOCES (bureaus of cooperative education services), and informal networks is mostly unconnected. It is also unconnected to any vision of teaching and learning. As one New York teacher complained in a recent meeting on professional development: "My district holds stress reduction workshops, but my stress comes from not knowing how to teach my students to meet the new standards! When will we deal with that?" The task just begun is to focus the energies of these disparate bodies on learning for the kind of teaching that can sustain a thinking curriculum for all students.

Opportunity-to-Learn Standards

Use of New York's learning standards to create a curriculum entitlement that could form the basis for school funding reforms has been advanced by a 1995 state court of appeals decision. The state's highest court essentially overturned the Levittown decision that has long stymied school finance changes in the state. The court found that the state has an affirmative duty to provide minimally adequate resources—facilities, supplies, competently trained teachers, and curriculum supports—to achieve the state's purposes for public education. The court also returned the case at issue to trial for evidence about how well the state's current funding system ensures this level of adequacy, a level that has now been much more clearly articulated by the state's new standards, curriculum frameworks, and performance assessments. This case is likely to result in a decision that requires the state to fund a set of system delivery standards, a key building block for equity to which I return in Chapter Eight.

In addition, the state began a process of rethinking its intervention program for failing schools, hoping to create a new approach focused on a change process for strengthening these schools rather than on a monitoring-and-inspection approach that collects statistics and requires reports but fails to activate real reform. And it has created a school quality review initiative that communicates standards of practice through a peer review strategy in schools. This process is intended to create deeper understandings of good practice among practitioners through an outside-in dialectic that stimulates inside-out reform. Both system delivery standards and school review processes are critical for ensuring that students have the opportunity to learn in the ways new standards demand. In the next chapter, I discuss how these new approaches to equity might be pursued.

## CHAPTER EIGHT

Ensuring Access to Knowledge

You can understand things better when you go among the wealthy. You look around you at their school, although it's impolite to do that, and you take a deep breath at the sight of all those beautiful surroundings. Then you come back home and see that these are things you do not have. You think of the difference.

*—New York City Sixteen-Year-Old
(quoted in Kozol, 1991, p. 104)*

Setting standards may send signals about the learning that is valued by society, but it will not create the conditions for learning where they do not already exist. And although reallocating resources can make a difference in some of these conditions, schools cannot spin gold from straw. The plain truth is that school funding policies in the United States do not begin to ensure that all students will have access to the teachers, materials, or ideas they need to learn. Although some U.S. schools have adequate resources that could be much more effectively spent, many others lack even the basic levels of funding needed to support the curriculum and teaching to which students should be entitled.

In 1988, annual spending in U.S. schools ranged from under $1,000 per pupil to over $50,000 per pupil (Picas & Bhimani, 1994, p. 115).

Although these figures represent the extremes, schools at the 90th percentile spend nearly ten times more than schools at the 10th percentile of expenditures. Heavy reliance on local property taxes to finance public schools makes systemic inequalities in education inevitable in most states. Districts with higher property values have greater resources with which to fund their schools, even when poorer districts tax themselves at proportionally higher rates. State aid rarely makes up the differences. Disparities also exist across states, with the wealthiest states spending nearly three times as much as the poorest ones (Educational Testing Service, 1991).

Studies demonstrate that these disparities "inflict disproportionate harm on minority and economically disadvantaged students," who are concentrated in the states and districts with fewest resources (Taylor & Piche, 1991, p. xi). The schools most affected tend to be urban schools that enroll large numbers of low-income students and recent immigrants and poor rural schools that have little tax base.

It is frequently difficult for those in positions of power, whose children attend affluent public or private schools, to imagine the extent of fiscal and intellectual impoverishment that characterizes the schools of many other people's children. Many are shockingly unsafe, lack basic materials and equipment, are intellectually vacuous, and are staffed by individuals who have had few opportunities to learn about children or teaching. Such inequalities have grown more pronounced since the early 1980s, leaving many districts in worse shape than they were twenty years ago. For example, in cities like Los Angeles and New York, following year after year of burgeoning enrollments colliding with year after year of budget cuts, class sizes routinely approach thirty-five or more students, and some high school teachers see nearly two hundred students a day. Schools often lack paper and textbooks as well as computers and science labs. Crumbling facilities and overwhelmed staff provide an inadequate physical and human infrastructure for student learning.

The costs of this inequality are increasingly high for our society as a whole as well as for the young people who are placed at risk by such schools. The victims of social inequality and education inadequacy are trapped in a growing underclass. They experience growing rates of crime, incarceration, structural unemployment, homelessness, drug use, and social dysfunction. Ultimately, everyone pays, financially and socially, the resulting costs to the broader society. In many ways unequal access to education threatens the foundation of democratic society.

Education reform must adjust its sights to focus on how unequal access raises persistent barriers to achievement. One flawed assumption of current reform thinking is that successful programs or practices can be lifted out of well-functioning well-resourced schools and plopped down (or "replicated") in poorly functioning underfunded ones with no loss of effectiveness. Another false assumption is that tough outcome standards for students are enough to ensure major reforms, as though schools and teachers have been holding out and need only be threatened with punishment in order to succeed. A final flawed belief is that education for disadvantaged students can be improved by tacking on special programs to their already inadequate and often damaging school experiences, rather than overhauling the schools they attend in the first place.

The truth is that many schools currently do not have the resources to provide the kind of education new standards demand. Profound differences in the capacities of schools and classrooms serving more and less advantaged children have become so ingrained that no quick-fix managerial reform—whether a fancy program, a teacher-proof curriculum, or an elaborate incentive scheme—can magically transform impoverished schools so that they produce better outcomes. Even if forward-looking standards and assessment systems were developed in all states and school systems, students served by inadequately prepared teachers in underfunded and poorly managed school organizations would still fail to achieve. Systemwide capacity building—that is, an overarching strategy to increase the supply of highly qualified teachers, the funds for under-resourced schools, and the ability of schools to use knowledge well—is absolutely critical to the success of students in U.S. schools.

SCHOOLING IN AMERICA: A LANDSCAPE OF EDUCATIONAL INEQUALITY

Inequality is deeply embedded in the American schooling system. Starting with its traditions of local control that leave school districts with unequal access to revenues, continuing with long-standing legal conventions for segregating African American, Latino, and Native American children and for spending less on their schools, and maintained by systems for tracking students of different backgrounds and aptitudes into qualitatively different experiences, the system rests on a foundation that assures unequal educational opportunity.

Access to Adequately Funded Schools

Despite its rhetoric about equality, the United States tolerates disparities in school funding and in access to good teaching that are far
greater than those in other developed nations. Much has been made
in recent years of the low performance of U.S. students on international assessments, especially in mathematics and science. Still more
striking is the finding from international studies that the spread of
achievement and of students' opportunities to learn is many times
greater in the United States than in other industrialized countries and
is comparable only to the level of disparity found in developing nations that do not yet provide universal access to education (McKnight
et al., 1987). Although the United States came sooner than many others to the task of educating a wide range of students in public schools,
it has yet to meet the challenge of providing equal access to quality education. What students have the opportunity to learn is typically a
function of where they live, what their parents earn, and the color of
their skin.

This institutionally sanctioned discrimination is older than the
United States itself. In his history of eighteenth-century colonial education Lawrence Cremin (1970) writes that "for all of its openness,
provincial America, like all societies, distributed its education resources unevenly, and to some groups, particularly those Indians and
Afro-Americans who were enslaved and even those who were not, it
was for all intents and purposes closed. . . . [B]y the end of the colonial period, there was a well-developed ideology of race inferiority to
justify that situation and ensure that it would stand firm against all
the heady rhetoric of the Revolution" (pp. 411–412).

Thus the ideology of racial inferiority—recently revived in *The Bell
Curve* (Herrnstein & Murray, 1994)—has long been used in this country to justify unequal access to knowledge. In nearly all of the South
and much of the North, white schools were allocated five to ten times
as much money as black schools until at least the 1950s. Most higher
education institutions were closed to nonwhites until the 1960s, and
some remained restricted until a decade thereafter (Kluger, 1976;
Meier, Stewart, & England, 1989; Schofield, 1991).

Educational experiences for low-income students and students of
color continue to be substantially separate and unequal. Most students
of color continue to attend schools where the student body is predominantly "minority" (Orfield, Monfort, & Aaron, 1989), and the

central city schools in which they are concentrated are typically funded at levels well below those of neighboring districts (Kozol, 1991; Educational Testing Service, 1991). Furthermore, schools with high concentrations of low-income and "minority" students often receive fewer resources than other schools within their districts (MacPhail-Wilcox & King, 1986). Even within schools, tracking systems segregate many low-income and nonwhite students, allocating still fewer education resources to them at the classroom level than the other students in the school receive (Oakes, 1985).

Jonathan Kozol's *Savage Inequalities* (1991) describes the striking differences between the public schools serving students of color in urban settings and their suburban counterparts. A typical example contrasts Goudy Elementary School, which serves a predominantly African American student population in Chicago, with the schools in the nearby suburb of nearly all white New Trier. While Goudy uses "15-year-old textbooks in which Richard Nixon is still president," has "no science labs, no art or music teachers . . . [and] two working bathrooms for some 700 children," New Trier provides its students with "superior labs . . . up-to-date technology . . . seven gyms [and] an Olympic pool" (pp. 63–65). Across the nation, some students attend schools with no science equipment or computers while others are hooked up to the Dow Jones to study stock exchanges; some sit in classes of nearly forty while others have classes of eighteen or less; some have no books to take home and few they can use in school while others have a wealth of materials with which to produce sophisticated work. Students notice the differences. As one New York City student said of his school, where holes in ceilings expose rusty pipes and water pours in on rainy days, "People on the outside may think that we don't know what it is like for other students, but we *visit* other schools and we have eyes and we have brains. You cannot hide the differences. You see it and compare" (Kozol, 1991, p. 104).

At least one message is clearly conveyed: some children are worth less in the eyes of society than others. Knowing the intricacies of school-funding formulas and state-level politics does not take away the sting or lessen the effects. And disparities in physical facilities are just the tip of the iceberg. Higher-spending districts consistently have smaller classes; higher-paid, better-qualified, and more-experienced teachers; and greater instructional resources, including a wider range of high-quality course offerings (Hartman, 1988; Ferguson, 1991; Educational Testing Service, 1991). In their review of resource allocation

studies MacPhail-Wilcox and King (1986) summarize the situation
this way: "School expenditure levels correlate positively with student
socioeconomic status and negatively with educational need when
school size and grade level are controlled statistically. . . . Teachers with
higher salaries are concentrated in high income and low minority
schools. Furthermore, pupil-teacher ratios are higher in schools with
larger minority and low-income student populations. . . . Educational
units with higher proportions of low-income and minority students
are allocated fewer fiscal and educational resources than are more affluent educational units, despite the probability that these students
have substantially greater need for both" (p. 425).

In state after state these patterns hold. In New York State, districts
with greater proportions of poor and minority students receive fewer
resources than others by virtually any measure—state and local dollars per pupil, student-teacher ratios, class size, teacher experience,
and teacher qualifications (Berne, 1994). In New Jersey, evidence presented in 1989 in a school finance reform case ongoing since 1973
demonstrated how the 2:1 spending ratios between affluent largely
white districts and poor largely minority city districts allow academic
course offerings in wealthy districts that are totally absent in poor predominantly black ones like Camden, East Orange, and Paterson (Educational Testing Service, 1991, p. 9).

In California the size and rigor of schools' college preparatory programs vary with the race and socioeconomic status of their students,
and some poor and minority students are taught by underqualified
teachers for virtually all of their school careers (California State Department of Education, 1984; California Commission on the Teaching Profession, 1985). A national study of mathematics and science
education found the same pervasive patterns of inequality were widespread (Oakes, 1990). Students in low-income high-minority schools
have fewer of every resource, ranging from computers and science lab-
oratories to texts and qualified teachers. Their chance of being taught
by a mathematics or science teacher who is fully certified and has a
degree in his or her field is under 50 percent.

Access to Knowledge: The Effects of Tracking

Deep-seated inequalities in access to knowledge are institutionalized
by curriculum disparities across schools and by tracking within
schools—that is, the differentiation of curriculum and course-taking

options based on presumptions about what students can or should learn. Schools serving predominantly minority and poor populations offer fewer advanced courses in academic subjects, and they have larger vocational programs (National Center for Education Statistics, 1985b; Rock, Hilton, Pollack, Ekstrom, & Goertz, 1985; Matthews, 1984; Oakes, 1990). As a result, minority students take fewer courses in English, mathematics, science, and foreign languages, even when they are college-bound (College Board, 1985; Pelavin & Kane, 1990).

Within integrated schools, tracking has created a form of education apartheid. The overrepresentation of poor and minority students in lower tracks is not solely a function of test scores and prior educational opportunities: researchers have found that even after controlling for test scores, race and socioeconomic status play a distinct role in determining assignments to courses and programs (Gamoran, 1992; Oakes, Selvin, Karoly, & Guiton, 1992; Useem, 1990; Cicourel & Kitsuse, 1963). As Oakes (1992) explains: "The extraordinarily complex connections between tracking and social stratification play out in two ways. First, schools with predominantly low-income and minority student populations tend to be 'bottom heavy.' That is, they offer smaller academic tracks and larger remedial and vocational programs than do schools serving whiter, more affluent student bodies. . . . The second link between tracking and students' race and social class is forged in racially mixed schools through the disproportionate assignment of African-American and Latino students to low-track classes" (p. 13).

Even within academic tracks minority students are less likely than others of similar ability levels to be assigned to honors courses, and within vocational programs they are enrolled earlier and more extensively in programs training for low-status occupations than are white students (Oakes, 1983).

Students placed in lower tracks ultimately achieve less than students of similar aptitude who are placed in academic programs or untracked classes (Gamoran & Mare, 1989; Oakes, 1985, 1990; Gamoran, 1990). Teacher interaction with students in lower-track classes is less motivating and less supportive and also less demanding of higher-order reasoning and responses (Good & Brophy, 1986). The interactions are also less academically oriented and more likely to focus on criticisms of students' behavior, especially for minority students (Eckstrom & Villegas, 1991; Oakes, 1985). Presentations are less clear and less focused on higher-order cognitive goals (Oakes, 1985). Learning tasks are less engaging and students are less engaged (Rosenbaum, 1976). Teaching practices are less effective (Boyer, 1983). Teachers prepare less (Rosenbaum, 1976), and they make minimal demands on students, thus diminishing the educational experiences offered (Powell, Farrar, & Cohen, 1985).

Starting with "ability grouping" in elementary schools, tracking in the United States is highly formalized by junior high school (Moore & Davenport, 1988), except in some middle schools that have begun to use heterogeneous grouping. Tracking persists in the face of growing evidence that it tends not to benefit high achievers and puts low achievers at a serious disadvantage (Oakes, 1985, 1986; Hoffer, 1992; Kulik & Kulik, 1982; Slavin, 1990). This persistence results in part from continuing deeply held views about racial, ethnic, and class inferiority and in part from the fact that few teachers have the skills to teach diverse groups effectively. Districts that have tried to detrack without confronting these realities have often found that teachers resent being asked to teach more challenging content to heterogeneous groups and feel insecure about their ability to do so. Where this is the case, detracked lower-status students often encounter more failure rather than greater success. Tracking also persists because good teaching is a scarce resource that tends to get allocated to the students whose parents or advocates have the most political clout. Typically, the most highly qualified teachers end up teaching the most enriched curricula to the most advantaged students. Thus although part of the reason for curriculum differentiation is the strongly held belief that only some students can profit from a thinking curriculum, another reason for the restricted access to challenging courses is the scarcity of teachers who can teach in the fashion such a curriculum demands.

I have seen these difficulties play out in many contexts over many years. In one desegregated magnet elementary school, for example, I noted that the primary-grade classrooms were distinctly identifiable by race. Although the school was predominantly minority, classes for "gifted and talented" students were almost entirely white. The mathematics classes were most distinct. In two classrooms teaching a highly conceptual curriculum—the Comprehensive System of Mathematics Program (CSMP)—there were no students of color. In the remainder a mechanical rote-oriented curriculum was being taught to predominantly minority classes. It was clear even in 1st grade which students were being prepared for algebra, trigonometry, and calculus and which were not.

I learned from the principal that the CSMP curriculum was reserved for "*highly* gifted" students. When I told her it had been developed with inner-city students in St. Louis and should be available to all the school's students, she emphatically agreed. She later secured resources so that the curriculum could be offered to all students the next year. And it was. But three years later, when I returned to the school, the old tracking system had been reinstated. When I asked what happened, the principal replied that most of the teachers found the more conceptual curriculum too difficult; they lacked the mathematics and teaching skills needed to use it well. And so tracking for students was revived, primarily as a means for dealing with unequal capacities of teachers.

Evidence suggests that teachers themselves are tracked, with those judged to be the most competent and experienced assigned to the top tracks (Oakes, 1986; Davis, 1986; Finley, 1984; Rosenbaum, 1976; Talbert, 1990; McDonnell, Burstein, Ormseth, Catterall, & Moody, 1990; Kaufman & Rosenbaum, 1992; Wheelock, 1992). Within a school the more expert experienced teachers, who are in great demand, are rewarded with opportunities to teach high-status students. Underprepared and inexperienced teachers are often assigned to the students whom others do not care to teach, which leaves them practicing on the students who would benefit most from highly skilled teachers. In addition poor rural and urban districts frequently hire teachers who are less well prepared and less well supported in their efforts to learn to teach. Thus the assignment of teachers within schools, across schools, and across districts reinforces inequality, creating differences in access to the knowledge well-prepared teachers rely on in offering high-quality instruction.

THE DISTRIBUTION OF GOOD TEACHING

This nation's belief that inequality in education is largely a function of students' innate abilities rather than the quality of schools and teaching has long been used to justify the continuation of greatly disparate educational offerings. As long as substandard schooling can hide undetected behind the mask of student ability differences, a circular excuse is created for the vast differentials in schooling outcomes that continue to exist.

How Curriculum Counts

In most districts it is still the case that from "gifted and talented" programs at the elementary school level through advanced courses in secondary schools, more skilled teachers offer richer, more challenging curricula to select groups of students on the theory that only a few students can benefit from such learning. Yet the distinguishing feature of such programs, particularly at the elementary level, is less their difficulty than their quality. Students in these programs are given opportunities to integrate ideas across fields of study, to think, write, create, explore, and develop their ideas. Though virtually all students would benefit from being similarly challenged, the opportunity for this sort of schooling remains acutely restricted. The result of rationing intellectually demanding curriculum to a very small proportion of students is that far fewer U.S. students ever encounter the kinds of content students in other countries typically experience (McKnight et al., 1987; Usiskin, 1987; Useem, 1990; Wheelock, 1992).

Of course individuals do have unique talents and aptitudes along many dimensions. However, given similar learning experiences that enable them to use their abilities, students show a far smaller spread of academic achievement than current practices in most schools produce. Research indicates that when students of similar achievement levels are exposed to more and less challenging material, those given the richer curriculum systematically outperform those placed in less challenging classes (Alexander & McDill, 1976; Oakes, 1985; Gamoran & Berends, 1987). Achievement differences among students of different racial and ethnic groups in such areas as mathematics, science, and foreign language are strongly related to differences in course taking (Pelavin & Kane, 1990). For students who have the opportunity to take similar courses, achievement test score differences by race or ethnicity narrow substantially (College Board, 1985; Jones, 1984; Jones, Burton, & Davenport, 1984; Moore & Smith, 1985).

A substantial body of research has found that much of the difference in school achievement among students is due to the effects of substantially different school opportunities and, in particular, greatly disparate access to high-quality teachers and teaching (see, for example, Barr & Dreeben, 1983; Dreeben & Gamoran, 1986; Dreeben & Barr, 1987; Darling-Hammond, 1985; Lee & Bryk, 1988; Oakes, 1985, 1990). These different learning experiences begin early on in school. In "Closing the Divide," Robert Dreeben (1987) describes the results of his study of reading instruction and outcomes for three hundred black and white 1st graders across seven schools in the Chicago area. Taking into account students' initial ability levels, Dreeben found that later differences in reading outcomes among students were almost entirely explained, not by socioeconomic status, race, or ability levels, but by the quality of instruction the students received: "Our evidence shows that the level of learning responds strongly to the quality of instruction: having and using enough time, covering a substantial amount of rich curricular material, and matching instruction appropriately to the ability levels of groups. . . . When black and white children of comparable ability experience the same instruction, they do about equally well, and this is true when the instruction is excellent in quality and when it is inadequate" (p. 34). However, the study also found that the quality of instruction received by black students was lower, on average, than that received by white students, thus creating a racial gap in aggregate achievement by the end of 1st grade.

Although most research on the relationship between learning opportunities and outcomes is correlational, experimental studies offer strong evidence that what students learn is substantially a function of the opportunities they are provided. A study that randomly assigned 7th-grade "at-risk" students to remedial, average, and honors mathematics classes found that at the end of the year, the "at-risk" students who took the honors class offering a pre-algebra curriculum outperformed all the other students in the original group (Peterson, 1989).

Another study of African American high school students randomly placed in public housing in the Chicago suburbs rather than in the city illustrates how school opportunities determine academic and later life success. Compared to their peers placed in city schools, the students who attended better-funded suburban schools were substantially more likely to take challenging courses, graduate on time, attend college, and secure good jobs (Kaufman & Rosenbaum, 1992).

How Teacher Knowledge Matters

It is becoming clear that differences in teacher expertise are a major reason for the difference in learning opportunities across schools and classrooms. In a recent large-scale study of more than one thousand school districts Ronald Ferguson (1991) demonstrated what wealthy folks already know: money matters in education. Student achievement increases with expenditure levels, and the strength of the effect is larger when spending focuses most pointedly on student instruction, especially on the quality of teachers. Ferguson found that the single most important determinant of student achievement was teacher expertise and experience. He also found that a small student-teacher ratio (eighteen or fewer students per teacher) was a statistically significant determinant of student outcomes, especially in the early grades. Many other studies have also found that small classes make a difference in student learning (Glass et al., 1982; Walberg, 1982; Centra & Potter, 1980; Educational Research Service, 1980). In effect Ferguson discovered that knowledgeable teachers working in personalized settings are the most important key to learning. He concluded that "what the evidence here suggests most strongly is that teacher quality matters and should be a major focus of efforts to upgrade the quality of schooling. Skilled teachers are the most critical of all schooling inputs" (p. 490).

Other studies confirm this conclusion. One comparison between a group of exceptionally effective elementary schools and a group of low-achieving schools with similar demographic characteristics in New York City found that differences in teacher qualifications and experience accounted for 90 percent of the variance in student reading and mathematics scores at grades 3, 6, and 8. Far more than any other factor, teacher expertise made the difference in what children learned (Armour-Thomas, Clay, Domanico, Bruno, & Allen, 1989).

In places where teachers are poorly trained, students tend to receive a steady diet of worksheets and rote drill guided by superficial texts. In large part as a function of the limited skills of their teachers, students in poor schools and those placed in the lowest tracks too often sit at their desks for long periods of the day, matching the picture in column a to the word in column b, filling in the blanks, copying off the board. They work at a low cognitive level on boring tasks profoundly disconnected from the skills they need to learn. Rarely are they given the opportunity to talk about what they know, to read real books, to construct and solve problems in mathematics or science (Oakes, 1985; Davis, 1986; Metz, 1978; Trimble & Sinclair, 1986; Cooper & Sherk, 1989). When their teachers know no other way to teach, what these students learn is quite different from what students learn in upper tracks and in schools where good teaching is widespread.

Effective teachers know how to develop programs that accommodate a variety of cognitive styles and learning rates, with activities that broaden rather than reduce the range of possibilities for learning (Strickland, 1985). They are successful at creating such programs because they understand child growth and development and the nature of cognition in specific fields or domains (Comer, 1988; Gardner, 1991). Even though the evidence clearly indicates that teachers' knowledge about both subject matter and teaching strategies makes a difference in what children learn (Darling-Hammond, 1992), a surprising number of teachers have not been fully prepared in the subject areas they teach, an even greater number have not had adequate preparation in teaching strategies and methods, and most have not received sufficient preparation in child development and learning theory (National Commission on Teaching and America's Future, 1996).

Because of the widespread belief that teacher knowledge does not matter (a logical complement to the belief that student ability matters most of all), U.S. policymakers have nearly always responded to teacher shortages by lowering standards so that schools can hire people who have had little or no preparation for teaching. Although no state will allow a person to fix plumbing, style hair, practice medicine, or write wills without completing training and passing an examination, more than forty states offer emergency and temporary licenses to teachers who do not meet these basic requirements (National Commission on Teaching and America's Future, 1996). The common belief that anyone can teach turns out to harm most intensely those students who most need good teaching (McMillen, Bobbitt, & Lynch, 1994).

Access to Qualified Teachers

Perhaps the single greatest source of inequity in education is this disparity in the availability and distribution of well-qualified teachers. Although the hiring of underprepared teachers is a U.S. tradition going back more than one hundred years, the practice was sharply reduced during the 1970s with a range of federal and state recruitment incentives and forgivable loans for college students preparing to teach under the National Defense Education Act, the Urban Teacher Corps initiative, and Master of Arts in Teaching programs created at many universities. By the end of the 1970s, almost no teachers were hired without preparation for teaching. However, the elimination of most of these recruitment incentives in 1981 led to renewed shortages of qualified teachers when student enrollments started to climb once again in the late 1980s.

As a consequence, in recent years more than 50,000 people without full preparation for their jobs have been hired into teaching annually. More than 12 percent of all new hires are unlicensed, and nearly 15 percent are admitted on substandard licenses (National Commission on Teaching and America's Future, 1996). The great majority of these underprepared teachers are hired in poor rural and urban schools, especially those serving large numbers of minority students (Choy, Henke, Alt, Medrich, & Bobbitt, 1994; Gray et al., 1993; Ingersoll, 1995; McMillen, Bobbitt, & Lynch, 1994; Pascal, 1987). However, the hiring of underqualified teachers is by no means restricted to these schools. As the National Commission on Teaching and America's Future (1996) recently found:

- Nearly one-fourth (23 percent) of all secondary teachers have less than a minor in their main teaching field. This is true for more than 30 percent of mathematics teachers (McMillen, Bobbitt, & Lynch, 1993).

- Among teachers who teach a second subject, 36 percent are unlicensed in the field, and 50 percent lack a minor in their field (National Center for Education Statistics, 1995c).

- Fifty-six percent of high school students taking physical science are taught by out-of-field teachers, as are 27 percent of those taking mathematics and 21 percent of those taking English (Ingersoll, 1995). The proportions are highest in high-poverty schools and in lower-track classes.

In nearly all cases, the least well prepared teachers are most likely to teach the least advantaged children. Although there are surpluses of qualified teachers for wealthy districts, nearly one-fourth of central city schools (23 percent) report they have difficulty filling vacancies with qualified persons. In these schools administrators use substitutes, eliminate course offerings, increase class sizes, or hire individuals who are not qualified to teach (Choy, Henke, Alt, Medrich, & Bobbitt, 1993).

At the same time, the reforms of the past decade have benefited children in more affluent schools. For every teacher hired without full preparation in 1991 (approximately 25 percent of total entrants), another was hired with a disciplinary major and a master's degree in education and was typically prepared by a school of education engaged in serious redesign of teacher education (National Commission on Teaching and America's Future, 1996).

States differ markedly in the attention they pay to teacher quality. In 1991, for example, more than 20 percent of newly hired teachers in Louisiana, Maryland, and Washington, D.C., failed to meet licensing standards, but states like Connecticut, Delaware, Kansas, Minnesota, and Wisconsin hired no unlicensed teachers. Although more than 50 percent of mathematics teachers in Alaska, California, and Hawaii had less than a minor in their subject, fewer than 15 percent of mathematics teachers in Connecticut, Kansas, and Minnesota lacked this level of preparation (National Commission on Teaching and America's Future, 1996).

Taken together these statistics illustrate the dual standard that increasingly characterizes entry to teaching, providing teachers of dramatically different qualifications to different students and exacerbating growing education inequalities between the rich and the poor. Although some children are spending their days with teachers who are more qualified and far better prepared than in years past, a growing number of poor and minority children sit in classrooms with teachers sorely unprepared for the task they face. This heightened inequality in opportunities to learn is occurring at the very time we most need to prepare all students more effectively for the challenges they will face as adults.

The shortage of expert teachers able to provide high-quality learning opportunities in all communities is a critical obstacle to narrowing the achievement gap, and it has several sources. As in other occupations, the relative attractiveness of salaries and working conditions influences the number of talented people who will choose the occupation, undertake rigorous preparation, and agree to work in a particular district. Noncompetitive salaries in urban and rural schools are clearly part of the reason these schools have difficulty recruiting and keeping qualified teachers. However, there are other problems as well. Districts often induce their own shortages of qualified teachers by their inefficient and cumbersome hiring processes. Many districts, especially large urban ones, have plenty of qualified applicants whom they do not ultimately hire because their antiquated hiring procedures are so difficult to navigate that candidates go elsewhere. In addition seniority transfer rules and late budget decisions often mean districts do not hire until late August or even September, when qualified recruits have already found other jobs (Wise, Darling-Hammond, & Berry, 1987; National Commission on Teaching and America's Future, 1996). Prospective teachers routinely report such unprofessional treatment during the hiring process as having their files lost, their requests for information unanswered or answered incorrectly, and their qualifications ignored.

Most disturbing, districts sometimes hire less qualified candidates over more qualified ones because they are cheaper, viewed as more compliant, or both. This has been a long-standing problem in teaching. As I described in Chapter Two, this long-standing attitude dates back to at least the nineteenth century when less well prepared teachers were often preferred because they would be more likely to follow orders. Today districts continue to reject candidates whose knowledge about teaching threatens bureaucratic authority. A Rand Corporation study, for example, found that many districts emphasize teachers' ability to "fit in" and their willingness to comply with local edicts over their professional expertise (Wise, Darling-Hammond, & Berry, 1987).

In addition urban school districts are highly bureaucratized and have tended to spend an even greater share of their funds than other districts do on services and staff outside the classroom, leaving less to spend on teachers. Those teachers they do hire are typically undersupported. The newest teachers are assigned to the neediest schools and students and left, without mentoring, to sink or swim. Many leave after a short time, and others learn to cope rather than to teach effectively (Darling-Hammond, Wise, & Gendler, 1990).

City schools are also often unattractive to better-prepared teachers because they frequently have unprofessional working conditions: in addition to large class sizes and few instructional resources, they tend to have low levels of teacher participation in decision making and dysfunctional organizational conditions. Most teachers say they have too little decision-making authority; those who teach minority and lower-income students in central cities are most likely to feel this way (Metropolitan Life, 1993)—unless they teach in restructuring schools (Harris & Associates, 1993). Therefore, increasing the pace of organizational reform in urban schools is key to their recruiting and retaining talented teachers.

It is as a consequence of all these factors that many children in poor schools are taught by a parade of short-term substitutes, inexperienced teachers who leave after only a matter of months, and underqualified teachers who know neither their subject matter nor effective teaching methods well (Darling-Hammond, 1992, 1995). This sets up the school failure that society predicts for low-income and minority children—a failure that society manufactures for them by its own refusal to deal effectively with the issues of teacher supply and quality.

TOWARD EQUAL
EDUCATIONAL OPPORTUNITY

If academic outcomes are to change, aggressive action must be taken to change the caliber of learning opportunities students encounter. These efforts must include equalization of financial resources, improvements in the supply of highly qualified teachers, and changes in teaching practices to provide adequate opportunities to learn.

Equalizing Resources

Efforts to equalize school funding have been under way for more than twenty-five years, with limited success. By 1990, courts in only ten of the thirty-one states where suits against existing funding patterns had been filed over two decades had found their state's school finance scheme to be unconstitutional (McUsic, 1991). Despite significant fiscal disparities in all these states, each court's "unique legal reasoning" (Taylor & Piche, 1991) brought a different ruling. Two concerns have often proved critical: first, whether local control is more important than equal funding across districts, and second, whether differences in per-pupil expenditures affect the quality of education a district offers. However, new answers to these questions and a new legal theory strengthened by the advent of performance standards are increasing the chances of success for such suits and are changing the kinds of remedies sought.

Local control over education has been so eroded by state regulation in recent years that it may hold decreasing sway in funding decisions. As the Texas Supreme Court wrote in its 1988 *Edgewood* v. *Kirby* decision: "The only element of local control that remains undiminished is the power of wealthy districts to fund education at virtually any level they choose, as contrasted with property-poor districts who enjoy no such local control. . . . Most of the incidents in the education process are determined and controlled by state statute and/or State Board of Education rule, including such matters as curriculum, course content, textbooks, hours of instruction, pupil-teacher ratios, training of teachers, administrators and board members, teacher testing, and review of personnel decisions and policies" (Wise & Gendler, 1989, p. 16). Parent and community involvement in the public schools remains an important local factor in successful education, but its existence does not depend on the continuation of inequitable financial resources for education. Indeed a more equitable distribution of resources might be considered a precondition for genuine local control. This view pertains in countries like Switzerland and Germany that fund schools much more equally but allow substantial local authority in important decisions about staffing and instruction.

Others have argued that school financing reform is unwarranted because "money doesn't make a difference." They argue that no definitive correlation has been shown between money spent and education quality, often citing James Coleman's (1966) *Equality of Educational Opportunity* and Eric Hanushek's later work (1989) in defense of that proposition. The Coleman report actually pointed out sources of inequality and argued they should be remedied. However, its statement that "schools bring little influence to bear on a child's achievement that is independent of his background and general social context" (Coleman et al., 1966, p. 325) became widely viewed as a claim that school funding does not affect school achievement. Later analyses pointed out that the strong correlation between students' backgrounds and their schools' resources makes it difficult to identify an independent effect of schooling on achievement (see, for example, MacPhail-Wilcox & King, 1986). Because poor students attend underfunded schools, the effects on achievement of student background are easily confounded with the effects of low school resources. And as Coleman later agreed, his analytic techniques had overestimated the effects of background and underestimated the effects of schooling.

The "no effects" findings in the Coleman report and other studies are also a result of the use of gross measures of inputs and outcomes averaged at the school or district level. More sophisticated analyses show how education spending does make a difference. When expenditures are disaggregated by function (Ferguson, 1991) and resources like teachers and curriculum are looked at in terms of the students they actually reach, the availability and use of school resources makes a big difference indeed. A reanalysis of data used by Hanushek concluded that if a typical school district increased its per-pupil spending by $500, student achievement would increase by 25 percentile points (Hedges, Laine, & Greenwald, 1994). Other recent studies have found that state investments in education affect both students' achievement scores (Wainer, 1993) and their later earnings (Card & Krueger, 1992).

Evidence that money matters can stimulate greater equalization. But states have many competing responsibilities. Another pressing question is how much is enough to accomplish the fundamental goals of public education? As standards are used to articulate clearer conceptions of what students need to learn to function in today's society and what schools need to do to support these levels of learning, a new wave of school finance lawsuits, like one recently won in Alabama, are demonstrating how resource disparities prevent schools from offering an education that is "adequate" to meet the state's expectations for student achievement.

Court decisions in such cases are requiring remedies that link levels of funding to minimum standards of learning and teaching. As suits brought on the adequacy theory establish that learning experiences depend on resources and influence academic outcomes, they simultaneously establish an opportunity-to-learn principle that could allow states to define a curriculum entitlement that would become the basis for both funding and review of school practices.

Opportunity-to-Learn Standards

The idea of opportunity-to-learn standards was first introduced by the National Council on Education Standards and Testing (NCEST), which argued for student performance standards but acknowledged they would result in greater inequality if not accompanied by policies ensuring access to resources, including appropriate instructional materials and well-prepared teachers (National Council on Education Standards and Testing, 1992, E12–E13). The council's Assessment Task Force proposed that states collect evidence on the extent to which their schools and districts provide an opportunity to learn the curricula implied by standards before the states used tests based on those standards as a prerequisite for school graduation or other decisions (National Council on Education Standards and Testing, 1992, F17–F18).

Opportunity-to-learn standards would establish, for example, that if a state's curriculum frameworks and assessments outline standards for science learning that require laboratory work and computers, certain kinds of coursework, and knowledge of particular content and teaching strategies among science teachers, then resources must be allocated and policies must be fashioned to give students these entitlements. Such a strategy would leverage both school improvement and school equity, providing a basis for state legislation or litigation where opportunities to learn are not adequately funded.

The concept of opportunity-to-learn standards has been controversial, in part because of the resource equalization it implies and in part because of concerns that such standards could lead to greater regulation of school inputs at a time when policymakers desire more focus on performance outcomes and when deregulation of many aspects of schooling seems called for. Some have imagined that opportunity-to-learn standards would repeat or even exacerbate the failings of accreditation practices that specify school inputs and procedures in great detail, impeding innovation without guaranteeing either quality of education or equity of learning opportunities. Conversely, advocates of opportunity-to-learn standards have argued that without such safeguards, performance standards will merely reify existing inequalities.

I believe that opportunity-to-learn standards can support the goal of equalizing access to high-quality education and that they can do so without creating highly constraining regulations if they set a floor of core resources, largely unconstrained in terms of how they are used, coupled with incentives for schools to work toward professional standards of practice that support high-quality learning opportunities. Enacted through a combination of funding commitments, indicators, and school review practices, such standards would be a basis for

- Information about the nature of the teaching and learning opportunities made available to students in different districts and schools across the state

- State legislation and, if necessary, litigation in support of greater equity in funding and in the distribution of qualified teachers

- Incentives for states and school districts to create policies that ensure adequate and equitable resources, curriculum opportunities, and teaching to all schools

- A school review process that helps schools and districts engage in self-assessments and peer reviews of practice in light of standards

- Identification of schools that need additional support or intervention to give adequate opportunities to learn to their students

The tension between establishing meaningful indicators and incentives for equalization and being flexible enough to accommodate many different strategies for providing quality education can be resolved by envisioning two different kinds of standards: *system delivery standards* that ensure critical resources for teaching and learning and *standards of practice* that guide work in schools. Standards for delivery systems should include a very small number of quantifiable resource measures that can be supported through school funding strategies and evaluated through straightforward indicators. So long as these measures do not constrain decisions about how to configure resources to deliver education, they may avoid the problem of overspecification and still promote equity. I would propose only two such standards:

1. All students should have equitable access to the school funding necessary to enact the state's learning standards.

2. All students should have access to well-prepared teachers and other professional staff who understand how to teach challenging content to diverse learners.

FUNDING ADEQUACY   Like the theory behind the "minimum foundation formula" for school aid developed in the early twentieth century, the first adequacy standard requires a costing out of the educational program implied by the state's expectations for education. In contrast to early foundation formula efforts that relied on output standards, however, the state's expectations should be outlined in curriculum frameworks that spell out what students are entitled to learn. The cost of this curriculum entitlement could be estimated based on analyses of the costs of education in schools and districts that are meeting the learning standards and adjusted for costs of living and special student needs, such as handicapping conditions or concentrated poverty. This strategy would provide a defensible beginning point for school funding reforms, but if the experience of past foundation approaches holds, the minimum might not keep pace with inflation, leading once again to growing inequality and decreasing adequacy of funding over time.

Another strategy (one that was ultimately adopted with some foundation funding plans) is to estimate the cost of the curriculum entitlement and peg it to a percentile level of district funding, so that future funding is driven by that percentile goal rather than being a fixed sum that quickly lags behind education costs. Allan Odden and William Clune have proposed one such plan, which also offers cost controls. It sets the foundation level of funding at the 90th percentile of rural spending and allows additional district spending based on a guaranteed tax base at the 90th percentile of statewide wealth (Clune, 1994). This approach ensures a high minimum standard; it allows districts to tax themselves to go beyond this standard; and it maintains state funding so that it does not slip below a defined level of adequacy.

ENSURING QUALIFIED TEACHERS   Once they have found a way to finance adequacy, the state and districts have an additional responsibility to see that whatever combination of resources is purchased results in the kinds of opportunities students need to learn to the new standards. As part of its duty of care to ensure that students are responsibly treated, the state has an obligation to provide well-qualified teachers to all students. As discussed earlier, money spent on knowledgeable teachers affects student learning much more directly than money spent on facilities or noninstructional staff. Thus the kinds of equalization policies likely to have the greatest effect on students' opportunities to learn are those that equalize districts' abilities to attract and hire well-qualified teachers.

In order to meet this standard, states should ensure that their strategies for educating and licensing teachers reflect the best available knowledge about how teachers can acquire the skills their students need them to have. The difficulty of satisfying this obligation through direct state regulation requires a new kind of policymaking. Richard Elmore and Susan Fuhrman (1993) explain that "as equality of opportunity comes to rest more squarely on the need for quality instruction, issues of how to enhance the professional competence of educators become more important. To ensure equal opportunity in today's context means enhancing, not limiting, the professional nature of teaching, and for that task state policy as it has been conceived in the past is hardly the best instrument. . . . We need new ways of conceiving the state role and the strategies at the state's disposal" (p. 86).

To better reflect current knowledge, state strategies will need to rely more on professional standard setting than direct regulation (Darling-Hammond, Wise, & Klein, 1995; Elmore & Fuhrman, 1993). A few states have established professional standards boards for teaching and require professional accreditation of preparation programs, as is the norm in fields ranging from medicine, architecture, and law to cosmetology and real estate services. In these cases state agencies "act less as direct regulators . . . and more as mobilizers of political and professional influence around important problems" (Elmore & Fuhrman, 1993, p. 93).

A more direct task for states and districts is the creation of incentives for recruiting well-prepared teachers for all schools. If some schools are found to lack qualified staff, states and districts should be held accountable for diagnosing the causes of the problem and developing policies and incentives to address them. Schools should be able to demonstrate that students in different courses of study have equitable access to qualified teachers. Schools and districts should also be evaluated on the extent to which they provide professional development opportunities equitably to all staff.

Connecticut's 1986 Education Enhancement Act provides a particularly useful illustration of how targeted and equalizing funding aimed at teachers' salaries can make good on this expectation. The state provided funds to districts according to an equalizing formula that raised minimum beginning teacher salaries statewide, and it simultaneously raised standards for teacher preparation and licensing. This strategy had substantial effects on both the supply and quality of teachers across the state. Within three years shortages of teachers evaporated, and the quality of entering teachers increased as licensing standards were strengthened. By 1989, many teaching fields showed surpluses, leading the state to consider ending its alternative certification program because it appeared no longer necessary (Bliss, 1992).

The introduction of more rigorous licensing standards stimulated improvements in teacher education across the state, and the establishment of a beginning teacher mentoring program supported the development of even greater expertise in the first years of teaching. Now Connecticut is developing a performance-based licensing assessment for beginning teachers modeled after the portfolio assessments of the National Board for Professional Teaching Standards. This should further support the development of teaching skill and the capacity of schools to offer the kind of curricular opportunities school reforms envision. Equalized funding for teachers coupled with professional standard setting is a strategy that invests directly in the front lines of teaching without creating onerous regulations that constrain districts' efforts to redesign schools.

A recent consent decree in Los Angeles used a similar strategy for equalizing schools' abilities to purchase qualified teachers. The Los

Angeles Unified School District was sued in 1990 because it assigned disproportionately large numbers of unprepared and inexperienced teachers to students in overcrowded predominantly minority schools. In part because of the disparities in staffing, these schools received fewer district funds than schools that were assigned more experienced and better-educated teachers. Under the consent decree, the district has agreed to allocate equal levels of noncategorical funding to schools so that they have more equal ability to hire qualified staff (*Rodriguez et al.* v. *Los Angeles Unified School District,* Superior Court of the County of Los Angeles #C611358; consent decree filed August 12, 1992). Allocating funds directly and equitably to schools rather than allocating staff positions on the basis of formulas or staffing ratios accomplishes two things at once: it puts schools more directly in charge of their decision making about resource allocations, and it equalizes their ability to hire high-quality teachers.

DECENTRALIZING FUNDING   As schools take greater charge of managing their budgets and redesigning their organizations, it makes sense that the largest share of state aid and district tax base funds should flow to them directly. Traditionally, in addition to taking a large share of school funding to pay for centralized services (which are not always managed efficiently), districts have tended to reallocate the remainder of that funding in ways that add many constraints to staffing, categorical program management, and the like, and that create more inequity for the most vulnerable students (for recent evidence see Hertert, 1993).

As Odden (1994) notes, direct funding of schools on a lump sum basis is already occurring in charter schools and some public school choice plans. In a direct funding approach, schools themselves allocate their funds, choosing which services—for example, transportation, accounting, purchasing, or professional development—they will buy from the district and which they will secure from other sources. A somewhat less radical approach is for states to allocate a large share of all education dollars directly to schools—Odden suggests 85 to 90 percent—and the remainder to district central offices, as the state of Hawaii does. All schools would receive equal per-pupil expenditures plus categorical allocations for special needs pupils and high rates of poverty.

Funding schools directly could help link policy and finance aimed at ensuring adequacy in students' opportunities to learn as these are enacted through professional standards of practice. Standards of practice are an alternative to stultifying input regulations that specify how schools should spend their money, organize their classes, and staff their programs. Based on professional knowledge about the teaching and schooling conditions under which children learn well, the goal of such standards is not to prescribe a set of specific teaching processes that can be regulated but to examine and promote appropriate practices based on professionwide knowledge about subject matter content and teaching. Examples of professional standards include those developed by the National Association for the Education of Young Children (1988) for guiding and assessing early childhood programs; by the professional subject matter associations, such as the National Council of Teachers of Mathematics, for guiding and assessing curriculum and assessment practices; and by the National Board for Professional Teaching Standards for guiding and assessing teaching. These standards of practice can be used to frame school-based processes of inquiry, self-evaluation, and problem solving as well as external reviews by practitioners.

Professional standards can be used to examine school and classroom practices through an expert lens that gauges the appropriateness of diverse approaches rather than promoting standardization. Peer review teams can be guided by leading questions as they look at teaching and learning: Is the curriculum rich and challenging? Does it support the development of critical thinking and performance skills? Does it reflect the curriculum standards? Is assessment continuous, reflective of the learning standards and informative for teaching? Is teaching developmentally and cognitively appropriate? Does it build on students' strengths and prior knowledge? And so on. This is the essential strategy of school inspectorate systems in countries like England and of peer review processes in professions like medicine, accounting, and law.

The School Quality Review

New York State's School Quality Review provides a useful example of how standards for learning can be linked to standards of practice in a fashion that takes account of local contexts and stimulates improvements in students' opportunities to learn. The review process generates the tension between ideals and reality that Peter Senge describes as essential for organizational learning: "The juxtaposition of vision (what we want) and a clear picture of current reality (where we are relative to what we want) generates what we call 'creative tension': a force to bring them together, caused by the natural tendency of tension to seek resolution. 'Learning' in this context does not mean acquiring more information but expanding the ability to produce the results we truly want. . . . . And learning organizations are not possible unless they have people at every level who practice it" (Senge, 1990a, p. 142).

The practitioner-led school review process is modeled, in part, after Her Majesty's Inspectorate (HMI) in Great Britain, though the process has been democratized and made more collegial in its trip across the Atlantic. In lieu of a lone inspector from the HMI office, teams of expert practitioners and community members look intently at teaching and learning experiences over a weeklong visit to a school. Similar practitioner-led review processes are under development in California, Illinois, and other states. After reviewing the school's goals, New York State school reviewers shadow students, sit in dozens of classrooms, sit in faculty meetings, look at students' work, examine school documents, and interview teachers, students, administrators, other school staff, and parents.

Following this intensive immersion in the teaching and learning work of the school, the team members aggregate their information, develop a collective perspective on what they have seen, and prepare an oral and written report to the school reflecting back to school members what they have observed. By helping schools look at the consonance and gaps between their visions and current realities, the review process motivates self-generated change as people recognize that there is work to be done to achieve their own goals.

This process differs from most accreditation procedures by directly examining practice, rather than reviewing documents, and by focusing on the quality of teaching and learning, rather than on measures like the number of library books or the paper credentials of staff. It also differs from accreditation or registration procedures in its affirmatively developmental stance. It is not used for monitoring or decision making about the school. It is used to provide feedback about how well the school is achieving its goals and enacting professional standards of practice. Its explicit goal is to stimulate staff thinking about ongoing school development and improvement. This goal is also supported by the fact that the external school quality review occurs on a five-year cycle, followed by annual self-reviews conducted by the school itself.

School quality review (SQR) is at the heart of an accountability strategy that promotes learning as the most direct and promising route to school change. Commissioner Thomas Sobol, who introduced the New York initiative with the help of former HMI inspector David Green, explained that it complements the other parts of the assessment and reporting system by allowing for diversity and stimulating ongoing improvement. So long as the state has means to deal with schools that are not performing, it can shift from an expensive noneducative checklist system to a learning-oriented approach:

> There's an analogy to the way the good teacher teaches a class. The good teacher does not organize and conduct the class so as best to prevent misbehavior by the few—with a lot of strict, confining rules and an air of intimidation. The good teacher creates a climate in which young people can discover their talents and discipline them and express them. And then deals with problems by exception.
>
> That's the kind of accountability system we think is appropriate for the vast preponderance of schools in the state. It doesn't presume that someone in central authority knows exactly how things should be done and the rest of you have to shape up and do it that way. What it does is engage people at a professional and human level that attempts to bring out the best in them. When you have that kind of attitude and activity going on in a school, you're likely to get good practice [Sobol, quoted in Olson, 1994, p. 27].

The experiences of many dozens of schools in New York demonstrate that the review is quite powerful as an instrument of organizational learning and change. Its use of the school's goals as well as external standards for examining practice and its approach to conveying information to the school and its community highlight what is actually going on in classrooms and public spaces, how these events affect children, and how these events enact or fail to enact the school's mission and professional practice. Its standards of practice employ the following four major lenses for examining teaching and learning (Ancess, 1996; Darling-Hammond, 1992):

- *School environment.* The school supports relationships that are respectful, trusting, and fair. It supports students' and adults' needs to be competent, to have a sense of self-worth, and to make sense of their world. It respects diversity in cultures, perspectives, and approaches to learning. Parents, students, teachers, administrators, and staff have opportunities for democratic participation in the life of the school.

- *Teaching and learning.* Teachers and staff know students well as individuals and learners. Students are taught in ways that are cognitively and developmentally appropriate and that respond to their individual experiences and learning needs. Teachers use an array of teaching strategies and adapt their teaching to support student success. Learning opportunities ensure equal access to high performance standards. Support is provided for all students to achieve.

- *Curriculum and assessment.* The curriculum fosters critical thinking, develops creative and performance capabilities, supports multiple intelligences and talents, and encourages cooperation and problem solving. Ongoing assessments of student learning support development and use appropriate and authentic measures of the goals being pursued as well as multiple sources of evidence.

- *Schoolwide inquiry and development.* Ongoing assessment of school practice supports students' progress, teachers' professional growth, and school improvement. Professional development and shared planning support teachers' needs and the school's vision. The school builds partnerships in the community to support students' health and development.

Using these lenses, reviewers look at evidence of student progress and accomplishments, how the teaching and learning environment supports learning, what kinds of teaching strategies are used, what kinds of learning opportunities different students experience, and how the school functions as a community. Questions serve as points of departure for the review. What kinds of learning are supported by classroom activities? How do the activities take account of students' diverse experiences? How do teachers actively engage students in their learning? How do students demonstrate their knowledge? What is the range and rigor of such opportunities? And so on.

Reviewers look for instances of practice that support the school's goals and exhibit good professional practice to hold up as exemplars in the report. Here, for example, is a description of effective practices from a review of Highland Elementary School in New York State: "Some teachers are implementing cooperative learning strategies in their classrooms. These activities actively engaged students with one another and with their tasks: During a reading extension activity, students were working in cooperative groups to compare and contrast living in Tonawanda to living in San Francisco. During a language arts lesson, student groups were creating a poster based on antonyms" (Ancess, 1996, p. 109).

This review report itself follows principles of good teaching and learning. By beginning with an affirmation of strengths, the report articulates and acknowledges norms of good practice, thereby helping teachers learn what these norms are and reflect on their own practice in light of these examples. The report's affirmative stance also creates a psychological climate of receptivity for its other observations. By giving concrete examples, the report provides clear descriptive feedback that is both educative and motivating. It also raises observations and questions like these for further work and consideration:

> Whole class learning is the dominant form of instructional experience for students at Highland. Students participate in recitations led by their teachers, communicating primarily the factual information for which recitation is a particularly appropriate format. They engage primarily in the same activity at the same pace using the same learning strategies. . . .
>
> *Questions for Consideration*: How can Highland provide students with more learning opportunities for problem-solving, critical and creative thinking within the total day in all subject areas? In a heterogeneous environment, how can learning opportunities and curriculum be structured to challenge the range of student interests and abilities and to increase students' opportunities for choice and responsibility in their learning? [Ancess, 1996, pp. 106, 108.].

Because of the openness engendered by this approach and the credibility that practitioners attach to the examination of practice, most teachers and principals in schools that have experienced the review have been motivated to undertake changes in their practice. At Highland Elementary school, for example, a complacent suburban working-class school with a highly experienced staff and little yen for change, teachers launched work on performance-based education and assessment after the review, along with a continuous self-review process based on surveys of teachers, students, and parents. The surveys asked teachers to indicate the frequency with which they used practices such as lecture, projects, and cooperative learning, and they asked students to report the kinds of learning opportunities they experienced. The survey data were the beginnings of schoolwide opportunity-to-learn indicators (Ancess, 1996).

Three years later, teachers still reported influences of the review on both the schools' practices and their own. The faculty engage in much more intensive learning-centered discussion and debate. Active learning for students *and* teachers is more noticeable throughout the school. These comments are typical:

> Some of us were already beginning to use different ideas like cooperative learning. [The SQR] has given us a safety net so that we are willing to try.

> The statement [in the SQR report] "solutions for improvement and renewal lie within" really hit home. It isn't like I haven't heard it before, but it really was a powerful declaration. As I think back over my 29 years of teaching, the SQR experience would have to be one of the highlights of my career [Ancess, 1996, pp. 53–54].

The school quality review brought several other benefits. It encouraged a more collective perspective for practitioners within the school and began the process of involving parents in a more meaningful way. Teachers commented that "we began looking at the boys and girls in our care as *ours* rather than as [belonging to individual] teachers in our own isolated classrooms" and that "the review brings teachers out of the classroom to begin working together" (Ancess, 1996, pp. 67–68).

After their involvement in the review and the attempt to reach out to them via surveys and school participation activities afterward, parents also reported feeling more involved as partners in the collective work of the school. Finally, the reviewers themselves—teachers, principals, parents, and community members—found the experience of conducting a review a powerful learning opportunity. As practitioners, they were able to examine and analyze practice in ways they had usually never before had the opportunity to do. They returned to their own schools with a deeper appreciation of the possibilities for practice, a more reflective stance, and a more extensive foundation of knowledge upon which to act.

Principles for School Improvement

The school quality review is but one example of a strategy for stimulating schoolwide inquiry and building capacity for change. Some reform networks, like the Coalition of Essential Schools, have organized their work around common principles and made them tangible through "critical friend" review processes. Other states have adopted different measures that have similar effects. For example, Maine's Innovative Educational Grants Program, which invites locally designed proposals for revising classroom and school practices, helps schools look at how to translate research into practice. Schools ask, What are we doing and why? They examine education research and convene professional conversations. Iowa has funded similar grants to stimulate schoolwide inquiry aimed at examining practice and its effects as a strategy for change. Ohio has established an extraordinarily successful "venture capital" fund that gives grants to schools that look honestly at their needs and problems, choosing professional development and school change strategies to address them.

All these efforts start from the assumption that creating ongoing occasions for reflection, self-assessment, and evaluation is a critical aspect of school improvement. Reviews of practice can create a forum for discussing the most important aspects of teaching and learning rather than leaving difficult issues unspoken and unaddressed. Conversations that are launched in this way break the barriers of bureaucratically imposed silence about teaching and learning and start the process of building professional and community norms, values, and knowledge that enable democratic education.

Strategies that seek to build school and teacher capacity reflect a key design principle for policies intended to support a right to learn. This principle emphasizes investments in knowledge building, including professional accountability and peer review systems, over direct regulation of practice (Elmore & Fuhrman, 1993).

In the pursuit of equity our goal should be to develop strategies that improve the core structures and practices of schooling rather than to layer additional programs and regulations on foundations that are already faulty. The pressures to respond to problems of poor performance with special categorical programs are great, and the tradition of succumbing to those pressures is well established in education as in other areas of national life. But special programs, with all their accouterments of new rules and procedures, separate budgets, and fragmented pullout programs will be counterproductive as long as the status quo remains significantly unchanged.

Initiatives to create special programs for "at-risk" children and youths, for example, cannot succeed if they do not attend to the structural conditions of schools, many of which originate with state and district policies, that place these children at risk in the first place. Leveling the education playing field by equalizing resources and ensuring capable teachers is a critical first step. The next essential actions are to supply supports for good practice and safeguards against harmful practices. These safeguards should provide proactive rather than punitive interventions in the downward spiral of failing schools—interventions that take a comprehensive view of resources and responsibilities so as to create new possibilities for schools and their students.

The solution to the problems of school failure, inequality, and underachievement do not lie within individual schools or fragments of the system, but will depend on major structural changes throughout the system as a whole. Such changes will require honesty and courage in facing the dirty laundry of education that has been allowed to accumulate, as well as foresight in adopting policies that seriously address the issues of professional accountability and systemwide restructuring. I turn to these issues next.

## CHAPTER NINE

Building a Democratic Profession of Teaching

The teacher remains the key. . . . Debates over educational policy are moot if the primary agents of instruction are incapable of performing their functions well. No micro-computer will replace them, no television system will clone and distribute them, no scripted lessons will direct and control them, no voucher system will bypass them.

—Lee Shulman, "Autonomy and Obligation"
(1983, p. 504).

Teachers, not assessments, must be the cornerstone of any systemic reform directed at improving our schools. . . . [Policymakers] have lost sight of the fact that "the teacher is a mediator between the knower and the known, between the learner and the subject to be learned. A teacher, not some [test], is the living link in the epistemological chain."

—George Madaus (quoting Parker J. Palmer),
A National Testing System (1992, p. 5).

When all is said and done, what matters most for students' learning are the commitments and capacities of their teachers. Teaching for understanding cannot be produced solely by spending more money or by requiring that schools use specific texts or curriculum packages, and it cannot be driven by mandating new tests, even better ones. Although things like standards, funding, and management are essential supports, the sine qua non of education is whether teachers know how to make complex subjects accessible to diverse learners and whether they can work in partnership with parents and other educators to support children's development. If only a few teachers have this capacity, most schools will never be able to produce better education for the full range of students who attend them. Widespread success depends on the development of a professionwide base of knowledge along with a commitment to the success of all students.

Over the last decade a quiet revolution in teaching has been under way. Teaching is evolving from an occupation that the public has historically considered routine "women's work" requiring little skill to a profession that enables its members to become as capable as the real demands of the work require. The teaching profession has begun to engage in serious standard setting that reflects a growing knowledge base about teaching and a growing consensus about what teachers should be able to do to help all students learn to high levels. Changes are under way in teacher preparation programs across the country, approaches to licensing and accreditation are being redesigned, and a new National Board for Professional Teaching Standards has created assessments for certifying accomplished teachers. Some school districts and grassroots networks have created partnerships to rethink schools. Yet these efforts, like those in other eras of reform, remain piecemeal—a good idea here and a thriving innovation there. They are as yet unconnected by a set of policies guaranteeing every child access to skillful teaching and every teacher access to the knowledge she needs to teach. Creating a web of always-available supports for students' and teachers' learning is the difficult, unglamorous, but absolutely essential work that will make the difference for school reform.

WHAT TEACHERS NEED
TO KNOW AND BE ABLE TO DO

What do teachers need to know to teach all students in the way new standards suggest? First of all, teachers need to understand *subject matter* thoroughly enough to organize it so that students can create useful cognitive maps of the terrain they are studying. Teachers need more than formulaic or procedural understanding of the core ideas in a discipline and how these help to structure knowledge, how they relate to one another, and how they can be tested, evaluated, and extended. Teachers also need to be able to use subject matter knowledge flexibly to address ideas as they come up in the course of learning. They need to understand how inquiry in a field is conducted and what reasoning entails—what counts as proving something in mathematics, for example, as compared with proving something in history (Ball & Cohen, in press). And they need to see ways that ideas connect across fields and to everyday life, so that they can select and use meaningful examples, problems, and applications.

Understanding subject matter in these ways provides a foundation for the *pedagogical content knowledge* (Shulman, 1987) that enables teachers to represent ideas so they are accessible to others. Knowledge of the domain of study is critical: the teacher needs to understand what ideas can provide important foundations for other ideas and how they can be usefully linked and assembled. Knowledge of the audience is also key: people will understand ideas differently depending on their prior experiences and context. A skillful pedagogue figures out what a particular audience is likely to know and believe about the topic under study and how learners are likely to hook into new ideas so as to create productive learning experiences. Knowledge about modes of cognition, information processing, and communication is also important, so that teachers can shape lectures, materials, learning centers, projects, and discussions in the ways most helpful to learners.

Framing productive experiences for students requires knowledge of *development*—how children and adolescents think and behave, what they are trying to accomplish, what they find interesting, what they already know, and what concepts they might have trouble with in particular domains at particular ages. Teachers should know how to encourage students' social, physical, and emotional growth as well as their cognitive development.

Teaching in ways that connect with students also requires an understanding of *differences* that may arise from culture, language, family, community, gender, prior schooling, and the other factors that shape people's experiences, as well as differences that may arise from the intelligences students rely on, their preferred approaches to learning, and any specific learning difficulties they may have. Teachers need to be able to inquire sensitively and productively into children's experiences and their understandings of subject matter so that they can interpret curriculum through their students' eyes and shape lessons to connect with what students know and how they learn well. To get nonstereotypic information, teachers need to know how to listen carefully and look at student work and also how to structure situations in which students write and talk about their experiences and what they understand. These activities build a teacher's *pedagogical learner knowledge* (Grimmett & MacKinnon, 1992), which grows as teachers examine how particular learners think and reason, how they learn best, and what motivates them.

An understanding of *motivation* is critical because achieving understanding is difficult. Teachers must know how to structure tasks and feedback so as to encourage extensive student effort without either relinquishing the press for understanding when the going gets tough or discouraging students so that they give up altogether. Motivating students requires not only general knowledge about how to engage young people and sustain their interest at different ages but also an understanding of what individual students believe about themselves and their abilities, what they care about, and what tasks are likely to give them the success that will keep them working hard to learn.

Teachers need several kinds of knowledge about *learning.* Because there are many kinds of learning—for example, learning in order to recognize information as opposed to learning in order to solve a problem or produce a piece of work—teachers need to think about what it means to learn different kinds of material for different purposes, how to support different kinds of learning with distinctive teaching strategies, and how to judge which kinds of learning are necessary in different contexts. Not everything can be learned deeply—that is, with opportunities for extensive application—but some things must be deeply understood as foundations for work that is to follow and as a means for developing specific skills and performances. Other ideas may be understood more superficially to create a map of the domain but nevertheless learned so that they meaningfully connect to other concepts.

Teachers need to understand what helps children (or anyone) learn in these different ways. They need to be able to *assess* students' knowledge and approaches to learning, to identify different learners' strengths and weaknesses, noting those who rely most on visual or oral cues, those who tend to reason from the specific to the general or vice versa, those who use spatial or graphic organizers and those who are text oriented, those who bring a highly developed logical-mathematical intelligence, and those who bring a strong aesthetic sense.

Using all this information well requires that teachers command *teaching strategies* that address a variety of ways to learn and a variety of purposefully selected goals for learning. In addition to regularly using multiple representations of content and pathways for learning, teachers need tools to work with the students in their classrooms who have specific learning disabilities or needs—the estimated 15 percent of students who are dyslexic or dysgraphic, who have particular visual or perceptual difficulties or difficulties with information processing. Useful teaching strategies exist for these relatively commonplace problems, but they have been rarely taught to "regular" education teachers. Moreover, because language is a major gateway to learning, teachers need an understanding of how students acquire language, whether it is a first or a later language. Teachers who understand language acquisition can build language skills and create accessible learning experiences, using strategies ranging from explicit teaching of key vocabulary and use of visual and oral cues to the creation of collaborative learning settings in which students use language extensively to accomplish specific tasks.

Teachers need to know about *curriculum resources and technologies.* They need to be able to connect their students with sources of information and knowledge that extend beyond textbooks—that allow for the exploration of ideas, the acquisition and synthesis of information, and the development of models, writings, designs, and other work products. The teacher's role will be to help students learn to find and use resources for framing and solving problems, rather than having students memorize the information contained in one source.

And teachers need to know about *collaboration.* They need to understand how to structure interactions among students so that powerful shared learning can occur. They need to be able to shape classrooms that sponsor productive discourse and that press for disciplined reasoning from students. They need to understand how to collaborate with other teachers to plan, assess, and improve learning within the school and also how to work with parents to learn more about individual children and to shape supportive experiences at school and home.

Finally, teachers need to be able to *analyze and reflect* on their practice, to assess the effects of their teaching and then refine and improve their instruction. When teaching for understanding, teachers must maintain two intertwining strands of thought at all times: how am I doing at moving the students toward high levels of understanding and proficient performance? and how am I taking into account what students know and care about as I move them toward the curriculum goals and develop their talents and social abilities? Teachers must continually evaluate what students are thinking and understanding and then reshape their plans, using what they have discovered as they build curriculum to meet their goals.

The knowledge demands that derive from the need to teach a much wider range of students for much higher standards of performance are new ones for most teachers. And when few teachers have experienced learning for understanding themselves, how can it be possible to establish a different kind of teaching on a wide scale? The only plausible answer is that we must develop much more powerful forms of teacher education: both before teachers enter the field and throughout their careers. This education must systematically give teachers experience with the kinds of knowledge and forms of practice just described, and it must be available to all teachers, not just a few. In short, I am suggesting we need to develop a profession of teaching.

THE PROS AND CONS OF PROFESSIONALISM

By sociologists' definitions, teaching is not now a profession. An occupation becomes a profession when it assumes responsibility for developing a shared knowledge base for *all* of its members and for transmitting that knowledge through professional education, licensing, and ongoing peer review. A profession seeks to ensure that its members understand and use standards of practice that put the interests of clients first and base decisions on the best available knowledge. In exchange for these assurances, societies grant professions substantial autonomy from government regulation and defer to them when making technical decisions. Policymakers turn to engineers to determine what specifications bridges ought to meet and rely on architects to decide the standards that will govern safe building construction. They ask the Board of Medical Examiners to set standards of knowledge for physicians and the Academy of Pediatrics to determine vaccination protocols. They typically do not ask teachers to make such determinations for their field, however, because they do not expect teachers to have the knowledge to do so.

As a policy strategy, professional accountability is aimed at ensuring that practitioners are sufficiently competent and committed to give the public high levels of confidence that these practitioners will behave knowledgeably and ethically. Public confidence is warranted only when a profession has ways to continually expand its knowledge and when it has specific methods of ensuring that the people it admits and allows to practice can be relied on to possess that knowledge, along with a commitment to public safety and well-being. Consequently, professions attach great importance to preparation, licensing, selection, induction, and evaluation of practitioners and to issues of research and knowledge building. They also use strategies like accreditation of professional schools and peer review within practice sites as means to review, critique, and improve practice. These strategies aim to ensure that decisions are *client oriented* and *knowledge based* rather than based on rules and procedures that frequently would prescribe a flawed course of action.

Professions attempt to meet these goals in different ways, and they are often far from perfect. Professionalism is not an end state for an occupation; rather it is a continual process of reaching for useful forms of accountability. Tensions exist between costs and quality, between public regulation and professional self-governance, between controls that ensure professional competence and those that create self-interested monopolies. Professions have succeeded to varying extents in socializing their members to an ethic of concern for clients and have sometimes lost public confidence due to "incomplete professionalization" (Brown, 1979), when their claims to authority exceed the actual spread of knowledge and skill.

Whenever self-regulation seems inadequate to assure access and quality, government regulation tends to increase. The resulting tug-of-war can currently be seen in the medical profession as governments and third-party payers have stepped in to set rules for practice aimed at reducing costs. Simultaneously, however, as the public has begun to perceive that these restrictions may be reducing doctors' abilities to do what is best for their patients, a countervailing pressure is building to lodge more decision making in the hands of doctors and to train doctors more thoroughly for the challenges of making the decisions raised by new life-saving technologies. Reconciling all of these tensions—which manifest themselves at different times for different professions—is a major social challenge. Yet it would be difficult to argue that society is less well served by the engineering knowledge or medical skill available to it today than it was when these occupations were unorganized, had produced little knowledge to guide practice, and had no means of ensuring that practitioners gained access to even the small amount of knowledge then available.

In his introduction to the 1910 Flexner report, which ultimately led to the total overhaul of medical training, Henry Pritchett, president of the Carnegie Foundation for the Advancement of Teaching, explained how knowledge could not advance under the ad hoc approach to medical education that existed in the early 1900s. With no means for accrediting medical schools or setting licensing standards, medicine was an unregulated enterprise that included a few serious medical colleges that had developed teaching hospitals and a large number of commercial schools that provided only a few months of training. The latter offered only memorized lists of symptoms and cures: "a coated tongue—a course of calomel; a shivery back—a round of quinine" (Flexner, 1910, p. 21). As a result, said Pritchett, "very seldom, under existing conditions, does a patient receive the best aid which it is possible to give him in the present state of medicine, and this is due mainly to the fact that a vast army of men is admitted to the practice of medicine who are untrained in sciences fundamental to the profession and quite without a sufficient experience with disease" (p. x). Although shortcomings in medical care still exist, the knowledge base of medicine and doctors' command of it are many times more extensive and reliable today than they were then, and adequate care—defined at a radically different level of expertise than eighty years ago—is much more accessible. When failures of medical knowledge occur today, they are viewed as scandalous only because expectations are so much higher than they could ever have been without a concerted effort to build a profession that has a base of knowledge and adheres to some standards of practice.

Teaching's claim to a common knowledge base is much like that of turn-of-the-century medicine. Much teaching looks like it did eighty years ago. Although a great deal more is known about how to teach effectively—especially for those students who do not learn easily—many teachers have not had access to this knowledge. And although some teachers are very well prepared, teachers as a group do not share a common set of ethical commitments and knowledge for teaching because preparation is uneven and frequently waived altogether, standards for teacher education and licensing vary wildly from state to state and are often unenforced, socialization into the occupation is weak, and bureaucratically operated school districts often require practices that are not professionally defensible. Teaching is the only licensed occupation—from medicine and law to cosmetology and plumbing—that routinely waives standards for entry. As a result, parents and the public have no guarantees about what their children's teachers might be expected to know and be able to do.

Whereas professions assume responsibility for defining, transmitting, and enforcing standards of practice, teachers currently have little control over standard setting. Except in thirteen states that have recently established professional standards boards and three states that require schools of education to be professionally accredited, authority for determining the nature of teacher preparation, the content of tests used for licensure, and the regulations that govern practice rests with legislatures and state departments of education. These governance structures tend to produce bureaucratic rather than professional standards, rarely up-to-date with advances in knowledge and based more on course tallies and paperwork trails than exacting methods for examining competence. Although nearly 1,300 schools of education are approved by their states for preparing teachers, only 40 percent of them are professionally accredited.

Meanwhile, most widely used tests for licensing tap very little of what might be called a knowledge base for teaching (Darling-Hammond, 1986b; Shulman, 1987; MacMillan & Pendlebury, 1985; Haney, Madaus, & Kreitzer, 1987). As Haertel (1991) notes: "The teacher tests now in common use have been strenuously and justifiably criticized for their content, their format, and their impacts, as well as the virtual absence of criterion-related validity evidence supporting their use. . . . These tests have been criticized for treating pedagogy as generic rather than subject-matter specific, for showing poor criterion-related validity or failing to address criterion-related validity altogether, for failing to measure many critical teaching skills, and for their adverse impact on minority representation in the teaching profession" (pp. 3–4). In short, educators have not yet been able to establish the kinds of accountability mechanisms that would guarantee that teachers are admitted to and retained in the profession based on their knowledge and ability to teach.

But is this a problem? Some argue that teaching should not become a profession. As some imagine it, a profession of teaching would be a self-serving, costly, unnecessary burden for society—one that would undermine democratic decision making and distance teachers from parents and communities by giving teachers dangerous powers. A host of issues arise. Would a profession of teaching emphasize technical knowledge at the expense of caring for students? Would teachers, armed with an aura of professional knowledge, be less sensitive to parents and more distant from communities than they are now? If standards for entry to teaching were enforced, would access to the profession be reduced for minorities? Would a monopoly on practice—one based on standards that do not predict competence—result? Could society afford the costs of better-paid teachers, as salaries would surely increase if preparation improved and standards were enforced? Is there really a knowledge base for teaching that would warrant any of these efforts?

Although I believe the current situation in which educators have substantial power without the safeguards of professional norms and knowledge is far more dangerous than a professional alternative, these concerns still deserve careful attention. Teaching is certainly susceptible to the same tensions as other professions. In fact, because it operates in a system that requires compulsory education of children in order to serve society's political, economic, and social needs, teaching is more heavily buffeted by these cross-currents than most other occupations. Teacher shortages battle with standards, as lay control offsets professional influence in defining what teachers will have the opportunity to learn and what they will be asked to do. In teaching and in other occupations, professionalization has often been seen as primarily concerned with power relations, autonomy, status, and compensation. Teachers, many have claimed, need and deserve more respect, more authority, and higher salaries.

These claims may well be true, but teaching will not deserve the trappings of professionalism until it constructs for itself a foundation for a profession: first, a strong and widely shared base of knowledge that is clearly related to improved learning and, second, a strong and widely shared commitment to the welfare of all children that is enacted in partnership with parents and communities. Empowerment must occur through *knowledge* rather than through new controls that would enfranchise teachers at the expense of others—especially parents—who have a deep interest in children's learning and success. Granting greater authority to educators who have little expertise or commitment to a professional ethic (as has happened already in some districts that have moved to site-based management) can lead to more harmful practices rather than more effective ones. Reliance on bureaucratic accountability cannot be reduced without strengthening professional accountability in its stead.

The concern that professionals may gain too much control over decisions and may distance themselves from their clients has been most often heard with respect to physicians. A better analogy for teaching might be the work of architects: professionals who know how to build a structure safely and effectively, who have insights into issues of design, who marshal the efforts of other parties involved in the construction process, and who negotiate the goals and course of the work with a client who is also deeply involved. Fortunately, the professional standards that are already emerging in teaching emphasize the importance of caring for students and of working in partnerships. They reject a view of the teacher as purely a technician and explicitly encourage the preparation of teachers who value the insights of parents and colleagues and collaborate with them in the interests of the child.

The Role of Government

Some argue that teaching differs from professions in which practitioners operate on a fee-for-service basis, noting that clients can choose professionals in the private sector but they can rarely choose their teachers. This, however, argues for *more* attention to competence and commitment rather than less. Parents should have a right to expect that when they are compelled by law to send their children to school, those children will be under the care of competent people who are committed to using the best knowledge available to meet the individual needs of that child—with no exceptions and no excuses. The alternative, a bureaucratic system of accountability, is what we have already tried and found ineffective. Parents have no reason to believe their children will be well served simply because standardized procedures have been promulgated and school staff must follow them whether or not they work well for students. And parents should not have to wonder whether the teachers to whom their children are assigned are competent.

Many other professionals do operate in the public sector (for example, physicians in public hospitals, army engineers, government accountants and lawyers). For these people, strong professional norms often provide a useful counterbalance to other forces that bear upon public bureaucracies, including incentives that encourage problem hiding and injudicious cost cutting. In these cases, public oversight occurs through publicly constituted boards, but these are obligated to respect professional standards of practice in their decision making. Weak professions—those lacking strong collective norms and knowledge—are not able to serve this counterbalancing function. For example, many unaddressed cases of child abuse have followed the imposition of professionally indefensible case management rules promulgated by child welfare agencies seeking to reduce costs. These rules met with little effective counterpressure from social workers until widely reported cases of child abuse created press-worthy scandals and public outrage.

Although strong professions sometimes serve the public well, there are a number of reasons why the modes of professionalization adopted by occupations such as medicine, law, accounting, and architecture are not fully adaptable to public school teaching. First, education is both a right and an obligation. Because education is a right, it must be made available to all on equal terms. Forms of professionalization that would deny services to some are not acceptable for teaching. In addition, education is compulsory to serve the state's needs for an educated citizenry: socialization to a common culture, literacy as a basis for democratic participation, and training to serve economic ends. Thus, there are limits to the controls that can be delegated to nongovernmental sources of authority, professional or otherwise.

The legitimate claims of governments, local communities, parents, and educators to determine the forms of education that are most suitable, most fair, and most effective for a wide range of goals cannot be ignored. Appropriate roles for each must be carved out in any systemic answers to reform. New approaches to governance and accountability need to allow teachers to practice professionally in the interests of students while they also preserve democratic traditions. Both goals can be met by public support and oversight of rigorous professionally defined standards of practice and by routinely engaging parents in making decisions and in sharing knowledge about their children.

Costs

Some argue that in the context of universal education we cannot afford to require all teachers to meet professional standards because we cannot sustain the costs of having to raise and equalize salaries. However, states like Connecticut, Minnesota, and Iowa have enacted high standards for teaching that they hold inviolable and have funded schools and schools of education in ways that produce adequate salaries and surpluses of qualified teachers even though their overall expenditures are lower than those of some other states that have not attended to these goals. Other countries also demonstrate that well-prepared teachers are affordable if most education funds are invested in classroom teaching rather than in a panoply of special programs and peripheral jobs that do not directly improve teaching (and are often created to offset the effects of inadequate teacher preparation). We could afford to prepare and hire well-qualified teachers if we directed our investments to the improvement of teaching rather than the maintenance of bureaucracies as they are currently structured.

Responsiveness

Images of heightened professionalism sometimes provoke fears that a professional cult will ignore the views of parents and local communities. Indeed, over many decades, the relative authority of parents and local communities has decreased along with the authority of educators as boards of education and state legislatures have exercised more controls over schooling. Although government agencies have gained great power over decisions affecting children and local schools, these decisions are often uninformed by professional knowledge. Meanwhile, frontline educators often have had little input into decisions made above them, and bureaucracies have secured the presumptions of professionalism without the knowledge that should accompany it. This messy situation evolved as scientific managers claimed authority for what was intended to be a professional bureaucracy, but did not infuse enough knowledge into school organizations at any level. Meanwhile, bureaucratic discouragements to the participation of frontline teachers and parents have reduced responsiveness up and down the line.

As a consequence of these failings, proposals for decentralization and choice in education are increasing—especially in large cities where bureaucracies have substituted coercion for both participation and competence. Both choice and decentralization are arguments for encouraging schools to better attend to the individual needs of students, and both are dependent on increased professionalism among teachers for their success. Ensuring good teaching while decreasing regulation will depend on assuring greater knowledge and commitment among fully professional educators.

Ultimately, the question is how to achieve accountability for student learning—which I define as responsible decision making based on knowledge and the best interests of the child. If teachers acquire greater knowledge about children, learning, and subject matter, their legitimate authority should increase as should their obligations to be responsive to student needs. Rather than making teachers less accountable, a clear focus on professional standards of practice would create a basis for redress of poor practice that does not exist in a bureaucratic system, which can only ask that procedures be followed. A more professional approach to education would also force districts to make decisions more responsibly and would encourage more involvement by both teachers and parents, rather than relying excessively on standardized procedures.

I recently saw another illustration of the limits of current rule-based approaches as two parents approached a suburban elementary school principal in the beginning of the year to discuss their children's different needs. One parent asked how she could work with the 4th-grade teacher to support her son's continued progress in mathematics, an area in which his skills were quite advanced. The principal replied that the teacher could only follow the 4th-grade curriculum, otherwise the children would be out of sequence for the 5th-grade curriculum the following year! (The teacher later told the parent privately that she would nonetheless try to supplement the curriculum for the child but would have to do so on the sly.)

Another parent asked how she could secure additional help for her child who had a specific visual-perceptual learning disability. The principal sent her to the school's resource room specialist. The specialist, however, explained that she used only one specific approach adopted by the district for "slow" readers. Using this approach, the specialist worked on reading problems with groups of children who drilled their sight vocabulary knowledge using flash cards. If the child's needs could not be addressed in this way, there would be no other option.

In a bureaucratic school, teachers are often restricted to a single math text or reading program that they must march through on rigid pacing schedules. Even if Johnny or Suzy is not succeeding, there is nothing more to be done. In a professionally organized school, teachers are expected to work with parents and colleagues to figure out what approaches are most likely to support students' success. Furthermore, in schools that are more professional *and* more democratic, workshops and seminars are open to educators and parents alike, knowledge about child development and teaching strategies is widely shared, and efforts are made to support learning in compatible ways at home and at school. Knowledge is used to empower parents and students as well as teachers, rather than to mystify clients so as to make professionals look smart.

Teaching needs to create its own form of professionalism that couples the benefits of knowledgeable and ethical practice with the strengths of close partnerships with parents and communities. Whereas some professions have secured specialized expertise and control of practice by distancing themselves from their clients, successful teaching must be embedded in community contexts and connected to students' lives. Professionalism in teaching must be joined with greater democracy in schooling, empowering parents and students as well as teachers to participate in communities of learning that speak to their needs and concerns. The goal must be to create schools that have their eyes on the child rather than on the bureaucracy above.

To create this level of responsiveness, both teacher preparation and teaching practice must be restructured. A profession of teaching must prepare and select teachers for both technical knowledge and dispositions to learn and collaborate. It must provide serious and sustained internships for beginners, create meaningful evaluation, and establish more useful opportunities for professional development. It must also develop ongoing peer review of practice in the context of collegial consultation that helps teachers learn from each other, expose and tackle problems, hear parents' concerns, and address students' needs. The norms that guide these processes are as important as the technical foundations of practice. The most critical are a commitment to student learning and a pledge to continue to search for knowledge that will support student growth and development.

Access and Knowledge

The most persistent questions are whether there is any set of knowledge and skills for teaching worth insisting upon and whether there are any defensible grounds for limiting access to teaching. How many times have I heard the indignant charge, "I have a degree in physics, but because of certification rules I cannot teach!" Or, "These licensing requirements would prevent Einstein from teaching in a public school!" That some current licensing requirements are trivial and cumbersome is a point easy to concede, and one I address further below. However, many such complaints reveal a belief that there should be no restrictions on who teaches, save perhaps some general gauge of subject matter knowledge. This view is widespread despite the fact that most people can recall brilliant professors who knew a great deal about their fields but could not teach what they knew to students as well as teachers who were abusive or incapable of organizing useful learning experiences.

As a parent and long-time teacher, I often want to remind proponents of this view that the Unabomber had a graduate degree in physics and we might be grateful that it did not qualify him to teach. I also want to suggest to them that there is little reason to believe that Einstein would have made a good elementary or secondary school teacher either. In fact, judging from his biography, I suspect he might have had a difficult time organizing the work of 3rd graders or even high school students. I also suspect he would have agreed that he should not be asked to assume such complex work without qualifications substantially closer to the demands of that job than those he possessed.

I also want to remind them that contrary to conventional wisdom, most people who enter teaching without training are not Einsteins. Although national data show that teacher education students in 1991 were more academically able than the average college student, unlicensed entrants to teaching had significantly lower levels of academic achievement than most college students and than those who prepared to teach (Gray et al., 1993). Studies have found that recruits in fields like mathematics and science who enter teaching with little or no preparation have lower grade point averages than entrants from schools of education and are much more likely to say that they entered teaching because jobs were available rather than that they wanted to work with children (Natriello, Zumwalt, Hansen, & Frisch, 1990; Stoddart, forthcoming).

But many people sincerely believe that anyone can teach or, at least, that knowing a subject is enough to allow one to teach it well. Others believe that teaching is best learned, to the extent it can be learned at all, by trial and error on the job. The evidence, however, strongly suggests otherwise. Reviews of research over the past thirty years, summarizing hundreds of studies, have concluded that even with the shortcomings of current teacher education and licensing, fully prepared and certified teachers are better rated and more successful with students than teachers without this preparation (Evertson, Hawley, & Zlotnik, 1985; Ashton & Crocker, 1986, 1987; Greenberg, 1983; Haberman, 1984; Olsen, 1985). These studies find that for success with students, a threshold level of subject matter knowledge is important and that knowledge of how to teach is even more important (for a review see Darling-Hammond, 1992). This is true for fields ranging from mathematics and science (Begle, 1979; Druva & Anderson, 1983; Davis, 1964; Taylor, 1957) to beginning reading (Hice, 1970; LuPone, 1961; McNeil, 1974) and early childhood education (Roupp, Travers, Glantz, & Coelen, 1979).

Teachers who are well prepared are better able to use teaching strategies that respond to students' needs and learning styles and that encourage higher-order learning (Perkes, 1967–1968; Hansen, 1988; Skipper & Quantz, 1987). Because the novel tasks required for problem solving are more difficult to manage than the routine tasks associated with rote learning, lack of knowledge about how to manage an active inquiry-oriented classroom can lead teachers to turn to passive tactics that dumb down the curriculum (Carter & Doyle, 1987; Doyle, 1986), busying students with workbooks rather than assigning more complex work that requires more skill to orchestrate (Cooper & Sherk, 1989).

Studies of teachers admitted with less than full preparation—ranging from no preparation to preparation through quick alternative certification routes of only a few weeks duration—reveal serious shortcomings. These recruits tend to be dissatisfied with their training; they have greater difficulties than fully prepared teachers in planning curriculum, teaching, managing the classroom, and diagnosing students' learning needs. They are less able to adapt their instruction to promote student learning and less likely to see it as their job to do so, blaming students when their teaching is not effective. Principals and colleagues rate them less highly on their instructional skills, and they leave teaching at higher-than-average rates. Most important, their students learn less, especially in areas like reading, writing, and mathematics that are critical to later school success (Bents & Bents, 1990; Hawk, Coble, & Swanson, 1985; Darling-Hammond, Hudson, & Kirby, 1989; Jelmberg, 1996; Darling-Hammond, 1992; Lenk, 1989; Feiman-Nemser & Parker, 1990; Gomez & Grobe, 1990; Grady, Collins, & Grady, 1991; Grossman, 1989; National Center for Research on Teacher Learning, 1992; Rottenberg & Berliner, 1990; Smith, 1991).

Even very bright people who are enthusiastic about teaching find that they cannot easily succeed without preparation, especially if they are assigned to work with children who need skillful teaching. Many studies of alternate routes into teaching have found that careful year-long programs with thoughtful coursework and intensively supervised internships produce much more satisfied, confident, and capable recruits who stay longer in the classroom than do the truncated programs that ignore coursework on child development, learning theory, and teaching methods (Darling-Hammond, 1992; Darling-Hammond, Hudson, & Kirby, 1989; Lutz & Hutton, 1989; Wright, McKibbon, & Walton, 1987). The "bright person myth" of teaching (Holmes Group, 1986), that is, the myth that smart people are automatically capable teachers, is just that.

The best recent example of a well-publicized program founded on this notion is Teach for America (TFA)—created to recruit bright college graduates to disadvantaged urban and rural classrooms for two years, en route to their ultimate careers in law, medicine, and other professions. TFA argued that its summer training programs of three to eight weeks duration (depending on the funding available in a given year) should be enough to authorize it to license its recruits and that they should not have to meet traditional state standards. In fact TFA's founder suggested that states should get out of the business of licensing teachers altogether (Kopp, 1992, 1993), issuing a forceful counterclaim to the idea of a teaching profession organized to educate candidates to meet common standards.

If anyone could prove that teachers are born and not made, these bright eager students, many of them from top schools, might have been the ones to do it. Yet four separate evaluations found that TFA's training program did not prepare candidates to succeed with students (Grady, Collins, & Grady, 1991; Popkewitz, 1994, 1995; Roth, 1993; Texas Education Agency, 1993), despite the noticeable intelligence and enthusiasm of many of the recruits. One evaluation, for example, found that "in general, the team found corps members to be bright young individuals, enthusiastic and highly dedicated. . . . [However], in observing the teaching of corps members, team members found an apparent lack of developmentally-appropriate techniques and strategies in the delivery of instruction" (Texas Education Agency, 1993, p. 17–18). Another stated that "although nearly unanimous in support of the corps member's enthusiasm and intelligence, the cooperating teachers were not as complimentary of their teaching abilities. There was a strong sense of wanting to separate the corps member's potential from her weakness in the classroom. . . . Most criticism of a corps member's teaching behavior (classroom management was the greatest area of concern, followed by insufficient knowledge of the fundamentals of teaching and learning) was qualified by the cooperating teachers' perceptions of limitations of the program in providing the corps member with adequate practice or theory to be successful" (Grady, Collins, & Grady, 1991, p. 20).

Many TFA recruits eventually concluded that their success, and that of their students, had been compromised by their lack of access to the knowledge needed to teach. Yale University graduate Jonathan Schorr (1993) was the first to raise this concern, saying: "I—perhaps like most TFAers—harbored dreams of liberating my students from public school mediocrity and offering them as good an education as I had received. But I was not ready. . . . As bad as it was for me, it was worse for the students. Many of mine . . . took long steps on the path toward dropping out. . . . I was not a successful teacher and the loss to the students was real and large" (pp. 317–318). Schorr argued that "just eight weeks of training . . . may be long enough to train neighborhood clean-up workers or even police auxiliaries but [it isn't] enough for teachers" (p. 316).

Others agreed:[1]

I felt very troubled about going into an elementary classroom having had 6 weeks [of training]. I didn't even know where to start. I was unprepared to deal with every aspect. . . . I had a lot of kids who were frustrated and I was frustrated because I wanted to help them and didn't have the training to do that [a recruit who left in the first year and later entered a teacher preparation program].

I could maybe have done a bad job at a suburban high school. I stood to do an awful job at a school where you needed to have special skills. I just didn't have the tools, and I didn't even know I needed them before I went in. I felt like, OK, I did the workshops; I know science; and I care about these kids. . . . You know, I had the motivation to help, but I didn't have the skill. It's sort of like wanting to fix someone's car and not having any idea how to fix a car. I wasn't equipped to deal with it, and I had no idea [a recruit who left in the first year and later went to medical school].

I stayed one year. I felt it was important for me to see the year out but I didn't necessarily feel like it was a good idea for me to teach again without something else. I knew if I wanted to go on teaching there was no way I could do it without training [a recruit who later entered a teacher preparation program].

Such feelings undoubtedly contributed to the high attrition rate of TFA recruits. TFA statistics show that of those who started in 1990, 58 percent had left by the third year, a two-year attrition rate more than twice the national average for new teachers, including those in cities. The Maryland State Department of Education reported that 62 percent of corps members who started in Baltimore in 1992 had left within two years. In North Carolina, where East Carolina University evaluated TFA recruits as the recommending agency for certification, only one candidate was recommended for certification in the first years of the program, one was recommended for dismissal, and the remainder were required to take additional coursework to make up for gaps left by their training. The university ultimately refused to consider any TFA recruits for certification in special education (where many school districts had placed them), feeling that allowing untrained teachers to work in such classrooms would contribute to exploitation of the handicapped.

Ultimately, although a minority of TFA recruits stayed on, and some of them found formal or informal routes to learn how to teach, few would argue that they were adequately prepared at the start or that they did justice to their initial classes of students.

Some people believe that these kinds of compromises in training are necessary to fill classrooms that would otherwise go unstaffed. Many TFA recruits, however, discovered otherwise:

> When we first got there, none of us had jobs, and a TFA person would go to the school board offices and try to find out if jobs were going to open up so that she could stick someone in before certified people found out about it. Then we found out that there were certified teachers without jobs, because you're in your community and you're teaching and you learn about that.

> I guess I was foolish. I was still under the impression that there was this classroom of kids that wasn't going to have a teacher, and if I didn't go they would have subs that would change every 2 days. And so I thought, I have to do this. And that was a complete false image because, at least in Louisiana, there were plenty of people that could have been hired.

> Most of us went in there pretty blind, having no idea of what was required of us, and most of us felt like these were teacher shortage areas or we wouldn't be competing. But it turned out a lot of us were competing with people who were certified for these jobs. When I left, they didn't have any trouble at all finding a replacement for me the day I quit. It was a certified teacher, and had they had the whole summer before, they could have found a certified replacement who would have stayed the whole year and who would have been much better than I.

> Here we were supposed to be teaching in shortage areas, and I met a woman who had ten or twelve years of teaching experience in elementary education, and she had applied for my position. Of course

she was going to cost several thousand dollars more a year so they didn't hire her . . . [but] the kids needed the training and experience she had. She ended up working at the [all-white] private school. Another woman who was certified got the job I left in the afternoon of the morning I resigned. That was troubling to me too, because then I thought, "what was I doing?" It makes me furious that teacher shortage areas are not defined by lack of people but by lack of money.

These recruits' concerns reflect the best of Teach for America: the honesty, sincerity, and commitment of many of the young people TFA brought into teaching—young people who sincerely wanted to make a difference but did not receive the knowledge and skills they needed to do so. These concerns also reflect the fundamental dilemmas of teaching in the United States—dilemmas that result from a long-standing disdain for teacher knowledge, a slipshod recruitment system, and a lack of investment in teacher recruitment and training. How can those who would teach be armed with the knowledge, skills, and commitments they need to succeed? How can resources be marshaled to underwrite their training and to fund the hiring of well-prepared teachers in all communities? In short, how can every student be guaranteed access to caring and competent teachers and every teacher be guaranteed access to high-quality preparation and professional development?

The answers, I believe, lie in the creation of professional standards for teaching, the development of more productive strategies for teacher learning, and a reconceptualization of the teaching career in concert with the redesign of schools.

STANDARDS FOR TEACHING

Probably the most important policy lever for improving teaching and learning is the recent development of professional standards that capture the important aspects of teaching. These standard-setting efforts are being led by the new National Board for Professional Teaching Standards, established in 1987 and the first professional body (a majority of its members are teachers) to set standards for accomplished teaching; the Interstate New Teacher Assessment and Support Consortium (INTASC, 1991), a consortium of thirty-two states working with teachers and teacher educators to develop "National Board–compatible" licensing standards; and the National Council for Accreditation of

Teacher Education (NCATE), which has been strengthening standards for teacher education programs, recently incorporating the performance standards developed by INTASC. These initiatives are the basis for a shared knowledge base reflected in sophisticated performance assessments that enable teachers to demonstrate skills and knowledge in real teaching contexts.

The three sets of standards share a view of teaching as complex, contingent, and reciprocal, that is, continually shaped and reshaped by students' responses to learning experiences. By examining teaching in the light of learning, they put considerations of effectiveness at the center of good practice. This view contrasts with that of the recent "technicist" era of teacher training and evaluation, in which teaching was seen as the technical implementation of set routines and formulas for behavior, which were disconnected from the needs and responses of students. The new standards and assessments explicitly address subject matter standards for students and the demands of learner diversity and also the expectation that teachers will collaborate effectively with colleagues and parents in order to improve their practice.

An analogue to the practice of board certification in medicine or accounting, the National Board for Professional Teaching Standards' examinations for certifying accomplished veteran teachers use a portfolio assessment completed over several months of classroom work augmented by performance tasks completed in an assessment center. Teachers demonstrate their practices through videotapes and other evidence of their teaching accompanied by discussions of their goals and intentions and samples of student work over time. They evaluate textbooks and teaching materials, analyze teaching events, assess student learning and needs, and defend teaching decisions based on their knowledge of curriculum, students, and pedagogy. The 500 teachers thus far certified by the National Board benefit not only from the recognition they receive for their expertise (sometimes in the form of increased compensation from their states or school districts) but also from the learning they experienced during the assessment.

Rick Wormeli, for example, an English teacher at Herndon Middle School in Virginia, credits the experience with changing his teaching. During the course of the assessment his close scrutiny of his work in light of the standards caused him to integrate other subjects into his lessons, rethink how he organized reading discussion groups, and scrap the vocabulary book that taught words out of context in favor of using words from his students' work. Even after he had finished the assessment, he continued to experiment with the changes he had begun. "I can't turn it off," he reports (Bradley, 1994, p. 25). Shirley Bzdewka, a teacher in Dayton, New Jersey, agrees. In addition to creating a group of colleagues with whom she continues to share ideas and solve problems, the assessment process deepened her approach to teaching: "I know I was a good teacher. But . . . I am a much more deliberate teacher now. I can never, ever do anything again with my kids and not ask myself, 'Why? Why am I doing this? What are the effects on my kids? What are the benefits to my kids?' It's not that I didn't care about those things before, but it's on such a conscious level now" (Bradley, 1995, p. 1).

These same effects on practice are reported by beginning teachers who have experienced the National Board–compatible assessments created by the INTASC consortium. The INTASC standards call for a staged set of examinations that tap knowledge about subject matter and about teaching and learning at the end of preservice education and then assess applied teaching skills when the candidate is practicing under supervision during an internship or induction year. The assessments examine how teachers plan and guide instruction around new standards for student learning, evaluate student learning and adapt teaching accordingly, use a variety of curriculum materials, and handle problems of practice. Tightly linked to subject area standards, the portfolio emphasizes content pedagogy along with the capacity to attend to student needs. For example, in mathematics, one assessment task requires teachers to plan an instructional unit structured around National Council of Teachers of Mathematics standards of mathematical problem solving, reasoning, communication, and connections; show how they use curriculum tools including manipulatives and technology; and reflect on and revise the instruction in practice. Other tasks require teachers to analyze student work and assess learning for purposes of planning, diagnosis, feedback, and grading.

A 7th-grade math teacher in Stamford, Connecticut, described how this assessment process was much more helpful to him than classroom observations. After he recorded each lesson every day for six weeks, he explained, "I would have to reflect on it—what I had done and how I would change the lesson to make it better, and [answer] basic questions like: How did I meet the needs of every student?" He recalled that "although I was the reflective type anyway, it made me go a step further. I would have to say, okay, this is how I'm going to do it differently. I think it made more of an impact on my teaching and was more beneficial to me than just one lesson in which you state what you're going to do. . . . The process makes you think about your teaching and reflect on your teaching. And I think that's necessary to become an effective teacher."

NCATE's new standards incorporate these ideals into expectations for what schools of education will prepare their candidates to do. Together the NCATE, INTASC, and National Board standards establish a continuum for what teachers need to know and be able to do from the time they prepare to enter teaching through their development of highly accomplished practice. The standards honor both rigorous approaches to content and supportive relationships with students grounded in deep understanding about learning and development. In the past few years, more than forty states have created partnerships with NCATE that encourage the use of NCATE's standards for reviewing schools of education. More than twenty states have adapted or adopted INTASC's standards for licensing, and more than fifteen states have agreed to give credit for relicensing or advanced certification to those who have been certified by the National Board. These actions lay the initial foundations for professional teaching standards that could ultimately influence practice; however, the real impact of standards has yet to occur—that is, their widespread use in making decisions about how institutions prepare teachers, how individuals are admitted to teaching, and how advancement in the field is acknowledged.

Legitimate questions can be raised about whether improving standards will create or exacerbate teacher shortages and whether standards will limit access to historically underrepresented groups, as the professionalization of medicine did many years ago. Interestingly, the reverse has historically been true in teaching. As Sedlak and Schlossman (1986) found in their historical study: "It has proved possible, time and again, to raise standards during periods of protracted shortage. Not only has the raising of standards not exacerbated teacher shortages, it may even—at least where accompanied by significant increases in teachers' salaries—have helped to alleviate them and, at the same time, enhanced popular respect for teaching as a profession" (p. 39).

During these periods of raised standards and salaries, representation of women and minorities remained stable or increased. However, declines in the entrance of minority candidates to teaching occurred during the 1970s and 1980s primarily because many able candidates defected from teaching when other professions previously closed to them opened up and teaching salaries declined (Darling-Hammond, Pittman, & Ottinger, 1988). As teaching salaries increased once again, along with standards, in the late 1980s and early 1990s, the numbers of minority entrants to teaching have increased once again, although not yet to levels that mirror the growing share of children of color in the nation's schools (Darling-Hammond, Dilworth, & Bullmaster, 1996).

Today there is no absolute shortage of teachers but a shortage in particular fields and locations. In fact nearly twice as many teachers are prepared as actually enter teaching each year. Spot shortages occur because of inattention to planning and recruitment: lack of national and regional information about vacancies, lack of reciprocity in licensing across states, and the paucity of incentives for recruiting teachers to the fields and locations where they are most needed. In addition nearly 30 percent of new teachers leave within a few years of entry, especially in the most disadvantaged districts that offer fewest supports, leading to continual pressure for hiring. The most pressing need is to equalize schools' resources and create a functional recruitment and induction system with incentives and supports for teaching in high-need areas (National Commission on Teaching and America's Future, 1996).

Finally, the most important concern in setting standards is that they must represent meaningful goals for candidates and colleges to pursue. The object in standard setting is not to increase the failure rates of candidates but to improve the caliber of their preparation for the real tasks of teaching. One of the most important aspects of the new teaching standards is that like standards in other professions, they bring clarity to the pursuit of teaching skills by focusing on the performance of critical teaching tasks rather than on lists of particular courses or tests of knowledge in forms too arcane and too distant from the way that knowledge is actually used. Teaching candidates consistently report that they learn from the new assessments—that the assessments actually help them develop and refine their skills. This means that these assessments are enhancing teachers' abilities and the overall capacity of the profession to do its work rather than merely rationing slots in a constrained labor market.

Implied in any performance-based licensing and accreditation system is the expectation that meaningful and rigorous assessments for licensing will be used with *all* candidates and that programs will need to demonstrate that they can successfully prepare their students to meet the standards. A way to enhance the probability that states will create such systems of licensing and accreditation would be to create state professional standards boards like those that govern all other professions. Composed of expert teachers (eventually this will mean those who are board certified), other educators, and members of the public, such boards can give serious attention to professional standard setting undistracted by political concerns. As John Goodlad has observed: "The states . . . [have] found themselves with a set of internally conflicting demands: Improve quality, but guarantee a body in every public classroom. . . . Temporary and emergency certificates ease the shortage in times of undersupply; while in times of oversupply, a glut of teachers removes any rising interest in providing incentives for the improvement of quality. The call for higher salaries is muted when many of those teaching have done little to be temporarily certified, just as it is muted when there are dozens of applicants for each vacancy" (1990, pp. 94–95).

Pressures to keep salaries low, allow patronage hiring, and preserve schools of education as cash cows for their universities tend to politicize standard setting and create incentives for the status quo. In addition, policymakers' lack of knowledge about what would make a real difference for teaching has allowed the continuation of licensing, hiring, and selection systems that often miss the point. For all these reasons, states that rely on legislatively directed state agencies to administer the agencies' own standards have proved largely incapable of closing down shoddy schools of education, creating and enforcing meaningful standards of entry to teaching, or inspiring substantial changes in practice. Creating and maintaining a press for quality teaching and learning—and an understanding of what quality consists of—will ultimately depend on the creation of governance structures that reflect professional knowledge and commitments along with public involvement and oversight. Standards boards for teaching are one such vehicle for advancing a coherent thoughtful agenda for change grounded in what students need their teachers to know rather than what political interests will comfortably support.

Building and sustaining a well-prepared teaching force will also require local, state, and federal initiatives to strengthen the teaching profession. Initiatives will be needed to recruit and prepare new teachers, to strengthen and improve teachers' initial preparation through meaningful reciprocal licensing systems and accreditation reforms, and to support teacher learning within schools.

The federal government has a leadership role to play in ensuring an adequate supply of well-qualified teachers just as it has had in ensuring an adequate supply of well-qualified physicians for the nation. When physician shortages were a major problem in the 1960s, Congress passed the 1963 Health Professions Education Assistance Act to improve the caliber of medical training, to create and strengthen teaching hospitals, to provide scholarships and loans to medical students, and to create incentives for physicians to train in shortage specialties and to locate in underserved areas. That sustained effort, continued for more than three decades, has had a substantial impact on the quality of medical care and training in this country and on the supply of physicians.

Similarly, federal initiatives in education should seek to *recruit new teachers,* especially in fields and locations facing shortages, through scholarships and forgivable loans for high-quality teacher education; *strengthen teachers' preparation* through incentive grants to schools of education to redesign programs so they meet higher standards; and *improve teacher retention and effectiveness* through funding internship programs for new teachers in which they receive structured coaching in professional development schools. Building useful learning opportunities throughout each teacher's career will require the involvement of every part of the system—and, as I describe in the following section, redesigning major parts of the system itself.

NEW STRATEGIES
FOR TEACHER LEARNING

Developing the kinds of knowledge I outlined at the beginning of this chapter will require most teachers to move far beyond what they themselves experienced as students and thus to learn in ways that are more powerful than simply reading and talking about new pedagogical ideas (Ball & Cohen, in press). Learning to practice in substantially different ways than one has ever before experienced can occur neither through theoretical imaginings alone nor through unguided experience alone. Instead it requires a tight coupling of the two.

Teachers learn just as their students do: by studying, doing, and reflecting; by collaborating with other teachers; by looking closely at students and their work; and by sharing what they see. This kind of learning cannot occur solely in college classrooms divorced from engagement in practice or solely in school classrooms divorced from knowledge about how to interpret practice. Good settings for teacher learning, in both colleges of education and schools, provide lots of opportunities for research and inquiry, for trying and testing, for talking about and evaluating the results of learning and teaching. The "rub between theory and practice" (Miller & Silvernail, 1994, p. 44) occurs most productively when questions arise in the context of real students and real work in progress where research and disciplined inquiry are also at hand.

Yet until recently many teacher education and ongoing professional development programs separated theory and application almost completely. People were taught to teach in lecture halls, from textbooks and teachers who frequently had not themselves ever practiced what they were teaching. Their courses on subject matter topics were disconnected from their courses on teaching methods, which were in turn disconnected from their courses on foundations and psychology. They completed this coursework before they began student teaching, which was a brief taste of practice typically appended to the end of their program with few connections to what had come before. In their student teaching classrooms, many encountered entirely different ideas from those they had previously studied because university- and school-based faculty did little planning or teaching together. Sometimes, cooperating teachers were selected with no regard for the quality or kind of practice they themselves engaged in. When prospective teachers finally entered their own classrooms, they could remember and apply little of what they had learned by reading in isolation from practice. Thus they reverted largely to what they knew best: the way they themselves had been taught.

In-service training programs were even less transformative. Large groups of teachers amassed in auditoriums after school had brief encounters with packaged prescriptions offered by outside consultants. Divorced from daily concerns and practice, these hit-and-run events were generally forgotten when the next day's press of events set in. Difficult problems of teaching and learning (How can I explain quadratic equations? What's keeping Ellen from being able to explain what she reads?) were never raised in these training contexts, much less explored and discussed.

Over the past decade many schools of education and school districts have begun to change these traditions. Stimulated by the efforts of the Holmes Group of education deans and the National Network for Educational Renewal, more than three hundred schools of education have created programs that extend beyond the confines of the traditional four-year bachelor's degree program, thus allowing more extensive study of the disciplines to be taught along with education coursework that is integrated with more extensive clinical training in schools. Some are one- or two-year graduate programs that serve recent graduates or midcareer recruits. Others are five-year models that allow an extended program of preparation for prospective teachers who enter teacher education during their undergraduate years. In either case the fifth year allows students to devote their energies exclusively to the task of preparing to teach through yearlong school-based internships that are woven together with coursework on learning and teaching.

A number of recent studies have found that graduates of extended (typically five-year) programs are not only more satisfied with their preparation, they are viewed by their colleagues, principals, and co-operating teachers as better prepared; are as effective with students as much more experienced teachers; and are much more likely to enter and stay in teaching than their peers prepared in traditional four-year programs (Andrew, 1990; Andrew & Schwab, 1995; Denton & Peters, 1988; Dyal, 1993; Long & Morrow, 1995; Shin, 1994).

Many of these teacher education programs have joined with local school districts to create professional development schools where novices' clinical preparation can be more purposefully structured. Like teaching hospitals in medicine, these schools are sites for state-of-the-art practice and are also organized to support the training of new professionals, extend the professional development of veteran teachers, and sponsor collaborative research and inquiry. Programs are jointly planned and taught by university- and school-based faculty. Cohorts of beginning teachers get a richer, more coherent learning experience when they are organized in teams to study and practice with these faculty and with one another. Senior teachers report that they deepen their knowledge by serving as mentors, adjunct faculty, co-researchers, and teacher leaders. Thus these schools help create the rub between theory and practice that teachers need in order to learn, and at the same time they create more professional roles for teachers and build teachers' knowledge in ways that improve both practice and ongoing theory building (Darling-Hammond, 1994).

These new programs typically engage prospective teachers in studying research and conducting their own inquiries through cases, action research, and the development of structured portfolios about practice. They envision the professional teacher as one who learns from teaching rather than one who has finished learning how to teach, and the job of teacher education as developing the capacity to inquire sensitively and systematically into the nature of learning and the effects of teaching. This is an approach to knowledge production like that John Dewey (1929) sought—one that aims to empower teachers with greater understanding of complex situations rather than to control teachers with simplistic formulas or cookie-cutter routines for teaching: "Command of scientific methods and systematized subject matter liberates individuals; it enables them to see new problems, devise new procedures, and in general, makes for diversification rather than for set uniformity. . . . This knowledge and understanding render [the teacher's] practice more intelligent, more flexible, and better adapted to deal effectively with concrete phenomena of practice. . . . Seeing more relations he sees more possibilities, more opportunities. His ability to judge being enriched, he has a wider range of alternatives to select from in dealing with individual situations" (pp. 12, 20–21).

When teachers investigate the effects of their teaching on students' learning and when they read about what others have learned, they come to understand teaching "to be an inherently problematic endeavor, rather than a highly routinized activity" (Houston, 1992, p. 126). They become sensitive to variation and more aware of what works for what purposes in what situations. Access to knowledge that is nuanced and contingent allows them to become more thoughtful decision makers.

Training in inquiry also helps teachers learn how to look at the world from multiple perspectives, including the perspectives of students whose experiences are quite different from the teachers' own, and to use this knowledge in developing pedagogies that can reach diverse learners. Learning to reach out to students—those who are difficult to know as well as those who are easy to know—requires boundary crossing, the ability to elicit knowledge of others and to understand it when it is offered. As Lisa Delpit (1995) notes, "we all interpret behaviors, information, and situations through our own cultural lenses; these lenses operate involuntarily, below the level of conscious awareness, making it seem that our own view is simply 'the way it is'" (p. 151). Teachers concerned with democratic education must develop an awareness of their perspectives and learn how to enlarge them to avoid the "communicentric bias" (Gordon, Miller & Rollock, 1990) that limits understanding of areas of study as well as of those who are taught.

These goals suggest a new relationship between research and practice. For most of this century, policymakers sought knowledge that would aid them in the remote control of teaching—generalizable dicta that would shape the design specifications for teaching via texts, curriculum packages, and teaching procedures. This trickle-down theory of knowledge envisioned that teachers could get all they needed from these tools and their teachers' manuals: five rules for a foolproof classroom management system or seven steps to a perfect lesson. When these directives and materials proved inadequate to the real complexities of teaching, teachers were left with whatever knowledge they had managed to accumulate on their own, largely from personal experience.

The kind of learning found in rich professional development settings has quite different features: it is *centered around the critical activities of teaching and learning*—planning lessons, evaluating student work, developing curriculum—rather than around abstractions and generalities; it grows from *investigations of practice* through cases, questions, analysis, and criticism; and it is built on *substantial professional discourse* that fosters analysis and communication about practices and values in ways that build collegiality and standards of practice (Ball & Cohen, in press). These elements are the building blocks for a seamless process of professional learning that begins in preservice education, continues through the early years of induction, and extends through years of developing accomplished practice. They are the common features of continual professional learning in a growing number of restructured schools in the United States and in schools elsewhere around the world.

Countries like Germany, Belgium, and Luxembourg have long required from two to three years of graduate study in education for prospective teachers on top of an undergraduate degree—sometimes with two disciplinary majors—in the subject(s) to be taught. Education courses include the study of child development and learning, pedagogy and teaching methods, plus an intensively supervised internship in a school affiliated with the university. Many other nations have recently launched similar reforms. In 1989, both France and Japan undertook major teacher education reforms to extend both university- and school-based training. In France, all candidates must now complete a graduate program of teacher education in newly created "university institutes for the preparation of teachers" that are closely connected to schools in their regions.

In Japan, graduate-level teacher education is encouraged but not required. There, as in Taiwan, a yearlong supervised internship, with a reduced teaching load that allows time for mentoring and additional study, is required for all entering teachers. By Japanese law, beginning teachers receive at least twenty days of in-service training during their first year on the job and sixty days of professional development. Master teachers are released from their classrooms to advise and counsel these beginning teachers. Early teaching experiences in both Japan and Taiwan involve new teachers in watching other teachers at length, discussing problems of practice, presenting and critiquing demonstration lessons, and with groups of colleagues, imagining and acting out how students might respond to certain presentations of material. In their study of mathematics teaching in Japan, Taiwan, and the United States, Stigler and Stevenson (1991) report that "[one of the] reasons Asian class lessons are so well crafted is that there is a very systematic effort to pass on the accumulated wisdom of teaching practice to each new generation of teachers and to keep perfecting that practice by providing teachers the opportunities to continually learn from each other" (p. 46). Because schools in other countries are structured for this kind of regular collegial exchange, teachers share knowledge and refine their practice throughout their careers.

Without such supports, learning to teach well is extremely difficult. Most U.S. teachers start their careers in disadvantaged schools where turnover is highest, are assigned the most educationally needy students whom no one else wants to teach, are given the most demanding teaching loads with the greatest number of extra duties, and receive few curriculum materials and no mentoring. After this hazing, many leave. Others learn merely to cope rather than to teach well. Not too much later, teachers are expected to know everything they will need for a career or to learn through workshops mostly on their own, with few structured opportunities to observe and analyze teaching with others. As one high school teacher who had spent twenty-five years in the classroom once told me: "I have taught 20,000 classes; I have been 'evaluated' thirty times; but I have never seen another teacher teach." With this degree of isolation common, is it any wonder that shared knowledge and standards of practice are so difficult to forge?

Some school districts have begun to create new models of induction and ongoing professional development for teachers and principals. They feature mentoring for beginners and veterans, peer observation and coaching, local study groups and networks for developing teaching within specific subject matter areas (like the National Writing Project or the Urban Mathematics Collaboratives), teacher academies that offer ongoing seminars and courses of study tied to practice, and school-university partnerships that sponsor collaborative research, interschool visitations, and a variety of formal and informal learning opportunities developed in response to teachers' and principals' felt needs.

For example, at Wells Junior High, a professional development school working with the University of Southern Maine,

> The whole notion of staff development was turned on its head. The emphasis shifted from outside consultants to in-house experts. Collaborative learning groups replaced the traditional lecture/demonstration format. Problem posing and problem solving supplanted the recipes and prescriptions for effective schools that teachers had heard for years and never managed to implement. . . .
>
> "Using the knowledge" became the starting point for developing a new view of staff development. The school staff redefined its use of the district's allocated workshop days. Rather than providing time for formal presentations by outside consultants, the days were used for teachers' review of research and for critical discussion and reflection. On one such day teachers spent two hours individually reading research about grouping. During another day, they worked in cooperative groups to share their perceptions on the research they had read. On yet another day, the staff met to engage in the process of consensus building with the goal of reaching a decision about grouping practices in the school [pp. 30, 31].

Similarly at Fairdale High School in Louisville, Kentucky, teachers' research coupled with shared decision making produced major changes:

> As part of a self-study, ten teachers followed ten children through a school day. When it was over, teachers said things like, "It was boring," or, "You know, this isn't a very humane place to be." Another teacher reported that no adult had spoken to the child she was following the entire day. . . . Another activity that brought teachers together was reading about education and teaching. The teachers who went to Gheens Academy read and began to trade articles from *The Kappan, Educational Leadership,* and *Education Week.* . . . Even before participative

management was initiated at Fairdale, the teachers started changing things. In 1987 a steering committee consisting of elected teachers, students, administrators, support staff, and parents adopted operating procedures and set up task forces to study, design, and implement program changes. . . . "Make no mistake about it," [the principal] said, "we are into culture building here. We are building a community culture outside and a professional culture inside" [Kerchner, 1993, p. 39].

In other schools, teachers have organized their learning around the development of standards and assessments of student work, evaluating both student learning and the effectiveness of their own teaching in the process. The result is a greater appreciation for what matters and what works as well as what needs to change to promote student success.

Professional development strategies that succeed in improving teaching share several features (Darling-Hammond & McLaughlin, 1995). They tend to be

- Experiential, engaging teachers in concrete tasks of teaching, assessment, and observation that illuminate the processes of learning and development
- Grounded in participants' questions, inquiry, and experimentation as well as professionwide research
- Collaborative, involving a sharing of knowledge among educators
- Connected to and derived from teachers' work with their students as well as connected to examinations of subject matter and teaching methods
- Sustained and intensive, supported by modeling, coaching, and problem solving around specific problems of practice
- Connected to other aspects of school change

These approaches shift from the old models of teacher training or in-servicing in which an expert imparts new techniques in drive-by workshops to a model in which teachers confront research and theory directly, are regularly engaged in evaluating their practice, and use their colleagues for mutual assistance. Growing evidence suggests that investments in this kind of professional development not only make teachers feel better about their practice, they also reap learning gains for students, especially in the more challenging learning new standards demand (Cohen, in press; National Foundation for the Improvement of Education, 1995, 1996; Lampert & Eshelman, 1995; Little, 1993; LeMahieu & Sterling, 1991).

REDESIGNING THE TEACHING CAREER

Teachers and administrators get smarter about teaching when they are involved in both planning and doing rather than in the distinct and mutually exclusive roles carved out for them by Frederick Taylor's bureaucracy. In restructured schools, virtually all professional staff, including principals, teach at least part of the time and virtually all engage in a variety of other roles in the time made available to them once a school invests more resources in teaching. Schools and students also benefit when teachers can continue to develop and improve their expertise in a variety of ways and do not have to leave the classroom in order to be promoted. A new vision of the teaching career is needed that rewards the knowledge and expertise of those who work closest to children as highly as the skills of those who work furthest away and that makes those skills more widely available, thus enabling teachers to take on complementary hyphenated roles as school and program leaders, curriculum developers, mentors, staff developers, teacher educators, and researchers while they remain teachers.

In contrast to bureaucratic schemes that "promote" a few teachers to roles in the bureaucracy from which they are supposed to direct and guide the work of others, new approaches redesign the work and responsibilities of all teachers so that they have opportunities to engage in decision making, knowledge production, peer coaching, and continual redesign of teaching and schooling. In schools like International High, Central Park East Secondary, Wheeler Elementary, the Key School, and many others, teachers assume roles once traditionally reserved for others as they shape programs for their students and professional development opportunities for themselves, inquire into the effects of their practice, advise one another, and manage curriculum change. These activities embedded in the daily work of teaching directly increase teachers' knowledge and skills much more than traditional workshops ever could (Smylie, 1994; Darling-Hammond, Bullmaster, & Cobb, 1995).

At different times, individual teachers may want to take on different tasks that contribute to the work of their colleagues and the school. In schools that provide time and space for a broader teaching role, like those that have restructured to provide at least ten hours a week for joint planning and collegial work, new leadership emerges in organic ways that resemble Howey's (1988) notion of career lattices, which permit "a dynamic interchange of roles and responsibilities" (p. 30) as needs for curriculum work, program development, research, and mentoring emerge within schools.

A few places have put many of the elements of effective teacher learning together and have begun to imagine and develop an entirely new teaching career (National Commission on Teaching and America's Future, 1996). In Cincinnati, Ohio, for example, new teachers begin their career in a five-year teacher education program developed by the University of Cincinnati in collaboration with the public schools. Candidates complete a bachelor's degree in their subject area as well as a master's degree in teaching. They engage in ongoing clinical experiences in professional practice schools that involve local schools and faculties as partners in the preparation of teachers and the redesign of schooling. Starting in their second year candidates conduct classroom observations, research studies, and tutoring in these local sites; by the fifth year they complete a full-year internship that combines half-time teaching responsibility with coordinated seminars under the joint supervision of university- and school-based faculty.

Following this in-depth preparation, new teachers are assigned a mentor who is an expert consulting teacher in Cincinnati's Career-in-Teaching program. They receive intensive help throughout their first year from this mentor, who has been selected through a rigorous evaluation process and who has released time to work with beginners on developing their practice. At the end of the year the consulting teacher assesses the new teacher's performance and recommends continuation or dismissal to a governing board of teachers and administrators. The program has resulted in lower attrition of beginning teachers, higher levels of competence, and greater selectivity in decisions about who remains in the profession (National Commission on Teaching and America's Future, 1996).

Interns proceed through a career continuum that links collegial coaching, a wide array of learning opportunities, serious evaluation based on professional standards, and compensation based on competence and performance. Their efforts to develop their expertise are supported in part by the Mayerson Academy, a professional development collaborative endowed by the business community, which offers courses, action labs, study groups, and seminars with and for educators. If new teachers are evaluated positively after three to four years as "residents," they become professional teachers. A formal evaluation by the school principal is required at the third and fifth years, when the teacher applies for career status, and then for tenure. Salary steps for experience at these junctures—and at years seventeen and twenty-two—are contingent on evaluation. Altogether there are at least six points at which salary advancement is linked to performance.

Those who wish to can apply for lead teacher status after seven or more years. About three hundred of Cincinnati's three thousand teachers have passed the rigorous evaluation process—four to six classroom observations by expert teachers, interviews of an applicant's colleagues, and an extensive application that reveals the candidate's philosophy and experience. Obtaining National Board certification is another means of becoming a lead teacher. Lead teachers serve as consulting teachers for beginners and for veteran teachers who are having difficulty and as curriculum developers, clinical faculty in the districts' teacher education partnerships, and leaders for school-based teams and departments while they continue their own teaching. Additional stipends are just part of the reward of lead teaching. As lead teacher Helen Buswinka explains: "Participating [as a lead teacher in a professional development school] has given me an occasion to think grandly about what it means to educate a teacher. In the process, my own vision of teaching has been nourished. As a member of both worlds, I am able to participate in the shaping of the next generation of teachers, to be part of the evolution of my profession" (National Commission on Teaching and America's Future, 1996, p. 97).

The evolution of the teaching profession is tightly interwoven with the future of U.S. schools and the opportunities that will be available to this nation's children. Democratic schools cannot evolve or survive without strong cords of commitment and shared learning that bind teachers to one another and powerful teaching that connects young people to their futures.

Note

1. Quotations from teachers are taken from interviews with them, unless otherwise noted.

## CHAPTER TEN

Conclusion

An Agenda for
Re-Creating Public Education

Education reformers in the late nineteenth and early twentieth centuries had many competing goals, among them the idealistic goal of educating every child, the practical goal of staffing the ongoing industrial revolution, and the social goal of producing a citizenry supportive of a changing society. The challenge of fulfilling these competing goals was coupled with the need to carry them out efficiently and cost-effectively. As schools were designed more and more along the lines of the mass-production factory, the drive to standardize instructional content and methods reshaped the original goals. Like Henry Ford's view in the early days of the assembly line that people could have any color car they wanted as long as it was black, children's right to an education became a right only to the kind of education the system found it most convenient to offer.

Over the past century, despite several subsequent reform efforts, the education offered has demanded that most children learn prescribed lists of facts and "basic" skills in isolated subject areas largely by rote learning methods; that teachers be trained to deliver these facts largely by lecturing to classrooms of children grouped to be similar in backgrounds and measured abilities; that at the end of this assembly line, the results be inspected by standardized short-answer and multiple-choice tests; and that failure to achieve be met with more of the same. The assumption has been that students who persist in failure are students who cannot learn.

Conversely, the education that we more and more require for fulfilling lives and a peaceful and productive society demands that children learn to understand concepts as well as facts, in classrooms where they link and apply ideas, produce their own work, and learn to cooperate productively with diverse peers. This requires in turn that teachers take account of children's abilities and needs in order to engage them in active in-depth learning and create a classroom setting that stimulates in-depth understanding; that the results be inspected by demonstrations of authentic performance; and that learning problems be met with thoughtful analysis and fresh approaches to helping individual children succeed. The assumption here is that all children can learn. The need is for teaching strategies and school organizations that make that possible.

Today several thousand restructured schools have managed to create democratic learning communities that succeed in ways not previously thought possible with diverse groups of students. As I have shown in the preceding chapters, research demonstrates that restructured schools produce high achievement with more students of all abilities and graduate more of them with better levels of skills and understanding than traditional schools do. We now know much about what schools structured for success look like. They organize teachers' and students' work together in ways that get beyond bureaucracy to produce

- Active in-depth learning
- Emphasis on authentic performance
- Attention to development
- Appreciation for diversity
- Opportunities for collaborative learning
- A collective perspective across the school
- Structures for caring
- Support for democratic learning
- Connections to family and community

To support this work they allocate the critical resources of staff and time to the central tasks of classroom teaching and teachers' learning.

We also now know that school reform cannot spread from individual schools to the entire education system until we change the policies and procedures that still govern most schools. Restructured schools have been operating largely under waivers from traditional school requirements. They have done so for one simple reason: *they cannot simultaneously meet those requirements and do the teaching that produces student success.* That should clearly tell us that it is time to change the requirements for everyone. Although valuable for individual schools and a few students, reforms like charter schools and most choice plans do not take this systemic view. Treating the failures of schools problem by problem is to treat the symptoms of illness one at time without addressing the underlying etiology of the disease. It will never result in a cure.

Throughout these chapters, I have suggested essential concerns for and characteristics of a new approach to school policymaking, and I summarize those in what follows. I have also emphasized how interdependent these policies are and how each relates to many aspects of schooling. The various aspects of reform must be woven tightly together as an entire tapestry. Pulling on a single thread will create a tangle rather than tangible progress. This necessary unity is the reason for my argument that change in policy and practice must be comprehensive, not piecemeal, if we are to avoid burdening schools with even more conflicting policies than they already face.

POLICYMAKING CHARACTERISTICS

First, the overall goal of education policymaking should be to develop the capacity of schools and teachers to create practices that reflect what is now known about effective ways to teach and learn. This means policies should emphasize professional learning and peer review of practice to build educators' individual and collective knowledge base.

Second, policymaking should set publicly adopted goals and enact professional standards rather than prescribe more and more details about how schools should be structured, staffed, and managed and how teaching should occur. In many areas of policy, less is definitely more productive for the long-run health of schools. Goals and standards can provide the grist for professional accountability processes that improve practice without overly constraining it.

Third, decisions about policy must grow out of a dialogue that incorporates teachers and other school staff, parents, researchers, and policymakers. At every level of the system, participation builds the knowledge and ownership that are essential to serious change.

ARENAS FOR REFORM

A major challenge is to develop policies that support learner-centered *and* learning-centered practice, that attend both to the needs of diverse students and the demands of challenging content. A set of interlocking initiatives is needed.

Curriculum

Curriculum policies should focus on defining core concepts and critical skills students need to learn and should avoid dictating long lists of items to be superficially covered. They should sort out the crucially important from the decidedly trivial, giving teachers latitude to teach in depth and to guide each child in joining the concepts to his or her existing knowledge and experience. Teachers who are enacting curriculum need curriculum guidance that is sufficiently permeable to be integrated with what they know about how children develop, how they learn, how they vary in cultural backgrounds and personal experiences, and what will enable and motivate them to develop their individual talents.

Assessment

Policies about assessment must ensure that what is being measured emphasizes genuine performance on tasks of true value rather than anemic proxies for important learning. If schools are to give students the ability to be "knowledge workers" and to be productive parents and community members, assessment policies should focus on supporting as well as measuring students' understanding and abilities to apply their knowledge, should encourage local involvement in assessment development and evaluation, and should use assessment results primarily as opportunities for educators to identify what is working and what is not as a basis for strengthening school programs. Assessment policies should not assume that merely measuring performance and adding punishments or rewards will result in positive change. The success of assessment policy depends greatly on curriculum and teacher development policies that support better teaching, on removing disincentives and barriers to good practice, and on strategies for collective inquiry that involve classroom teachers and other educators in assessment of teaching and learning.

Professional Teachers

Policies must also recognize how teacher education must change to address the new mission of teaching. Teaching *all* children for high levels of understanding will require more intensive teacher training, more meaningful licensing systems, and more thoughtful professional development. These policies are the first step for moving past the assumption that learning depends mostly on the child's ability and has little to do with the teacher's ability. Teachers must be helped to acquire the knowledge they need to teach powerfully. This includes conceptual knowledge of subject matter; knowledge about children's cognitive, social, and personal development; understanding of learning and motivation; appreciation for the diversity of children's experiences and approaches to learning and knowledge of varied teaching strategies to address them; skill in using collaborative learning techniques, new curriculum tools and technologies, and sophisticated assessments of learning; and the capacity to work collectively and reflect on practice with other teachers. The policy goals should be to ensure that all children have access to skillful teachers, to make the teaching profession more attractive to talented young adults, and to produce humane and intellectually lively learning communities for both students and teachers.

Teacher Evaluation

Teacher evaluation systems, likewise, should both support and assess good practice through peer review processes that use vivid professional standards focused on the connections between teaching and learning. These systems should encourage active learning, teaching adapted to students' needs, planning with other teachers, using student feedback and assessments to adjust teaching approaches, and focusing on challenging tasks and content while developing multiple pathways to knowledge.

Of course these teacher policies must be supported by complementary policies about curriculum and assessment along with policies about levels of staffing and school scheduling that give teachers the time and opportunity to apply their professional knowledge effectively.

School Funding and Resource Allocation

If this society truly wants all children to have an opportunity to learn at the level newly adopted standards suggest they should, then school funding policies must change so that the poorest schools have the resources to hire well-qualified teachers and to provide personalized settings that allow the active in-depth learning that does make a difference.

We also need to take a hard look at how traditional schools are staffed as compared to restructured schools and schools in other countries with better student achievement. As education results have faltered, the reaction has been to increase bureaucratic controls and specialization, producing a flow of staff and dollars out of classrooms and into side offices and peripheral functions. Schools need policies that reverse that flow, moving both people and funds back into the classroom. New resource allocation policies should be connected to policies that increase teachers' preparation and decision-making ability and that seek to maximize the use of teachers' talents in helping one another and the organization learn to teach in the ways demanded by new goals for curriculum and assessment.

Structures for Learning

These reallocations of staff and funds must go hand-in-hand with policies for creating smaller schools and more personalized settings. Policies that enforce traditional staffing patterns, class schedules, and narrow course divisions must be reshaped so that students and teachers can spend more time together, teaching can deal with concepts across subjects, and teachers have time to plan together and share their areas of expertise. Policies should also foster the development of heterogeneous and democratic classrooms that offer students more opportunities to learn about and with one another, about reaching goals in concert with others, and about gaining knowledge from others who are different from themselves. Policies aimed at reducing tracking and the proliferation of programs for special education students must be linked with policies for developing teachers who have the knowledge and skill to handle the multiple demands of these restructured classrooms and to profit from their colleagues' additional expertise.

Collective Perspective

Education policies should support the development of a collective perspective in schools: at the classroom level as students engage in collaborative learning and at the school level as teachers and parents engage in setting shared standards and values, goals, and assessment practices. In order to create a cohesive community and a consensus on how to proceed, schoolpeople must have the occasion to engage in democratic discourse about the real stuff of teaching and learning. Policies must preserve a substantive role for local decision makers and encourage rather than bypass participation by stakeholders in assessing and reshaping their own schools.

Accountability

Policies in all these areas should also incorporate new approaches to accountability. In addition to the student accountability suggested by new learning standards and the teaching accountability embedded in new professional standards, state and local officials must assume accountability as well. They should guarantee that all schools' resources and staffing are adequate for them to meet the new standards being established for learning and teaching. Accountability based on the setting of procedures will not do the job of ensuring good education for students. Both opportunity-to-learn standards and practitioner-led school quality reviews are needed to help ensure each student will have caring and challenging teaching in a personally attentive, stimulating setting with appropriate resources.

AN AGENDA FOR CHANGE

In many respects it is misleading to describe policies as though they were discrete units or self-contained ideas. In practice it is critical to consider policies and practices together, as a *unified agenda for change*, if we are to succeed in enacting a genuine right to learn. It is also critical to remember that reform is never completed, because everyone continually changes, and everyone continually learns, experiencing fresh insights from practice, from research, and from the synergy of teachers, administrators, students, parents, and others inquiring together. Although policy supports are essential, reform can never be enforced from the top down, because people must create change in locally appropriate ways at the school and classroom level. The importance of both context and commitment mean that local invention must be supported by policies that provide a mix of top-down support and bottom-up initiatives.

This agenda for change is an ambitious one, much more daunting than any of the single solutions frequently proffered in the name of reform. Rebuilding the system of U.S. public education so that it can provide a genuine right to learn is not a task for publicity hunters or the faint of heart. It is exceedingly difficult work that will take many years of struggles and setbacks as well as insights and epiphanies to accomplish. But the rewards will be reaped at every step along the way with every child who experiences greater accomplishment and ability to contribute to the lives of others. For those parents, grandparents, teachers, policymakers, researchers, and community members who have the courage and fortitude for this task, I dedicate this book.

TO YOU

To sit and dream, to sit and read,
To sit and learn about the world
Outside our world of here and now—
    our problem world—
To dream of vast horizons of the soul
Through dreams made whole,
Unfettered free—help me!
All you who are dreamers, too,
Help me make our world anew.
I reach out my hands to you.
                    —*Langston Hughes*

~~~ References

Aiken, W. M. (1942). *Adventure in American education: Vol.1. The story of the Eight-Year Study.* New York: HarperCollins.

Alexander, K. L., & McDill, E. L. (1976). Selection and allocation within schools: Some causes and consequences of curriculum placement. *American Sociological Review, 41,* 963–980.

Allington, R. L., & McGill-Franzen, A. (1992). Unintended effects of educational reform. *Educational Policy, 6*(4), 397–414.

Ancess, J. (1995). *An inquiry high school: Learner-centered accountability at the Urban Academy.* New York: National Center for Restructuring Education, Schools, and Teaching, Teachers College, Columbia University.

Ancess, J. (1996). *Outside/inside, inside/outside: Developing and implementing the school quality review.* New York: National Center for Restructuring Education, Schools, and Teaching, Teachers College, Columbia University.

Anderson, R. H., & Pavan, B. N. (1993). *Nongradedness: Helping it to happen.* Lancaster, PA: Technomic.

Andrew, M. D. (1990). The differences between graduates of four-year and five-year teacher preparation programs. *Journal of Teacher Education, 41*(2), 45–51.

Andrew, M. D., & Schwab, R. L. (1995, Fall). Has reform in teacher education influenced teacher performance? An outcome assessment of graduates of eleven teacher education programs. *Action in Teacher Education, 17*(3), 43–53.

Andrias, J., Kanevsky, R. D., Streib, L. Y., & Traugh, C. (1992) *Exploring values and standards: Implications for assessment.* New York: National Center for Restructuring Education, Schools, and Teaching, 1992.

Appalachia Educational Laboratory. (1996, February). Five years of reform in rural Kentucky. *Notes from the Field: Educational Reform in Rural Kentucky 5*(1).

Apple, M. W. (1990). *Ideology and curriculum* (2nd ed.). New York: Routledge.

Armour-Thomas, E., Clay, C., Domanico, R., Bruno, K., & Allen, B. (1989). *An outlier study of elementary and middle schools in New York City: Final report.* New York: New York City Board of Education.

Ashton, P., & Crocker, L. (1986). Does teacher certification make a difference? *Florida Journal of Teacher Education, 3,* 73–83.

Ashton, P., & Crocker, L. (1987). Systematic study of planned variations: The essential focus of teacher education reform. *Journal of Teacher Education, 38,* 2–8.

Bagley, W. C. (1910). *Classroom management.* Old Tappan, NJ: Macmillan.

Bagley, W. C. (1925). *Determinism in education.* Baltimore: Warwick & York.

Ball, D., & Cohen, D. (in press). Developing practice, developing practitioners: Toward a practice-based theory of professional education. Paper prepared for the National Commission on Teaching and America's Future.

Banks, J. (1993). Multicultural education: Historical development, dimensions and practice. In L. Darling-Hammond (Ed.), *Review of research in education* (Vol. 19, pp. 3–49). Washington, DC: American Educational Research Association.

Barr, R., & Dreeben, R. (1983). *How schools work.* Chicago: University of Chicago Press.

Barton, P. E., & Coley, R. J. (1996). *Captive students: Education and training in America's prisons.* Princeton, NJ: Educational Testing Service.

Baumrind, D. (1967). Child care practices anteceding three patterns of preschool behavior. *Genetic Psychology Monographs, 75,* 43–88.

Begle, E. G. (1979) *Critical variables in mathematics education.* Washington, DC: Mathematical Association of America and National Council of Teachers of Mathematics.

Ben-Peretz, M. (1975). The concept of curriculum potential. *Curriculum Theory Network, 5*(2), 151–159.

Bensman, D. (1994). *Lives of the graduates of Central Park East Elementary School: Where have they gone? What did they really learn?* New York: National Center for Restructuring Education, Schools, and Teaching, Teachers College, Columbia University.

Bents, M., & Bents, R. (1990, April). Perceptions of good teaching among novice, advanced, beginner, and expert teachers. Paper presented at the meeting of the American Educational Research Association, Boston.

Benveniste, G. (1987). *Professionalizing the organization: Reducing bureaucracy to enhance effectiveness.* San Francisco: Jossey-Bass.

Berliner, D. C. (1986). In pursuit of the expert pedagogue. *Educational Researcher, 15,* 5–13.

Berliner, D. C., & Biddle, B. J. (1995). *The manufactured crisis: Myth, fraud, and the attack on America's public schools.* Reading, MA: Addison-Wesley.

Berman, P., & McLaughlin, M. W. (1978). *Federal programs supporting educational change: Vol. 8. Implementing and sustaining innovations.* Santa Monica, CA: Rand.

Berne, R. (1994). Educational input and outcome inequities in New York State. In R. Berne & L. O. Picus (Eds.), *Outcome equity in education.* Thousand Oaks, CA: Corwin Press.

Berry, B. (1995). School restructuring and teacher power: The case of Keels elementary. In A. Lieberman (Ed.), *The work of restructuring schools: Building from the ground up.* New York: Teachers College Press.

Bliss, T. (1992). Alternate certification in Connecticut: Reshaping the profession. *Peabody Journal of Education, 67*(3), 35–54.

Bobbitt, J. F. (1913). *The supervision of city schools: Some general principles of management applied to the problems of city-school systems: Twelfth yearbook of the National Society for the Study of Education.* Bloomington, IL: National Society for the Study of Education.

Bond, H. M. (1934). *The education of the Negro in the American social order.* Englewood Cliffs, NJ: Prentice Hall.

Bouvier, A. (August 5, 1995). Personal communication.

Boyer, E. L. (1983). *High school: A report on secondary education in America.* Princeton, NJ: The Carnegie Foundation for the Advancement of Teaching.

Braddock, J. H., & McPartland, J. M. (1993). The education of early adolescents. In L. Darling-Hammond (Ed.), *Review of research in education* (Vol. 19, pp. 135–170). Washington, DC: American Educational Research Association.

Bradley, A. (1994, April 20). Pioneers in professionalism. *Education Week,* pp. 18–21.

Bradley, A. (1995, November 22). What price success? *Education Week,* p. 1.

Bredekamp, S. (1987). *Developmentally appropriate practice.* Washington, DC: National Association for the Education of Young Children.

Brown, A. L. (1994). The advancement of learning. *Educational Researcher, 23*(8), 4–12.

Brown, E. R. (1979). *Rockefeller medicine men: Medicine and capitalism in America.* Berkeley: University of California Press.

Bryk, A., Lee, V., & Smith, J. B. (1990). High school organization and its effects on teachers and students: An interpretive summary of the research. In W. H. Clune & J. F. Witte (Eds.), *Choice and control in American education: Vol. 2. The practice of choice, decentralization and school restructuring.* Philadelphia: Falmer Press.

Buechler, M. (1996, January). *Charter schools: Legislation and results after four years.* Bloomington: Indiana Educational Policy Center.

Bumiller, E. (1995, Sept. 6). Are surgeon 'report cards' fair? *New York Times.*

Bussis, A. M. (1982). Burn it at the casket: Research, reading, instruction, and children's learning of the first R. *Phi Delta Kappan, 64,* 237–241.

Bussis, A., Chittenden, E., & Amarel, M. (1976). *Beyond surface curriculum.* Boulder, CO: Westview Press.

Calfee, R. (1981). Cognitive psychology and educational practice. In D. Berliner (Ed.), *Review of research in education* (Vol. 9, pp. 3–74). Washington, DC: American Educational Research Association.

California Commission on the Teaching Profession. (1985). *Who will teach our children?* Sacramento, CA: Author.

California State Department of Education. (1984). *California high school curriculum study: Path through high school.* Sacramento: Author.

Callahan, R. E. (1962). *Education and the cult of efficiency.* Chicago: University of Chicago Press.

Card, D., & Krueger, A. B. (1992). Does school quality matter? Returns to education and the characteristics of public schools in the United States. *Journal of Political Economy, 100,* 1–40.

Carlson, R. O. (1965). *Adoption of educational innovations.* Eugene: Center for Advanced Study of Educational Administration, University of Oregon.

Carnegie Council on Adolescent Development. (1989). *Turning points: Preparing youth for the 21st century.* New York: Carnegie Corporation of New York.

Carnegie Forum on Education and the Economy. (1986). *A nation prepared: Teachers for the 21st century.* Washington, DC: Author.

Carrajat, M. A. (1995). *Why do academically able Puerto Rican males drop out of high school?* Unpublished dissertation, Teachers College, Columbia University.

Carter, K., & Doyle, W. (1987). Teachers' knowledge structures and comprehension processes. In J. Calderhead (Ed.), *Exploring teacher thinking* (pp. 147–160). London: Cassell.

Centra, J. A., & Potter, D. A. (1980). School and teacher effects: An interrelational model. *Review of Educational Research, 50*(2), 273–291.

Central Park East Secondary School. (1990). *Senior institute handbook.* New York: Author.

Central Park East Secondary School. (n.d.). *A public high school: Central Park East Secondary School.* New York: Author.

Chamberlin, D., Chamberlin, E. S., Drought, N., & Scott, W. (1942). *Adventure in American education: Vol. 4. Did they succeed in college?* New York: HarperCollins.

Cheeseboro, M. (1990). Differential consequences of environmental complexity on internal organizational complexity of school systems in Switzerland and the United States. Unpublished manuscript.

Choy, S. P., Henke, R. R., Alt, M. N., Medrich, E. A., & Bobbitt, S. A. (1993). *Schools and staffing in the United States: A statistical profile, 1990–91.* Washington, DC: National Center for Education Statistics, U.S. Department of Education.

Chubb, J., & Moe, T. (1990). *Politics, markets, and America's schools.* Washington, DC: Brookings Institution.

Cicourel, A. V., & Kitsuse, J. I. (1963). *The educational decision makers.* Indianapolis: Bobbs-Merrill.

Clandinin, J. (1986). *Classroom practice: Teacher images in action.* Bristol, PA: Falmer Press.

Clune, W. H. (1993). The best path to systemic educational policy: Standard/centralized or differentiated/decentralized. *Educational Evaluation and Policy Analysis, 15*(3), 233–254.

Clune, W. H. (1994). The shift from equity to adequacy in school finance. *Educational Policy, 8*(4), 376–394.

Coalition of Essential Schools. (1990, March). Performances and exhibitions: The demonstration of mastery. *Horace, 6*(3), 1–4.

Coffman, L. D. (1911). *The social composition of the teaching population.* New York: Teachers College, Columbia University.

Cohen, D. K. (1995). What standards for national standards? *Phi Delta Kappan, 76,* 751–757.

Cohen, D. K. (1996). Rewarding teachers for student performance. In S. H. Fuhrman & J. A. O'Day (Eds.), *Rewards and reform: Creating educational incentives that work* (pp. 60–112). San Francisco: Jossey-Bass.

Cohen, D. K., & Barnes, C. A. (1993). Conclusion: A new pedagogy for policy. In D. K. Cohen, M. W. McLaughlin, & J. E. Talbert (Eds.), *Teaching for understanding: Challenges for policy and practice* (pp. 240–275). San Francisco: Jossey-Bass.

Cohen, D., & Hill, H. (1997, March). Policy, practice, and learning. Unpublished paper prepared for the American Educational Research Association Annual Meeting, Chicago, IL.

Cohen, D. K., McLaughlin, M. W., & Talbert, J. E. (Eds.). (1993). *Teaching for understanding: Challenges for policy and practice.* San Francisco: Jossey-Bass.

Cohen, E. G. (1986). *Designing groupwork: Strategies for the heterogenous classroom.* New York: Teachers College Press.

Coleman, J., Campbell, E., Hobson, C., McPartland, J., Mood, A., Weinfield, F., and York, R. (1966). *Equality of educational opportunity.* Washington, DC: U.S. Government Printing Office.

Coleman, J., & Hoffer, T. (1987). *Public and private high schools: The impact of communities.* New York: Basic Books.

College Board. (1985). *Equality and excellence: The educational status of black Americans.* New York: Author.

Comer, J. P. (1988). Educating poor minority children. *Scientific American, 259*(5), 42–48.

Comer, J. P. (1994). *A brief history and summary of the School Development Program.* Unpublished manuscript.

Comer, J. P., Haynes, N. M., & Hamilton-Lee, M. (1989). School power: A model for improving black student achievement. In W. D. Smith & W. E. Chun (Eds.), *Black education: A quest for equity and excellence* (pp. 187–200). New Brunswick, NJ: Transaction.

Comer, J. P., Haynes, N. M., Joyner, E. T., & Ben-Avie, M. (1996). *Rallying the whole village: The Comer process for reforming education.* New York: Teachers College Press.

Commission on Chapter 1. (1992). *High performance schools: No exceptions, no excuses.* Washington, DC: Author.

Conley, S., & Odden, A. (1995). Linking teacher compensation to teacher career development. *Educational Evaluation and Policy Analysis, 17*(2), 219–237.

Consortium on Productivity in the Schools. (1995). *Using what we have to get the schools we need: A productivity focus for American education.* New York: Author.

Cooper, B., Sarrel, R., & Tetenbaum, T. (1990, April). *Choice, funding, and pupil achievement: How urban school finance affects students.* Paper presented at the meeting of the American Educational Research Association, Boston.

Cooper, E., & Sherk, J. (1989). Addressing urban school reform: Issues and alliances. *Journal of Negro Education, 58*(3), 315–331.

Corbett, E. (1971). *Classical rhetoric for the modern student.* New York: Oxford University Press.

Cremin, L. A. (1965). *The genius of American education.* New York: Vintage Books.

Cremin, L. A. (1970). *American education: The colonial experience 1607–1783.* New York: HarperCollins.

Cuban, L. (1990). Reforming again, again, and again. *Educational Researcher, 19,* 3–13.

Cubberley, E. P. (1909). *Changing conceptions of education.* Boston: Houghton Mifflin.

Curtis, M., & Glaser, R. (1981). Changing conceptions of intelligence. In D. Berliner (Ed.), *Review of research in education* (Vol. 9, pp. 111–150). Washington, DC: American Educational Research Association.

Cusick, P. (1979, January 5). A study of the value/belief patterns of teachers and administrators. *News and Notes* (pp. 2–4). Institute for Research on Teaching, Michigan State University.

Darling-Hammond, L. (1985). *Equality and excellence: The educational status of black Americans.* New York: College Board.

Darling-Hammond, L. (1986a). A proposal for evaluation in the teaching profession. *Elementary School Journal, 86*(4), 1–21.

Darling-Hammond, L. (1986b, Fall). Teaching knowledge: How do we test it? *American Educator,* p. 46.

Darling-Hammond, L. (1988, Summer). Teacher quality and educational equality. *The College Board Review,* pp. 16–23, 39–41.

Darling-Hammond, L. (1990a). Achieving our goals: Superficial or structural reforms. *Phi Delta Kappan, 72,* 286–295.

Darling-Hammond, L. (1990b). Instructional policy into practice: The power of the bottom over the top. *Educational Evaluation and Policy Analysis, 12*(3), 233–241.

Darling-Hammond, L. (1990c). Teacher professionalism: Why and how. In A. Lieberman (Ed.), *Schools as collaborative cultures: Creating the future now* (pp. 267–290). Bristol, PA: Falmer Press.

Darling-Hammond, L. (1990d). *Teacher supply, demand, and quality: A mandate for the national board.* Paper prepared for the National Board for Professional Teaching Standards.

Darling-Hammond, L. (1990e). Teachers and teaching: Signs of a changing profession. In R. Houston, M. Haberman, & J. Sikula (Eds.), *Handbook of research on teacher education* (pp. 267–290). Old Tappan, NJ: Macmillan.

Darling-Hammond, L. (1991). The implications of testing policy for educational quality and equality. *Phi Delta Kappan, 73,* 220–225.

Darling-Hammond, L. (1992). Teaching and knowledge: Policy issues posed by alternate certification for teachers. *Peabody Journal of Education, 67*(3), 123–154.

Darling-Hammond, L. (1993). Reframing the school reform agenda: Developing capacity for school transformation. *Phi Delta Kappan, 74,* 753–761.

Darling-Hammond, L. (Ed.). (1994). *Professional development schools: Schools for developing a profession.* New York: Teachers College Press.

Darling-Hammond, L. (1995). Inequality and access to knowledge. In J. Banks (Ed.), *Handbook of research on multicultural education* (pp. 465–483). Old Tappan, NJ: Macmillan.

Darling-Hammond, L. (1996). Restructuring schools for high performance. In S. H. Fuhrman & J. A. O'Day (Eds.), *Rewards and reform: Creating educational incentives that work* (pp. 144–192). San Francisco: Jossey-Bass.

Darling-Hammond, L., & Ancess, J. (1994). *Graduation by portfolio at Central Park East Secondary School.* New York: National Center for Restructuring Education, Schools, and Teaching, Teachers College, Columbia University.

Darling-Hammond, L., & Ancess, J. (1996). Authentic assessment and school development. In J. B. Baron & D. P. Wolf (Eds.), *Performance-based student assessment: Challenges and possibilities: Ninety-fifth yearbook of the National Society for the Study of Education.* Chicago: University of Chicago Press.

Darling-Hammond, L., Ancess, J., & Falk, B. (1995). *Authentic assessment in action: Studies of schools and students at work.* New York: Teachers College Press.

Darling-Hammond, L., Ancess, J., MacGregor, K., & Zuckerman, D. (in press). *Inching toward systemic reform: The coalition campus schools project in New York City.* New York: National Center for Restructuring Education, Schools, and Teaching, Teachers College, Columbia University.

Darling-Hammond, L., Bullmaster, M., & Cobb, V. (1995). Rethinking teacher leadership through professional development schools. *The Elementary School Journal, 96*(1), 87–106).

Darling-Hammond, L., Dilworth, M. E., & Bullmaster, M. (1996, January). *Educators of color.* Paper presented at the invitational Conference for Recruiting, Preparing, and Retaining Persons of Color in the Teaching Profession, Washington, DC, Office of Educational Research and Improvement, U.S Department of Education.

Darling-Hammond, L., Hudson, L., & Kirby, S. N. (1989). *Redesigning teacher education: Opening the door for new recruits to mathematics and science teaching.* Santa Monica, CA: Rand.

Darling-Hammond, L., & Kirby, S. N. (1985). *Tuition tax deductions and parent school choice: The case of Minnesota.* Santa Monica, CA: Rand.

Darling-Hammond, L., & McLaughlin, M. W. (1995). Policies that support professional development in an era of reform. *Phi Delta Kappan, 76,* 597–604.

Darling-Hammond, L., Pittman, K., & Ottinger, C. (1988). *Career choices for minorities: Who will teach?* Paper prepared for the National Education Association/Council for Chief State School Officers Task Force on Minorities in Teaching.

Darling-Hammond, L., with Sclan, E. (1992). Policy and supervision. In C. D. Glickman (Ed.), *Supervision in transition: 1992 yearbook for the Association for Supervision and Curriculum Development* (pp. 7–29). Alexandria, VA: Association for Supervision and Curriculum Development.

Darling-Hammond, L., Snyder, J., Ancess, J., Einbender, L., Goodwin, A. L., & Macdonald, M. B. (1993). *Creating learner-centered accountability.* New York: National Center for Restructuring Education, Schools, and Teaching, Teachers College, Columbia University.

Darling-Hammond, L., & Wise, A. E. (1985). Beyond standardization: State standards and school improvement. *Elementary School Journal, 85*(3), 315–336.

Darling-Hammond, L., Wise, A. E., & Gendler, T. (1990). *The teaching internship: Practical preparation for a licensed profession.* Santa Monica, CA: Rand.

Darling-Hammond, L., Wise, A. E., & Klein, S. (1995). *A license to teach: Building a teaching profession for 21st century schools.* Boulder, CO: Westview Press.

Darling-Hammond, L., Wise, A. E., & Pease, S. R. (1983). Teacher evaluation in the organizational context: A review of the literature. *Review of Educational Research, 53,* 285–237.

David, J. (1990). Restructuring in progress: Lessons from pioneering districts. In R. F. Elmore & Associates, *Restructuring schools: The next generation of educational reform* (pp. 209–250). San Francisco: Jossey-Bass.

Davis, C. R. (1964). *Selected teaching-learning factors contributing to achievement in chemistry and physics.* Unpublished doctoral dissertation, University of North Carolina, Chapel Hill.

Davis, D. G. (1986, April). *A pilot study to assess equity in selected curricular offerings across three diverse schools in a large urban school district: A search for methodology.* Paper presented at the meeting of the American Educational Research Association, San Francisco.

de Geus, A. P. (1988, March-April). Planning as learning. *Harvard Business Review,* pp. 70–74.

Dearborn, W. F. (1928). *Intelligence tests: Their significance for school and society.* Boston: Houghton Mifflin.

Deci, E. L. (1976). The hidden costs of rewards. *Organizational Dynamics, 4*(3), 61–72.

Defazio, A., & Hirschy, P. D. (1993). *Integrating instruction and assessment.* New York: International High School.

Delpit, L. (1995). *Other people's children: Cultural conflict in the classroom.* New York: New Press.

Deming, W. E. (1986). *Out of the crisis.* Cambridge, MA: Massachusetts Institute of Technology Center for Advanced Engineering Study.

Denton, J. J., & Peters, W. H. (1988). *Program assessment report: curriculum evaluation of a non-traditional program for certifying teachers.* Unpublished report, Texas A&M University.

Dewey, J. (1916). *Democracy and education.* Old Tappan, NJ: Macmillan.

Dewey, J. (1929). *The sources of a science of education.* New York: Liveright.

Dewey, J. (1956). *The school and society.* Chicago: University of Chicago Press. (Original work published 1900)

Dobrzynski, J. H. (1996, July 21). The new jobs: A growing number are good ones. *New York Times,* sec. 3, pp. 1, 10–11.

Dornbusch, S., Ritter, P., Leiderman, P., Roberts, D., & Fraleigh, M. (1987). The relation of parenting style to adolescent school performance. *Child Development, 58,* 1244–1257.

Doyle, W. (1986). Content representation in teachers' definitions of academic work. *Journal of Curriculum Studies, 18,* 365–379.

Dreeben, R. (1987, Winter). Closing the divide: What teachers and administrators can do to help black students reach their reading potential. *American Educator,* pp. 28–35.

Dreeben, R., & Barr, R. (1987, April). *Class composition and the design of instruction.* Paper presented at the meeting of the American Education Research Association, Washington, DC.

Dreeben, R., & Gamoran, A. (1986). Race, instruction, and learning. *American Sociological Review, 51*(5), 660–669.

Drucker, P. F. (1986). *The frontiers of management.* New York: Harper-Collins.

Drucker, P. F. (1994, November). The age of social transformation. *Atlantic Monthly,* pp. 53–80.

Druva, C. A., & Anderson, R. D. (1983). Science teacher characteristics by teacher behavior and by student outcome: A meta-analysis of research. *Journal of Research in Science Teaching, 20*(5), 467–479.

Du Bois, W.E.B. (1970a). Education and Work. In P. S. Foner (Ed.), *W.E.B. Du Bois Speaks* (pp. 55–76). New York: Pathfinder. (Original work published 1930)

Du Bois, W.E.B. (1970b). The freedom to learn. In P. S. Foner (Ed.), *W.E.B. Du Bois Speaks* (pp. 230–231). New York: Pathfinder. (Original work published 1949)

Duchastel, P. C., & Merrill, P. F. (1977). The effects of behavioral objectives on learning: A review of empirical studies. *Review of Educational Research, 43*(1), 53–69.

Dunkin, M., & Biddle, B. (1974). *The study of teaching.* Austin, TX: Holt, Rinehart and Winston.

Dyal, A. B. (1993). *An exploratory study to determine principals' perceptions concerning the effectiveness of a fifth-year preparation program.* Paper presented at the meeting of the Mid-South Educational Research Association, New Orleans.

Ebmeier, H., Twombly, S., & Tweeter, D. J. (1991). The comparability and adequacy of financial support for schools of education. *Journal of Teacher Education, 42*(3), 226–235

Eckstrom, R., & Villegas, A. M. (1991). Ability grouping in middle grade mathematics: Process and consequences. *Research in Middle Level Education, 15*(1), 1–20.

Educational Research Service (1980). *Class size: A summary of research.* Reston, VA: Author.

Educational Testing Service. (1989a). *Crossroads in American education.* Princeton, NJ: Author.

Educational Testing Service. (1989b). *A world of differences: An international assessment of mathematics and science.* Princeton, NJ: Author.

Educational Testing Service. (1990). *Learning to write in our nation's schools: Instruction and achievement in 1988 at grades 4, 8, and 12.* Princeton, NJ: Author.

Educational Testing Service (1991). *The state of inequality.* Princeton, NJ: Author.

Eliot, C. W. (1909). Educational reform and the social order. *School Review, 17,* 217–222.

Elkind, D. (1988). *The hurried child* (rev. ed.). Reading, MA: Addison-Wesley.

Elkind, D. (1989). Developmentally appropriate practice: Philosophical and practical implications. *Phi Delta Kappan, 71,* 113–117.

Elley, W. B. (1992). *How in the world do students read?* Hamburg: International Association for the Evaluation of Educational Achievement.

Elmore, R. F. (1979–1980). Backward mapping: Using implementation analysis to structure program decisions. *Political Science Quarterly, 94,* 601–616.

Elmore, R. (1983). Complexity and control: What legislators and administrators can do about implementing policy. In L. S. Shulman & G. Sykes (Eds.), *Handbook of teaching and policy* (pp. 342–369). White Plains, NY: Longman.

Elmore, R. F. (1996). Getting to scale with good educational practices. In S. H. Fuhrman & Jennifer A. O'Day (Eds.), *Rewards and reform: Creating educational incentives that work* (pp. 294–329). San Francisco: Jossey-Bass.

Elmore, R. F. (in press). *Staff development and instructional improvement: Community District 2, New York City.* Paper prepared for the National Commission on Teaching and America's Future, Teachers College, Columbia University.

Elmore, R. F., & Fuhrman, S. H. (1993). Opportunity to learn and the state role in education. In *The debate on opportunity-to-learn standards: Commissioned papers.* Washington, DC: National Governors' Association.

Elmore, R. F., & Associates. (1990). *Restructuring schools: The next generation of educational reform.* San Francisco: Jossey-Bass.

Evertson, C., Hawley, W., & Zlotnik, M. (1985). Making a difference in educational quality through teacher education. *Journal of Teacher Education, 36*(3), 2–12.

Ewert, O. M., & Braun, M. (1978). Ergebnnisse und Probleme vorschulischer Foerderung. In *Struktu foerderung im Bildungswesen des Landes Nordrhein-Westfalen. Eine Schriften-reihe des Kultusministers: Vol.34. Modellversuch Vorklasse in NW-Abschlussbericht.* Köln: Greven.

Faber, A., & Mazlish, E. (1987, Summer). How to talk so students will listen and listen so students will talk. *American Educator, 11*(2), 37–42.

Faber, A., & Mazlish, E. (1995). *How to talk so kids can learn at home and at school.* New York: Fireside.

Feiman-Nemser, S., & Parker, M. B.(1990). *Making subject matter part of the conversation or helping beginning teachers learn to teach.* East Lansing, MI: National Center for Research on Teacher Education, University of Michigan.

Feistritzer, C. E. (1993). *Report card on American education: A state-by-state analysis.* Washington, DC: National Center for Education Information.

Ferguson, R. F. (1991, Summer). Paying for public education: New evidence on how and why money matters. *Harvard Journal on Legislation, 28*(2), 465–498.

Fine, M. (1991). *Framing dropouts: Notes on the politics of an urban public high school.* Albany: State University of New York Press.

Fine, M. (1994). *Chartering urban school reform.* New York: National Center for Restructuring Education, Schools, and Teaching, Teachers College, Columbia University.

Finley, M. K. (1984). Teachers and tracking in a comprehensive high school. *Sociology of Education, 57,* 233–243.

Flexner, A. (1910). *The Flexner report on medical education in the United States and Canada 1910.* Princeton, NJ: The Carnegie Foundation for the Advancement of Teaching.

Flinders, D. J. (1989). *Voices from the classroom: Educational practice can inform policy.* Eugene, OR: ERIC Clearinghouse on Educational Management.

Florida Department of Education. (1989). *Manual for coding teacher performance on the screening/summative observation instrument: Florida Performance Measurement System.* Tallahassee: Author.

Foner, P. S., & DuBois, S. G. (1970). *W.E.B. DuBois speaks,* (Vol. 2). New York: Pathfinder.

Fowler, W. J. (1992, April). *What do we know about school size? What should we know?* Paper presented at the meeting of the American Educational Research Association, San Francisco.

Freire, P. (1970). *Pedagogy of the oppressed.* New York: Seabury Press.

Fuhrman, S. H. (1993). The politics of coherence. In S. H. Fuhrman (Ed.), *Designing coherent education policy: Improving the system.* San Francisco: Jossey-Bass.

Fullan, M. (1991). *The new meaning of educational change.* New York: Teachers College Press.

Fullan, M. (1994). *Turning systemic thinking on its head.* Paper prepared for the U.S. Department of Education.

Gagnon, P. (n.d.). *Systemic reform of schools: From national standards to the classroom down the hall. A primer with examples.* Unpublished manuscript, U.S. Department of Education.

Gallagher, J. J. (1967, January). Teacher variation in concept presentation. *BSCS (Biological Sciences Curriculum Study) Newsletter,* No. 30.

Gamoran, A. (1990, April). *The consequences of track-related instructional differences for student achievement.* Paper presented at the meeting of the American Educational Research Association, Boston.

Gamoran, A. (1992). Access to excellence: Assignment to honors English classes in the transition from middle to high school. *Educational Evaluation and Policy Analysis, 14*(3), 185–204.

Gamoran, A., & Berends, M. (1987). The effects of stratification in secondary schools: Synthesis of survey and ethnographic research. *Review of Educational Research, 57,* 415–436.

Gamoran, A., & Mare, R. (1989). Secondary school tracking and educational inequality: Compensation, reinforcement or neutrality? *American Journal of Sociology, 94,* 1146–1183.

Garbarino, J. (1978). The human ecology of school crime: A case for small schools. In E. Wenk (Ed.), *School crime* (pp. 122–133). Davis, CA: National Council on Crime and Delinquency.

Garcia, E. (1993). Language, culture, and education. In L. Darling-Hammond (Ed.), *Review of research in education* (Vol. 19, pp. 51–98). Washington, DC: American Educational Research Association.

Gardner, H. (1983). *Frames of mind: The theory of multiple intelligences.* New York: Basic Books.

Gardner, H. (1991). *The unschooled mind: How children think and how schools should teach.* New York: Basic Books.

Gardner, H., Torff, B., & Hatch, T. (1996). The age of innocence reconsidered: Preserving the best of the progressive tradition in psychology and education. In D. R. Olson and N. Torrance (Eds.), *Handbook of education and human development: New models of learning, teaching, and schooling* (pp. 28–55). Cambridge, MA: Blackwell.

Gardner, H., & Winner, E. (1982). First intimations of artistry. In S. Strauss (Ed.), *U-shaped behavioral growth* (pp. 147–168).

Gemignani, R. J. (1994, October). *Juvenile correctional education: A time for change: Update on research* (US. Department of Justice, Office of Juvenile Justice and Delinquency Prevention). *Juvenile Justice Bulletin,* n.p.

Ginott, H. (1970). *Teacher and child.* New York: Avon.

Glaser, R. (1990). *Testing and assessment: O tempora! O mores!* Pittsburgh: University of Pittsburgh, Learning Research and Development Center.

Glaser, R., & Silver, E. (1994). Assessment, testing, and instruction: Retrospect and prospect. In L. Darling-Hammond (Ed.), *Review of research in education* (Vol. 20, pp. 393–419). Washington, DC: American Educational Research Association.

Glass, G. V., Coulter, D., Hartley, S., Hearold, S., Kahl, S., Kalk, J., & Sherretz, L. (1977). *Teacher "indirectness" and pupil achievement: An integration of findings.* Boulder: Laboratory of Educational Research, University of Colorado.

Glass, G. V., Cahen, L. S., Smith, M. L., & Filby, N. N. (1982). *School class size: Research and policy.* Thousand Oaks, CA: Sage.

Glasser, W. (1984). *Control theory.* New York: HarperCollins.

Glasser, W. (1990). *The quality school: Managing students without coercion.* New York: HarperCollins.

Glasser, W. (1992, May 13). Quality, trust, and redefining education. *Education Week*, p. 25.

Glickman, C. (in press). *Democracy as education: Revolution, change, and the real renewal of America's schools.* San Francisco: Jossey-Bass.

Goldsberry, L., with Holt, A., Johnson, K., MacDonald, G., Polinquin, R., & Potter, L. (1995). The evolution of a restructuring school: The New Suncook case. In A. Lieberman (Ed.), *The work of restructuring schools: Building from the ground up* (pp. 136–156). New York: Teachers College Press.

Gomez, D. L., & Grobe, R. P. (1990, April). *Three years of alternative certification in Dallas: Where are we?* Paper presented at the meeting of the American Educational Research Association, Boston.

Good, T. L., & Brophy, J. E. (1986). *Educational psychology* (3rd ed.). White Plains, NY: Longman.

Good, T. L., & Brophy, J. E. (1987). *Looking in classrooms* (4th ed.). New York: HarperCollins.

Goodlad, J. I. (1984). *A place called school.* New York: McGraw-Hill.

Goodlad, J. I. (1990). *Teachers for our nation's schools.* San Francisco: Jossey-Bass.

Gordon, E. W., Miller, F., & Rollock, D. (1990). Coping with communicentric bias in knowledge production in the social sciences. *Educational Researcher, 19,* 14–19.

Gottfredson, G. D. (1986). *You get what you measure, you get what you don't: Higher standards, higher test scores, more retention in grade* (Report 2a). Baltimore: Center for Research on Elementary and Middle Schools, Johns Hopkins University.

Gottfredson, G. D., & Daiger, D. C. (1979). *Disruption in 600 schools.* Baltimore: Center for Social Organization of Schools, Johns Hopkins University.

Grady, M. P., Collins, P., & Grady, E. L. (1991). *Teach for America 1991 Summer Institute Evaluation Report.* Unpublished manuscript.

Gray, L., Cahalan, M., Hein, S., Litman, C., Severynse, J., Warren, S., Wisan, G., & Stowe, P. (1993). *New teachers in the job market: 1991 update.* Washington, DC: U.S. Department of Education, OERI.

Green, G., & Stevens, W. (1988). What research says about small schools. *Rural Educators, 10*(1), 9–14.

Green, T. F. (1980). *Predicting the behavior of the educational system.* Syracuse, NY: Syracuse University Press.

Green, T. F. (1983). Excellence, equity, and equality. In L. S. Shulman & G. Sykes (Eds.), *Handbook of teaching and policy* (pp. 318–341). White Plains, NY: Longman.

Greenberg, J. D. (1983). The case for teacher education: Open and shut. *Journal of Teacher Education, 34*(4), 2–5.

Greene, M. (1984). *Education, freedom, and possibility.* Inaugural lecture as William F. Russell Professor in the Foundations of Education. New York: Teachers College, Columbia University.

Greene, M. (1992, April). *The passions of pluralism.* Paper presented at the meeting of the American Educational Research Association, San Francisco.

Grimmett, P., & MacKinnon, A. (1992). Craft knowledge and the education of teachers. In G. Grant (Ed.), *Review of research in education* (Vol. 18, pp. 385–456). Washington, DC: American Educational Research Association.

Grossman, P. L. (1989). Learning to teach without teacher education. *Teachers College Record, 91*(2), 191–208.

Haberman, M. (1984, September). *An evaluation of the rationale for required teacher education: Beginning teachers with or without teacher preparation.* Prepared for the National Commission on Excellence in Teacher Education, University of Wisconsin-Milwaukee.

Haertel, E. H. (1991). New forms of teacher assessment. In G. Grant (Ed.), *Review of research in education* (Vol. 17, pp. 3–29). Washington, DC: American Educational Research Association.

Haley, M. (1924). Why teachers should organize. *NEA addresses and proceedings, 43rd Annual Meeting, St. Louis.* Washington, DC: National Education Association.

Haller, E. J. (1990). School size and program comprehensiveness: Evidence from high school and beyond. *Educational Evaluation and Policy Analysis, 12,* 109–120.

Haller, E. J. (1992). High school size and student discipline: Another aspect of the school consolidation issue? *Educational Evaluation and Policy Analysis, 14*(2), 145–156.

Haller, E. J. (1993). Small schools and higher-order thinking skills. *Journal of Research in Rural Education, 9*(2), 66–73.

Hambleton, R., Jaeger, R., Koretz, D., Linn, R., Millman, J., & Phillips, S. (1995). *Review of the measurement quality of the Kentucky Instructional Results Information System 1991–1994.* Frankfort, KY: Office of Educational Accountability.

Haney, W., & Madaus, G. (1986). *Effects of standardized testing and the future of the national assessment of educational progress* (Working paper prepared for the NAEP [National Assessment of Educational Progress] Study Group). Chestnut Hill, MA: Center for the Study of Testing, Evaluation, and Educational Policy, Boston College.

Haney, W., Madaus, G., & Kreitzer, A. (1987). Charms talismanic: Testing teachers for the improvement of American education. In E. Z. Rothkopf (Ed.), *Review of research in education* (Vol. 14, pp. 169–238).

Hansen, J. B. (1988). *The relationship of skills and classroom climate of trained and untrained teachers of gifted students.* Unpublished doctoral dissertation, Purdue University.

Hanushek, E. A. (1989). The impact of differential expenditures on school performance. *Educational Researcher, 18(4),* 45–62.

Harris, L., & Associates (1993). *A survey of the perspectives of elementary and secondary school teachers on reform* (Prepared for the Ford Foundation). New York: Louis Harris Research, 1993.

Harris, W. T., & Doty, D. (1874). *A statement of the theory of education in the United States as approved by many leading educators.* Washington, DC: U.S. Government Printing Office.

Harris, J., & Sammons, J. (1989). *Failing our children: How standardized tests damage New York's youngest students.* New York: New York Public Interest Group.

Hartman, W. T. (1988). District spending disparities: What do the dollars buy? *Journal of Education Finance, 13(4),* 436–459.

Hawk, P., Coble, C. R., & Swanson, M. (1985). Certification: It does matter. *Journal of Teacher Education, 36(3),* 13–15.

Hawthorne, R. K. (1992). *Curriculum in the making: Teacher choice and the classroom experience.* New York: Teachers College Press.

Hedges, L. V., Laine, R. D., & Greenwald, R. (1994). Does money matter? A meta-analysis of studies of the effects of differential school inputs on student outcomes. *Educational Research, 23(3),* 5–14.

Herrnstein, R. J., & Murray, C. (1994). *The bell curve: Intelligence and class structure in American life.* New York: Free Press.

Hertert, L. (1993). *School finance equity: An analysis of school level equity in California.* Unpublished doctoral dissertation, University of Southern California.

Hice, J.E.L. (1970). The relationship between teacher characteristics and first-grade achievement. *Dissertation Abstracts International, 25*(1), 190.

Hill, L., & Weaver, A. (1994). A multicultural curriculum in action: The Walt Disney Magnet School. In *Teachers' voices: Reinventing themselves, their profession, and their communities.* New York: National Center for Restructuring Education, Schools, and Teaching, Teachers College, Columbia University.

Hill, P. T., Foster, G. E., & Gendler, T. (1990). *High Schools with character: Alternatives to bureaucracy.* Santa Monica, CA: Rand.

Hirsch, E. D., Jr. (1996). *The schools we need and why we don't have them.* New York: Doubleday.

Hirschy, D. (1990a). Address to the faculty of Grover Cleveland High School, Buffalo, NY. In *Insights: Thoughts on the process of being international.* Long Island City, NY: International High School.

Hirschy, D. (1990b). The new schedule. In *Insights: Thoughts on the process of being international* (pp. 6–9, 18–19). Long Island City, NY: International High School.

Hoffer, T. B. (1992). Middle school ability grouping and student achievement in science and mathematics. *Educational Evaluation and Policy Analysis, 14*(3), 205–227.

Holland, J. G. (1960). Teaching machines: An application of principles from the laboratory. *Journal of the Experimental Analysis of Behavior, 3,* 275–287.

Holmes, C. T., & Matthews, K. M. (1984). The effects of nonpromotion on elementary and junior high school pupils: A meta-analysis. *Review of Educational Research, 54,* 225–236.

Holmes Group. (1986). *Tomorrow's teachers: A report of the Holmes Group.* East Lansing, MI: Author.

Hornbeck, D. W. (1992, May 6). The true road to equity. *Education Week Commentary,* pp. 32, 25.

Horowitz, D. L. (1977). *The courts and social policy.* Washington, DC: Brookings Institution.

Horwitz, R. A. (1979). Effects of the "open" classroom. In H. J. Walberg (Ed.), *Educational environments and effects: Evaluation, policy and productivity* (pp. 275–292). Berkeley, CA: McCutchan.

Houston, H. M. (1992). Institutional standard-setting in professional practice schools: Initial considerations. In M. Levine (Ed.), *Professional practice schools: Linking teacher education and school reform* (pp. 124–132). New York: Teachers College Press.

Howey, K. R. (1988). Why teacher leadership? *Journal of Teacher Education, 39*(1), 28–31.

Howley, C. B. (1989). Synthesis of the effects of school and district size: What research says about achievement in small schools and school districts. *Journal of Rural and Small Schools, 4*(1), 2–12.

Howley, C. B., & Huang, G. (1991, July). Extracurricular participation and achievement: School size as possible mediator of SES influence among individual students. *Resources in Education,*

Huberman, A. M., & Miles, M. B. (1986). Rethinking the quest for school improvement. In A. Lieberman (Ed.), *Rethinking school improvement: Research, craft, and concept* (pp. 61–81). New York: Teachers College Press.

Hughes, L. (1994). "To you." In Rampersad, A. (Ed.), *The collected poems of Langston Hughes.* New York: Knopf.

Hudson Institute. (1987). *Workforce 2000: Work and workers for the 21st century.* Indianapolis, IN: Author.

Ingersoll, R. M. (1995). Schools and staffing survey: Teacher supply, teacher qualifications, and teacher turnover, 1990–1991. Washington, DC: National Center for Education Statistics, U.S. Department of Education.

International Association for the Evaluation of Educational Achievement. (1988). *Science achievement in 17 countries: A preliminary report.* New York: Teachers College, Columbia University.

Interstate New Teacher Assessment and Support Consortium [INTASC]. (1991). *Model standards for beginning teacher licensing & development: A resource for state dialogue* (Working draft). Washington, DC: Council of Chief State School Officers.

Jackson, P. W. (1968). *Life in classrooms.* Austin, TX: Holt, Rinehart and Winston.

Jaeger, R. M. (1991). Legislative perspectives on statewide testing. *Phi Delta Kappan, 73,* 239–242.

Janesick, V. (1977). An ethnographic study of a teacher's classroom perspective. Unpublished doctoral dissertation, Michigan State University.

Jelmberg, J. (1996, January/February). College-based teacher education versus state-sponsored alternative programs. *Journal of Teacher Education, 47,* 60–61.

Johnson, S. M. (1990). *Teachers at work: Achieving success in our schools.* New York: Basic Books.

Joint Committee on Teacher Planning for Students with Disabilities. (1995). *Planning for academic diversity in America's classrooms.* Lawrence: Center for Research on Learning, University of Kansas.

Jones, L. V. (1984). White-black achievement differences: The narrowing gap. *American Psychologist, 39,* 1207–1213.

Jones, L. V., Burton, N. W., & Davenport, E. C. (1984). Monitoring the achievement of black students. *Journal for Research in Mathematics Education, 15,* 154–164.

Kagan, S. L., & Newton, J. W. (1989, November). Public policy report: For-profit and nonprofit child care: Similarities and differences. *Young Children, 45,* 4–10.

Kahne, J. (1994). Democratic communities, equity, and excellence: A Deweyan reframing of educational policy analysis. *Educational Evaluation and Policy Analysis, 16*(3), 233–248.

Kamii, C. (1982). Encouraging thinking in mathematics. *Phi Delta Kappan, 64,* 247–251.

Kamin, L. (1974). *The science and politics of IQ.* New York: Wiley.

Kaufman, J. E., & Rosenbaum, J. E. (1992). Education and employment of low-income black youth in white suburbs. *Educational Evaluation and Policy Analysis, 14*(3), 229–240.

Kearns, D. T. (1988). An education recovery plan for America. *Phi Delta Kappan, 69,* 565–570.

Kentucky Legislative Research Commission. (1990). *A guide to the Kentucky Education Reform Act of 1990.* Frankfort, KY: Author.

Kerchner, C. T. (1993). Building the airplane as it rolls down the runway. *School Administrator, 50*(10), 8–15.

Kidder, T. (1989). *Among schoolchildren.* Boston: Houghton Mifflin.

Kimbrough, J., & Hill, P. T. (1981). *The aggregate effects of federal education programs.* Santa Monica, CA: Rand.

Kluger, R. (1976). *Simple justice.* New York: Knopf.

Klugman, E., Carter, S., & Israel, S. (1979). *Too many pieces: A study of teacher fragmentation in the elementary school.* Boston: Wheelock-Malden Teacher Corps Collaborative.

Knapp, M. S., Shields, P. M., & Turnbull, B. J. (1995, June). Academic challenge in high-poverty classrooms. *Phi Delta Kappan, 76,* 770–776.

Kohn, A. (1993). *Punished by rewards.* Boston: Houghton Mifflin.

Kopp, W. (1992). Reforming schools of education will not be enough. *Yale Law and Policy Review, 10,* 58–68.

Kopp, W. (1993, December 1). *Proposal for a strategic alliance between TFA, Inc., and Columbia University.*

Koretz, D. (1988). Arriving in Lake Wobegon: Are standardized tests exaggerating achievement and distorting instruction? *American Educator, 12*(2), 8–15, 46–52.

Koretz, D., Stetcher, B., & Deibert, E. (1992). *The Vermont portfolio program: Interim report on implementation and impact, 1991–92 school year.* Santa Monica, CA: Rand.

Koretz, D., et. al. (1992, December 4). *The reliability of scores from the 1992 Vermont Portfolio Assessment Program: Interim report.* Santa Monica, CA: Rand Institute on Education and Training.

Kornhaber, M., & Gardner, H. (1993). *Varieties of excellence: Identifying and assessing children's talents.* New York: National Center for Restructuring Education, Schools, and Teaching, Teachers College, Columbia University.

Kozol, J. (1991). *Savage inequalities: Children in America's schools.* New York: Crown.

Kulik, C. C., & Kulik, J. A. (1982). Effects of ability grouping on secondary school students: A meta-analysis of evaluation findings. *American Education Research Journal, 19,* 415–428.

Lampert, M., & Eshelman, A. S. (1995, April). *Using technology to support effective and responsible teacher education: The case of interactive multimedia in mathematics methods courses.* Paper presented at the meeting of the American Educational Research Association, San Francisco.

Lankford, H., & Wyckoff, J. (1995). Where has the money gone? An analysis of school district spending in New York. *Educational Evaluation and Policy Analysis, 17*(2), 195–218.

Lawler, E. E., III. (1986). *High-involvement management: Participative strategies for improving organizational performance.* San Francisco: Jossey Bass.

Lawler, E. E., III (1992). *The ultimate advantage: Creating the high-involvement organization.* San Francisco: Jossey-Bass.

Lee, V. E., & Bryk, A. (1988). Curriculum tracking as mediating the social distribution of high school achievement. *Sociology of Education, 61,* 78–94.

Lee, V. E., Bryk, A., & Smith, J. B. (1993). The organization of effective secondary schools. In L. Darling-Hammond (Ed.), *Review of research in education* (Vol. 19, pp. 171–267). Washington, DC: American Educational Research Association.

Lee, V. E., & Smith, J. B. (1994). High school restructuring and student achievement: A new study finds strong links. *Issues in Restructuring Schools* (Newsletter, Center on Organization and Restructuring of Schools, University of Wisconsin), *7,* 1–5, 16.

Lee, V. E., & Smith, J. B. (1995). *Effects of high school restructuring and size on gains in achievement and engagement for early secondary school students.* Madison: Wisconsin Center for Education Research, University of Wisconsin.

Lee, V. E., Smith, J. B., & Croninger R. G. (1995). Another look at high school restructuring: More evidence that it improves student achievement and more insight into why. *Issues in Restructuring Schools* (Newsletter, Center on Organization and Restructuring of Schools, University of Wisconsin), 9, 1–9.

LeMahieu, P. G., & Sterling, R. (1991). *CHARTing educational reform: An interim report of evaluations of the Collaborative for Humanities and Arts Teaching.* Philadelphia: Collaborative for Humanities and Arts Teaching.

Lenk, H. A. (1989). *A case study: The induction of two alternate route social studies teachers.* Unpublished doctoral dissertation, Teachers College, Columbia University.

Lepper, M. R. (1981). Intrinsic and extrinsic motivation in children: Detrimental effects of superfluous social controls. *Aspects of the development of competence: Minnesota Symposia on Child Psychology, 14,* 155–214.

Lepper, M. R., & Greene, D. (1978). *The costs of reward: New perspectives on the psychology of human motivation.* Hillsdale, NJ: Erlbaum.

Lieberman, A. (1995). *The work of restructuring schools: Building from the ground up.* New York: Teachers College Press.

Lieberman, A., Darling-Hammond, L., & Zuckerman, D. (1991). *Early lessons in school restructuring.* New York: National Center for Restructuring Education, Schools, and Teaching, Teachers College, Columbia University.

Lieberman, A., Falk, B., & Alexander, L. (1994). *A culture in the making: Leadership in learner-centered schools.* New York: National Center for Restructuring Education, Schools, and Teaching, Teachers College, Columbia University.

Lightfoot, S. L. (1975). *Worlds apart.* New York: Basic Books.

Lightfoot, S. L. (1983). *The good high school: Portraits of character and culture.* New York: Basic Books.

Lindsay, P. (1982). The effect of high school size on student participation, satisfaction, and attendance. *Educational Evaluation and Policy Analysis, 4,* 57–65.

Lindsay, P. (1984). High school size, participation in activities, and young adult social participation: Some enduring effects of schooling. *Educational Evaluation and Policy Analysis, 6*(1), 73–83.

Lipsky, M. (1980). *Street-level bureaucracy: Dilemmas of the individual in public service.* New York: Russell Sage Foundation.

Little, J. W. (1993) Teacher development in a climate of educational reform. *Educational Evaluation and Policy* Analysis *15*(2), 129–151.

Lockwood, A. (1993, Spring). National standards: Who benefits? *Focus in Change, 11,* 1–14. Madison: National Center for Effective Schools, University of Wisconsin.

Long, J. C., & Morrow, J., (1995). Research analysis of professional development school graduates and traditional phase I and phase II graduates. Unpublished manuscript. Paper presented at the Annual Meeting of the Association of Teacher Educators, Detroit, MI.

Lortie, D. C. (1975). *Schoolteacher: A sociological study.* Chicago: University of Chicago Press.

LuPone, L. J. (1961). A comparison of provisionally certified and permanently certified elementary school teachers in selected school districts in New York State. *Journal of Educational Research, 55,* 53–63.

Lutz, F. W., & Hutton, J. B. (1989, Fall). Alternative teacher certification: Its policy implications for classroom and personnel practice. *Educational Evaluation and Policy Analysis, 11*(3), 237–254.

Lynd, R. S., & Lynd, H. M. (1929). *Middletown: A study in contemporary American culture.* Orlando, FL: Harcourt Brace.

MacMillan J. B., and Pendlebury, S., (1985). The Florida Performance Measurement System: A consideration. *Teachers College Record, 87,* pp. 69–78.

MacPhail-Wilcox, B. & King, R. A. (1986). Resource allocation studies: Implications for school improvement and school finance research. *Journal of Education Finance, 11,* 416–432.

Madaus, G. F. (1988). The influence of testing on curriculum. In L. Tanner (Ed.), *Critical issues in curriculum* (pp. 83–121). Chicago: University of Chicago Press.

Madaus, G. F. (1991). The effects of important tests on students: Implications for a national examination system. *Phi Delta Kappan, 73,* 226–231.

Madaus, G. F. (1992). *A national testing system: Manna from above? A historical/technological perspective.* Chestnut Hill, MA: Boston College, Center for the Study of Testing, Evaluation, and Educational Policy.

Madaus, G. F., Kellaghan, T., Rakow, E. A., & King, D. J. (1979). The sensitivity of measure of school effectiveness. *Harvard Educational Review, 49*(2), 207–230.

Madaus, G. F., et al. (1992). *The influence of testing on teaching math and science in grades 4–12.* Chestnut Hill, MA: Boston College, Center for the Study of Testing, Evaluation, and Educational Policy.

McDonald, J. (1993). Planning backwards from exhibitions. *Graduation by exhibition: Assessing genuine achievement.* Alexandria, VA: Association for Supervision and Curriculum Development.

McDonnell, L. M., Burstein, L., Ormseth, T., Catterall, J., & Moody, D. (1990). *Discovering what schools really teach: Designing improved coursework indicators.* Washington, DC: U.S. Department of Education.

McGregor, D. (1960). *The human side of enterprise.* New York: McGraw-Hill.

McKeachie, W. J., & Kulik, J. A. (1975). Effective college teaching. In F. N. Kerlinger (Ed.), *Review of research in education* (Vol. 3, pp. 165–209). Itasca, IL: Peacock.

McKnight, C. C., Crosswhite, F. J., Dossey, J. A., Kifer, E., Swafford, J. O., Travers, K. J., & Cooney, T. J. (1987). *The underachieving curriculum: Assessing U.S. school mathematics from an international perspective.* Champaign, IL: Stipes.

McLaughlin, M. W. (1987). Learning from experience: Lessons from policy implementation. *Educational Evaluation and Policy Analysis, 9(2),* 171–178.

McLaughlin, M. W. (1990). The RAND change agent study revisited: Macro perspectives and micro realities. *Educational Researcher, 19(9),* 11–16.

McLaughlin, M. W. (1994, Fall). Somebody knows my name. *Issues in restructuring schools* (Newsletter, Center on Organization and Restructuring of Schools, University of Wisconsin), *7,* 9–11.

McLaughlin, M. W., Irby, M. A., & Langman, J. (1994). *Urban sanctuaries: Neighborhood organizations in the lives and futures of inner-city youth.* San Francisco: Jossey-Bass.

McMillen, M. M., Bobbitt, S. A., & Lynch, H. F. (1994, April). *Teacher training, certification, and assignment in public schools: 1990–1991.* Paper presented at the meeting of the American Educational Research Association, New Orleans.

McNeil, J. D. (1974). Who gets better results with young children— Experienced teachers or novices? *Elementary School Journal, 74,* 447–451.

McNeil, L. (1986). *Contradictions of control.* New York: Routledge.

McUsic, M. (1991, Summer). The use of education clauses in school finance reform litigation. *Harvard Journal on Legislation, 28(2),* 307–340.

Mann, D. (1987). Can we help dropouts? Thinking about the undoable. In G. Natriello (Ed.), *School dropouts: Patterns and policies.* New York: Teachers College Press.

Massachusetts Advocacy Center and the Center for Early Adolescence. (1988). *Before it's too late: Dropout prevention in the middle grades.* Boston: Author.

Matthews, W. (1984). Influences on the learning and participation of minorities in mathematics. *Journal for Research in Mathematics Education, 15,* 84–95.

Meier, D. (1987, June). Central Park East: An alternative story. *Phi Delta Kappan, 68*(10), 753–757.

Meier, D. (1995). *The power of their ideas: Lessons for America from a small school in Harlem.* Boston: Beacon Press.

Meier, K. J., Stewart, J., Jr., & England, R. E. (1989). *Race, class, and education: The politics of second-generation discrimination.* Madison: University of Wisconsin Press.

Melton, R. F. (1978, Spring). Resolution of conflicting claims concerning the effect of behavioral objectives on student learning. *Review of Educational Research, 48*(2), 291–302.

Mercer, J. R. (1989). Alternative paradigms for assessment in a pluralistic society. In J. A. Banks & C. M. Banks (Eds.), *Multicultural education* (pp. 289–303). Needham Heights, MA: Allyn & Bacon.

Metropolitan Life. (1993). The American teacher 1993. New York. Author.

Metz, M. H. (1978). *Classrooms and corridors: The crisis of authority in desegregated secondary schools.* Berkeley: University of California Press.

Miles, K. H. (1995, Winter). Freeing resources for improving schools: A case study of teacher allocation in Boston Public Schools. *Educational Evaluation and Policy Analysis, 17,* 476–493.

Miller, L., & Silvernail, D. L. (1994). Wells Junior High School: Evolution of a professional development school. In L. Darling-Hammond (Ed.), *Professional development schools: Schools for developing a profession* (pp. 28–49). New York: Teachers College Press.

Ministry of Education, Science, and Culture. (1983). *Course of study for lower secondary schools in Japan.* Government of Japan.

Mishel, L., & Teixeira, R. A. (1991). *The myth of the coming labor shortage: Jobs, skills, and the incomes of America's workforce 2000.* Washington, DC: Economic Policy Institute.

Mohrman, S. A., Wohlstetter, P., & Associates. (1994). *School-based management: Organizing for high performance.* San Francisco: Jossey-Bass.

Moore, D., & Davenport, S. (1988). *The new improved sorting machine.* Madison: University of Wisconsin, National Center on Effective Secondary Schools.

Moore, E. G., & Smith, A. W. (1985). Mathematics aptitude: Effects of coursework, household language, and ethnic differences. *Urban Education, 20,* 273–294.

Mullis, I. V., Jenkins, F., & Johnson, E. G. (1994, October). Effective schools in mathematics: Perspectives from the NAEP 1992 assessment (Report No. 23-RR-01). Washington, DC: National Center for Education Statistics.

Murnane, R. J., & Levy, F. (1996a). *Teaching the new basic skills.* New York: Free Press.

Murnane, R. J., & Levy, F. (1996b). Teaching to new standards. In S. H. Fuhrman & J. A. O'Day (Eds.), *Rewards and reform: Creating educational incentives that work* (pp. 257–293). San Francisco: Jossey-Bass.

National Assessment of Educational Progress (NAEP). (1981). *Reading, thinking, and writing: Results from the 1979–80 national assessment of reading and literature.* Denver: Author.

National Association for the Education of Young Children (NAEYC). (1988, January). NAEYC position statement on developmentally appropriate practice in the primary grades, serving 5 through 8 year olds. *Young Children,* pp. 64–84.

National Center for Education Statistics. (1982a). *The condition of education, 1982.* Washington, DC: U.S. Department of Education.

National Center for Education Statistics. (1982b). *Digest of education statistics.* Washington, DC: U.S. Department of Education.

National Center for Education Statistics. (1985a). *The condition of education.* Washington, DC: U.S. Department of Education.

National Center for Education Statistics. (1985b). *High school and beyond: An analysis of course-taking patterns in secondary schools as related to student characteristics.* Washington, DC: U.S. Government Printing Office.

National Center for Education Statistics. (1987). *Digest of education statistics, 1987.* Washington, DC: National Center for Education Statistics, U.S. Department of Education.

National Center for Education Statistics. (1993a). *The condition of education, 1993.* Washington, DC: U.S. Department of Education.

National Center for Education Statistics. (1993b). *NAEP 1992 reading state report for New York.* Washington, DC: U.S. Department of Education.

National Center for Education Statistics. (1994a). *Digest of education statistics, 1994.* Washington, DC: U.S. Department of Education.

National Center for Education Statistics. (1994b). *1990–91 schools and staffing survey: Selected state results.* Washington, DC: U.S. Department of Education.

National Center for Education Statistics. (1994c). *Report in brief: National Assessment of Educational Progress (NAEP) 1992 trends in academic progress.* Washington, DC: U.S. Department of Education.

National Center for Education Statistics. (1995a). *Digest of education statistics, 1995.* Washington, DC: U.S. Department of Education.

National Center for Education Statistics. (1995b). *Extracurricular participation and student engagement (Education policy issues: Statistical perspectives* series). Washington, DC: U.S. Department of Education.

National Center for Education Statistics. (1995c). *The condition of education.* Washington, DC: U.S. Department of Education.

National Center for Research on Teacher Learning. (1992). *Findings on learning to teach.* East Lansing, MI: Author.

National Commission on Excellence in Education. (1983). *A nation at risk.* Washington, DC: U.S. Government Printing Office.

National Commission on Teaching and America's Future (NCTAF). (1996). *What matters most: Teaching and America's future.* New York: Author.

National Council of Teachers of Mathematics. (1989). *Curriculum and evaluation standards for school mathematics.* Reston, VA: Author.

National Council on Education Standards and Testing (NCEST). (1992). *Raising standards for American education.* Washington, DC: U.S. Government Printing Office.

National Education Association. (1992). *Status of the American public school teacher, 1990–1991.* Washington, DC: Author.

National Foundation for the Improvement of Education (NFIE). (1995). *Touching the future.* Washington, DC: Author.

National Foundation for the Improvement of Education (NFIE). (1996). *Teachers take charge of their learning: Transforming professional development for student success.* Washington, D.C.: Author.

National Governors' Association. (1986). *Time for results: The governors' 1991 report on education.* Washington, DC: Author.

National Institute of Education. (1977). *Violent schools–safe schools: The safe school study report to Congress.* Washington, DC: Author.

National Research Council. (1982). *Ability testing: Uses, consequences, and controversies* (A. K. Wigdor & W. R. Garner, Eds.). Washington, DC: National Academy Press.

National Science Board (U.S.), Commission on Precollege Education in Mathematics, Science, and Technology. (1983). *Educating Americans for the 21st century.* Washington, DC: National Science Foundation.

Natriello, G., Zumwalt, K., Hansen, A., & Frisch, A. (1990). *Characteristics of entering teachers in New Jersey.* Revised version of a paper presented at the 1988 meeting of the American Educational Research Association.

Nelson, F. H., & O'Brien, T. (1993). *How U.S. teachers measure up internationally: A comparative study of teacher pay, training, and conditions of service.* Washington, DC: American Federation of Teachers.

New York City Board of Education. (1994). *Allocation guidelines 1994–95.* New York: Author.

New York State Council on Curriculum and Assessment. (1994). *Learning-centered curriculum and assessment for New York State.* Albany: New York State Education Department.

New York State Education Department. (1990). Report of school district mandates. Unpublished manuscript. Albany: State Education Department.

New York Study Group on Outcome Equity. (1993). *The road to outcome equity: Final report of the study group on outcome equity* (R. Berne, Ed.). Albany: New York State Education Department.

New York Times. (1991, November 6). Letters to the editor.

Newmann, F. M., Marks, H. M., & Gamoran, A. (1995, April). *Authentic pedagogy and student performance.* Paper presented at the meeting of the American Education Research Association, San Francisco.

Newmann, F. M., & Wehlage, G. G. (1995). *Successful school restructuring: A report to the public and educators by the Center on Organization and Restructuring of Schools.* Madison: Board of Regents of the University of Wisconsin System.

Oakes, J. (1983, May). Limiting opportunity: Student race and curricular differences in secondary vocational education. *American Journal of Education, 91*(3), 328–355.

Oakes, J. (1985). *Keeping track: How schools structure inequality.* New Haven, CT: Yale University Press.

Oakes, J. (1986, June). Tracking in secondary schools: A contextual perspective. *Educational Psychologist, 22,* 129–154.

Oakes, J. (1987). *Improving inner-city schools: Current directions in urban district reform* (Center for Policy Research in Education, Joint Note series). Santa Monica, CA: Rand.

Oakes, J. (1989). What educational indicators? The case for assessing the school context. *Educational Evaluation and Policy Analysis, 11*(2), 181–199.

Oakes, J. (1990). *Multiplying inequalities: The effects of race, social class, and tracking on opportunities to learn mathematics and science.* Santa Monica, CA: Rand.

Oakes, J. (1992, May). Can tracking research inform practice? Technical, normative, and political considerations. *Educational Researcher, 21*(4), 12–21.

Oakes, J., Selvin, M., Karoly, L., & Guiton, G. (1992). *Educational matchmaking: Academic and vocational tracking in comprehensive high schools.* Santa Monica, CA: Rand.

O'Day, J. A., & Smith, M. S. (1993). Systemic school reform and educational opportunity. In S. H. Fuhrman (Ed.), *Designing coherent education policy: Improving the system*. San Francisco: Jossey-Bass.

Odden, A. (1994). *Trends and issues in American school finance*. Paper prepared for the Carnegie Corporation, Consortium for Policy Research in Education, University of Wisconsin-Madison.

Office of Research, U. S. Department of Education. (1993, April). *What's wrong with writing and what can we do right now?* (Education research report). Washington, DC: U.S. Department of Education.

Ogbu, J. (1992). Understanding cultural diversity and learning. *Educational Researcher, 21*(8), 5–14.

Olsen, D. G. (1985). The quality of prospective teachers: Education vs. noneducation graduates. *Journal of Teacher Education, 36*(5), 56–59.

Olson, L. (1994). Critical Friends. *Education Week, 13*(32), 20–23, 26–27.

Orfield, G. F., & Ashkinaze, C. (1991). *The closing door: Conservative policy and black opportunity*. Chicago: University of Chicago Press.

Orfield, G. F., Monfort, F., & Aaron, M. (1989). *Status of school desegregation: 1968–1986*. Alexandria, VA: National School Boards Association.

Organization for Economic Cooperation and Development (OECD). (1995). *Education at a glance: OECD indicators*. Paris: Author.

Oxley, D. (1989, Spring). Smaller is better. *American Educator*, pp. 28–31, 51–52.

Palinscar, A. S., & Brown, A. L. (1984). Reciprocal teaching of comprehension—Fostering and monitoring activities. *Cognition and Instruction, 1*(2), 117–175.

Palmer, P. J. (1983). To know as we are known: A spirituality of education. San Francisco: HarperCollins.

Pascal, A. (1987). *The qualifications of teachers in American high schools*. Santa Monica, CA: Rand.

Pecheone, R., Falk, B., & Darling-Hammond, L. (in press). *Technical report on the 1996 pilot assessments in New York State*. New York: National Center for Restructuring Education, Schools, and Teaching, Teachers College, Columbia University.

Pelavin, S. H., & Kane, M. (1990). *Changing the odds: Factors increasing access to college*. New York: College Board.

Perkes, V. A. (1967–1968). Junior high school science teacher preparation, teaching behavior, and student achievement. *Journal of Research in Science Teaching, 6*(4), 121–126.

Peterson, P. (1979). Direct instruction reconsidered. In P. Peterson & H. Walberg (Eds.), *Research on teaching: Concepts, findings, and implications* (pp. 57–69). Berkeley, CA: McCutchan.

Peterson, P. (1989). Remediation is no remedy. *Educational Leadership, 46*(60), 24–25.

Peterson, P. (1990, Fall). Doing more in the same amount of time: Cathy Swift. *Education Evaluation and Policy Analysis, 12*(3), 277–296.

Peterson P. L., & Clark, C. M. (1978, Fall). Teachers' reports of their cognitive processes during teaching. *American Educational Research Journal, 15*(4), 555–565.

Philbrick, J. D. (1856, September). Report of the superintendent of common schools to the [Connecticut] general assembly, May 1856. *American Journal of Education, 2*, 261–264.

Piaget, J. (1970). *Science of education and the psychology of the child.* New York: Penguin Books.

Picus, L. O., & Bhimani, M. (1994, July). Determinants of pupil/teacher ratios at school sites: Evidence from the schools and staffing survey. In *Schools and staffing survey: Papers presented at meetings of the American Statistical Association* (pp. 114–120). Washington, DC: National Center for Education Statistics, U.S. Department of Education.

Pittman, R., & Haughwout, P. (1987). Influence of high school size on dropout rate. *Educational Evaluation and Policy Analysis, 9*, 337–343.

Popkewitz, T. S. (1994, June 30). Personal communication.

Popkewitz, T. S. (1995). Policy, knowledge, and power: Some issues for the study of educational reform. In P. Cookson and B. Schneider (Eds.), *Transforming schools: Trends, dilemmas, and prospects* (pp. 413–455). New York: Garland.

Poplin, M., & Weeres, J. (1992). *Voices from the inside: A report on schooling from inside the classroom.* Claremont, CA: Institute for Education in Transformation, Claremont Graduate School.

Porter, A. C. (1989). External standards and good teaching: The pros and cons of telling teachers what to do. *Educational Evaluation and Policy Analysis, 11*(4), 343–356.

Porter, A. C., Archbald, D. A., & Tyree, A. K. Jr. (1991). Reforming the curriculum: Will empowerment policies replace control? In S. H. Fuhrman & B. Malen (Eds.), *The politics of curriculum and testing: The 1990 yearbook of the Politics of Education Association* (pp. 11–36). Bristol, PA: Falmer Press.

Powell, A. G., Farrar, E., & Cohen, D. K. (1985). *The shopping mall high school.* Boston: Houghton Mifflin.

Pressey, S. L. (1926). Simple apparatus which gives tests and scores and teaches. *School and Society, 23*, 373–376.

Price, J., Schwabacher, S., & Chittenden, T. (1992). *The multiple forms of evidence study: Assessing reading through student work samples, teacher observations, and tests.* New York: National Center for Restructuring Education, Schools, and Teaching, Teachers College, Columbia University.

Public Agenda. (1994). *First things first: What Americans expect from the public schools.* New York: Author.

Public Education Association. (1992). *Small schools' operating costs: Reversing assumptions about economies of scale.* New York: Author.

Raab, C. M. (1993). *Reviewing biology with sample examinations, Revised edition.* New York: Amsco School Publications.

Ratzki, A. (1988, Spring). Creating a school community: One model of how it can be done. *American Educator,* pp. 10–17, 38–43.

Raywid, M. A. (1990). Rethinking school governance. In R. F. Elmore & Associates, *Restructuring schools: The next generation of educational reform* (pp. 152–206). San Francisco: Jossey-Bass.

Redefer, F. L. (1950). The Eight-Year Study . . . after eight years. *Progressive Education, 28,* 33–36.

Resnick, L. (1987a). *Education and learning to think.* Washington, DC: National Academy Press.

Resnick, L. (1987b). Learning in school and out. *Educational Researcher, 16,* 13–20.

Rock, D. A., Hilton, T. L., Pollack, J., Ekstrom, R. B., & Goertz, M. E. (1985). *A study of excellence in high school education: Educational policies, school quality, and student outcomes.* Washington, DC: National Center for Education Statistics, U.S. Department of Education.

Rosenbaum, J. E. (1976). *Making inequality: The hidden curriculum of high school tracking.* New York: Wiley.

Rosenbaum, J. E. (1980). Social implications of educational grouping. In D. C. Berliner (Ed.), *Review of research in education* (Vol. 8, pp. 361–401). Washington, DC: American Educational Research Association.

Rosenholtz, S. J. (1987). Education reform strategies: Will they increase teacher commitment? *American Journal of Education, 95*(4), 534–562.

Rotberg, I. C., & Harvey, J. C. (Eds.). (1994). *Federal policy options for improving the education of low-income students: Vol. 2. Commentaries.* Santa Monica: Rand.

Roth, R. (1993, Summer). Teach for America 1993 Pre-Service Institute program review. Unpublished evaluation.

Rothman, A. I., Welch, W., & Walberg, H. J. (1969). Physics teacher characteristics and student learning. *Journal of Research in Science Teaching, 6,* 63.

Rothstein, R., & Miles, K. H. (1995). *Where's the money gone? Changes in the level and composition of education spending.* Washington, DC: Economic Policy Institute.

Rottenberg, C. J., & Berliner, D. C. (1990, April). *Expert and novice teachers' conceptions of common classroom activities.* Paper presented at the meeting of the American Educational Research Association, Boston.

Roupp, R., Travers, J., Glantz, F., & Coelen, C. (1979). *Children at the center: Summary findings and their implications.* Cambridge, MA: Abt Associates.

Rowan, B. (1996). Standards as incentives for instructional reform. In S. H. Fuhrman & J. A. O'Day (Eds.), *Rewards and reform: Creating educational incentives that work* (pp. 195–225). San Francisco: Jossey-Bass.

Sarason, S. (1982) *The culture of the school and the problem of change* (rev. ed.). Needham Heights, MA: Allyn & Bacon.

Sato, N. (1994, November). *Reflections from an ethnographic study of Japanese elementary schools.* Washington, DC: American Association for Higher Education Fifth National Conference on School/College Collaboration.

Schalock, D. (1979). Research on teacher selection. In D. C. Berliner (Ed.), *Review of research in education* (Vol. 7). Washington, DC: American Educational Research Association.

Schlechty, P. C. (1990). *Schools for the 21st century: Leadership imperatives for educational reform.* San Francisco: Jossey-Bass.

Schmidt, W., McKnight, C., & Raizen, S. (1996). *A splintered vision.* Kluwer Academic Publishers.

Schmoker, M., & Wilson, R. B. (1993). Transforming schools through total quality education. *Phi Delta Kappan, 74,* 389–394.

Schoenfeld, A. H. (1988). When good teaching leads to bad results: The disasters of "well taught" mathematics courses. *Educational Psychologist, 23*(2), 145–166.

Schofield, J. W. (1991). School desegregation and intergroup relations. In G. Grant (Ed.), *Review of research in education* (Vol. 17, pp. 335–409). Washington, DC: American Educational Research Association.

Schorr, J. (1993, December). Class action: What Clinton's National Service Program could learn from "Teach for America." *Phi Delta Kappan, 75,* 315–318.

Secretary's Commission on Achieving Necessary Skills (SCANS). (1991). *What work requires of schools.* Washington, DC: U.S. Department of Labor.

Sedlak, M., & Schlossman, S. (1986, November). *Who will teach? Historical perspectives on the changing appeal of teaching as a profession* (R-3472). Santa Monica, CA: Rand.

Senge, P. (1990a). *The fifth discipline: The art and practice of the learning organization.* New York: Doubleday.

Senge, P. (1990b). The leader's new work: Building learning organizations. *Sloan Management Review, 32,* 7–23.

Senge, P. (1992). Building learning organizations. *Journal for Quality and Participation, 15*(2), 30–38.

Shaver, J. P., Davis, O. L., & Helburn, S. W. (1979). The status of social studies education: Impressions from three NSF studies. *Social Education, 43,* 150–159.

Shepard, L. A. (1991). Will national tests improve learning? *Phi Delta Kappan, 73,* 232–238.

Shepard, L., & Smith, M. L. (1986, November). Synthesis of research on school readiness and kindergarten retention. *Educational Leadership,* pp. 78–86.

Shimahara, N. K. (1985). Japanese education and its implications for U.S. education. *Phi Delta Kappan,* 418–421.

Shin, H. (1994, April). *Estimating future teacher supply: An application of survival analysis.* Paper presented at the meeting of the American Educational Research Association, New Orleans.

Shulman, L. (1983). Autonomy and obligation. In L. Shulman & G. Sykes (Eds.), *Handbook of teaching and policy* (pp. 484–504). White Plains, NY: Longman.

Shulman, L. (1987). Knowledge and teaching: Foundations of the new reform. *Harvard Educational Review, 57*(1), 1–22.

Sizer, T. R. (1984). *Horace's compromise: The dilemma of the American high school.* Boston: Houghton Mifflin.

Sizer, T. R. (1991, May). No pain, no gain. *Educational Leadership,* pp. 32–34.

Sizer, T. R. (1992). *Horace's school: Redesigning the American high school.* Boston: Houghton Mifflin.

Sizer, T. R., McDonald, J. P., & Rogers, B. (1992, Winter). Standards and school reform: Asking the basic questions. *Stanford Law and Policy Review 4,* 27–35.

Skager, R. W., & Braskamp, L. A. (1996, November). *Changes in self-ratings and life goals as related to student accomplishment in college.* Iowa City, IA: American College Testing.

Skinner, B. F. (1954). The science of learning and the art of teaching. *Harvard Educational Review, 24,* 86–97.

Skinner, B. F. (1961). *Cumulative record.* Englewood Cliffs, NJ: Appleton-Century-Crofts.

Skipper, C. E., & Quantz, R. (1987, May-June). Changes in educational attitudes of education and arts and science students during four years of college. *Journal of Teacher Education,* pp. 39–44.

Slavin, R. E. (1990). Achievement effects of ability grouping in secondary schools: A best evidence synthesis. *Review of Educational Research, 60*(3), 471–500.

Slavin, R. E. (1995). *Cooperative learning: Theory, research, and practice* (2nd ed.). Needham Heights, MA: Allyn & Bacon.

Smith, E. R., & Tyler, R. W. (1942). *Adventure in education: Vol. 3. Appraising and recording student progress: Evaluation, records, and reports in thirty schools.* New York: HarperCollins.

Smith, F. (1986). *High schools admission and the improvement of schooling.* New York: New York City Board of Education.

Smith, J. M. (1990, February). School districts as teacher training institutions in the New Jersey Alternate Route Program. Paper presented at the Annual Meeting of the Eastern Educational Research Association, Clearwater, FL.

Smith, M. L. (1991). Put to the test: The effects of external testing on teachers. *Educational Researcher, 20*(5), 8–11.

Smith, M., & O'Day, J. (1990). Systemic school reform. In S. H. Fuhrman & B. Malen (Eds.), *The politics of curriculum and testing: 1990 Yearbook of the Politics of Education Association* (pp. 233–267). London: Taylor and Francis.

Smylie, M. A. (1994). Redesigning teachers' work: Connections to the classroom. In L. Darling-Hammond (Ed.), *Review of research in education* (Vol. 20, pp. 129–177). Washington, DC: American Educational Research Association.

Snyder, J., Bolin, F., & Zumwalt, K. (1992). Curriculum implementation. In P. W. Jackson (Ed.), *Handbook of research on curriculum* (pp. 402–435). Old Tappan, NJ: Macmillan.

Snyder, J., Lieberman, A., Macdonald, M. B., & Goodwin, A. L. (1992). *Makers of meaning in a learning-centered school: A case study of Central Park East Elementary School.* New York: National Center for Restructuring Education, Schools, and Teaching, Teachers College, Columbia University.

Soar, R. S. (1977). An integration of findings from four studies of teacher effectiveness. In G. D. Borich (Ed.), *The appraisal of teaching: Concepts and process* (pp. 96–103). Reading, MA: Addison-Wesley.

Sobol, T. (1992, February). Keynote address to the annual meeting of the American Association of School Administrators, San Diego.

Social Security Administration. (1996). *1996 annual report of the board of trustees of the federal old age and survivors insurance and disability insurance trust funds.* Baltimore: Social Security Administration.

Soo Hoo, S. (1990). School renewal: Taking responsibility for providing an education of value. In J. L. Goodlad & P. Keating (Eds.), *Access to knowledge: An agenda for our nation's schools* (pp. 205–222). New York: College Board.

State University of New York. (1992). *SUNY 2000: College Expectations* (Report of the Task Force on College Entry-Level Knowledge and Skills). Albany: Author.

State University of New York. (1994, March 25). *Trustees resolution.* Albany, NY: Author.

Stedman, L. C. (1996). The achievement crisis is real: A review of "The Manufactured Crisis." *Educational Policy Analysis Archives, 4*(1), 1–13.

Sternberg, R. (1985a). *Beyond IQ.* New York: Cambridge University Press.

Sternberg, R. (1985b). Teaching critical thinking: Part I. Are we making critical mistakes? *Phi Delta Kappan,* 194–198.

Stigler, J. W., & Stevenson, H. W. (1991, Spring). How Asian teachers polish each lesson to perfection. *American Educator,* pp. 12–47.

Stoddart, T. (forthcoming). An alternate route to teacher certification: Preliminary findings from the Los Angeles Unified School District Intern Program. In E. Ashburn (Ed.), *Alternative certification for teachers.* Washington, DC: U.S. Department of Education.

Strauss, S. (Ed.). (1982). *U-shaped behavioral growth.* Orlando: Academic Press.

Strickland, D. (1985). Early childhood development and reading instruction. In C. K. Brooks (Ed.), *Tapping potential: English and language arts for the black learner* (pp. 880–101). Urbana, IL: National Council of Teachers of English.

Stufflebeam, D. (in press). Overview and assessment of the Kentucky Instructional Results Improvement System (KIRIS). In J. Millman (Ed.), *Grading teachers, grading schools.* Thousand Oaks, CA: Sage.

Sykes, G. (1983). Public policy and the problem of teacher quality. In L. S. Shulman & G. Sykes (Eds.), *Handbook of teaching and policy* (pp. 97–125). White Plains, NY: Longman.

Talbert, J. E. (1990). *Teacher tracking: Exacerbating inequalities in the high school.* Stanford, CA: Center for Research on the Context of Secondary Teaching, Stanford University.

Talmage, H., & Rasher, S. P. (1980). Unanticipated outcomes: The perils to curriculum goals. *Phi Delta Kappan, 62,* 30–32, 71.

Taylor, F. W. (1911). *The principles of scientific management.* New York: HarperCollins.

Taylor, T. W. (1957). *A study to determine the relationships between growth and interest and achievement of high school students and science teacher attitudes, preparation, and experience.* Unpublished doctoral dissertation, University of North Texas.

Taylor, W. L., & Piche, D. M. (1991). *A report on shortchanging children: The impact of fiscal inequity on the education of students at risk* (Prepared for the Committee on Education and Labor, U.S. House of Representatives). Washington, DC: U.S. Government Printing Office.

Texas Education Agency. (1993). *Teach for America visiting team report.* Austin: Texas State Board of Education Meeting Minutes, Appendix B.

Tietze, W. (1987). A structural model for the evaluation of preschool effects. *Early Childhood Research Quarterly, 2,* 133–153.

Todd, H. M. (1913). Why children work: The children's answer. *McClure's Magazine, 40,* 68–79.

Trimble, K., & Sinclair, R. L. (1986, April). *Ability grouping and differing conditions for learning: An analysis of content and instruction in ability-grouped classes.* Paper presented at the meeting of the American Educational Research Association, San Francisco.

Tucker, M. (1992, June 17). Quoted in "The roundtable: A new 'social compact' for mastery in education." *Education Week* (special report).

Tyack, D. (1974). *The one best system: A history of American urban education.* Cambridge, MA: Harvard University Press.

Tyack, D., & Tobin, W. (1994). The grammar of schooling: Why has it been so hard to change? *American Research Journal, 31,* 453–479.

Tyson-Bernstein, H. (1988). *A conspiracy of good intentions: America's textbook fiasco.* Washington, DC: Council for Basic Education.

U.S. Department of Education. (1993). *Education in the states and nations.* Washington, DC: Author, National Center for Education Statistics.

U.S. Department of Labor. (1986). *Current population survey, 1986–87.* Unpublished data.

Useem, E. L. (1990, Fall). You're good, but you're not good enough: Tracking students out of advanced mathematics. *American Educator, 14*(3), 24–27, 43–46.

Usiskin, Z. (1987). Why elementary algebra can, should, and must be an eighth grade course for average students. *Mathematics Teacher, 80,* 428–438.

Victoria Ministry of Education. (1988). *The school curriculum and organisation framework: P–12*. Victoria, Australia: Ministry of Education.

Vygotsky, L. S. (1962). *Thought and language* (E. Hanfmann & G. Vaker, Eds. & Trans.). Cambridge, MA: MIT Press.

Wainer, H. (1993). Does spending money on education help? *Educational Researcher, 22*(9), 22–24.

Walberg, H. (1982). What makes schooling effective. *Contemporary Education: A Journal of Review, 1*, 22–34.

Walberg, H. J., & Rothman, A. I. (1969). Teacher achievement and student learning. *Science Education, 53*, 256–257.

Walker, J., & Levine, D. U. (1988, Winter). The inherent impact of non-promoted students on reading scores in a big city elementary school. *Urban Review, 20*(4), 247–252.

Watson, J. B. (1913). Psychology as the behaviorist views it. In W. Dennis (Ed.), *Readings in the history of psychology*. Englewood Cliffs, NJ: Apple-Century-Crofts.

Weber, M. (1958). *From Max Weber: Essays in sociology* (H. H. Gerth & C. W. Mills, Trans. & Eds.). New York: Oxford University Press. (Original work published 1946)

Wehlage, G. G., Rutter, R. A., Smith, G. A., Lesko, N., & Fernandez, R. R. (1989). *Reducing the risk: Schools as communities of support*. Bristol, PA: Falmer Press.

Westbury, I. (1992). Comparing American and Japanese achievement: Is the United States really a low achiever? *Educational Researcher, 21*, 18–24.

Wheelock, A. (1992). *Crossing the tracks*. New York: New Press.

Whitford, B. L. (1996, September 23). Personal communication.

Whitford, B. L,. & Gaus, D. M. (1995). With a little help from their friends: Teachers making change at Wheeler School. In A. Lieberman (Ed.), *The work of restructuring schools: Building from the ground up* (pp. 18–42). New York: Teachers College Press.

Whitford, B. L., & Jones, K. (in press). Assessment and accountability in Kentucky: How high stakes affects teaching and learning. In A. Hargreaves, A. Lieberman, M. Fullan, & D. Hopkins (Eds.), *International handbook of educational change*. Netherlands: Kluwer.

Wiggins, G. (1989, April). Teaching to the (authentic) test. *Educational Leadership*, pp. 41–47.

William T. Grant Foundation, Commission on Work, Family, and Citizenship. (1988). *The forgotten half: Non-college youth in America*. Washington, DC: Author.

Wilson, S. (1990). A conflict of interests: The case of Mark Black. *Educational Evaluation and Policy Analysis, 12*(3), 309–326.

Winkelmann, W., Hollaender, A., Schmerkotte, H., & Schmalohr, E. (1979). Kognitive Entwicklung und Foerderung von Kindergarten und Vorklassenkindern. Bericht uber eine laengsschnittliche Vergleischsuntersuchung zum Modellversuch des Landes Nordrhein-Westfalen (2 Vols.). Kronberg: Scriptor.

Wise, A. E. (1979). *Legislated learning.* Berkeley: University of California Press.

Wise, A. E., Darling-Hammond, L., & Berry, B. (1987). *Effective teacher selection: From recruitment to retention.* Santa Monica, CA: Rand.

Wise, A. E., Darling-Hammond, L., McLaughlin, M. W., & Bernstein, H. T. (1984). *Case studies for teacher evaluation: A study of effective practices.* Santa Monica, CA: Rand.

Wise, A. E., & Gendler, T. (1989). Rich schools, poor schools: The persistence of unequal education. *College Board Review, 151,* 12–17, 36–37.

Wohlstetter, P., Smyer, R., & Mohrman, S. A. (1994). New boundaries for school-based management: The high involvement model. *Educational Evaluation and Policy Analysis, 16*(3), 268–286.

Wolcott, H. F. (1977). *Teachers vs. technocrats.* Eugene: University of Oregon Center for Educational Policy and Management.

Wright, D. P., McKibbon, M., & Walton, P. (1987). The effectiveness of the teacher trainee program: An alternate route into teaching in California. Sacramento: California Commission on Teacher Credentialing.

Yelon, S. L., & Schmidt, W. H. (1973, Spring). The effect of objectives and instructions on the learning of a complex cognitive task. *Journal of Experimental Education, 41*(3), 91–96.

Yinger, R. J. (1978, July). *A study of teacher planning: Description and a model of preactive decision making.* East Lansing, MI: Institute for Research on Teacher Learning.

Zahorick, J. A. (1970). The effect of planning on teaching. *Elementary School Journal, 71,* 143–151.

Zancanella, D. (1992). The influence of state-mandated testing on teachers of literature. *Educational Evaluation and Policy Analysis, 14*(3), 283–295.

— Name Index

~~~ Subject Index